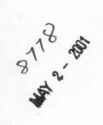

FRANKENSTEINS OF FRAUD

The 20th Century's Top Ten White-Collar Criminals

by

Joseph T. Wells

Frankensteins of Fraud
Published by the Obsidian Publishing Company, Inc.
Copyright 2000

Printed by
Thomson-Shore Printing Company, Inc., Dexter, Michigan

Obsidian Publishing Company
800 West Avenue
Austin, Texas 78701
(800) 245-3321

Printed in the United States of America
1 2 3 4 5 6 7 8 9 0
ISBN   1-889277-25-8
Library of Congress Catalog Card Number 00-100668

Photo Credits
The following photos and illustrations are used with permission from the
copyright holders:

pages xvi, 112, 144, 170: © AP/WIDE WORLD PHOTOS; page 22:
© Archive Photos; pages 214, 288, 328: © Reuter's/Archive Photos; page
70: © 1929 Time, Inc., reprinted by permission; page 260: © Philadelphia
Inquirer/Ron Tarver.

To Margaret, Tina, and the memory of Bill.
Thanks for believing in me.

Foreword

Mary Shelley's novel *Frankenstein* tells us a good deal about the thought processes that drove the flagrant law breakers who are meticulously and vividly portrayed in Joseph T. Wells' *Frankensteins of Fraud*. Why did they flaunt the law, mock decency, and steal relentlessly and without remorse? "Through the whole period during which I was the slave of my creature, I allowed myself to be governed by the impulses of the moment," Frankenstein declares in Mary Shelley's novel. So did Michael Milken, Charles Ponzi, Eddie Antar, Ivar Kreuger, and the other villains portrayed by Wells in this absorbing study of major fraudsters. These upper echelon crooks never had enough, and they could only retain their sense of self by feeding their greed and lust for more and more.

There is a dynamic to fraud captured in these portraits of some of the most renowned and reviled practitioners. Writing of a conman, the novelist Doris Lessing portrays the force that propels and keeps fraudsters at their work: "His strength was—and I could feel just how powerful that strength was—this terrible, compelling anxiety that he should be able to force somebody under his will," Lessing observes. "It was almost as if he were pleading silently, in the moment when he was tricking a victim: Please let me trick you; please let me cheat you; I've got to, it's essential for me."

Sociologist Robert Merton, a preeminent figure in the study of the processes that lead to the kind of behavior documented in *Frankensteins of Fraud*, pointed out that a good deal of crime in the United States grows out of our overwhelming emphasis on money and the fact that there are barriers that cannot be surmounted by most people to obtain the kind of money they'd like to possess. Most of us come to terms with that reality: we settle for the best that we can do and we find our happiness in things that do not carry exorbitant price tags. Others give up, and anesthetize themselves with drugs and alcohol. There are relatively few like the culprits portrayed here who feel compelled to make their fortune by stomping on others and living lives that they know might at any moment end in disaster—public exposure and disgrace, a prison term, or suicide, the agony-saving way out.

Merton also pointed out that there is what he called an "anomia of success." It "arises when progressively higher aspirations are fostered by each temporary success and by the enlarged expectations visited upon financially successful persons by associates." Similarly, another well-known sociologist, Daniel Bell, has written: "Wants by their nature are unlimited and insatiable." More simply put, someone else will always have a larger house, a better car, or a bigger yacht than you. The Frankensteins of Fraud are driven to batter their way to an impossible goal—having it all.

Getting away with their scandalous law-breaking was seen by people such as Kreuger, Robert Vesco, and Michael Milken as a test of their mettle. That they could outfox others told them that they were smarter, shrewder, better—and deserving of the wealth that they accumulated. They became addicts. The first shot of criminal success may have come almost inadvertently, like the first shot of heroin injected casually at a wild party. But the need for more became insatiable: they were hooked, riding on a merry-go-round that went so fast that they could never get off.

This book complements Wells' encyclopedic *Occupational Fraud and Abuse* (1997), a pioneering inventory and discussion of a wide range of illegal acts that are the professional and vocational concerns of the 25,000 members of the Association of Certified Fraud Examiners. Wells' work in founding and parenting the Association, combined with a background of fraud investigation for the Federal Bureau of Investigation, an accounting background, and a quick and penetrating intellect all serve to make this book the most comprehensive and useful exploration of fraud at the highest levels. Besides that, the book is a pleasure to read—well-researched, well-written, and with sophisticated and sensible interpretations of the facts that have been gathered.

Mary Wollstonecraft Shelley, the author of *Frankenstein*, was born in London on August 30, 1797; her mother, also named Mary, died of puerperal fever just 11 days after her first child's birth. Mary Wollstonecraft had written several well-regarded books looking toward greater liberties for women. Mary's father, William Godwin, was a prolific author who also wrote with an eye toward making the world a more decent place and those in it more decent people. Both her parents and Mary herself particularly deplored the kinds of exploitative behavior engaged in by the high-level con artists portrayed in *Frankensteins of Fraud.*

When she was just short of 17 years old, and pregnant by him, Mary ran away to the continent with Percy Bysshe Shelley, a man who was on his way to lasting fame as one of England's premier poets. Shelley, from an aristocratic family, had been educated at Eton and briefly at Oxford before he was tossed out (or, as the English gently put it, "sent down" from the university). He was five years older than Mary, and deserting a pregnant wife and a child to elope with her. When his wife committed suicide by drowning two years later, Shelley married Mary, in part to be able to present an image of respectability in an unsuccessful lawsuit to obtain custody of his two children.

Frankenstein, Or the Modern Prometheus, was published in three volumes in London in 1816. The subtitle, *The Modern Prometheus*, derives from the Greek benefactor who, in legend, stole fire from the gods on Mount Olympus and delivered it to mankind. He was chained to a rock by Zeus for what was regarded as a traitorous act and an eagle plucked pieces from his liver daily, which grew back during the night, until he finally was rescued by Hercules. *Prometheus Unbound* would be the title of Shelley's most famous collection of poems, and the story of Prometheus had been detailed by Mary's father in a book for children. It also was the title of a poem by Byron.

Shelley died by drowning while returning home on a boat that sank in the Bay of Spezia in July 1822, eight years after he had run off with Mary. She lived another 29 years before succumbing to a brain tumor at the age of 53 on February 1, 1851.

Some interesting ties exist between Wells' *Frankensteins of Fraud* and Shelley's classic novel. Kenneth Neill Cameron, a leading Shelley scholar in America, was married to Mary Bess (Owen) Cameron, the author of *The Booster and the Snitch* (1964), still the best study ever done of department store shoplifting. Mary

Bess Owen had been a graduate student working with Edwin H. Sutherland at Indiana University at the time that Sutherland introduced the term "white-collar crime" into the English language during a speech in Philadelphia in 1938. The typewritten version of Sutherland's speech has a handwritten note on it: "Written by Mary Bess Owen, and slept through by Lois Howard [another graduate student]." When I talked to Mary Cameron about eight or so years ago in New York City, where she had been a dean at Hunter University, she said that Sutherland was only being playful with the inscription, but that she had been influential in pushing him toward studying the wrongdoings of people in power, in part because of values that she had gotten from her husband-to-be, who in turn had derived some of them from the ideas of Percy Shelley and his wife.

Sutherland was the mentor of Donald Cressey, one of the founding forces of the Association of Certified Fraud Examiners and a close friend of the author of *Frankensteins of Fraud*. Cressey, who died about a decade ago, would have been enormously pleased with this book. He had no tolerance for indecency, and he would have taken pleasure in seeing the despicable behavior of these Frankensteins of Fraud held up to a penetrating light, showing them to be what they actually were, rather than what they pretended to be.

Specialists in fraud detection will find a great deal of information and insight in this book that should prove valuable for their work. The details of scamming may change, but the essential tactics and attitudes persist. General readers too will find the stories fascinating portraits of the worst side of some of the worst people of recent times. For lay persons and specialists alike, *Frankensteins of Fraud* will prove not only instructive, but also a wonderfully good read.

Gilbert Geis
Professor Emeritus
Department of Criminology, Law and Society
University of California, Irvine

Preface

The ten *Frankensteins of Fraud* in this book represent the worst monsters of 20th century capitalism. Their fiendish financial schemes wreaked havoc on society, and destroyed many more people than Mary Shelley's Creature did. Most of us—myself included—first met the Frankenstein monster as children at the movies or on our TV screens. The story was simple—an evil hideous creature, fashioned from dead bodies by Viktor Frankenstein, went berserk.

But there's much more to the tale than that.

The book *Frankenstein* (1816) was the brainchild of Mary Wollstonecraft Shelley. She was only 19 at the time, recently married to the celebrated poet Percy Bysshe Shelley. Mary's motive for writing her first (and most famous) novel was, believe it or not, boredom. During a wet and confining summer in Switzerland, Mary, her husband, and their friend, Lord Byron, each decided to write a ghost story—as a sort of a writing competition amongst themselves. Mary won the contest, and her book was published the same year.

When Mary died in 1851, she could not have imagined that her work would live on indefinitely. But so it has in the nearly 200 years since this classic novel was written. However, in the interim, the Frankenstein created by Mary Shelley became the Boris Karloff-like monster invented in Hollywood. And although both versions of the Creature were physically repulsive, Shelley's character wasn't always so bloodthirsty.

He got that way, the monster claims, from seeing injustice all around him; people were not able to look past his frightening countenance to the real person underneath. So when society—and his own creator—rejected him, the Creature felt his wrath was justified. Confronting Dr. Viktor Frankenstein, the Creature laments:

> *"Oh, Frankenstein, be not equitable to every other,*
> *and trample on me alone, to whom thy justice, and*
> *even thy clemency and affection, is most due.*
> *Remember that I am thy creature. I ought to be Adam,*
> *but I am rather the fallen angel, whom thou drivest*
> *from joy for no misdeed. Everywhere I see bliss,*
> *from which I am irrevocably excluded. I was benevolent*
> *and good; misery made me a fiend."*

The moral is that almost no person, including this fiendish murderer, considers himself evil. Just as the Creature blamed his transgressions on others, you will see that the *Frankensteins of Fraud* believed their illegal conduct was someone else's fault—banks, insurance companies, the government, the public. Some argue that is the nature of man: when we do something bad, our conscience forces us to justify the act.

The Frankensteins of Fraud in this book would say (rightfully) that the greed of their victims gave them life. Dr. Frankenstein's greed for fame gave birth to a monster. On screen, the creator is portrayed as a lunatic. But in the novel, the Doctor is—in Harold Bloom's words—a "moral idiot;" he does not realize the implications of his actions.

Similarly, the 20th-century victims described in these pages did not intend to give life to heinous financial schemes. But they did. It is no coincidence that the central theme for what you are about to read can be traced to the epigraph for Mary Shelley's classic work, which was inspired by a line from John Milton's *Paradise Lost*.

> *"Did I request thee, Maker, from my clay*
> *to mold me man? Did I solicit thee from*
> *darkness to promote me?"*

Shelley's simple point is that we create our own monsters, and the same goes for *Frankensteins of Fraud*.

The selection of the financial monsters for this book was not an easy task because the 20th century produced a bumper crop of them. There are a number of reasons; one is paramount. Prior to the 1900s, most profit-making organizations were privately held. But because of globalization and other considerations, companies started raising more and more capital through outside investors. Since the price investors are willing to pay depends on their perception of the potential profit, it didn't take long for unscrupulous businessmen (and a few businesswomen) to figure out that the higher return they promised, the more money they raked in.

This fictitious promise—providing attractive and often outrageous profits—has become the hallmark of fraud over the last 100 years. The list of investment swindles alone is staggering. Indeed, the cases rejected for this book—Charles Keating, the Reverend Jim Bakker, Robert Maxwell, Billy Sol Estes, and many more—point out the stiff competition to be included in the top ten white-collar criminals of the 20th century.

To the anti-fraud scholar, which I have been (in one form or another) over the past 30 years, some of the choices for the *Frankensteins of Fraud* are obvious. In the beginning of the century, one needs to look no further than the notorious Charles Ponzi. During the summer of 1920 alone, he collected over $20 million from thousands of investors by promising to double their money in 90 days. He was so successful that he is one of the few people to have a crime named for them—the Ponzi scheme.

At the end of the 20th century, another obvious choice is junk-bond king Michael Milken. He was not only successful at committing a multi-billion dollar financial fraud, he served less than two years in prison for his crimes. He's still alive and financially well today. Some even consider Milken a victim. Indeed, his expertise is in high demand for big bucks.

Other choices for inclusion in *Frankensteins of Fraud* may not be so readily apparent. You may have never heard of some of them. However, as you read, you will discover how these monsters all drew from the same bag of tricks to beguile their victims.

I first noticed this characteristic during the early years of my career in fraud detection and deterrence. Since this is my seventh book, many readers already know that I began as an FBI agent specializing in the investigation of financial crimes. Because I was previously a practicing CPA, it was a natural fit. After nearly ten years, I left for the private sector to become an anti-fraud consultant. And 12 years ago, I became board chairman of the Association of Certified Fraud Examiners, which I helped found.

In three decades, I've investigated and studied literally thousands of cases of fraud and corruption. So I've basically learned how little I know. As a result, I've called on some of the greatest minds in the field to help make the selections for *Frankensteins of Fraud.*

There are a number of people responsible for this book, but two were vital. The first is Dr. Gil Geis, professor emeritus in criminology from the University of California, Irvine. Gil traces his roots in white-collar crime research directly to the masters themselves, Sutherland and Cressey. Dr. Geis has authored 13 books, hundreds of articles, and has conducted more original fraud research than any living expert. As a result, his counsel in establishing the "top ten" list was invaluable.

The second person responsible for *Frankensteins of Fraud* is Brett Holloway-Reeves, or "Dash" as I affectionately call him. Dash did much of the original research; prepared story drafts; assisted in the editing; and conducted multiple interviews. That he is not listed as co-author is a testament to my extreme vanity, regardless of the fact that I alone am responsible for any errors or omissions.

Thanks goes to Elsie Airhart, Jackie Kizer, Michael Alleman, Martin T. Biegelman, Giacomo J. "Jack" Bologna, Dick Carozza, Claude K. Chappelear, Sharon Chaumont, Marita Crawford, Isabel M. Cumming, Renae Dockins, Orrin Fuelling, John D. Gill, Richard Goldberg, Anne Graham, Carrie Gregor, Carrsyn Gregor, Jennie Gregor, Rusty Gregor, John J. Hickey, Paul Hayes, Thomas D. Hubbard, Jennifer Huth, "Izzy," David Katz, Matt Kinsey, Jackie Kizer, Scott Landry, G. Michael Lawrence, Philip C. Levi, Donald S. LeVie, Jr., Robert J. Lindquist, Katherine McLane, Ann McGrath, David McKay, Elaine Cressey Ohlen, Charles M. Peck, DuWayne Pheffer, Brian Reeves, Randall Sanborn, Harrison Saunders, Nikki Seibert, Abe Shalot, Ronnie Simonds, Judith Smith, Judy Smith, Denise Stretton, Delores Tuttle, John Warren, Paul Weissman, and Hester Young.

I must also acknowledge the assistance of key staffers at the Association of Certified Fraud Examiners—my partners Kathie Green and Jim Ratley; and my brainy and beautiful assistant, Jeanette LeVie. Without the three of them and my loving wife, Judy, I would never have the time or the inspiration to write.

Joseph T. Wells
Austin, Texas
June, 2000

Contents

CASSIE L. CHADWICK.
1904.

Cassie Chadwick

(1857 - 1907)

CHAPTER 1

The Trial:
Cassie Chadwick

"Shall I create another, like yourself, whose joint wickedness might desolate the world? ...Your evil passions will be renewed, and you will then have a companion to aid you in the task of destruction."
—*Viktor Frankenstein*

On a cool sunny afternoon in late April 1905, U.S. Attorney John J. Sullivan paced in front of the jury box. Twelve men listened as Sullivan framed for them their duty. "There is no law in this country so well settled as the law governing conspiracies to rob national banks without the use of dynamite," Sullivan proclaimed, his spirits buoyed by the nodding heads of the jurymen. "You have before you today, what twelve men may in this country never have had before them in all criminal history—a criminal of conspicuous note—a notorious and dangerous character—the fate of whom never was determined before by any jury in any court, this *Duchess of Diamonds*, the most dangerous criminal known to human society today."

From across the courtroom she glared, enveloped in black, as if she mourned for her own wretched person. Beneath a black silk taffeta shawl she wore a black dress, also silk, its hemline obscuring the laces of her stiletto-heeled boots. Wide combs, their teeth carved in ebony wood, pulled her gray-striped hair back severely from her face, where her reedy lips frowned. Occasionally her mouth twitched as Mr. Sullivan snapped one epithet after another into the brittle air of the courtroom. Beside the woman's chair, a parasol leaned against a black hat, its narrow brim fashioned from Milan straw, topped by a floppy crown of layered silk.

As if Viktor Frankenstein had granted his Creature's wish and used his unholy powers to animate a *female* body, here sat this woman. She had defied moral principles and the banking laws of the state of Ohio during a lifetime of treachery and lies. Her eyes, witnesses testified, exerted "hypnotic powers." It was rumored she could bestir the invisible magnetic forces which governed the earth, aiding her to sway men's souls and open their wallets. Poor men threw every dollar they could grab—and their lives—at this woman's feet. Rich men gave her millions. Over the years, she had incarnated a harem of aliases: Lydia Devere, Alice Bestado, Mazie Bagley, Madame Hoover. She was called *Lady Bountiful*, the *Queen of Swindlers*, the *Duchess of Diamonds*—in sum, *The Most Notorious Woman of Her Age*. A tabloid biography, hastily published on the eve of the sensational trial, offered:

The History and Story
OF THE DOINGS OF THE
Famous
Mrs. Cassie L. Chadwick
THE SO-CALLED
"Queen of Finance"
SHOWING
How She Fleeced the Bankers

Approaching 50 years old, Cassie Chadwick might be forgiven if the spark of her sexual engine had dimmed. Her once excitatious bosom now formed an undifferentiated mass, its folds strapped uncomfortably beneath a steel-wired corset. Wrinkles had gathered her skin, causing her once pert features to take on a simian cast. Yet, Mr. Sullivan warned the men of the jury, "Some of you may be feeling the force of her hypnotic eyes even now."

Cassie Chadwick's seductive charms, it would seem, extended beyond merely physical attributes. Hadn't she, even in her matronly years, persisted in tempting one man after another to his doom? Hadn't she driven poor Leroy Chadwick away from Cleveland, the city that gave him life and wealth? Hadn't she ushered Charles Beckwith, small-town banker and trustee for Oberlin College, to an early grave? Well, hadn't she?

The Duchess of Diamonds

For six months prior to the trial, Cleveland buzzed with the name of Cassie Chadwick. She'd been escorted from the train by federal deputies the previous December 1904, direct from The Tombs prison in New York City. She'd been held for a week in The Tombs and was feeling the strain. On the train ride west, she'd begun to fret. "What do the people think of me in my home city? Are they all against me? Will there be a crowd to stare at me?" She gave a loud cry and then flooded several deputies' handkerchiefs. Then, in the space of two minutes, she sat upright and commented gaily about the deep snowfall thus far in a chilly winter.

Cleveland gossips noted that Leroy Chadwick had not bothered to return from Paris, despite having several weeks' notice about his wife's predicament. When he was asked about the accusations against his wife—that she'd conned several millions from bankers using forged notes—Leroy could think only of himself. "There is no truth in the report that Mrs. Chadwick settled a large sum on me," he announced, though no one had asked. "Anyone would be able to see that I am not a man who has received millions from his wife. Do I look like a man of millions?" In fact, Leroy looked like a man who never made a decision more grave than whether to have eggs or fruit for breakfast, and who spent a considerable portion of his day waxing his mustache. Cassie rendered her own defense in a public statement just after New Year's 1905.

> *Public clamor has made me a sacrifice. Here I am, an innocent woman hounded into jail, while a score of the biggest businessmen in Cleveland would leave town tomorrow if I told all I know. Yes, I borrowed money, but what of it. I will even admit I did not borrow in a business-like way. I wish now I had followed old rules a little closer. But you can't accuse a poor businesswoman of being a criminal can you?*

Jail ain't a bad place to be, Cassie argued, if you're regarded as the Most Notorious Woman of the Age. "Let me make it plain why I do not seek bail," she declared.

> *It is not because I cannot raise the funds. Only today I received a special delivery letter from one of the wealthiest men in the country, who has known me since I was twelve years old. In this letter he assured me that despite the penalty of publicity, he would sign my bond for any amount. I shall refuse this kind offer. For while I am in jail I am free from the annoyance of curious*

> *people. If I were living at home or in a hotel under bail, I could*
> *not hire men enough to protect me from the affronts of these*
> *people. I shall stay with Sheriff Barry at least until the*
> *bankruptcy case is settled. I have not wrongfully obtained money*
> *from anyone, and I will repay every dollar of my indebtedness.*

Cassie's situation was causing a particular stir along Euclid Avenue, the tony neighborhood that played host to most of Cleveland's "400," i.e., the richest and most influential members of the city, including the man responsible for Cleveland's growth into an industrial metropolis, John D. Rockefeller. Cassie had never been popular among the "400," who found her haughty in her person and tacky in her taste. She gained one of her enduring nicknames from a Euclid Avenue resident, none other than James Chadwick, her husband's brother. "Her hair, streaked with gray, was piled high and glistened with diamonds," James told the court's inquiry. "A double necklace of diamonds circled her full throat. There were diamonds on her shoulders and diamonds on the front of her dress. She struck me as a handsome woman, then, though at other times I thought her plain. The most remarkable thing about her was her eyes. They were brown, I think, though when I looked in them I was at once filled with such a feeling of strange excitement I cannot swear to the color."

A Toronto jeweler reported that Cassie had more than a passing affection for baubles. "We sold her in all 56 rings, in addition to various other articles of jewelry. She knew how to buy jewels. She paid us $3,000 for the last ring. To get this jewel I traveled more than 12,400 miles, having to cover much of Europe before finding a ring I thought would take her fancy. This ring was a peculiar marquise setting, and contained probably the largest diamond ever brought into Canada. I bought her many other treasures in the way of rare jewelry while on the same trip."

Little Girl Lost

Cassie Chadwick was not the madam's real name. She was christened Elizabeth Bigley. Born in 1867, Elizabeth was the baby girl in a family of three girls and two boys. Her father, Daniel Bigley, worked as a section hand maintaining the railroad while Alice Bigley raised the children on a small farm outside Woodstock, Ontario. Elizabeth was a sickly child, born with a lisp and a susceptibility to chills. A fever at age three left her all but deaf in her right ear. The deafness and her lisp combined made Elizabeth appear retarded to many people, but the child was craftier than most her age. She often bragged to her classmates at Woodstock's little schoolhouse that she was going to grow up and become the richest woman in the Dominion of Canada and answer only to Queen Victoria.

Elizabeth had several brushes with the law. At age 16, she caused a stir in the nearby hamlet of Hamilton by representing herself to area dressmakers as a European debutante on holiday. She'd acquired some of the latest fashions by passing around a card printed with a few dollars stolen from her mother's egg money:

Miss Lydia Bagley
Heiress to $15,000

A few years later, she made a similar spree through shops around Woodstock, endorsing checks in a flamboyant script, "Mrs. E. G. Thomas." She was recently widowed, Elizabeth told the storekeepers, and was spending a few dollars of her husband's estate to assuage her grief. She bought a necklace and some earrings—nothing terribly expensive, just costume jewelry—and several dresses, some $250 total. She'd also had a reed organ, costing $150, toted into the tiny apartment she rented along Maple Street. When pressed to make the checks good, Elizabeth presented her creditors with a letter from a London attorney, one Reuben Kipp, who vouched that Mrs. E.G. Thomas had been bequeathed $1,800 in her husband's estate.

The Kipp letter, local prosecutors easily determined, was a forgery. A meager bank account in the name of "E.G. Thomas" in Toronto had been cleaned out long ago. However, with the Bigley family agreeing to stand good for the debt, and seeing all the merchandise was returned intact, a judge took pity on poor half-deaf, lisping Elizabeth. After a single morning's questioning, Elizabeth was declared not guilty by reason of insanity, based on her utter ignorance of banking fundamentals—like balancing a checking account—and because she continually made faces at the jury.

"It's not that I'm crazy," she explained to her sister, named Alice like their mother. "It was just a way for the judge to let me go without having to punish me." Alice had agreed to let Elizabeth live with her and her husband in Cleveland, hoping the girl would find brighter prospects than she had in the little towns of southern Ontario.

It wasn't Elizabeth's first time in the big city, though. In Toronto, for a year or so after her trial in Woodstock, Elizabeth had paid her rent by working as one of the *ribbon girls*, so called because "their attempts at finery consist chiefly of a bright red ribbon worked into the hair of one, and the blue neck ribbon of the other," in the words of one observer. Homeless, penniless, many of them clueless, these girls from the hinterlands and from far across the Atlantic avoided 16-hour shifts in a textile factory by offering themselves on the pickup circuit.

Fed up with life as a ribbon girl, Elizabeth came to live with her sister Alice in the spring of 1880, at No. 503 Superior Street, Cleveland, Ohio.

Elizabeth found employment with a group of other young women learning the milliner's art. They all lived in a large house at 359 Superior Street, just down from Alice's apartment, and very near the docks. She also told fortunes, using the name *Madame La Rose.*

The Chadwick Estate, 8214 Euclid Avenue

It all sounded so unlikely, Clevelanders chirped in the spring of 1905. Almost half a million people lived in Cleveland now. A number of Cleveland streets had been paved and rival street-car companies vied for passengers' pennies. How could a half-deaf, lisping girl rise from the obscurity of the Canadian backwoods to walk among the celebrated "400"? Maybe the rumors were true. This woman had made a deal with the Devil, giving her sway over men. Dr. Leroy Shippen Chadwick, a widower starved for companionship, had thus been taken in by a wily old whore with hypnotic powers.

The couple was married in February 1897. They visited Windsor, Ontario, where Cassie—the former Mrs. C.L. Hoover—was introduced to Leroy's daughter, Darla Chadwick, who was attending boarding school in Canada. On the Sunday following their return west, Leroy dropped the bomb on the Cleveland "400." As one narrator later described it, "Dr. Chadwick appeared at church and with him was his wife.... His friends could not understand it, but the subject of his marriage was never mentioned. They took their curiosity home with them and smothered it in the culture to which they had been reared."

Breaking the silence years later, a Euclid Avenue denizen told how the new Mrs. Chadwick had squeezed what was left from poor old Leroy's broken heart. "Chadwick was our family physician," the man said. "He was the closest friend of our family, until he married this woman. At the time, he was a struggling doctor, who'd almost been ruined by poor business dealings and the settling of his wife's estate. He was in much trouble over tangled finances when he got married. Afterward, we saw him only occasionally. The marriage, we all in the old circle supposed, was a sort of business arrangement."

Indeed, Leroy Chadwick sought neither companionship nor sexual favors from the woman he called Madame Hoover. Leroy was broke, he confessed to Madame, and he had no plan for what he'd do once the news came out. Madame Hoover assured her friend— who occasionally visited because her massages helped him with his severe back pain—that she could solve his money problems. All Leroy had to do was marry her and give her control of the estate. She'd mingle the few funds Leroy had left with her own considerable wealth and both of them would prosper. Leroy said sure. As long he continued receiving his monthly stipend, he didn't care where the money came from.

For Christmas 1900, Leroy and Cassie's third Christmas together as a married couple, she insisted they leave the house early for a long evening of dinner, a musical at the Lyric Opera House, and a carriage ride afterward. Poor Leroy was all but tuckered out when he finally made it back to 8214 Euclid—to a house he hardly recognized. "This is my Christmas present to you," she announced. As a correspondent noted, "The old furnishings of the house had been torn out and the trappings were now more elegant than they had ever been." The windows were now framed by heavy drapes of a burgundy shade with gold trim. There were six matching Watteau cabinets, piled with chinaware and knick-knacks. There were miniatures galore. Cassie had changed the carpets to Persian rugs. She'd bought oil paintings and wood-carvings and statues. She had changed the fixtures in the bathroom and hung electric lights. "Merry Christmas!" Cassie said again, jolting Leroy with a jab to the ribs.

His father had built the house on a purposefully modest plan. The Chadwicks were not the ostentatious sort. Even the polished towers of the exquisitely preserved pipe organ, an antique costing $9,000 that Cassie thought sure would get a rise out of her husband, could not relieve the shock gripping Leroy's befogged mind. The once plain, roomy halls of the Chadwick house were stuffed to overflowing. It had been transformed in a single evening into the most baroque of curio shops. The eye found no rest amid the clutter, each mound spilling into the next.

Among the goods noted by Cassie's visitors: "a plaster cast of a Negro boy holding a card tray," "a sofa with sealskin upholstery," "a huge oil painting of pigs drinking from a trough." Madame's personal jewelry chest contained eight drawers, brimming with pearls and diamond oddities worth at least $100,000. Guests also noted her affection for clocks, as evidenced by a sampling of clocks in every form, big and small, including novelty clocks, like the fire engine that not only displayed the time but also boasted fully working bells, wheels, and a whistle. In her several Watteau cabinets, Cassie kept 5-cent figurines crowded elbow to rib with lavishly detailed porcelain miniatures. In one corner stood a glass chair, shaped like a seashell; on the opposite side of the room, a "musical chair" played a tune whenever a guest sat down.

During Cassie's trial in 1905, an anonymous female writer persuaded the deputies guarding the Chadwick home to turn their backs for a couple of hours. In a breathless report to readers across the Midwest, the woman described what she found inside. "There was a mite of a monkey, a fairy in a seashell, and a pair of tiny Indian shoes. They might have cost 10 cents each. They might have cost a small fortune. Across the room, another handsome cabinet. Inside stood an array of marble statues about eight inches high. They were so nearly alike and there were so many of them they might have been bought by the hundred."

In what was once a roomy parlor, Cassie had installed a grand piano. Just behind the instrument there glared "the largest oil painting in the house." The visitor complained, "The picture was so large and the room so small that I couldn't get far enough from it to make out what it represented. There were a lot of men in it. To the right of this gargantuan scene, a mite of a painting depicted the finding of baby Moses in the bulrushes. To the left, a bull fight had been carved into a plank of ivory—there slouched the wounded bull, the frenzied horses, the cheering crowd, all in ivory. Even the drops of blood showed, all in a scene no more than two feet long by 16 inches high."

Mr. Carnegie, Please

Two years after Leroy received his heart-attack of a Christmas gift, Cassie was experiencing some pains of her own. She'd stretched the Chadwick credit as far as it would go. Leroy was enjoying the latest leg of a European tour he'd begun shortly after that fateful Christmas night. He was safely tucked away in a Paris hotel, but unless Cassie kept paying the bills, they'd all end up in the poor house.

So in the spring of 1902, Cassie engaged an attorney named Virgil P. Kline to accompany her to New York City. Mr. Kline agreed to assist Mrs. Chadwick on a purely personal basis, his professional duties being taken up with his position as "the leading lawyer of Ohio and attorney for the Standard Oil Company," in the words of a regional history. Cassie told Kline she was the niece of Frederick Mason, who worked in Andrew Carnegie's financial organization. Uncle Frederick had died, though, and Mr. Carnegie now held Cassie's inheritance in a trust as instructed by Mason's will. That's where they were headed now, to Carnegie's home at Fifth Avenue and 91st Street, Manhattan. Knowing the great man's reputation for privacy, Kline agreed to wait in the carriage until Cassie had okayed their appointment. After some 20 minutes, Kline saw his companion return, aflush with excitement. She had been expecting about $7.5 million in the trust fund. But Mr. Carnegie had added a considerable amount of securities and had grown the stake to nearly $11 million! Hopping into the carriage with more than her usual sleekness of foot, Cassie nearly spilled the contents of a box onto Kline's lap; he saw the box contained notes on the Caledonia Railroad of Scotland and a deed of trust signed by Andrew Carnegie. The deed alone was for the amount of $10,246,000!

Cassie shivered throughout the ride back to their hotel, several times taking Kline by the arm and wetting his sleeve with her tears. Before they parted that evening, she had shared a secret with Virgil Kline that she'd never told anyone. "She was not the niece of Frederick Mason, but the natural daughter of Mr. Carnegie himself. This great wealth was given to her that the 'Steel King' might do justice to her." Cassie inquired about what bankers in Cleveland might be trusted. Kline agreed to make her personal introduction to Mr. Iri Reynolds, president of Wade Park Bank.

After a fairly lengthy interview, in which Cassie grilled Mr. Reynolds about his bank's history and lending practices, she took him into her confidence. "I can't speak my father's name, but you've heard of him." She allowed him to glimpse the edge of the deed she held, signed *Carnegie.* She explained her shock to learn from her Uncle Fred that her parent was seated so highly. And she had been even more shocked when he bestowed on her a set of Caledonia Railroad bonds.

It was clear to Iri Reynolds that the woman before him was no spoiled brat, slurping up daddy's money. She conducted herself with dignity; and she spoke intelligently of the methods of finance, asking probing questions about the bank's own investment portfolio. The attorney who recommended her, Virgil Kline, had praised Cassie's knowledge of ancient Greece, one of Kline's philological passions. The two of them had talked about Greek history and archaeological curiosities for hours. Cassie had exhibited "abstruse information" that Kline had seldom encountered outside the university, and had never seen in a woman.

Against the Caledonia bonds that Mrs. Chadwick sealed inside an envelope, Iri Reynolds let her have a $30,000 line of credit for expenses. She handed him the envelope and the deposit slip which she'd completed during their conversation. Reynolds felt his hand tremble, torn as he was between doing the proper, bankerly thing—verifying the documents—and doing the thing Mrs. Chadwick clearly expected him to do—shake her hand and wish her good day.

****

The men who loaned Cassie money were amply repaid. For a $25,000 loan, given three months to repay, she'd toss in $5,000 for interest and fees. Those spiked interest rates didn't usually accrue at the First National. But Cassie was a special case. By one accounting, on some $750,000 she borrowed from Cleveland banks, Cassie paid $233,000 in fees and interest, as she began chasing her bad loans by getting loans at new institutions.

At trial, despite her notoriety for multiple acts of fraud-by-hypnosis, Mrs. Chadwick was charged with only one crime. The one would symbolically stand in for all the others. According to the charge, Mrs. Chadwick had bankrupted the Citizens National Bank of Oberlin, a tiny operation near Oberlin College, by persuading the bank's president, one Charles T. Beckwith, to act as her business manager. Beckwith had paid off debts that Cassie Chadwick made at other banks during her legendary shopping expeditions, using more than $100,000 of his own funds as well as the banks' money.

After hearing from Iri Reynolds that Cassie held $11 million in notes in a Cleveland bank—and after hearing, "unofficially," who Cassie's father was—Beckwith talked his clerk A.B. Spear into joining the speculation. Some bankers just can't keep a secret. Both men received a salary of $10,000 a year as co-managers of the Chadwick estate. The salaries were nothing, Beckwith and Spear told each other, compared to what they'd reap once the Carnegie funds came under their full control. The Oberlin Bank, capitalized at $60,000, was but a rowboat scooting them toward a yacht.

The Sad Tale of Joe Lamb

The chorus of Cassie's wretched deeds told of a life spent a step ahead of her latest lie. She had fallen out with her sister Alice when she was caught, as Elizabeth Bigley, having pawned Alice's new furniture for $300. Of course the furniture wasn't worth more than $100, but Elizabeth had pawned it to three different brokers.

In 1882, she was married as Lydia Springsteen to a Cleveland doctor. Though William Springsteen was a particularly down-and-out and drunken doctor, seeing a few patients in his back-stair walkup, he nevertheless made good pickings for Elizabeth as she learned a trade more satisfying and lucrative than prostitution, namely fraud. The marriage lasted but 12 days before Springsteen was faced with a pile of bills. "You said your rich Irish relatives sent you all those presents!" he railed. When the three pawnbrokers came round, each with a claim to Alice York's furniture and a charge against Elizabeth Bigley, Springsteen sent his little woman packing.

It was said that Cassie spent most of the year 1883 in convalescence with a kindly Lutheran family in Erie, Pennsylvania. She was calling herself Mazie Bagley. To gain the couple's aid, she'd performed a trick she learned in the Toronto train stations, slicing her gums with a razor and fainting, somewhere very near an obviously good Samaritan. Mazie, a "young heiress," promised to pay her hosts back with interest once she reached Cleveland. However, as the good folks of Erie learned,

> Mazie Bagley has passed peacefully away, putting her full trust in God, at 2:30 o'clock on March 27, 1884. Poor Mazie's remains were taken to their native home in Canada for interment and were followed to their last resting place by a large and sorrowing concourse of friends.

Elizabeth couldn't resist a parting shot in a less cultured voice.

> I thought you had heard. She was a splendid girl, but unfortunately weakminded.

However, of all the tales resounding through the streets of Cleveland during her celebrated trial, the most revealing involved a poor man named Lamb and an ambitious lawyer who branded a woman for life.

****

During the mid- to late 1880s, in the person of Madame Lydia Devere, Elizabeth left her mark on the city of Toledo, known as Cleveland's rougher cousin. In some parts of town, Madame Devere was the toast. First in a house on Washington Street, near 12th, and later at Broadway and Clayton, Madame cut a swath through Toledo's gusto-charged underworld. At Madame's, said a popular account, "There was high revel by night and well into the morning. Men jollied each other over their beer about the banquets and social sessions with *The Devere* and her comely associates, for the Madame, a prepossessing woman herself, usually had an attractive friend to assist at the entertainment."

Madame Devere retained enough charms to enthrall a clerk and to establish herself as a temptress of distinction. Joseph Lamb delivered packages and sorted mail for a small firm in downtown Toledo. To his eyes, Madame Devere was a lady who'd suffered some bad luck, but who nevertheless refused to give up her optimism. As Joe recounted later, Lydia told him she'd married young and moved to England with her husband, who was killed in a riding accident. "After her return to America, she had settled at Rochester. There she married a young physician and they enjoyed every luxury. But the husband, she said, was not satisfied, and later entered a career of debauchery. In a single year he squandered more than $50,000 in riotous living. She left him and removed to Cleveland. Some time later he was arrested for forgery, Madame said. While he was in prison he committed suicide, I believe she said by drinking concentrated lye."

It was terrible, the way some men treated a lady such as Madame. Joe, who was himself married and the father of five little girls, promised to do everything he could to prevent Madame's further suffering. He helped out with a few dollars here and there—five, ten, twenty dollars, then a hundred, then two hundred. When Joe came to Madame's rooms one afternoon and found her in feverish convulsions, he ached himself in sympathy. But he had no way to get the $2,000 Madame said she needed for an operation, a *womanly* operation, she'd confided in a quivering voice.

Confessing to detectives later, his shoulders bowed into the shape of a harness, Joe Lamb related how he used the last few hundred dollars in his savings account to leverage Madame her money: "On February 1, 1888, I got $200 for her on a personal note from the Ketcham National Bank. On February 6, I got $300 more from the same bank. February 20, I got $500 by having my friend J. J. Mattocks endorse a note with me. In exchange for these sums, Madame gave me her note for $1,000, due one year afterward. I also gave her at this time my personal note for $275, payable three months afterward. This note she claimed she gave to her physician. It turned up in the Second National Bank; I learned that she had bought a sealskin sack with the money.... During this week alone, I had raised for her $1,785, and had only her note for $1,000."

When Joe's credit ran out, Madame still pushed for more. She presented him with a government bond for $25,000 in the name of Richard Brown of Cleveland. Joe was supposed to take the bond to his bank, where he could cover his notes and open an account for Madame. Then they'd write checks, paying off the debts at the other banks where Joe had borrowed. Their total obligation was crawling past $10,000 and generating interest by the day.

A bank clerk at Second National spotted Madame's forgery on the bond and had both Joe Lamb and Lydia Devere arrested. "The day of my arrest," Joe recalled, "I pleaded with her, begged her to come to some understanding with the banks. For four hours I talked with her, but she was indifferent. At last, in a passionate outburst of rage, when I again begged her to submit to the bankers, she said, 'I will do nothing of the sort!' She told me I should go and get a lawyer and bring him to her house. We would manufacture a story that would save us both. I told her no. I said I had done nothing that I feared. She was terrible mad, called me everything, and said I was the biggest fool in existence. I said, 'I know I have been a fool and a dupe.' It was now her turn to beg. She cried, weeping, for me to please send for the lawyer. But I said no."

Irvin Belford, in the course of winning an acquittal for Joe Lamb, simultaneously convicted Lydia Devere and marked her for the rest of her life as a sorceress. With a smug grin and mock humility vying for his features, attorney Belford told how he won his first big case. "I was preparing to make my final plea for Joe Lamb when I read that a prominent French physician had claimed much for hypnotism in the treatment of cases. It was clear, in Lamb's case, that this woman had exerted some remarkable influence over him. Various prominent men and attorneys have told me they felt themselves decidedly uneasy whenever they were subjected to her presence. She had some way of securing their assent to almost anything that she proposed. The ease with which she got ahold of prominent men was wonderful. I remember one old man, very wealthy, who gave her $1,000 and a diamond stud worth

$500 without any security, not even a promissory note. After the trial was done and Lamb acquitted, a great deal was written to the effect that we had made hypnotism a defense in America, as the Frenchman had done on the Continent."

During the trial, Belford didn't hesitate to direct the courtroom's gaze at Joseph Lamb's wife and five daughters, arrayed in a bench near the front. It was said that during Belford's summation "the spectators were moved to tears and even the jurymen wept." Cassie Chadwick was sentenced to nine years in the Ohio State Penitentiary. Joe Lamb was acquitted.

The Trial of Cassie Chadwick

In April 1905, while his wife faced her accusers and a salacious mob in a Cleveland courthouse, Leroy Chadwick was playing a $9,000 pipe organ in the display window of a New York music store. The organ had once belonged to Leroy, a present from his wife. These days he drew a weekly salary for playing standards on the instrument as curiosity seekers stood giggling on the sidewalk.

For Cassie, the last few days of April would mean life or death. She'd already been to prison once, serving nine years for leading poor Joe Lamb to the slaughter. She couldn't take it again. The woman known as Cassie Chadwick, née Elizabeth Bigley, was distinguished not only as a notorious fraudster, but as the first woman imprisoned in Ohio's penitentiary system.

In one of the few moments she allowed herself to show fear, Cassie told her defense attorney, "If they send me to prison, I'll die, Mr. Dawley. I don't mean I'll die 'inside myself.' I mean I'll die, literally." Jay P. Dawley, a respected barrister with somewhat large, kindly eyes and a tuft of goat-like beard on his chin, promised to do all he could. But the odds and the evidence were mounting against them. On the positive side, Dawley told his tearful client, the banker Charles Beckwith couldn't testify against her, since he'd died in February with a wicked case of pneumonia. A.B. Spear, Beckwith's clerk and fellow accomplice, was taking the Fifth Amendment.

On the negative side, prosecutor John Sullivan had documents written in Cassie's own hand. In a matter involving Fay & Wurst, a New York City law firm who'd performed some work on Cassie's behalf, Mr. Fay had informed Mrs. Chadwick that his firm required the $10,000 they were owed right away. Fay wrote to say he was passing through Cleveland and he'd receive her check personally if she'd have one ready. Cassie hastily dispatched a note to the

Citizens National Bank of Oberlin, addressed to the clerk, A.B. Spear:

> *Could we arrange this matter of Mr. W. and Mr. F. in this way: they don't even know that I have ever met you or done any business with you. I think I might say I was going to make a loan through your bank in connection with the College. Now this he would not repeat because he wants to act for me in every way he can in the future. I would not tell him anything that would ever show that we had ever done any business. I would ask you to certify my check dated October 10th, and this would get the matter out of their hands. I could then get the funds on the goods in the East to meet the check, and you would not be anything out, so if you will draw the check for $15,000 and certify it on your checks I can sign it and he will be none the wiser.*
>
> *Now I will pay you and Mr. B. well for this favor, and am sure it will be safe, and you need not let them know anything about matters. There will be nothing for you folks to say, only that the check will be good on that date....*
>
> *I send you also my note dated to cover the F&W certified check, and a small commission for your kindness. I think by advice of my attorney I am myself going to be able to do something which will be of great interest to us all. He will prepare the papers today. I was sick and did not get it arranged yesterday.*
>
> *Please phone me if you can do this. If you do this, I save. What I save, I give you.*
>
> *Very truly, C.L.C.*
>
> *Postscript. I mean I will tell them that I had a deal with the college that will pass through your bank, which is true for I have had, and if they help me further then it will be through you.*

The next day, Cassie followed up her note with clarification:

> *My Dear Mr. Spear and Beckwith:*
>
> *I just said [to Fay and Wurst] I would be receiving funds from a deal that would go through your bank in connection with the College. You need only listen to him. I don't think he will ask any questions. I don't want him to be in possession of any facts. I think best not to. It will only be necessary to you to say that you will renew the paper. Mr. Fay said he was going to take the check*

up and show it to you, and ask you to renew their paper on the strength of the check not being payable before November 1st.

Hoping this will pass off all safe, with many thanks to you both,

Very gratefully, C.L. Chadwick

P.S. He is going first thing in the A.M. He remarked that you would be surprised to see the check in his hands, so you better look surprised. If you do not say it, you can look it.

Lawyer Dawley promised Cassie he'd do everything he could to keep her out of jail. But if she did in fact possess any powers of mesmerism, Dawley thought to himself, this would be a good time to exert them.

****

1903 turned into 1904 and 1904 was inching toward 1905 and Mrs. Chadwick had still not transferred the Carnegie funds into the Citizens National Bank of Oberlin like she'd promised. Charles T. Beckwith was palsied with fear. Cassie remained, as always, calm. She'd arranged a bridge loan, she said to Beckwith in her most soothing lisp, through a prominent man in Massachussetts. Beckwith no longer trusted Cassie's talk of "prominent men." Though she and Beckwith had never discussed Andrew Carnegie personally, Cassie had insinuated the man into nearly every conversation. Cassie told Beckwith that she'd spoken with the Reverend Charles Eaton, pastor of the Euclid Avenue Baptist Church, whose most famous congregationalist was John D. Rockefeller. Cassie had shared with the Reverend the story of her illegitimate parentage ("a prominent industrialist in the Pittsburgh region") and her present money woes. Eaton sent her to his brother John Eaton, a Boston lawyer, who arranged for Cassie to meet with an industrialist and financier named Herbert Newton, of Brookline, Massachussetts.

Using a promissory note from Beckwith, itself backed by the phony bonds in Iri Reynold's vault, Cassie got Newton to loan her $79,000 from his personal account. She also left Brookline with a promissory note, redeemable at any bank, for an additional $50,000. For the $129,000 she agreed to repay $190,000, plus $800 which Newton included to defray her traveling expenses between Cleveland and Brookline.

But Herbert Newton hadn't become a rich man in the back-biting world of industrial America by playing bullshit. He had driven vicious bargains—like $62,000 interest for a $130,000 loan—and he'd held the man across the table to the terms. He made no exceptions for Mrs. Chadwick. In early November 1904, he demanded she at least pay the interest due. She wired to say she couldn't do so right away. Afterward she did not respond to Newton's calls or wires, so the old gentleman traveled to Cleveland himself, where Cassie offered to cover the debt with a new note.

Newton filed suit against Cassie on November 22, 1904. Word shot from Boston westward that Cleveland's celebrated spendthrift—who had thrilled scores of bankers by paying back-alley interest for front-door loans—was soon to bust. Two Cleveland banks followed Newton's lead with their own suits, for $67,000. A pile-on ensued. Elyria Savings Deposit Bank demanded $10,000; the American Exchange Bank of New York City, $29,000; a Pittsburgh industrialist, James Woods Friend, was owed $75,000; the Euclid Avenue Savings Bank and Trust of Cleveland, $38,000. The debits kept piling up, past $2 million.

Though Iri Reynolds kept quiet publicly, he admitted to the board of Wade Park Bank that he'd loaned Mrs. Chadwick $17,000 in bank funds and $10,000 of his own. That wasn't so bad for an institution Wade Park's size, but the direct loans were the least significant aspect of the relationship. As depositors would soon learn, all of Mrs. Chadwick's loans were drawn against her bonds at Wade Park. The Wade Park board was forced to announce that no withdrawals of more than $100 could be made without 60 days' notice, lest a run should shut down the bank altogether.

There were depositor assaults on many banks, including the little Citizens National Bank in Oberlin. Chairman William Bedortha, pitching in with Beckwith and Spear, kept customers happy until nearly sundown on the Saturday following Newton's lawsuit. But on Monday, November 28, 1904, a sign greeted anxious travelers who approached the bank's shuttered doors: "Closed Until Further Notice." Beckwith rode straightaway to 8214 Euclid, crying, begging, eventually sinking to his knees. Cassie recoiled, jabbering, "I'll pay, I'll pay, I'll pay! But I can't pay now."

Beckwith howled from the floor, "You must! I must take the funds with me back to Oberlin. We can visit Mr. Reynolds, at Wade Park. You have the securities there." Beckwith pleaded with his chilly-eyed mistress, "I don't care for my own money. But the bank's money, it belongs to others. Its loss means the loss of my honor. I am too old to face disaster now."

Repulsed by Beckwith's slobbering on her dress and hands, Cassie turned defiant. "I can't pay now. I cannot pay now! Good day, Mr. Beckwith." When Beckwith still wouldn't rise, she gave him several checks, totaling $50,000. These were made out to her by other parties, and endorsed by Mrs. Chadwick in Beckwith's presence. He'd have to hold the checks a week, Cassie said when Beckwith rose to his feet. The declaration nearly sent him back to the floor. After leaving the Chadwick house, Beckwith took the checks to the banks they were drawn on, where they were each denied.

At an emergency meeting of the bank board, attended also by the Trustees of Oberlin College, Beckwith swore, "These loans are backed by a note for $500,000 endorsed by a man who can pay it as easily as you or I would pay a nickel at the fruit stand." When pressed for detail, he shook from head to toe, twisting his thin frame like a crepe myrtle in a blizzard, crying, "I can't, I can't. If I lose home, honor, reputation, everything, I must keep locked in my breast this secret. I am bound by an oath I cannot break." Chairman Bedortha was furious, calling Beckwith a fool and worse, but the misery-ridden banker would not give up his secret.

Herbert Newton had no such scruples. He told the courts and the press that he'd been assured by Beckwith that the debt was underwritten by the name of Andrew Carnegie.

Once the Carnegie rumor came out, Beckwith and Iri Reynolds had no more wiggle room. They had to produce the bonds or else. As Reynolds fumbled with the key to Cassie's safe deposit box, he said that yes, long ago he should have opened the envelope given to him by Mrs. Chadwick and verified its contents, "but to do so would have evidenced a distrust I did not feel." Reynolds emerged from the vault with a stack of personal checks and a poorly worded, poorly printed Deed of Trust signed in a poorly forged version of Andrew Carnegie's handwriting.

> Known [sic] all men by these presents [sic], that I, Andrew Carnegie, do hereby acknowledge that I hold in trust for Mrs. Cassie L. Chadwick, wife of Dr. Leroy S. Chadwick of 1924 Euclid avenue [sic], city of Cleveland, county of Cuyahoga, and the state of Ohio, propety [sic] assigned and delivered to me for said Cassie L. Chadwick by her uncle, Fredrick [sic] R. Mason, in his lifetime (now deceased) which property is of the appraised value of ten million two hundred and forty-six thousand dollars, $10,246,000.

Through his attorneys, Carnegie issued a terse statement: "I never heard of, nor saw, Mrs. Chadwick or Mme. Devere. I have never had any dealings of any nature with Mrs. Chadwick or Mme. Devere. I never signed a note for $500,000 or any other amount;

and if there is such a note bearing my signature in existence, it is a forgery."

The following day, Cleveland's *Plain Dealer* reported that Charles T. Beckwith was suffering extreme *nervosa*:

> *Beckwith's modest home bore a sign saying "Rooms for Rent Here." He was distraught. When a friend sent him flowers, he burst into tears: "Is it still possible I have one friend left? Is it possible that there is still a single person in the world who has a kindly feeling for me?"*

"I am a broken, dishonored old man," Beckwith sobbed. "It is now too late. All is lost.... If I could relieve the sorrow and suffering that I caused, I could die in peace."

Closing Arguments

Cassie's best hope, as attorney Jay P. Dawley explained to her quietly, was the jury. Composed of 11 farmers and a real estate salesman, the group might resent a cadre of wealthy men ganging up on a woman of advanced age (the life expectancy of a woman at that time averaging 47 years). It would also help if Cassie had someone to sit beside her, Dawley suggested, someone offering moral support and a sympathetic figure for the jury to focus on. Leroy Chadwick was still playing his organ in New York City, so Cassie was alone. However, she had a son, she revealed to Dawley. Born in 1886, sometime after Mazie Bagley and before Madame Devere, the boy was named Emil. He'd been raised by Cassie's mother, Alice Bigley. Dawley arranged to have 19-year-old Emil Bigley join his mother, whom he'd seldom seen, at the defendant's table for the duration of the trial.

His arms spread wide before the jury box at the end of testimony, Dawley groaned, "A woman stands alone on one side of this courtroom." Turning to the defendant's table, he gestured toward Cassie. His eyes drooped in sadness as he watched her clutching a black handkerchief, her gaze fixed with horror on the courtroom floor. "Arrayed against her on the other side are all the forces of the great, the powerful, the magnificent United States government, the strongest, the mightiest, the most feared government in the world. And this tremendous crushing power stands as the accuser of this one weak woman...."

In *his* turn, John J. Sullivan began by praising Andrew Carnegie. Sullivan told how Carnegie had not wanted the innocent victims at Oberlin College to suffer for Charles Beckwith's folly, so Mr. Carnegie had covered the bank's losses with a personal check. After a thank-you visit with Oberlin College's president, Henry King, Carnegie donated another $165,000 to expand the college's library.

But John Sullivan warned his jury not to allow Mr. Carnegie's beneficence to obscure the real and enduring threat of the woman called Cassie Chadwick. He reminded them of Deputy Sheriff Porter, who had guarded Mrs. Chadwick. Porter had said, "Every time she looked at me I became dizzy. I can't understand those eyes of hers. The first time Mrs. Chadwick got a good, square look at me I began to blink under the piercing gaze, until I was forced to turn my eyes in another direction. I grew dizzy from the effect, but something, I don't know what it was, would make me return my gaze to hers."

"You have the opportunity to do right today. And you have the opportunity to do wrong. Whatever *you* may do, I feel I have done, in my humble way, the best that I know, to convict a criminal of such conspicuous note, a notorious and dangerous character, the most dangerous criminal known to human society today."

Awaiting the verdict, Cassie was among the most composed persons in the court. The jury reviewed the case for five hours, during which time Cassie sat at the trial table, clad in ripples of black silk, with Emil at her side. Only a few spectators were left when the jurors returned.

A writer in the Cleveland *Plain Dealer* narrated the announcement of the verdict:

"'Guilty,' the clerk read, and the sound of that word was like a shot. But Mrs. Chadwick was hard of hearing; and of all the persons there, she alone had not heard. Emil put his arms around his mother's neck and whispered in her ear. A spasm of pain crossed her face; her head gradually fell forward, and for a moment she was silent. It was as though the blow had crushed her completely. A few tears welled from her eyes and trickled down her cheeks. She put her handkerchief before her face to stop the sudden flow, but it was useless. Her weeping grew until she was sobbing like a child. Thinking his client hadn't made out the wording, Dawley leaned over to tell her, 'We have lost, Mrs. Chadwick.'"

When the bailiff approached, she became agitated, awkwardly stumbling from her seat, reaching for either her parasol or Emil's arm, it wasn't clear which. "Let me go!" she screamed as the bailiff's hand cupped her elbow. "Oh my God! Let me go. I'm not guilty, I'm not guilty. Let me go."

****

Cleveland attorney John A. Smith, tired of the legends, told the *Plain Dealer* in 1919 that Cassie's magic came from a quite natural source: "I don't want anyone to talk to me about hypnotism or anything of that kind. The quality and quantity of her nerve can only be estimated when it is remembered that she left the penitentiary [in 1893], settled within 100 miles of her former operations; married a respectable man, created an elaborate establishment on Euclid Avenue; made a play for society, and won out to some extent. She numbered the financiers of the city among her intimate friends; she borrowed upwards of $1 million and faked it for years. Mrs. Chadwick had not a figure that charmed; her person evoked sympathy, if noticed at all. Her face did not attract, but it did appear to indicate honesty. Her eyes cast no spell. They were sharp, seeing eyes, the windows of her clever brain. From her lips came no blandishment, but a ready story. She made words fit any situation, vanishing obstacles with her woman's tongue."

On a cool sunny afternoon in late April 1905, Elizabeth Bigley, the Canadian farm girl who grew up to become Cassie Chadwick, the most notorious woman of her time, was sentenced to ten years in the Ohio State Penitentiary. She died there in October of 1907.

Charles Ponzi

(1882 - 1949)

CHAPTER 2

Meet Mr. Ponzi:
Charles Ponzi

"Listen to my tale; when you have heard that, abandon or com-
miserate me, as you shall judge that I deserve. But hear me."
—*The Creature*

**MEET MR. PONZI,
THE CHAMPION GET-RICH-QUICK WALLINGFORD
OF AMERICA**
—*Chapter title in Charles Ponzi's self-published autobiography*

Ponzi scheme. **An investment swindle in which high profits are promised from fictitious sources and early investors are paid off with funds
raised from later ones. [After Charles Ponzi (1882-1949), Italian-born
speculator who organized such a scheme (1919-1920)].**
—*American Heritage Dictionary*

Charles Ponzi claimed to have left his home in
Parma—a picturesque city in northern Italy known as
the birthplace of Giuseppe Verdi and *parmigiano*
cheese—perforce. Charles' early memories were haunted
by the visitors who approached his mother's house on a
dark fall night. "I had just closed a lucrative business
deal," he said. "Maybe too lucrative." The *mano negro*, or
Black Hand, had no patience with a 21-year-old upstart
speculator who strutted around like a dandy in a
stageshow. Carlo could leave the country or pay the
considerable cost of having offended the most ruthless
criminal organization in all Europe.

The young fellow threw his belongings into a satchel,
scraped together a few lire, and caught a ship bound for
the U.S.A. "Dearest Momma," he promised, "I'll get rich

and send for you. Give me a year. You will be so proud when I'm done." Imelda Ponzi prayed her boy was telling the truth.

In the hard times they were living, Imelda's only child had fallen into gambling, and the gossips around Parma whispered other things too vicious to repeat to his mother. But Imelda knew. Charles had taken to thieving and forging names on checks. He'd briefly attended the University of Rome, vowing to become an "eminent jurist" like Imelda's father. But he'd caroused more than he'd read, and more than his tiny trust fund could support.

"I was in bed during school hours," the erstwhile student confessed. "In the evenings, I visited the theaters, restaurants, and dance halls. I wanted to dress in the best fashion and tried to keep up the pace set by fellow students whose wealth far outdid mine." When his money dried up, Charles headed home to Momma.

Besides the bags Imelda packed for his hasty departure, Charles also carried money from a council of family members. Charles' father was killed in a boating accident when the boy was only three, so it fell to Imelda's brother to deal with the wayward young man.

"We're not rich," his uncle lectured Charles. The family lived comfortably off the income of several hotels, but still.... "Your debts have been disposed of, and this time, for the last time. No more shysters badgering the family, no more police visits, no more watching my sister cry her eyes out. No more, period." It wasn't only the Black Hand that wanted the boy gone; it was his family.

On the 15th of November 1903, Charles greeted Boston Harbor. He liked to point out—telling the story again and again—that it was a Sunday. From the prow of the boat, he waved his hat to the tiny figures on the dock. A steady drizzle fell amidst the fog. No one noticed young Charles debarking. He was shorter than most of the other men and huddled for warmth in a smart blue suit Imelda had given him for the trip. Charles told himself he needed no welcoming committee. However dismal the skies above his hatless head (he had lost his thick fur cap in a dice game), he imagined himself entering Boston as a rich man.

Charles was anything but rich. He'd blown his grub stake playing *bocci* during the long boat ride. Of the $200 his uncle had pressed on him, he now possessed $2.50. He'd crossed the ocean with a one-way ticket. His friends, his mother, and everything he had ever known were a world away. But then so was the sour luck of his youth.

Stretching on his heels to make his 5' 2" frame look like 5' 3", Charles said to himself, "I'm gonna make history. History and a fortune." He repeated the words like a catechism, wondering if a hotel would let him stay a week before he had to pay.

Things remained bleak for some time. A year came and went without noticeable improvement in Charles' financial status. Up and down the coast, from New York to Maine and back to Boston, he passed through a whirl of menial jobs—a grocery store, an insurance company, a macaroni factory, anywhere he could make a buck without getting too dirty (no railroading or ditch digging for Charles).

Carlo wrote faithfully home to his mother, Imelda, warning her not to let her affairs get so complicated that she could be detained from their reunion in America. He stood poised on the edge of a fortune.

More likely, (and his mother wasn't fooled) he was poised at the edge of a table while men—no better, some clearly much more stupid than himself—ordered appetizers and cocktails. He made a big show of memorizing their requests to the letter, shunning paper and pen like a veritable lion-tamer of waiters.

"Many's the time," Charles reflected, "I fell into some game of chance and watched my fortune accumulating, literally, in coins and bills at my feet, only to have it snatched away."

Charles claimed he was a naïf taken in by cheaters.

Adding Two and Two

BY ADDING TWO AND TWO TOGETHER, MR. PONZI DEVELOPS AN ANALYTIC MIND AND ARRIVES AT THE INEVITABLE HOUR

By 1906, three years into his American sojourn, Charles had soured on the country. Frustrated and all but broke, he grabbed a train to Montreal. So far no venture had borne fruit for Momma 'Melda's boy, but Charles felt his optimism flickering again as he chugged across the Canadian border. He was growing a mustache to look more mature. As soon as he found lodging, he promised himself, he'd start canvassing Montreal.

"My day will come," he wrote in his letters home. Then, as he'd prophesied, Charles saw a notice in an afternoon newspaper for something called the Zarossi Company. His eyes lit up like fireworks on the Fourth of July.

He'd heard about Joseph Zarossi in the Italian neighborhoods of Boston. At a large July 4th celebration the year before, Zarossi was all the talk. Zarossi had left Boston for Montreal, his old friends had gabbed excitedly, and now ran his own cigar factory. It was a small concern, to be sure. But Zarossi had become a prosperous man.

With sparkling mien, Charles took a street car to Montreal's warehouse district, found the address, and bounced up a flight of concrete steps into Zarossi's office. He extended one hand toward Zarossi and waved with the other toward the clerk at the front desk.

Charles looked scrawny to the fleshly Signori Zarossi. Charles seemed too young to know much about business. But at least, Zarossi said to himself, the boy isn't ogling every inch of the landscape with fresh-off-the-boat eyes, clutching his hat in his hand, and shuffling his feet.

"I'm good with figures, and I translate like a scholar," Charles intoned. He included in a brief biographical recitation how his family had dispatched him across the Atlantic to act as a financial emissary. Once Charles established himself as a businessman, he would officially be named the North American representative of his family's considerable wealth.

"Guiseppe Zarossi," Charles' host said, beaming, and extending his chubby hand.

"Carlo Bianchi," Charles replied, a precaution in case Zarossi's old-country contacts might have heard about Carlo *Ponzi's* youthful indiscretions. But Charles needn't have worried. He and Zarossi spoke the same language—not only their native Italian, but also the language of men who dream big, unafraid to blow everything on a turn of fortune's wheel.

Zarossi treated Charles like one of his family. Secretly Zarossi had prayed for a boy every time his wife conceived. He doted on his four girls, but longed for a son with Charles' energy and quickness of mind. The Zarossi girls also showered Charles with attention. All the family loved Charles.

But, true to form, Charles' luck did not hold. The Zarossi Company was failing, he soon learned. Zarossi had borrowed money, at criminal interest rates, to stay afloat. Considering his creditors and their collection methods, bankruptcy might be the least of Zarossi's worries. Oh well, Charles thought, any club that'd have me for a member....

Zarossi asked if the Bianchi family, with its sizable fortune, might want to invest and help put the bank right again? Huh?

Charles said he would try.

In a few days he told Zarossi that the Bianchi family wouldn't be able to intervene, not just now anyway, but he suggested other avenues. He introduced his friend to Angelo Salviati, a schoolmate Charles knew from Parma. Salviati could barely sign his name and read little beyond street signs and decimal points, but he knew just what the Zarossi Company needed.

Salviati fanned a column of bills before Joseph Zarossi's face. "You make money—with money," he lectured. Salviati's fingers were stained yellowish brown from the Turkish cigarettes he continually puffed. He laid the money on the table. "*Rich* is a club, and the only way you get in, you buy your way in."

Salviati helped his new partners reorganize Zarossi Company into the Banco Zarossi. Thousands of immigrants were fanned out across North America, all of them squeezing every penny so they could send money back home for other relatives to come over, or to pay the debts the family had fled in the first place. Banks happily assisted in the transfers. As the dispatch crawled across the Atlantic, financiers placed the money into short-term investments, including speculation in foreign currency.

With just a couple of twists, Salviati demonstrated, you could turn the international transfer to even greater advantage. First, you promise better returns on your deposits than the other guys allow. If they're giving three percent, you give five. Second, you massage your connections. For the Banco Zarossi that meant catering to the Italian enclaves. "These banks, run by the Anglos and the Greeks and the Jews, they're stealing our people blind," Charles and his cohorts broadcast through the Italian neighborhoods. The Banco Zarossi paid better rates, and kept the business in the family, so to speak.

Finally, as Salviati instructed his new partners, the overseas exchange becomes especially lucrative if you hold the money just a little longer than usual, say a month instead of two weeks. Money has value over time. A delay is as good as cash. Who's to notice?

Lots of people noticed. Some Banco Zarossi transfers never arrived at their destination; some arrived but not without hefty bites clipped from the balance. A successful transfer through the Banco Zarossi might take an entire summer for consummation, or it might not go through at all.

Meantime Zarossi had extended loans to various Salviati associates in some high-risk projects bubbling "out West." The projects fizzled. Charles knew they were hung, and said so. Thanks to the help they'd received from Salviati, the bank would definitely fail. And Zarossi would be charged with embezzlement. That is, if the mob raging at the office doors—many of whom knew the banker and his grinning young assistant personally—didn't draw and quarter them first.

Salviati told Zarossi to run. "I'll handle the receivership. Carlo and I, we'll pay off the creditors, probably for pennies on the dollar. When my associates come through with the repayments on the loans, we'll contact you in America and split the proceeds."

Zarossi protested, "What about my girls? My wife and four girls. I cannot become a fugitive with a family to support."

"I'll take care of them," Carlo volunteered. "They're safe with me." It was all he could think of at the time. He didn't trust Salviati and didn't relish acquiring a ready-made family, but at least he wasn't waiting tables.

He *was* waiting, though. Long hours of nothing but *wait*. By Charles' calculations, he'd inherited all of Zarossi's liabilities, including the fretful Mrs. Zarossi and four worrisome daughters, while all the assets stayed bound in legal documents.

Salviati counseled Charles to be patient. He was dying of languor. Every evening as he entered the Zarossi's house on the Rue des Chenes, he found himself pinned by four pairs of hopeful eyes, longing for news of their father.

Finally, his friend Salviati suggested Charles might check on some associates "out West."

Sans farewell, he prepared to exit Montreal early one Monday morning. As he approached the station he was stopped by police who wanted to know how much money he was carrying. They questioned him about the past two days. Did he cash a check on Saturday afternoon? Yes, Charles answered. And was that check for $423.58, endorsed by one Damien Fournier of the Dominion Warehousing Company? Carlo conceded that he had gone with a friend to cash a check, for $423.58, but he said it was his friend, not he, who cashed the check.

"You're a crappy liar and crappier forger," the police officers replied.

Charles' mind flashed back to the Saturday just passed. Salviati was leaning against the wall next to the teller's window. He'd handed Charles a check and swiveled his head away while Charles slid the check through the teller's window.

"I've arranged a loan," Salviati had assured Charles, "through Damien Fournier." Charles knew Fournier. The man had moved a lot of cigars for Joseph Zarossi back in the good old days when Zarossi conducted business for a living. Salviati said Fournier had given him the check they were cashing in exchange for some office equipment.

The police officers snorted at Charles' story. They'd questioned Fournier, and he denied loaning money to anyone connected with Zarossi. Fournier said the check was stolen and his signature was forged. He'd fingered Carlo Bianchi right away. "I know Bianchi all too well," Fournier told the officers. "He's a snake." Fournier described Charles precisely, down to the face-stretching grin, the caterpillar mustache which Charles cupped obsessively with his lower lip, and the flick of the wrist he liked to deploy in his banter.

But this is only Monday, Charles kept thinking. *How can the authorities know about a check I just cashed on Saturday?* The check shouldn't have reached Fournier's bank until Tuesday at the earliest. Salviati must have ratted him out, he reasoned. Salviati had now cleverly dumped both his partners—Zarossi on the lam, Charles in the slam—and absconded with the remains of their banking venture.

Uncle Sam Plays a Trick

Charles was unceremoniously escorted to the St. Vincent de Paul Penitentiary. That $400 check had purchased him three years of hard time. "From the sack of corn leaves and cobs which served as a mattress to the basement dungeons, that prison was indeed a place of penance and punishment," Charles wrote decades later.

Charles got out of St. Vincent's after serving 20 months of his 36-month sentence. Within days, however, he was again hauled into custody, this time in Plattsburg, New York for smuggling five Italian immigrants into America. Charles told everybody who would listen, from the Canadian customs officers to the jailer guarding his tiny cell, that he had simply agreed to help five Italian immigrants make their rail journey into America. He was only a friendly escort for the much taller, non-English speaking gentlemen in his company. He had no papers himself since he had been out of circulation. And the money in his pockets? A loan from the friend who had introduced him to the five traveling gentlemen.

The assistant U.S. attorney said he would recommend a fine. "Though," he reminded Mr. Ponzi, "I could ask for as much as two years jail time for each alien you have brought across." When Charles pointed out that an ex-con looking for work wasn't in a position to pay a fine, the lawyer assured him the fine would be small. Charles could make it up with easy time, say, the month he'd already served.

When he at last stood before a judge, Charles had been in the Plattsburg jail for better than three months. The men he had been traveling with, meanwhile, had been dubbed government witnesses, provided with a federal stipend, and sheltered in a nearby rooming house. Soon they would be handed work visas for legal entry into the United States.

What the hell, Charles thought, it can't get any worse. I'll plead guilty, they'll sentence me to 90 days, which I've already done, and they'll set me free on time served. The U.S. attorney pointed to where Charles should sign the guilty plea and handed him a pen. Once the documents were stamped, Charles was ushered before a federal judge.

"Two years and $500," barked his honor.

****

Charles was removed from the Plattsburg jail and shuttled to the United States Penitentiary in Atlanta, Georgia. After three months of dirt and mildew in Plattsburg, the bars flecking paint like dandruff onto the always damp stone floor, Charles rejoiced to see his Atlanta digs. In Plattsburg, he had languished among thieves and brawlers, living in conditions a short step above bestial. His peers in Atlanta occupied special housing for business-type offenders. (They were white-collar criminals, though criminologist Edwin Sutherland hadn't coined the term yet.)

There Charles first met the best and brightest cons America had to offer. Charles had learned the fundamentals of crime in Boston's ghettoes and Montreal's warehouse alleys. The Atlanta penitentiary became his graduate school.

Charles rapidly made cozy arrangements for himself in his new home. In exchange for special food and privileges, he agreed to monitor his cellmate, who was suspected of capital as well as financial crimes. But Charles wasn't just a rat. While spying for the establishment, he also kept his fellow inmates informed about the warden's office, where he worked as translator and lackey.

In Atlanta, the months jingled by like pocket change. One afternoon, the warden came in grinning and asked Charles to type up a pardon; when the obsequious little clerk sat down at the typewriter, he discovered his own name in the recipient's line. Charles was released on early parole after serving a little more than a year.

Fresh out of the pen, he caught a train to Birmingham. An old acquaintance from Boston had set up a bogus medical practice in the mining regions of Alabama. The friend's practice involved filing large-sum claims against the region's largest coal companies, then settling with company lawyers for considerably less than he had at first declared his due. Charles translated some documents for his friend but barely gave the scam a glance. Corporate blackmail held no excitement for a man of his disposition. The process was too long and arduous. He wanted something to get his blood up.

Next stop, a town called Blocton. Charles concocted his most practical scheme ever for this overgrown Alabama mining camp. The roads stayed muddy nearly all year, with ruts deep enough to swallow an entire buckboard. Even the best homes in Blocton had no running water, much less electricity. "This is the 20th century," Charles informed a gathering of the area's considerable Italianate population. "With the simplest of engineering, we can harness the water that runs through the hills above the town. A gasoline engine can pump running water into the houses, stores, and offices below, and also operate a small dynamo, producing electricity. An ordinary bond issue pays for the reasonable costs of set-up, and the utility's output not only pays for itself, it generates a profit!...that is, a surplus!...for civic projects." (And, as Mr. Ponzi never tired of pointing out in later years, it was all completely aboveboard—no mirrors, no legerdemain—his one pure, respectable idea.)

Blocton loved the idea. What they didn't care for was the smart-mouthed schemer who strutted into town like Lord Fauntleroy, prepared to take a cut of their electrical co-op for telling them how to use their land. The citizens formed the co-op themselves and sent Mr. Ponzi packing.

That isn't exactly how Charles remembered his Blocton trip though. He claimed the humanitarian impulses which often mar an otherwise business-like heart led to his downfall. A nurse tending consumptive coal miners was burned severely along her right side when a gasoline engine exploded, Charles said. The regional doctor announced that only a skin graft would save the woman's arm from amputation. But, the doctor complained, "I can't find anybody who will give up as little as an inch of skin."

"How many inches do you need altogether?" Charles asked the doctor.

"Forty or 50, I guess."

"You have found them," Charles announced. "I will give you all the skin you need." When next he woke, he found himself with raw, aching legs and the skin literally stripped from his back. According to Charles' version, the selfish townspeople of Blocton tricked him out of his power plant while he convalesced from the operation.

Who knows? Maybe he was tarred and feathered and preferred to think of his wounds as heroic. At any rate, Charles' boots were made for walking.

"In 1913, I went to Pensacola, Florida as a sign painter," he recounted. "The next step was Mobile, Alabama, where I was under contract to paint a houseboat." (He never did say if he actually painted the boat.)

"While in Mobile, I saw an advertisement from the University of Alabama seeking a librarian and secured the job after making application at the medical college." Charles drew $30 a month, and enjoyed the work, but he split academia for good "when the president of the university fired me." A dispute of some sort arose— Charles wouldn't say what—which the president settled by declaring "a lack of funds" for the librarian's post.

A hurricane bombarded the Gulf Coast during the fall of 1915, and Charles trailed its wreckage from Mobile to New Orleans. He took a job painting signs instead—he liked thinking up the right words and inventing new ways to write the letters to catch people's attention. The only drawback to sign painting? People didn't care much for creativity. They wanted stenciled letters, black on a white background. Nothing fancy, nothing cute. Charles despaired that his life was doomed to monotony, whether he was lying on a prison bunk or tiptoeing to dot the little *i* on *L'Hotel Ignatius*.

He hopped a train and ended up in Wichita Falls, Texas, translating documents for an exporter who sold cars and trucks to foreign countries. Whatever happened to Charles in Wichita Falls, he never wanted to talk about it. The Wichita Motors Company reported, when they were contacted sometime later by federal authorities, "He left us after a few months, secured passage to New York as Italian reservist, but from his correspondence understand he left steamer in Boston, jumping overboard and swimming ashore. Is highly educated, brilliant mind and memory, but given to pipe dreams. Quick to resent any infringement on what he considered his rights. Was efficient worker."

****

When he arrived at this point in his story, Charles always paused. "Boston Harbor," he sighed, slumping his shoulders. He had returned from the Texas prairie to the filthy streets of Boston, where he'd begun. He was without money and without prospects. More than ten years into his American sojourn, and still he had no place to offer his mother.

Charles washed dishes and clerked at hotels. One evening at the Boylston Street subway station he spied a young girl talking with a woman whom Charles recognized as a neighborhood piano teacher. Charles realized he had seen the girl a few days before coming out of her father's business, the Guecco Brothers grocery wholesaling warehouse. Charles mentioned to the teacher that he had heard the girl play in a recital, and had been transported by her gentle way with the keys.

When the woman turned to introduce her pupil, Charles nearly swooned: "that picture of loveliness and kindness and clean vivacity.... One look into her deep, dark, smiling eyes...at that pretty round face, framed in a background of gorgeous curls...at her whole fascinating ensemble...."

Her name was Rose Guecco. She had not yet turned 20 when Charles, almost 38 years old, started telling her how much time he spent pondering her whole fascinating ensemble. "A few days after we met, I telephoned Miss Guecco and asked her if she would go to a moving picture theatre in Somerville that evening. Also, I told her I was determined to marry her."

Rose giggled. "Don't be a tease."

"I'm absolutely serious."

"Then you must be crazy!"

Rose wasn't simple. Her father had paid for six months of business school, where she learned bookkeeping. No, Rose was no dummy, but she radiated a hopefulness that burned furiously when fanned by someone like Charles. Each day for a solid year, Charles had flowers and soda pop delivered to Rose at the sewing factory where she clerked. Rose believed her Charlie could do anything.

It was Rose's puppy-dog eyes, which seemed to perpetually emit a silent but palpable sigh, that persuaded her Poppa to take Charles into the grocery business. "The business was failing," as Rose told the story later, "and Charlie took hold in an effort to put father on his feet."

Charlie joined the Guecco brothers that spring, after he and Rose spent their two-day honeymoon in a New York hotel. By January 1919, the business was bankrupt.

He and Rose moved from her parents' house in Somerville to a box of an apartment in the city. Charles nevertheless had not given up on the grocery business. "Our assets were about $6,000, and the liabilities mounted to $11,000. I asked the bankruptcy attorneys to let me borrow the $6,000 assets, promising that in 12 months I would meet all the obligations. The attorneys said no."

Charles took a position as a clerk at J.R. Poole's, an import-export business. There he performed anesthetizingly routine tasks without any prospect of advancement or opportunity.

Rose, poor dear, kept books for the factory in Somerville and kept her young girl's eyes smiling for her husband. Charles talked incessantly in the evenings, his monologue limited mainly to two topics: how he could make a million like any other juke-joint fool, and how much Rose would love his mother. Imelda still diligently answered her Carlo's letters, her effusions equalled only by her son's inflated promises.

Charles was reading aloud from the latest Parma dispatch when a police officer showed up at their door. Rose squeaked at the sudden knocking. The police officer said he was sorry to inform Mr. Ponzi that his wife's parents had both been killed in an automobile accident. Rose collapsed onto the floor, her face in her hands, weeping and shaking her head from side to side.

****

Charles quit his job at J.R. Poole and opened his own business. Foreign deals were booming since the war. He had done the paperwork for transactions worth hundreds of thousands at Poole's. He would do the same for himself. He put down a small security deposit for an office, promising to pay full rent in the coming months, and bought some chipped, tawny furniture on credit.

But Charles brought no clientele with him from Poole's, nor any contacts. It was almost like being in jail again, willing the phone to ring but hearing only the squeak of his chair. During these depressing hours Charles pored over the literature on the import-export industry. Finding the material woefully inadequate, he determined to fill the void. Charles decided he would publish an industry newspaper for international merchants: *The Trader's Guide.*

It wasn't a bad idea—the guide offered general trading news and advertising for each major port city along the East Coast. But the publication struggled because Charles had no money, and no moneyed contacts in publishing, shipping or investing. Charles had only ideas.

"It's just a matter of time," he said to Henry Chmielinski, the president of the Hanover Trust Company. Charles begged for $2,000 so he could keep his *Guide* afloat. He had two guys selling ads and laying out demonstration copies of the newspaper, but they were going to quit if he didn't pay them some wages.

At the Hanover, Chmielinski halted Ponzi's spiel. "Your account is frankly more of a bother than a benefit to us," Chmielinski observed. He suggested Charles try other avenues of finance.

"I Saw the Money"

MR. PONZI FINALLY DISCOVERS
AN UNTRODDEN PATH TO WEALTH AND TAKES IT

Charles finally got his payoff by cornering the market in postage stamps. It was 1920. Millions of European refugees flocked to America, Canada, and Brazil. Family members left their kin in the night. They would die apart from everyone, their only contact a letter now and then, with a few dollars enclosed. Families longed for the mails, clutching the crumpled paper like sacred texts.

The Universal Postal Union arranged to move all those letters, business documents and messages across national lines by issuing Postal Reply Coupons. You bought a Postal Reply Coupon in your host country and enclosed it in your letter. Your mother, once she got your letter, exchanged the Postal Reply Coupon for stamps at her local post office. Your reply arrived in a few weeks, or it might take longer—the UPU couldn't work miracles—but it usually arrived.

As soon as he'd spotted the financial opportunity in Reply Coupons, Charles began spreading the word. He posed for a photograph in his offices, cocking his head to the side, as if he were shading his face beneath his thick brown hat. It was a pose meant to say, *Dollar-Bill*. Between his teeth he dangled a cigarette holder, with smoke extending like ribbons along the collar of his pudgy overcoat. Charles raised his hat to passersby as he emerged from the Niles Building. In a fist he clutched the crown jewel of his ensemble, a Malacca cane, which he tapped on the concrete as he walked.

Charles told his fellow North-Enders that during December of 1919 he had been playing the mails. "Everybody's heard of the Postal Union. They print coupons like these I'm holding here. Postal reply coupons—so you can send a letter back home, or anywhere in the world. You can trade this coupon for a stamp from any country. I send my mother coupons with every letter home.

"Now, in cooperation with certain large businesses in our city, I am making a fortune on the postal reply coupon. Stocks are too risky. Forget it. And bonds, what are they paying? How much, can anyone tell me? Bonds are paying six percent, maybe? Savings accounts at Tremont Trust, they'll give you four and a half cents on the dollar. Give them a hundred dollars and they'll give you back $104.50.

"I can beat that into the ground!" Charles shouted, whacking his cane against the floor. "My investors get 50 cents on the dollar! Place a hundred dollars with the Securities Exchange Company, and you take out one-fifty. Put that one-fifty in, you'll get back two-twenty-five. That's right, in six months, you can more than double your money."

How could he pay 50 percent when banks couldn't manage five? "Exchange rates," Charles explained. "Every morning I go down and check to see how the lira is doing against the dollar. Usually you get five lire for a dollar. This morning I checked; and with the war just ended, it takes 20 lire to make a dollar."

While currency exchange rates were bouncing around like popcorn, Charles pointed out, the postal reply coupon always bought one stamp. "Here's what I do," Charles said.

- *I send my cousin in Parma $1.*
- *He exchanges the dollar for lire. With the 20 lire (2,000 centesimi) we can buy 66 postal reply coupons (worth 30 centesimi each, the cost of a letter-sized stamp in Italia).*
- *Back in America, each of the coupons buys one stamp, face value 5 cents. I redeem all 66 coupons for $3.30 worth of stamps.*
- *The magic happens in the exchange rate. In America, my dollar buys 20 postal coupons. But if I exchange the dollar for lire, and buy the coupons in Italy, then return and buy the stamps in America, I get $3.30 worth of stamps for that same $1. My profit margin is 230 percent!*

"Yeah, but $3.30 worth of stamps is still stamps," an attentive listener offered.

"Precisely," Charles replied.

- *So I sell the stamps at a 10-percent discount through my contacts with the larger firms downtown. Deducting the discount, I've got $3 cash now from the $1 I started with.*
- *Now let's say, I got that first dollar from you. I will pay you back your dollar, plus 50 cents interest. Since I just sold $3 worth of stamps, I have a dollar and 50 cents for myself. I'm going to spend a third of that on my offices and processing overhead, and a third on commissions and bonuses to my salespeople, and*

then, ladies and gentlemen, I'm going to pocket the other third and take my wife for a stroll.

> $ 3.00   *Sale of Stamps*
> −1.00   *Initial Investment*
> −0.50   *Interest to Investors*
> $ 1.50   *Overhead and Profit*

Presto!

There you have it, brimming with flim and flam, the original Ponzi scheme, the "Coke Classic" of American crime. What Charles saw in the Postal Reply Coupon tells you a lot about what sort of man he was. The proposal had an element of goofiness about it; the logic held up, provided you didn't dig too deep. Charles had seen that, while national currencies were fluctuating like crazy, the UPU's coupons were always good for *X* amount of stamps.

Charles named his concern the Securities Exchange Company, noting with pleasure how the capital letters he'd painted on the office door formed an almost complete circle, with a small dollar sign at the bottom acting as a link.

Plenty of swindlers before him had used the basic pattern of Charles' ploy. In the 1880s, a group called Lawrence & Co. touched off a scandal with what became known as *The Royal Bounce.* Small investors put their money into Lawrence's investment pool. Not long afterward they received a statement in the mail indicating that their stock was soaring. Many people heaved in whatever money they had been holding back in the name of caution.

Then they got the Royal Bounce, a letter sadly informing them that the stock had gone belly up and there was little or nothing left to recover from the fund. We've lost, too, the letter said, nevertheless inviting the recipient to send more money to the fund so that "losses may soon be forgotten in the larger gains."

Charles' most immediate forbearer in fraud was known as 520-Percent Miller. Born William Miller, the former brokerage clerk insinuated himself into the small Protestant churches where the Dutch, German, and Swedish immigrants of Brooklyn worshipped. He earned his nickname from 1889 to 1891, by promising to pay $5.20 for every dollar invested in his stock picking system. As Miller indeed began to pay miraculous returns to a few prominent congregationalists, the rest couldn't shove their way in fast enough. Somber churchmen—men who spurned gambling parlors and lotteries and didn't feel all that comfortable with raffles—handed over their life savings to 520-Percent Miller.

In just over a year, he snared $2 million, until a reporter got wise to Miller's scam and publicly branded him "a fly-by-night stock operator." When Miller couldn't produce any money for his panicked investors, he was given the next five years to do penance in Sing Sing prison.

As Charles' boat was docking in 1903, fraud remained a thriving industry, growing apace with the boom-and-bust U.S. economy. America was suffering growing pains: more people, more industry, more money, more of the woes that came with all of the above. The early decades of the 20th century spawned a plague of scams. *Financial World* magazine documented more than $600 million squandered between 1904 and 1911 on phony oil wells and mining scams. Journalists exposed one phony promotion after another.

The upheaval—and the economic kick—of World War I gave fraudsters even more fodder. *The New York Times* noted, "Since the armistice, Boston has been infested with agents seeking to interest small investors by promising big profits."

Charles acknowledged to his listeners there were a lot of cons stalking the neighborhoods. "But," he hastily added, "I'm not playing stocks or building factories. This is a simple exchange, a kink in the system that no one has noticed before. It's a stamp." Charles held up the rough, pulpy square of paper for his audience.

Mainly, Charles understood, "You show them the money." That much 520-Percent Miller got right. The difference between a Ponzi swindler and a regular old thief is that the Ponzi gives back some of his victims' money. He broadcasts a share of the loot back into the crowd. The thrilled recipients then assure every friend they've got—"*I saw* the *money.*"

In Charles' day and our own, the best ruse occurs in broad daylight. A millionaire con doesn't try to pick your pocket; he offers you *his* wallet.

Driving the Locomobile

MR. PONZI DISPROVES THE THEORY THAT THERE CANNOT BE A PROFIT WITHOUT A CORRESPONDING LOSS

Charles toured his old haunts—the dice games, card games, and back rooms of the speakeasy era. He talked the man who leased him his office furniture into becoming the SEC's first investor. Joseph Daniels gave him $200 cash, and Charles gave the pawnbroker a promissory note for $300, redeemable in 90 days.

Charles presented his gambling buddies with a handful of postal coupons, waving them like a peacock airing his tail. "Good as money," he beamed. Greed sometimes finds its best friend in Hope, and Charles' compatriots were brimming with both. Charles collected $870. He promised to pay in three months, and if he didn't, the investors knew where to find him.

In March 1920, Charles made a production of counting out each payoff in $5 bills, speaking the numbers aloud, some in Italian, some in English. It wasn't hard, afterward, to persuade the customers, such as his friend Signori Congiusti, to let the money ride. Congiusti had turned more profit on his money in three months than he would have reaped in a year with the Hanover Bank.

Congiusti said, "No, you keep the money," and returned the bills to Charles' waiting hand. The men let their laughter feed on itself. With their glee bouncing palpably off the walls, Charles folded the bills into the breast of his new suit. He turned to Congiusti's friend, who had come along for the visit and was already fishing his savings from his pants pocket. "Please take this $100," the man supplicated, placing the bills gently into Charles' hand. "It is all I have now, but soon I will get more, and I will see you then."

It's easy to see why Charles' prey fell so hungrily into what he offered. What's harder to divine is how Charles ever thought he could get away with it. He told himself he'd scare up the funds to pay everyone, or he'd concoct a painless way to close out the game without having to pay. Something. Several times he had the chance to run, with more than $7 million stashed in banks. He held an open passport to Italy, still his home country. But Charles stayed put.

He knew one thing: he had not the time, the network, or the inclination to actually try selling hundreds of thousands of stamps to businesses at a discount. He was hauling in too much money to worry about that, that—detail! Maybe, he reasoned, I can buy a few companies, sell them at a huge profit and pay off most of the investors. Then I'll close the SEC and use my clout to swing the next big deal.

He told himself he was really only borrowing from the investors' pool. This meant he was paying interest to make his gambling buddies proud—50 cents on the dollar—but that's hindsight, and hindsight don't count in a Ponzi scheme. It's all about getting swept up in the moment.

The moment was sweeping Ponzi along like the Charleston. He handed Joseph Fowler, Esq., $5,000 in cash and instructed the lawyer to be available should the SEC need legal assistance. He already had several stringers working for him, selling at a ten percent commission, and he told them to bring their friends by the office. Though he hired one or two salespeople a day, Charles' scheme sold itself; he just needed some bodies to count the money and fill out the receipts.

When 18-year-old Lucy Meli arrived to take up her secretary's position, she answered yes, she knew basic bookkeeping, whereupon Charles dropped his "records" onto her desk. He nodded at the file cards, three or four stacks of them, and snapped open the binder clips on an oblong loose-leaf ledger, a holdover from the ill-fated *Trader's Guide*. Lucy smiled and wondered what to do next.

After a week of reorganizing the "records," Lucy made her report. Charles had matched the $870 he received in December with $900 in January. He brought in $5,000 during February, and now, with the arrival of spring, the pace was leaping to nearly $1,000 a day, almost $30,000 for the entire month! The best Lucy could tell (and who could know for sure?) by mid-April Charles would owe about $53,000 on the notes he'd sold since January.

Charles decided to party. He bought a house and five acres in Lexington, the very swankiest of Boston suburbs, known as a "banker's colony" because of the financiers among its population. Charles' house sat at the corner of Fair Street, in view of the trolley line. He made no attempt to avoid the neighbors' inquiries about who was moving into their midst. He wanted them to know. The house sat braced by an enormous second-story porch that stretched 36 yards long, ending on the east side with a circular overlook. Wrought-iron patio furniture invited visitors to chat over drinks and cigarettes. Three latticed gables, each three windows wide, overlooked the shrub-bordered sidewalks like sentries. To the rear on the west side, a matching cottage served as servant's quarters or a guest house, whichever the resident preferred.

The owner was asking $30,000, but Charles made him a better offer. "I'll give you $10,000 cash, right here," Charles said, pulling the stacks of money from his kidskin satchel, "and I'll give you $20,000 in Securities Exchange notes. Now, in 45 days you come down to my office—on School Street, you've heard of it, surely—and I'll give you at that point, $30,000 for the $20,000 in notes. You see? When the 20 matures, you'll keep an extra 10,000 on the deal."

The man nodded enthusiastically. Suddenly, with dollars fluttering like doves from out of his shirtsleeves, people paid attention to Charles. No more Carlo this, Carlo that, no more (as the broker Fournier had called him in Montreal) Bianchi the snake!

He informed Rose she was heretofore a lady of leisure. She would politely resign from her job and ask her supervisor over for tea. Posing for photographers in a black silk dress, her shawl held tastefully over her shoulders by a thin silver clasp, Rose beamed. She stroked a fern with her fingers, and leaned her head awkwardly, as if she wondered what all the fuss was about. The *Post*'s gossip columnist wrote,

> There has been no small degree of feminine envy coupled with admiration directed toward the unusually pretty wife of the "postal coupon king." Mrs. Ponzi jumped from the position of mistress of a modest home in Somerville to the charming hostess of a spacious country estate in Lexington, and all within the short period of a few months.

If Rose wanted to go somewhere, a chauffeur would carry her in their new Locomobile. The sapphire-blue monster of a car glowed in the sharp spring sunlight. The Locomobile weighed nearly 6,000 pounds. In case of accident, the company assured its buyers, "It's the other car you should be concerned about, not the Locomobile." The hand-rubbed leather seats, coaxed to a buttery shade of tan, were stuffed with horsehair and held six passengers in splendorous comfort. Elsie DeWolfe, the trendy New York designer, had seen to the car's aesthetic dimensions. Charles led Rose by the hand around its broad snout of a grille, pointing at the cut-glass side lamps, the Tiffany shade covering the dome light, and the silk roller shades on the windows. "This trim," he nearly sang, "is sterling silver. If you need to converse with the driver, there's an electric telephone at your side. And, for m'lady's convenience...." Charles reached through the door and flicked open a compartment in the roof, dropping down a makeup case and mirror. Rose shrieked and leapt back from the car, giggling and clapping her hands.

"All for just over $10,000, because I paid cash. It's $12,000 on the showroom floor," Charles added, and Rose shrieked again.

"Charlie! We didn't make $10,000 between us last year!"

"It's the *Duce* of automobiles, Rosa. Remember that Cadillac we rode in last week? It was $4,600, the most expensive model they had. But for double the price, you get quality. Locomobile only makes four cars a day. You know how many cars come rolling off the line at Ford and General Motors every day? Hundreds, Rosa. But a Locomobile takes time."

Rose interrupted his pitch with a slow wet kiss. When she leaned back, her cheeks aglow, Charles added, "Nothing can touch this specimen of a machine, *mia flora*, nothing."

The stormy days were over, Charlie assured his young wife. In April, 150 souls carried $141,000 into Ponzi's makeshift office. Ms. Meli and the staff of young clerks, some of whom could barely add and subtract, nearly went berserk. Money viewed in bulk massages the viewer's reality. Nothing's the same after you've beheld a chimney stack of dollar bills. Charles' staff gasped at the sight of money towering from shelves and desktops, at the drawers that wouldn't close because they bulged with legal tender. The entire office reeled from the effects, the clerks' voices becoming funhouse silly, their faces stretched tired at the end of the day from laughing.

The haul for May approached $500,000. More than 1,500 new customers placed their funds with the Securities Exchange Company.

Charles rebuffed his skeptics in law enforcement. Boston police officers weren't what you would call up-to-date on international goings-on. "It had to be explained to them," Charles recounted, "that the Universal Postal Union was not a 'Local,' that is, a *Union Local*. Like the Hod Carriers. And that the coupons themselves were not clippings from Liberty Bonds."

Many police officers who dropped in on Charles left behind a piece of their salary. It was a sure thing, a legal thing, a grand thing this little man had created, as if from thin air.

****

That summer Boston danced to Ponzi's tune.

It was the summer of cheering in the streets, hails and salutes greeting Charles as he sat proudly behind his Japanese chauffeur (who was not a tall man), waving to well-wishers from the Locomobile. It was the summer of money.

It was the summer of lines stretching around the corner, of citizens with cans under their arms, clutching handsewn purses, begging for Ponzi's clerks to stay open only a few more minutes.

It was the summer when the garbage cans in Charles' office were requisitioned by an anthill of clerks, so they could stash the money that overflowed their desk drawers. When an extra office in the Niles Building wasn't enough. When substations, 30 across the city, sprang up, and stations in other towns were established to meet the ardorous demand.

"Today all Boston is get-rich-quick mad over him," wrote Marguerite Mooers Marshall of the *New York Evening World*. "Did I say Boston? My mistake. I should have said the entire New England, from Calais, Maine, to Lake Champlain, from the Canadian border to New Jersey."

That summer a hall closet was piled to the ceiling with $10 and $20 bills, all in neatly stacked, rubberbanded bricks, a wall of cash staring back at the nosy passersby who peeked inside. One million dollars a week swelled the drawers and cabinets and anywhere a slab of bills could be tucked.

Imelda was to join them in June on the first available Atlantic crossing. Imelda was packing two large trunks and saying goodbyes to the family in Parma as one who has, against long odds, proved her point. Her Charles had made good.

He did have his detractors. Men in vested coats, with tasteful cuffs and pure-gold watch chains, all their earthly pleasures dependent on dutifully paying out 4 or 5 cents on the dollar—bankers, whose depositors were flocking to Ponzi like so many pigeons. Everywhere, people talked about "Ponzi's Bank."

"What have I got at your bank, about $500,000?" Charles asked Henry Chmielinski, president of the Hanover Trust. Charles knew. It was $473,806.42. In the same vaults that couldn't spare him $2,000 a year before, he now had half a mill. The man who'd called Charles' account "a bother" now addressed him as "Sir—Mr. Ponzi, sir." When Charles asked Chmielinski if he remembered their first meeting, the man professed total ignorance.

Charles dismissed the issue. "It's true, isn't it," Charles asked, "that you're about to issue 2,000 new shares in this institution?"

Before the astounded Chmielinski could ask how Charles knew that, Charles cut him off, demanding that 1,500 of the shares be sold to him. Charles Ponzi was offering to buy his way into the Hanover. The shares would go for $125 each, Chmielinski confirmed: about $190,000 for the lot. Charles nodded. Take it out of my account.

"Director Ponzi," Charles said. Charles not only wanted the shares, he wanted a directorship to go with them, since he now owned a fourth of the bank.

The Hanover involved only two other major shareholders and they agreed with Chmielinski: they couldn't refuse Ponzi. They would have to let him in. Otherwise, his deposits would walk, to be followed by a horde of customers trailing the one-man circus.

The Tremont Trust, one of the Hanover's peers and an anti-Ponzi stronghold, declared war on Charles with a series of newspaper ads.

The text explained in large type:

REAL DOLLARS

ARE STILL MADE IN THE OLD-FASHIONED WAY

—WORKING AND SAVING. A REAL DOLLAR CANNOT BE MADE FROM BUBBLES.

OUR LAST MONTHLY INTEREST DIVIDEND WAS 5-1/2 %

AND WAS PAID FROM OUR EARNED AND COLLECTED INCOME

AS ARE ALL OUR MONTHLY DIVIDENDS.

Charles immediately got the Tremont's president, Simon Swig, on the telephone. "Say, Mister Swig, if I was to deposit a few hundred thousand dollars at the Tremont, you wouldn't have any objections, would you?" Swig allowed they were always glad to accommodate depositors.

"Mighty fine," Charles replied, and dispatched 150,000 of his very real dollars to the Tremont vaults. "That oughta keep the old badger down," he declared. Behind his back, the bankers could call him "that circus monkey on School Street," but soon he would be a full-fledged financier.

Meanwhile, Charles was writing big checks. It was his *only* hope. He would score big with a legit operation, then use the money to pay off as many investors as possible, and return the latest investors' money short, i.e., without interest, before their 90-day terms had ended. Or maybe if he built up enough holdings in verifiable assets, he could borrow against those assets, sell some off if necessary, and use *that money* to pay off the Securities Exchange Company debts.

To his interest in the Hanover, Charles added shares of Fidelity Trust, South Trust, and the Tremont Trust—which, nevertheless, continued to run ads sneering obliquely at "Ponzi's Bank." He bought the Carney Building on Tremont Street and leased two full floors of the Niles Building to expand his main office. He bought himself an apartment in the township of Winthrop and one in the West End. He bought C & R Construction Company and set the men to work building an entire complex of apartments, priced affordably so the little guy could live in them. Mr. Ponzi would *not* be a slumlord. On a whim, he bought the Napoli Macaroni Factory, just so he could joke to journalists, "I'll never run out of macaroni!"

Charles personally handled the acquisition of J.R. Poole's, Inc., the import-export company where he had earned $16 a week just months before. "How many shares do you have outstanding?" Charles asked, "because that's how many I'm buying."

Charles had no time for scratching about in other people's business, but he did have partner problems. He didn't have a partner, it's true. But Joseph Daniels filed a lawsuit alleging that he'd helped found the Securities Exchange Company with a loan of $230 worth of furniture and $200 in cash. Daniels had provided the beat-up desks that first hunkered in the dusty School Street office, and he had let Charles have a couple hundred dollars to spark interest in the postal coupons. It wasn't just a loan, Daniels maintained now that the spunky promoter was drowning in cash: "We were partners. I put up capital and property." On July 2, deputies handed Charles a notice demanding $1 million.

The *Boston Post* called. Charles told the reporter, "When I opened, I bought furniture from Daniels; but he never left any money with me for investment." Charles said he had nothing to fear from Daniels' lawsuit.

One of the readers perusing the next morning's *Post* was Joseph Allen, the newly installed bank commissioner of Massachusetts. "Why have I never heard of this Ponzi?" Allen wondered. "Where did he come from? Who are his associates? How is he doubling people's money?" Commissioner Allen called to ask Boston's hottest financier to drop by the statehouse, a courtesy call to be sure. The Securities Exchange Company didn't refer to itself as a bank or offer any banking services. Therefore, absent a complaint—and there were none—the commissioner's office had no jurisdiction for poking into Ponzi's business.

"We simply have, as they say, a curiosity," the commissioner explained. Allen's curiosity remained unsated even after he and two assistants spent the better part of an hour talking with Charles. After pattering as usual about postal coupons and how money chased money, Charles bade the commissioner goodbye. He tapped his cane as he pranced through the offices to his car, enjoying the Malacca's whack echoing in the high-ceilinged hallways. Busy with $450,000 in receipts from the weekend, Charles gave the meeting no further thought.

He couldn't get near his offices that day. The publicity from Daniels' suit had brought out even more thousands of the Boston masses than usual. It wasn't an angry mob. These were *new* investors. Charles realized headily that the yells from the crowd were people wanting in! As outliers recognized the Locomobile, word swept through the lines. *He's here! Ponzi's here!* Charles had his chauffeur park, and he climbed on top of the huge blue car. He loved the view.

"Faced with adversity," Mr. Ponzi lectured the crowd, "the average man quits. But not top-notchers! They gobble up banks faster than a turkey does mush. And their gizzards never feel congested."

The crowd hurrahed until Charles disappeared into his offices.

That day more than 30,000 citizens handed over their savings to Mr. Ponzi. According to the figures he quickly scrawled on his dry-cleaning bill, the Securities Exchange Company was holding $15 million in notes. On this, the biggest day of his life, did Charles feel remorse or humility, watching millwrights and working mothers lined up like the damned, shoving their way into his scheme? No.

"I had given them the best show that was staged in their territory since the landing of the Pilgrims! I had given them the most brazen exhibition of sheer nerve that had ever been witnessed in the world of finance! I had given them the longest ride, the most mileage for their money they had ever got before or since! It was easily worth 15 million bucks to watch me put the thing over!"

The Fur Flies

MR. PONZI, PEEVED AT THE "MONEY LENDERS," DECLARES WAR ON THEM AND BEGINS HOSTILITIES

Simon Swig was not impressed. From the Tremont Trust, the dour Mr. Swig called Charles. "It is time for frank talk, sir. I believe the large sums of money pouring in on you from the public has turned your head. That is, you've become unreasonable on the subject of finances. During the entire time you've deposited money here, you have not issued or received a foreign draft, or a New York draft for that matter. All you have done is take in money from the public. You have not once shown me anything that looks like a profit. Any man who can pay ten percent to agents for bringing in money on which he pays 50 percent in 45 days, and then doesn't put the money to work earning something, then he must have a bankroll bigger than Rockefeller's."

"Yes, and how is the royal family?" Charles carped.

Swig replied, "I cannot stand any further requests for information about your enterprise. I can no longer have this institution associated with you or your businesses. I ask that you immediately remove your funds from this institution."

"What about the $160,000 attachment from the lawsuit?" Charles replied hopefully.

"How badly do you need the money?" Swig asked.

"Swig, I don't need it all. It's the goddamn principle, that's all. I've worked hard for my millions."

Charles took to the streets, calling in his funds. He started with the Tremont, where he noisily demanded the full amount of his deposits, immediately, in cash. "Ten 10-thousand-dollar bills will suffice...."

From there Charles toured all of Boston's banks. He barged through door after door, upbraiding clerks furiously, packing large denominations of cash into his briefcase, or failing that he took cashier's checks.

If his ploy worked, he reasoned, all his problems would wash out with the tide. First he siphoned all his funds from the smaller banks in the region. He then let it be known he had "no confidence" in the institutions.

In Charles' plan, depositors would follow his lead and cart their money out of the banks to—where else?—the Securities Exchange Company. When the banks began to fail, Charles would scoop up their shares for little or nothing. Then he could use his new assets to write off the SEC notes, and he was home free.

To launch the plan, he announced a contest between his bank—"MY BANK, The Hanover"—and its peers. "One thousand dollars to the depositor who recruits the most new clients to the Hanover," Charles explained. He was talking to his friend, Judge Dominick Leveroni, who presided over juvenile court and dispensed legal advice to Charles on the side. "What's to stop me?" Charles asked. "I'm using my own money. It's simple. I've had these referral cards printed. Every time someone brings in a new depositor, we stamp their card. At the end of the month, the person who steers the most business our way wins $1,000. Commissioner Allen can't possibly oppose me.... Can he?"

Leveroni thought not, "Not if you're using your own money."

Commissioner Allen's staff reluctantly admitted, "No, there's nothing we can do to stop you," though they advised against it.

With the depositorship of the Hanover canvassing the neighborhoods, Charles figured, his rivals would be crippled inside of a month. Then he would reap the pickings, buying the wrecked banks and restoring them to solvency with cash from the Securities Exchange Company.

The Tremont Trust fired off another ad in response to the depositors' contest. The text never named the culprit, but everyone understood who Simon Swig's target was:

> Our advertisements speak frankly.
> We do not mislead for the purpose of getting depositors.
> Gold bricks are not offered,
> but a just and reasonable interest is paid,
> such as belongs to the people.

Buy up every inch of newspaper space you want, Charles thought. But "don't underestimate people talking." People talking built the Securities Exchange Company, Charles knew. That same power, *people talking*, would coax the cash out of his rival banks. When two people brought two people.... Just keep the people talking....

****

OH BOY! WHAT A FIGHT! THE FUR IS STILL FLYING AND YOU CAN'T TELL WHICH IS WHICH!

Charles explained to his fellow directors that he was building this respectable but unremarkable Hanover Trust into the most popular bank in New England. Already the contest was spurring deposits! (Admittedly some people withdrew their money a few days later and took it to School Street.)

The directors weren't listening. They had other things to talk about. Hawking checking accounts like canolis was not their favorite topic.

"Banking Commissioner Allen, you know him, don't you, Mr. Ponzi?" asked Chmielinski. Allen wasn't present but Chmielinski gestured as if the man were even now shifting in his seat. "The Commissioner has brought a great deal of attention to bear on our operations here, largely, as he himself will tell you, because of the substantial shares owned by you, and because he's concerned how this institution might be affected by setbacks in your personal finances. Do I make myself clear, sir?"

"I see no point of concern," Charles replied.

As Chmielinski drew it out, the banking commissioner was demanding some guarantee that Mr. Ponzi's operations as a trader, or whatever he was, wouldn't endanger the bank. Charles' hand shook as he signed the documents which Chmielinski had just sealed: an agreement authorizing the Hanover Trust Company to hold Charles' money, some of it anyway, in reserve.

"How much do you want?" Charles asked.

"One-point-five million dollars," Chmielinski replied.

Rage and shame burned Charles' face as he climbed into the Locomobile. They actually *hoped* he would bust! They were hounding him when they should've been toasting his success. Goddamn bankers!

Judge Leveroni told Charles, "You've got to keep the public on your side. They're all you have." Leveroni made Charles a lunch date with William McMasters, a publicity man, one of the newfangled professionals who earned their keep by swaying people's opinions. McMasters strutted into Charles' offices chomping a cigar and nosing around like a postal inspector. McMasters knew the most powerful people in Boston personally, not just judges and wardheelers, but bankers, lawyers, businesspeople of every stripe.

McMasters demanded a detailed accounting of the SEC, inside and out. "What's really happening here?" he exclaimed. He declined when Charles suggested that the contract be made payable in notes from the SEC.

McMasters prepared a batch of 10,000 pamphlets at Charles' request and arranged for the circulars to be mailed to every individual in the region with a bank account. He also canvassed the *Post* and other newspapers to have them run stories on this banking revolution. McMasters cultivated warm relations with the press, but the papers weren't interested.

Mr. Ponzi is Betrayed

Charles never saw it coming. He stayed so busy puffing his chest and scrambling from one crisis to the next that he didn't anticipate that his enemies—the banking establishment and its cronies—would dare call him a liar. Richard Grozier had recently risen from reporter to city editor at the *Post*. He had never liked Ponzi's circus barker act, and he knew in his gut the SEC wasn't turning millions on postage stamps. Grozier took aim at Ponzi's operation by eliciting commentary from one of Boston's premier citizens, the man said to have created financial journalism as we know it, Clarence Barron.

Barron consulted with the most influential people of his generation. "What They Told Barron" became a catchphrase, a tribute to the man's insider status. He owned Dow Jones & Co. and *The Wall Street Journal*, and in the summer of 1920 he was about to launch *Barron's, The National Financial Weekly*.

Both Barron and Charles were braggarts who used money to get the respect they couldn't command with their person alone. But while Clarence Barron was dug in deep with old money, Charles wouldn't last through the rainy season.

On the last Monday in July 1920, the *Post* frontpaged its story:

**CLARENCE BARRON QUESTIONS THE MOTIVE
BEHIND PONZI'S SCHEME**

Theoretically you could turn a profit on the UPU coupons, Barron admitted. But that's the only truth in the operation. You could never make more than a few thousand, not just because of the trouble of offloading the stamps and tracking the various conversions driving the process, but because there simply weren't enough coupons out there. France, Romania, and Spain had left the system several months before. A cursory check with the UPU showed they had a few hundred thousand dollars worth of stamps in circulation, nowhere near the $10 million to $15 million Ponzi claimed to be trading. *So where was Ponzi getting his coupons?*

Furthermore, the U.S. Postal Service had announced weeks earlier, on July 2, that postal reply coupons would not be redeemed in lots larger than ten. *Where, then, was Ponzi turning his coupons into stamps?*

Finally, Barron asked, if Ponzi is doubling everyone else's money, why does he keep his own funds in regional banks? The *Post* knew that Ponzi kept millions on deposit in seven or eight New England banks, and those accounts were growing. *How could a man paying 100 percent interest every 90 days stomach drawing four or five percent a month?*

Barron concluded, "Right under the eyes of our government court officials, Mr. Ponzi has been paying out U.S. money to one line with deposits made by a succeeding line." The so-called financial wizard of School Street turned out to be another goldbrick salesman.

****

The summer of money was ending. All the doors that had flown back on their hinges for Charles were slamming shut. William McMasters told his client he had been approached by Massachusetts District Attorney Joseph C. Pelletier. Now that Barron had provided an opening, Pelletier seized the opportunity. Shutting down Ponzi would reap the D.A.'s office plenty of favor among upper-crust Bostonians. Not to mention the fact that it would be a pleasure to fell a colossal ego like Ponzi's.

McMasters persuaded Charles to talk with Pelletier, unofficially. In Pelletier's office, Charles prepared for battle. But Pelletier refused to clang swords with the bantam wannabe financier. As McMasters later recounted, "Pelletier seized the moment to give Ponzi a severe calf-down for spreading the idea that the D.A. and the Banking Commissioner were personally vested in the SEC." Charles cringed and gushed with apology.

Pelletier nodded at Charles' explanations of the coupon business. He nodded at the excoriations of bankers. He nodded as Charles evoked the worthy names of Boston society vested in the SEC. Pelletier knew that Charles liked to refer to his hoards of money in overseas banks.

"Could you get that money back promptly enough if you needed it to cover notes?" the D.A. asked.

"I don't need to get it back," Charles snapped. "I've got plenty of funds on hand to pay all my notes."

Pelletier arched his eyebrows.

"Could you settle all your depositors' accounts today if you had to?" Pelletier asked.

"Absolutely! I'd have a surplus of $2 million. You know, I see by the way you keep raising your eyes there, you don't believe me. I tell you what—give me until Saturday to put my affairs in order. On Saturday I'll stop taking new funds and we'll have an auditor, of your choosing, Mr. Pelletier, to verify my solvency. How's that?"

Pelletier had no intention of playing apprentice to the so-called wizard of finance. "See here, Ponzi, I think your scheme is crooked.

If you think for a minute I'm going to allow you to take in money for the rest of the week you are crazy. At the speed you're going now, you'd take in $10 million and pledge to pay back $15 million. I don't need a complaint filed against you. I'm charged with protecting the public's interest, and that's what I'm doing. Your operations stop today and my auditor goes to work as soon as possible."

Charles asked for at least a day, but McMasters interrupted him. "No, you close today," McMasters said, with a reassuring look at the district attorney.

"Very well," Charles assented. "I'll accept no more funds until the auditor's report."

McMasters nodded to his client and Charles left for his next appointment at the office of the state attorney general, J. Weston Allen. Charles hoped he could talk Allen into making Pelletier lighten up. Allen said he not only knew about Pelletier's audit, but shared the D.A.'s "concern." Charles learned that Massachusetts Governor Calvin Coolidge had arranged for a federal auditor to assist Pelletier's inquiry, a man named Edwin L. Pride.

Charles kept his grin and his cool. McMasters listened, amazed, as his client improvised responses to the second grilling of the day. "He answered every question with gusto," McMasters amazedly told his friends, "chattering for over three hours in the fourth dimension of finance and romance."

Outside the statehouse, Charles asked McMasters, "How did I do?"

McMasters said, "You don't need a publicity agent, you need a lawyer."

"Do you think so?" Charles asked.

"I do, and I will phone him tonight."

It's not the end of the world, Charles thought, but mortal fear was gripping his bowels. As soon as he reached his offices, he called Rose. In this fight to the death, he told his faithful pup, he had only one weapon. "Barron and his ilk have stirred up rumors, and some weak come-latelys have demanded their money. By God, they got it, too. Not one of my clients ever went begging when they asked for their funds. But there's as many or more gathered outside who are pulling for our side, Rose," he said.

And he wasn't lying. There were people waiting to make new deposits, and long-standing depositors defending the Ponzi name. "Yes, I know, dear, the banks and the newspapers and the attorneys and commissioners...they want to shut us down so bad, they're trembling. But we've got something they don't, Rose. We've got the people."

Taking the phone to the streetside window, Ponzi waved to the crowd sweating outside his offices.

"Three cheers for Ponzi!" they roared.

"Three groans for the *Post!*" he called back.

"I think we could use some 'wet' blood in the statehouse, don't you?" Charles teased a group of journalists, referring to his immigration status.

That Monday afternoon, Ponzi had the people on his side. But a mob is a fickle mistress, as a gambling man ought never to forget. When Tuesday's paper announced Pelletier's audit, School Street erupted.

WE WILL NOT BE ACCEPTING NEW DEPOSITS, read the sign above the wicket cages. It might as well have said, THE RUN STARTS HERE.

****

The next two days turned School Street into a battle zone. Women fainted from exhaustion, fights broke out, and the crowds grew more restless as they grew larger. Charles saw "a huge line, people four abreast, stretching from the City Hall Annex, through City Hill Avenue and School Street, to the entrance of the Niles Building, up stairways, along the corridors."

As the run gained force, herds of people shoved desperately against the large glass doors of the Niles Building until they shattered the panes, raining shards of glass on everyone nearby and lacerating several victims who were slammed into the broken door frames. On Tuesday afternoon, so many depositors were sardined inside Charles' front office that one could hardly move. Suffocating heat engulfed the anxiety-ridden crowd. To prevent another disaster, police officers clawed their way inside the office, then removed the throngs of people and stationed them behind barricaded walkways along the street. Four people were hospitalized.

Charles was busy filing a $5-million libel suit against Clarence Barron and the *Post*. To handle the overflow crowds, he leased the Bell-in-Hand, a well-known barroom which was also housed in the Niles Building, and had clerks passing money through a hastily constructed cashier's booth in the exit doorway. The SEC was refunding at least 1,000 claims a day, about $60,000 by each afternoon's closing.

Charles managed a quivering guffaw when McMasters showed him the article. By Thursday the SEC had redeemed all but the most recent notes, those issued in the previous 45 days. "Now we've taken care of those disgruntled souls, we can get back to business," he told his stern-faced rep. McMasters knew differently. During the last month and a half, Ponzi had sold nearly 30,000 notes, about as many as he had issued during the previous six months. Plus, customers in June and July were buying larger and larger notes as the scheme gained momentum. Giving back a few thousand a day was nothing compared to what the Ponzi clerks would see as the flood of recent notes started coming due.

Meanwhile, Edwin Pride's audit team was flailing beneath the Ponzi books, "approximately 40,000 note cards, several bound notebooks, and sundry looseleaf sheets of paper, actually," according to Pride. Charles clung blissfully to his ignorance. He babbled wildly to reporters about racist conspiracies and the plans he had for revolutionizing American business. He contacted a shadowy "investor" from New York who had once offered to buy him out for $10 million. Charles could not admit he was a small-time fool whose fall had been predestined by the nature of his rise. But even Charles' optimism would run out of sand sooner or later.

On August 2, just a week after Barron's remarks provoked the run, Charles read the morning *Post:*

PONZI IS HOPELESSLY INSOLVENT

The article itself spoke more directly.

> *Charles Ponzi is unbalanced on one subject—his financial operations. He thinks he is worth millions. He is hopelessly insolvent. He does not have sufficient funds to meet his notes. He has sent no money to Europe, nor received money from Europe recently.*

Later that day, the author told an audience of local dignitaries, "Ponzi's no financial wizard. He can hardly add.... He sits with his feet on the desk smoking expensive cigars in a diamond holder and talking complete gibberish about postal coupons." The speaker, one William McMasters, admitted that he had served the last few weeks as the idiot's public representative.

I had to throw the switch, McMasters said, or share the cell awaiting Mr. Ponzi. "Let him stop glittering generalities about his wealth and tell his note holders how much he owes and where the money is to meet it."

Bianchi the Snake Returns

In Boston, thousands flocked to School Street. Some came to bury Charles, some to praise him. All pressed *en masse* against his doors, threatening once more to shatter the recently replaced glass. Charles rode gamely in from Lexington to face the music. He promised he would not only deliver on his notes, he would bring about nothing less than the "downfall of an autocratic clique that has been allowed to prey on the credulity of the public."

That Tuesday, Charles' clerks paid off 300 or 400 notes, then barricaded the offices, assuring everyone they would open early Wednesday. Like a consummate politician, Charles kept obsessively to his business as usual. He babbled to the press about his new venture, a hybrid that crossed his profit-sharing bank idea with a line of mothballed ships he was buying from the Navy surplus yard.

Wednesday evening Charles had Rose and Imelda don their best dresses and accompany him to a variety show. Newsreel photographers had swarmed about their Lexington home over the last several days. The Ponzis were gonna be in pictures.

The *Post* reporter wrote, "Ponzi hired a box close to the stage at Keith's and saw himself in the movies for the first time." In the reel a long shot followed a crowd of people to the Ponzi home, where Charles stood on the front steps, his arms around his mother and his loving bride.

According to the reporter, "Ponzi liked the newsreel very much and was further elated by the applause of the audience. Then came a comedy act with a few flattering allusions to Ponzi. This tickled him more."

Despite his seemingly nonstop public displays, gossips throughout Boston wagged that Charles had skipped town. Many of his associates, including a friend from the Atlanta penitentiary named Louis Casullo and Rose's uncle John Dondero, had indeed left as soon as the audit began. Charles, according to the most popular story, had satcheled $2 million into his car and headed for Sarasota Springs, New York. He planned to win himself out of trouble, using a deck of cards and a chorus of *Hail Marys*.

That sounded like Charles all right; but he never left Boston. He stubbornly stayed put and in the open. His friends and enemies alike kept constant tabs on him. A steady procession of automobiles rode past his house, morning and night. Curious streetcar riders hung out the windows as they passed within view of the Ponzi home, and many debarked at the next stop, walking up the hill to get a closer look.

****

Meanwhile the *Post* dug up a mugshot of one Charles Bianchi, an Italian national who had served time in Montreal for forging a check. The man in the photograph wore a mustache while Charles Ponzi was clean shaven. The man stared at the camera with deeper, fuller eyes than Charles Ponzi, whose hair was starting to thin and showing swirls of gray, but the image had been taken 12 years before, as Bianchi was processed into St. Vincent's Penitentiary. The *Post* had a photographer brush a mustache onto a recent shot of Charles Ponzi and lower the receding hairline. It was clearly a match.

Charles pathetically challenged the story. He claimed he had done secret work for the Italian government in Canada. He was threatening to file yet another lawsuit against the paper. But there was no doubt Bianchi and Ponzi were the same man. Dominico Defrancesco, who had clerked in the Banco Zarossi 12 years before, nearly bounced off the walls of his tiny home when he recognized the mug shot.

"I know that man, too, he is, his name—Bianchi!" shrieked Mrs. Defrancesco.

"Bianchi!" repeated her husband, haltingly. "Sure, sure," the man stuttered, nearly raising out of his chair. "Only he shave off the mustache. Sure, I work in the same office. I lose some of my own money." Defrancesco called Bianchi "a sporty feller" and added: "He never liked to work, and was always talking of millions and wearing a nice white collar and nice clothes. I was just the clerk that write out the papers. I lost some of my own money. But I do not worry. I have worked and I would rather go out with the pick and the shovel than be Bianchi."

Canadian inspectors confirmed the identification. As manager of the Banco Zarossi, this Bianchi had hundreds of immigrant families sending money back home. "The game was to give a receipt and then when the money didn't come, the families in Italy would write and complain and then the folks here would make a holler, and then some of the money that was coming in would be used to really send over a draft," the inspectors explained. "The old game of paying the second fellow with the first fellow's money; and then, when there was a reckoning, Zarossi skipped out to Mexico."

Apparently ready to come clean, Charles summoned reporters to his house late on Thursday night for a bombshell announcement, he claimed. When the writers appeared, Charles brandished a gun from his front porch. "My guards' power is limited!" he shouted. "But mine is unlimited. When I shoot, I shoot to hit! Get away or there'll be some tall shooting." The reporters drew back to the bottom of the hill, where they could still see the front light burning on the Ponzi porch.

An audit team at the Hanover Trust meanwhile had turned up further troubles. Charles had already written checks for $500,000 against the $1.5 million CD he had pledged there. Worse, the auditors also found loans made to Charles' "straw men," such as Charles *Pizzi*, for as much as $160,000 each. These were the bank loans Charles guaranteed with notes from his Securities Exchange Company. Later he confessed, "I had the notes signed by 'dummies,' employees of the bank and others. Then the dummies endorsed the certificates over to the Hanover as collateral. The bank discounted the notes and credited the amount to my account." The proceeds of the various loans were traced to accounts in Charles' name and several in the name of Lucy Martelli, the not-so-clever alias Charles devised for his secretary, Lucy Meli.

Banking Commissioner Allen fumed at the gross violation of the law. Ponzi grumbled, "Maybe it was a violation. Maybe it wasn't."

Allen charged that many "bad loans," like Charles' dummy guarantees, permeated the books. "Practically every employee and most of the directors have funds invested with the Securities Exchange Company," the Commissioner wrote. "As commissioner of banks, I have no supervision over the affairs of Charles Ponzi. The moment I learn, however, that he is overdrawing his account in a trust company, which *is* under my supervision, it is my duty to interfere." The doors of the Hanover were padlocked and chained.

Charles openly scoffed outside the bank. "I told Allen a lot of bull—all bull! And he has been looking it up. If I talk to him again, I'll tell him a lot of bull."

But Edwin Pride, federal auditor, brooked no bull. Charles left the Hanover to meet with Pride in a conference room at the state house.

"How much are my liabilities?" Charles asked.

"About $7 million," Pride said. Then, Pride asked: "How much do you believe you have in assets?"

"About $4 million," Charles answered. Pride adjusted his rimless spectacles. When Charles saw the auditor was waiting for him to speak, he blurted, "Gee, I must be insolvent."

Friday's newspapers announced:

THE GIGANTIC PONZI BUBBLE HAS BURST

At Charles' arraignment, observers noted that Ponzi's trademark cigarette holder was missing from his ensemble, as was the customary rubberband of a smile. "The only familiar thing about him was his cane," noted one observer. "But he no longer carried the item at a jaunty angle. It hung—just hung—from his arm." Charles stood mute as the judge bound him over for mail fraud and bank fraud.

While deputies led Charles away, Rose and Imelda wept, promising they would never rest until Charles walked free. "He is my husband," Rose bravely asserted. "He is a big man who will face the danger of having his skin grafted on a woman he didn't know and will serve a prison term to absolve a friend. To meet my husband is to like him, at the least. To know him is to love him."

Imelda and Rose both declared their beloved's innocence. "Who knows Charlie better than we?"

The two women also began packing their bags as government agents informed them that the house in Lexington, along with all other Ponzi assets, would be seized. The *Post* marked the day with an exclusive interview, Imelda Ponzi's first and only public words concerning her son. With her white hair pulled into an intricate knot, the 69-year-old woman sat in an overstuffed easy chair, plying her crochet hook.

"Everything I own," Imelda declared, "straight down to the skirt around my waist, I would willingly give if it would help to make my boy straight with the world."

Rose added, "There has been talk of my gowns and my jewels. I have no jewels except my wedding ring. Since we have come here I have bought exactly three dresses—two little black silk dresses and a white satin suit. There would not be any gowns to take."

For weeks thereafter, agents swarmed the house, searching for hidden vaults, secret passageways, and rigged bookshelves. Boston legend said Ponzi's walls were lined with Liberty Bonds, millions worth, but the agents found no magic hideaways and no valuables beyond the lavish furnishings Charles had showered upon his women.

Rose sobbed as she stepped into her taxi, never once looking back at the magnificent house. "I just wish my poor mother were here."

Doing the Dipsy-Doodle

And still the people lined School Street, many of them grumbling, starting fights, threatening to make spaghetti out of the erstwhile wizard. But just as many cheered for Ponzi, who had shaken fistfuls of money at the Boston establishment. Sadly, those who stood most loyally by Charles' scheme were the poor working immigrants who could least afford to lose.

"You're the greatest Italian of them all!" somebody boomed from a streetcar, spying Charles outside the courthouse.

"No, Columbus and Marconi. Columbus discovered America. Marconi invented the wireless," Charles answered.

"Yeah, but you discovered money!" the voice called back, and hurrahs faded down the street with the car.

During the trial, Charles was held in Plymouth Jail. Crowds trailed him as he shuffled between his cell and the courthouse. The authorities treated Charles almost like an associate. Photos of the diminutive hustler walking next to the tall, ample-chested sheriff circled the nation.

Even after his several trials and convictions, many of Charles' victims remained loyal to him, despite the 12 cents on the dollar they were mailed by the receivership. William McMasters opined that once bitten by the quick-fix bug, investors were incurable. (The trend continues to our own day. It's not greed alone, though, but pride that renders victims incapable of basic reason. Ponzi players often find it easier to defend their assailant than admit they've bedded down with a con.)

Charles' luck in the courts matched his ill-starred attempts at the gaming table. He plunked down $100,000 for a defense attorney, Daniel Coakley, known as "one of the deftest and least scrupulous lawyers in Massachusetts." Coakley advised his client to plead guilty to the federal charge of mail fraud. Charles would draw short time and avoid the wrath of the state of Massachussetts, which was clamoring to try him for larceny.

Appearing in Charles' defense, William McMasters appealed to the federal judge for leniency. McMasters testified that during the short time he worked for Ponzi, he watched a man gripped by the very mania he'd helped create. "I called him unbalanced at the time. And it was true. He was nutty then, your Honor, but he's not nutty now." Others, including his wife and mother, pled for mercy on Charles' behalf, citing his kind nature and the philanthropic works he had performed with his money.

Such words notwithstanding, the judge decreed a five-year sentence. Rose fainted and had to be carried from the courtroom.

Charles looked with queasy eyes at his attorney. "Five years doesn't sound like short time," he told Dan Coakley.

Charles returned to the Plymouth County Jail that day, as he had returned every day for months. Since the feds had no facility of their own in Massachusetts, Charles would remain housed in Boston for the duration of his sentence. Rose was happy she would be able to visit daily. Charles worried they were keeping him under wraps for the next big hit. He began a fervid study of the law and undertook his own defense in a rash of bankruptcy proceedings and civil suits.

After logging three-and-a-half of his five years, Charles was released by the U.S. government. Immediately state authorities picked him up and launched a new trial. Attorney Dan Coakley, who had assured Charles the state would forego a separate prosecution, had nothing to offer his former client but sympathy. Shortly after Charles' original guilty plea, the attorney was disbarred for his role in a blackmail scandal.

All but broke, Charles represented himself before the Massachussetts court. "The promise of profits is not larceny," Charles averred. "It is merely a promise, and a promise may or may not be kept according to the circumstance." Without the state's meddling, all would have gone swimmingly. Not one investor went unpaid, Charles truthfully stated, until the authorities, under pressure from the banking establishment, shut him down.

Charles pointed out that a man he knew from the Atlanta penitentiary—Charles Morse, an embezzling banker who kept on trading stocks from inside the prison—was currently a prosperous financial analyst in the Midwest. "It's the same here," Charles Ponzi demanded. "I've served my time, I deserve another chance." The jury acquitted on four counts, but couldn't decide on the remaining 18 charges. A second trial ensued.

In February 1925, the state won its case. Charles was branded "a common and notorious thief" and assigned a penalty of seven to nine years imprisonment. The summer of money had definitely ended.

Charles told Rose they would fight to the end. He quickly filed an appeal while Rose and Imelda were raising $14,000 bail money.

Mr. Ponzi Meets Ma Ferguson

The fall of 1925 came to Boston with a blast of cool air. When the recently reunited lovers weren't working, they were entertaining. Friends, supporters, and sleaze hounds mobbed the apartment which Imelda had rented for her boy and Rose.

One afternoon Charles' visitors included an old friend, a schoolmate who brushed away Charles' handshake and hugged him savagely, the ashes of his cigarette falling down Charles' back onto the tiled floor. It was Charles' accomplice in the Banco Zarossi. Only he didn't call himself Angelo Salviati anymore; he was now Calcadonio Alviati.

While on a business trip to Boston, Alviati had read in the *Post* about his old friend's troubles. They both agreed it was a wretched newspaper. They agreed that they had aged. Charles' hair loss had crossed the line into full-on baldness, save for a little gray swipe on each side; and he had grown flabby laying about in prison. Alviati had shrunk. His face was gaunt, made more so by his oiled-down hair. His voice had thinned and he stopped the conversation several times for convulsive coughing, the price for his love of fine Turkish tobacco. Neither spoke of their time together in Montreal.

Alviati told Charles he had an opportunity for him. "Land values in southern Florida have increased by 560 percent in just the last four years, Carlo. While you were serving time, I've been getting rich." The next day, Charles informed Rose he would be sending for her soon, but for the present he had business to tend to in Florida.

Actually Alviati wasn't doing that well. He and his wife Maria had only been in Jacksonville for about a year. And the heat was getting to them, so to speak. Grand juries were convening to investigate the land boom. Offices were being raided in the middle of the night and promoters driven from their homes in their bedclothes to answer questions. The boom was about to bust, but Charlie didn't have a clue.

He skipped bail in May and headed for Florida. A few weeks later Rose received an envelope with a small stack of shareholder's notes made out in her name. She recognized her husband's handwriting but had never heard of the company she partly owned—something called the Charpon Land Syndicate. Charpon was CHARles PONzi's latest venture. With three prison terms under his belt, Mr. Ponzi had nevertheless not ceased to scheme.

He gave his name in Jacksonville circles as Charles Borelli. With the remaining funds he had saved from the SEC, he purchased 100 acres of land in Columbia County. He paid $16 an acre. Charles and Alviati named it the Rosa Maria tract, after each of their wives. The Charpon Syndicate divided the land into 24 lots per acre, which they sold for $10 each. Total yield, $240 an acre.

So what if the lots were mosquito-infested marshes unreachable except by pirogue or by poling a johnboat. Alviati explained that they weren't selling to homebuyers; they were selling to investors, people who expected to sell the land to someone else, who would probably sell it again. Charles worked up a song and dance to convince suckers that a single $10 investment would bring them $5.3 million in two years. If you were thinking short term, Charpon also offered a special deal. You put up the money for your lots, say ten lots, at $100. In 60 days, you either claimed a 100-percent profit by selling the lots for $200 through the Syndicate or you owned the land outright and began making payments. Oh yes! The Ponzi Plan was back in action!

Charles Borelli made his first sale on November 9, 1925. By the time he sent for Rose in February of the next year, he had collected $7,000. Slow by his standards, but this was a tough game.

Charles had also attracted attention. Socially, most business people in Jacksonville had learned by now that their Signor Borelli was in fact the infamous Mr. Ponzi. It only took a little time before sheriff's deputies learned this also. In April, just as Rose was arriving for her second visit, Charles got a tip that the Jacksonville authorities were about to arrest him. He suggested to Rose that they see Tampa.

They spent two nights at the Horizons Hotel before Charles' attorney called from Jacksonville. "I've been asked to bring you in. The deputies are waiting here now."

Charles and Rose, along with Calcadonio and Maria Alviati, were charged with not registering with the State of Florida and not purchasing a $150 license. The charges against Rose and Maria were dropped almost immediately. Calcadonio was convicted within two days and extradited to face a similar charge in Boston for recruiting Charles and others there into the land scam racket.

Charles, whose luck had run hot and cold, held his breath. A jury found him guilty and sentenced him to one year's hard labor in the Florida State Penitentiary at Raiford. Judge James Peeler denied Charles' motion for a new trial. Peeler did grant him 60 days to file an appeal and freed him on $1,500 bond.

Peeler might as well have booked Charles' ship. A week after the verdict, Charles received a telegram informing him that the Massachussetts Supreme Court had rejected his appeal and was ordering him to appear for sentencing. Charles got himself a deckhand's job on the Italian freighter *Sic Vos Von Vobis*, which was bound for Genoa, Italy, after stopping at various ports on the Gulf Coast.

The Florida authorities easily anticipated Charles' move and alerted law officers in Houston, Texas, the *Vobis'* next port. Sheriff Binford wired back:

> *DO YOU WANT CHARLES PONZI? ADVISE RETURN WIRE*
> *QUICK, ADVISE FINGERPRINT CLASSIFICATION AND IF*
> *ANY REWARD.*

There was no reward, Binford learned, but he put a man on it anyway. This Ponzi bird was causing a national stir, and there might be some good publicity for the dude who bagged him. Deputy George Lacy narrowly missed the *Vobis*, arriving as the ship was steaming out of Galveston Bay. With Binford's permission, Deputy Lacy drove to New Orleans and waited there.

As soon as the *Vobis* docked, Lacy sent a message from the U.S. Customs office, saying they had to register Charles Borelli's luggage for international travel. A simple technicality, the ship's steward explained to Charles, who was finding his smooth hands and flabby chest were not suited to a deckhand's life. Charles spotted Lacy's cowboy hat and tried to bolt, but customs officers grabbed him and motioned for Lacy to bring cuffs.

Charles' court-appointed attorney told him he had a good chance of slipping his bonds. His extradition hearing would be presided over by the first woman governor of Texas, Miriam "Ma" Ferguson. Ma's husband, James "Pa" Ferguson, had been impeached as governor on corruption charges. Ma ran in his place and won in 1924. Charles learned that Ma Ferguson was known for issuing a string of clemencies. She'd once ordered a clearly guilty defendant, who was appealing his conviction for murder, "Make a check for $1,000 and you're a free man."

Charles told the dour-faced governor that he, an Italian citizen, had been kidnapped from an Italian vessel. He ought to be released immediately to return to his homeland. Governor Ma allowed that she had never been to Italy, nor could she understand a word of the Eye-talian language. "The King's English was good enough for Jesus, and it's good enough for me," she quipped. Ma added that she wouldn't make any decision on Charles' case until after the gubernatorial primary at the end of July.

Ma Ferguson lost the primary (although she mounted a successful comeback run in 1933) and Charles lost his motion. Because Charles was still subject to an outstanding warrant in

Massachusetts, Boston deputies were notified to come and get their man.

While he was waiting for his escorts, Charles telegraphed Calvin Coolidge, who had served as governor of Massachussetts before being elected U.S. President in 1922. As governor, Coolidge had personally ordered the shutdown of Charles' Securities Exchange Company in August 1920, as Charles well knew. But logical discernment had never ranked high on Charles' personal inventory. He addressed the President directly, pleading":

> *PERSONALLY KNOWING EVENTS DOINGS AND PERSONS ON BEACON HILL MAY I ASK YOUR EXCELLENCY FOR OFFICIAL OR UNOFFICIAL INTERVENTION IN MY BEHALF?*
>
> *THE PONZI CASE HAS ASSUMED THE PROPORTIONS OF A NATIONAL SCANDAL FOSTERED BY THE STATE OF MASSA-CHUSSETTS WITH THE FORBEARANCE OF THE FEDERAL GOVERNMENT.*
>
> *I CANNOT SILENTLY SUBMIT TO FURTHER PERSECUTION BUT FOR THE BEST INTERESTS OF ALL CONCERNED I AM WILLING TO SUBMIT TO IMMEDIATE DEPORTATION.*
>
> *WILL YOUR EXCELLENCY GIVE HIS CONSIDERATION TO THE EVENTUAL WISDOM OF MY COMPROMISE ?*
>
> *CHARLES PONZI*
>
> *HARRIS COUNTY JAIL*

He Bids Farewell

Charles never got a reply from President Coolidge, but he *was* deported. First though, the U.S. Attorney in Boston agreed to have Charles serve seven years in a Massachussetts state pen. There, Charles raised white mice, which the state sold to laboratories for medical experiments, and he read legal books. He was furloughed just once during his stay, to attend Imelda's funeral.

While in prison, Charles redoubled his ire at the government and fought the deportation proceedings against him. Rose was working as a secretary and bookkeeper for the Coconut Grove nightclub. On her days off she served as Charles' paralegal, shuttling lawbooks and appeal briefs to the visitors' window. When Charles was at last released from prison in February of 1934, Rose helped him get a job at a grocery wholesaler. He made $25 a week and spent most of his free time writing to Governor Joe Ely asking for a pardon.

But despite their best efforts, the Ponzis lost. Charles was arrested in September by immigration officials, who feared he would flee again. The deportation was set for October 7. Charles told reporters from his cell that Rose wasn't coming with him; he'd send for her as soon as he arrived in Rome.

On the appointed day an official entourage walked Charles to his ship. Nearly 12 years of prison life, combined with the uncertainties ahead, dampened even Charles' fabled spirits. He held his shoulders stiffly, as if he were trying to keep his pudgy cheeks from overflowing. He had grown pale from too little sunlight and exercise and was now completely bald except for a small patch of hair just above each ear. He needed glasses to read and sign the deportation order, which he held trembling in his hand.

The scene resembled the usual Ponzi carnival. A small crowd had gathered. Newspaper reporters snapped pictures of the 52-year-old man who had so infamously burned Boston. Charles posed obligingly but his eyes no longer danced and his smiles were forced. He suggested that three of the seven deputies observing the deportation should stand alongside him for a photo, and they did.

During the official news conference he spoke from a velvet chair, explaining that besides $500 in travel money his friends had kicked in an extra $100 to upgrade his ticket to first class. As the ship's horn signaled departure time, Charles declared, "I went looking for trouble and I got it. I wish success to President Roosevelt on his recovery program."

He cleared his eyes with his handkerchief. Squaring his shoulders, Ponzi donned a puffy golfer's cap, gave the Fascist salute, and left America forever.

Mr. Ponzi's Last Big Adventure

Now that he was back in the motherland, Charles wanted to meet Italy's dictator, Benito Mussolini. Charles' second cousin—Colonel Attilio Biseo, Mussolini's personal pilot—got the two together. Mussolini wanted to hear about how the little man had stung Americans for more than $20 million, but *Il Duce* had little patience for Charles' fiscal recommendations.

For several years Charles bounced between jobs. He was a bookkeeper for a movie company. He sold construction materials. Mostly he sponged off friends and relatives, stayed drunk, and proved nightly that he was still one of the world's worst gamblers. He wrote often to Rose, promising to send for her and asking her if she would borrow $2,000 from her American friends. Charles had a manuscript, *The Rise of Mr. Ponzi*. He needed enough cash to publish it himself, since none of the big-leaguers, according to Charles, would tell the truth of his ordeal.

Rose didn't come through with the money. Instead she filed for divorce. She had waited and hoped and struggled, without the help of her husband and bereft of her family, and she had finally run out of patience. "When he had millions, when he had a mansion, when he had cars, I stuck with him," she boldly told reporters. "When he was down, when he was in prison, I stuck with him. I feel that I have proved my loyalty through thick and thin." But Rose was tired. She was 36 years old. She might marry again, if she chose to. (She never did.)

Charles flew into a rage when he was notified of the divorce, which was granted to Rose on the grounds that her husband was a convicted criminal. He called a news conference and announced he was publishing a book. Tentatively titled *The Boston Merry-Go-Round*, the story would contain disclosures walloping enough to fell the entire Massachussetts power structure. Shouting, shivering with tears and bordering on incoherence, Charles told the few reporters who would listen, "I'm going to hell, and I'm going to take a lot of people with me."

But he didn't. He kept on scheming, as always. He was still shopping his first book, *The Rise of Mr. Ponzi*, hoping to finance its publication with a subscription company. With 1,000 shares of Charles Ponzi Publishing, costing $20 a share, subscribers stood to make...you guessed it...*100 percent interest.* "I don't think I'm under an illusion that 25,000 copies should sell in New England alone," Charles brayed.

Finally he managed, through a friend in New York, to have a Brooklyn printer typeset 1,000 copies and glue them into cheap yellow bindings. But Charles lacked the $235 balance due. He phoned a reporter at the *Boston Post*, suggesting the paper run a notice: "If a hundred people send $2.50 to the printer, each of them will receive a copy of the book at a bargain price and be among the first to savor its revelations." The *Post* declined.

In 1939 Charles was eking out what living he could as a translator for hotels in Venice and Rome. His cousin, Colonel Biseo, wanted to know if Charles might prefer to join him in Rio de Janeiro. Mussolini had given the Colonel full powers to establish

LATI, an airline between Brazil and Italy. Maybe Charles would like to be business manager for the Italian national airline?

The airline gig in Rio was Ponzi's final payoff. Charles bought himself a home in a tony strip called Spanema Beach. He hobnobbed with the Italian ambassador, was chauffeured wherever he wished to go, and was perpetually attended by two manservants. Once more, Charles tasted the high life.

Then he faced the hangover. Representatives of the Brazilian State Department showed up in Charles' doorway one afternoon. Colonel Biseo's little airline was not just jogging passengers from Rio to Rome. LATI was helping smuggle Brazilian diamonds for the Fascist cause. As for the passengers on LATI's flights, many of them were spies or escaped military figures.

Charles was livid. No one had given him a cut! He offered to help the Brazilians with their investigation. In exchange for 25 percent of anything recovered, he'd name names and itineraries. They passed. The representatives intended to wait for Biseo's next visit, arrest him, and impound the airline's property until the diamonds were returned.

Charles sent a letter to the American embassy. Give me a U.S. visa, he said, and I'll break this thing wide open for you. The Americans didn't want to hear anything about international smuggling operations. They were staying as far out of this war as possible. Charles called the newspapers and offered to sell them the LATI scoop. They also declined. As always, when Charlie had a cow he tried to milk her until she dropped.

On December 8, 1941, all Italian military personnel in Rio were called home. The Japanese had triggered U.S. involvement in World War II with a sneak attack on Pearl Harbor the day before. *Il Duce* had more pressing concerns than a smuggling operation with its cover blown.

Charles was out on his ear, but decided to stay in Rio. Against his nature, he had saved some money the last few years, which he used to buy himself a rooming house. This venture, like so many of his others, flopped. Charles' neighbors complained that his roomers, all women, tended to entertain a steady march of male friends. It was one of *those* houses, not unheard of in Rio, but not usually perched in the middle of Spanema Beach.

Charles unloaded the house and started a chain of hot-dog stands. He had moved to an apartment in the Copacabana area. A photo from that time shows him lying in the sand, wearing all white, his smile glinting to match the dome of his head, perusing a copy of *The Rise of Mr. Ponzi*. Apparently, he bought the Brooklyn shop's print run with money he had saved during his stint at LATI.

The hotdog stands were a wash. Charles sold very few hotdogs, and his operators stole handfuls of what he did take in. In 1947, he sold his beachside apartment and rented a filthy room in a working-class suburb. He found work, $300 a month steady income, translating documents for an exporting firm. The monster was slipping, though. His work was sporadic, and his translations were ridden with grammatical errors and haphazard renderings of simple turns of phrase.

After a year with the exporting firm, a stroke paralyzed his left side. Charles now required constant nursing care, so he became a resident of the local charity ward. An operation for cataracts saved some of the sight in his right eye but also caused it to swell in its socket. While the bulbous eye wandered uncontrollably around the room, Charles lay back in his bed, looking like a puffed-up lizard searching for food. He could still move his right side, but he spent most days flat on his back, chattering incessantly with his nearly toothless mouth to the nurses and occasional visitor. If no one else came around, Charles talked to his roommate, an elderly black man who had been catatonic for at least 15 years. Each morning the nurses dutifully moved the man to the wheelchair at the end of his bed, where he spent his days with his head angled at the ceiling.

A ward of the state, unknown beyond a few local friends, Charles conceded nothing to his old nemesis, Fortuna. He planned to hire himself out as a business consultant when he got well, he said. Opportunities were exploding around the world, as Europe and Japan rebuilt their war-scarred industries. He was putting out feelers for a scheme to swindle the Soviet Union out of $2 billion by promising to help agents smuggle gold deposits out of South America. "What a joke on the Communists! May Stalin rot in hell," Charles wheezed. He wrote a few paragraphs each day for the second volume of his memoirs, *The Fall of Mr. Ponzi*. He was naming names this time.

"This is a helluva story," the monster said to his roommate.

The other man sat in his chair, as he sat all day, every day, staring at the ceiling, mute, immobile, uncomprehending; but with his head cocked so you could have sworn he was listening to Charles.

"A helluva story."

TIME

The Weekly Newsmagazine

TÄNDSTICK·KONUNG KREUGER
He made the match.
(See BUSINESS)

Volume XIV

Number 18

Ivar Kreuger

(1880 - 1932)

CHAPTER 3

Keeper of the Flame:
Ivar Kreuger

"Was man, indeed, at once so powerful, so virtuous, and magnificent, yet so vicious and base? He appeared at one time a
mere scion of evil principle and at another as all that can be
conceived of as noble and godlike."
—*The Creature*

"*Silence*," Ivar Kreuger once hissed to a news
correspondent. The man was badgering Kreuger about
the secret to winning big in business. Kreuger repeated
his answer, effectively ending the interview. "Silence,
silence, and more silence."

In 1922, when ministers of the French government
were desperately searching for a loan, they asked this
monster if he would help. Kreuger was among the richest
men alive, acting as a kind of freelance World Bank. He'd
loaned millions to Spain, Romania, Poland—to a host of
countries, large and small—helping to rebuild the
wreckage of the First World War. While France's Prime
Minister Pinochet sawed a finger across his mustache,
angling for his share of Kreuger's generosity, Kreuger sat
at the head of a runway-sized mahogany table and said
nothing. He returned each man's questioning look with
his own expectant stare.

Sunlight angled through the tall windows, flashing on
the pale corners of Kreuger's widow's peak. He stretched
his long legs beneath the table. He drew back his jacket
lapel and retrieved a cigarette case. He laid the case on
the table with its raised silver *K* facing up. With his index
finger he flipped the case open, as a poker player reveals
a card. Again he reached into his coat, its gray stripes
thin as foil, almost invisible against the material's basic
black, and produced a box of matches. He set the

matches beside the cigarette case. His arm now fully extended, Kreuger pinched a cigarette between his finger and thumb. He craned the cigarette over the matchbox and tapped. He tapped again and again, setting a dirge-like rhythm, catching the eye of each man at the table, offering a smile, a nod, an encouraging blink. Every time the cigarette struck the box top, the matches rattled inside.

The box was stamped by the Swedish Match Company. Though he dabbled in businesses of every sort, matches made Kreuger king. He held monopoly contracts throughout the world, furnishing entire nations with their matches. People usually cooked with wood or gas; electricity was just coming into its own and the Bic hadn't been invented yet. Everybody needed a quick source for fire. If Kreuger couldn't persuade a country to grant him a monopoly to sell his matches, he arranged concessions that allowed him to compete tariff-free with the nation's own producers; then he gradually swallowed up his rivals. Just before his death, this modern Prometheus controlled four-fifths of the world's supply of matches, and was known everywhere as *The Swedish Match King*.

It seemed like a cosmic joke. In the early decades of the 20th century, the world's most powerful businessman rested his empire on matches. Not automobiles. Not oil. Not industrial technology or corporate finance. Matches. "A commonplace, unexciting object," Kreuger admitted. "But it doesn't matter what you make. Just so you make lots of them. And you control every one."

Just so, Kreuger floated over the French negotiators, riding a cloud of silence in perfect calm. Tapping his cigarette on a matchbox. Waiting for what they would give him.

Prime Minister Pinochet got a $75-million loan, stabilizing the dangerously volatile franc. Ivar Kreuger secured unlimited rights to ship luxury matches—instead of cheap wartime knockoffs—into the French market. Not to mention that Ivar won bragging rights for having rescued one of the world's great states. *Europe's Saviour*, his admirers in the press hoorahed. The Match King had worked his magic again.

Kreuger gained the world's affection not by warmth and charisma but by exerting financial wizardry. When the American stock market crashed on October 29, 1929, whose face gazed stoicly from the cover of that week's *Time* magazine? Ivar Kreuger's. Even in a charcoal drawing, his taut features projected an air of...patience. The patience of rock, and of the water that, drop by drop, wears the rock into sand.

As the Great Depression spread across continents, Kreuger took a hit like everyone else. But he never panicked. Laudatory articles extolled the Kreugerite attitude in the *Saturday Evening Post* and the *Literary Digest*. Whatever the hysteria in the markets, however many would-be tycoons somersaulted from their office ledges, Kreuger abided. Visiting America, he assured President Hoover that the financiers were overreacting. It would take strong, disciplined men such as the two of them, he told Hoover, to coax the country back into shape.

Kreuger's stocks and bonds continued to be the most widely traded in the world because unlike most post-Crash operations, Kreuger's holding company never stopped shelling out money. He seemed amused at the chaos swirling around him and kept right on paying annual dividends as high as 20 percent on the dollar.

"Making money is a child's game," Kreuger quipped privately. "The fortune of nations can be made to turn on apparently trivial things. I have made countries swing upon a match. It could just as well be hairpins or buttons."

No References Required

Karl Marx once warned that the insatiably thirsty force of capitalism hovered over Europe, threatening to destroy her. He might have used Ivar Kreuger for the "Wanted" poster.

Nobody ever proved that Ivar drew his strength from a supernatural force—greed and conniving sufficed—but one could be forgiven for regarding Ivar as spooky because he played the role so well. His face kept a wanness even in summer. His lips seemed to have been touched-up in pastel pink. A native of Sweden, Ivar sported the proverbial Nordic temperament, with a sense of humor charitably called wry. He preferred long sleeves and oblique lighting. Posing for photographs, he'd stiffly face the camera. His brown eyes appeared both dead and alive: empty, bored, distracted, but nevertheless smoldering, designing.

Ivar Kreuger kept people guessing. At the negotiating table he answered any query flatly, if not directly, his brittle tone indicating the answer was final. If a financier badgered Ivar too much about audits and verification of funds, he'd simply stop doing business with that man. People knew that Ivar walking out the door meant lots of money trailing in his wake; they learned to relax their standards when the Swede came calling. If Ivar said he had collateral, then he had collateral.

Ivar moved human beings as deftly as he handled his cash flow. In 1923, for example, he phoned a man named Karl Lange. Ivar knew Lange was looking for a job, because Ivar sat on the board of the Bank of Stockholm, which had just fired the young officer for embezzlement. It seemed that Mr. Lange had established an alias account and made himself a small loan with Bank of Stockholm funds. The board, by unanimous vote, promptly gave Lange the boot. Privately, though, Ivar didn't take such a stern view of "informal appropriations."

"No," he assured Lange over the phone, "I'm certainly *not* calling to harrass you. I can use your help. I want you to work for me." Lange thought he must have a bad connection. One of the men who fired him was offering him a job. What else could Lange say but, thank you Mr. Kreuger? No one was else was calling.

Over the following years, Lange quietly visited Swedish cities and pushed the sale of Kreuger stock. Giving brokers double commission, for example, kept the Swedish Match Company's shares moving briskly. So did hints dropped about future issues, confidential warnings that the market was about to fluctuate, and "bonus" payments for managers who could throw an entire sales team onto the Kreuger bandwagon. If he had to, Lange simply bought thousands of shares of Kreuger stock under assumed names, simulating a briskly traded stock even when the shares were stagnant. Playing the lackey, first skittishly and later with relish, Karl Lange worked brokerage firms to his master's advantage. Lange's support of Kreuger & Toll, Ivar's major holding company, ensured that the venture maintained a prominent position in each trading city.

Lange was later promoted to work Berlin, a challenging financial landscape in the wake of a world war. But his big job came in 1925, a couple of years into his tenure as a Kreuger operative. Ivar was enjoying a monopoly in Poland for the production of matches. What he needed was a deal locking in the *sale* and *distribution* rights as well. That way Ivar would control every stage of the match's life in Poland, from harvesting the trees and manufacturing the sticks through the strike against the window sill. A good old-fashioned iron-sided trust.

But the deal had fallen through. Ivar had enemies as well as friends in the Polish Diet, and this time his enemies won out. He wouldn't get his exclusive rights, and there would be a tariff on all foreign matches, including those sold by the Swedish Match Company. Bad news, Ivar acknowledged. But he went ahead and made the deal.

As if he had never had his proposal rejected, Ivar formed a company called Garanta, to handle all the Polish match work. Garanta listed its home as Amsterdam, because Holland's banking laws were especially user-friendly—at the time, Dutch banks dealt in all currencies, they required no annual auditing of operations, and they levied no taxes on undistributed profits. Ivar wrote a letter to a large Dutch bank, explaining he needed an account through which he could move funds with maximum discretion. The bank obliged.

To fund his new venture, Ivar threw 450,000 shares onto the New York Stock Exchange. The shares were quickly snapped up, not because anyone gave a damn about Garanta but because the offering was launched under the name of Kreuger & Toll. The man might as well have been Midas. According to the prospectus Ivar floated, his New York subsidiary, the International Match Company (IMCO) would pass the first $17 million of the stock sale to Garanta in October 1925. The following July, IMCO would send $8 million more.

But Ivar had no intention of letting such a huge pile of cash simply waddle to its destination. He had the will and the means to snatch $25 million in full view of the investing public, and he was definitely going to do so.

Keep your eye on the ball, reader:

- IMCO, which sold the shares on Garanta's behalf, wouldn't actually make a cash payment to Garanta.

- The Swedish Match Company, Kreuger's flagship, owed money to IMCO. Swedish Match would reduce its IMCO debt by sending Garanta the $25 million due from the stock sale.

- Only, Swedish Match didn't send the money. Ivar drew up the paperwork for the transaction—lowering Swedish Match's debt to IMCO, clearing IMCO's obligation to Garanta, and crediting Garanta's account with the payment. Then he used the cash for "other things."

The Match King won on three fronts: he personally laid hands on a wad of liquid assets; Swedish Match reduced its debt to a subsidiary by half; and the New York-based IMCO carried the Garanta financing as an asset, recording interest payments at a healthy rate of 24 percent a year. The interest payments were never collected, of course; this was a totally fictitious transaction, except for the real cash from American investors. Garanta was a shell company—no one but Ivar ever saw the account books. He dictated

Garanta figures into the general ledger while his assistants nodded and scribbled. The balance was whatever Ivar said it was.

All Ivar needed to swing his $25-million swindle was a signature from the ex-embezzler and current Kreuger stooge, Karl Lange. Ivar met with Karl in Amsterdam, congratulating him: "You've just been named executive director of Garanta." He showed Karl a stack of papers describing the financial transactions of the company. As Karl sat down with the documents, Ivar placed a balance sheet on top of the stack and handed him a pen.

"Sign it," Ivar commanded.

"There's a lot of money here," Karl protested, "I'd like to look it over before I put my name on it." Ivar stared at him, surprised by the catch in Karl's voice.

"I mean," Karl said defensively, "how are we supposed to balance the books if we don't have the loan money on hand? It's not here." Karl pointed to the numbers on the gridded page before him.

"Just debit it to me," Ivar said. In this, one of his favorite tactics, Ivar closed off an irritating inquiry by offering his personal guarantee.

"Debit it to my personal account," he repeated when Karl remained motionless.

"At least it would be nice to know where all that money's going."

Ivar gave Karl a stare that asked, *Do you really want to know?* "It's being spent, very discreetly, on unsettled Polish political conditions," Ivar answered finally. "You can go to Poland and see for yourself if you don't believe me. But this can't be talked about."

Karl signed the page and shut his mouth. Ten years later he would remember the night from a jail cell.

Ivar was dead by then. At least he was rumored dead. Certain people suggested the Match King had staged the scene, then vanished to parts unknown, perhaps Indonesia. Ivar's Stockholm tobacconist swore that, years after Ivar's last rites, he received a special order for Ivar's custom Havana cigars. The request was wired from Sumatra; and nobody, the tobacconist announced with a knotty finger in the air, ordered *those* cigars in the precise quantity that Mr. Kreuger did.

Ivar Kreuger spent a lifetime making things up as he went along. So who's to say? His death could have been a part of the show.

24 Hours a Day

When Ivar was five years old, according to family legend, he recited verbatim a sermon he had just heard. Then, encouraged by his listeners' enthusiasm, he repeated the same sermon backwards. Ivar's parents found the performance impressive, even if the backwards part sounded somewhat strange. Otherwise, he was an unremarkable boy. Bright but not outgoing. He was once caught cheating on an exam. Another time he pranked a chemistry teacher by neutralizing the contents of an experiment. He was not exactly a natural-born shocker, this Ivar.

His mother, *nee* Jenny Forssman, said of her eldest son, "He ate three meals regularly a day and one at midnight and never cried if he was fed late, or, for that matter, about anything." Early on she noticed a reclusiveness and something brooding about her son's dark eyes. Perhaps she recognized her own steely gaze. In what passed for effusiveness Mrs. Kreuger summed up young Ivar: "He took care of himself and was just an angel."

Ivar's father, Ernst, was a successful industrialist who numbered among his holdings a controlling interest in a few match factories. Ernst had done well on his own, but he had inherited the bulk of his fortune from his grandfather, Peter Edvard Kreuger, Ivar's great-grandfather. Peter Kreuger helped fund many of the factories that ushered Sweden into the Industrial Revolution. He was able to pass on an inheritance of baronial proportions to his grandson, Ivar's father, including textile operations, a papermaking plant, and a facility for making safety matches.

Sweden was the birthplace and the chief Western manufacturer of the safety match. Gustaf Erik Pasch, a chemist, was working for Sweden's first match factory in 1844 when he got the idea to swap the poisonous yellow phosphorus in the matchhead for a benign red phosphorus. Since Pasch's match would ignite only when the tip was rubbed against the striking surface on the box, it was called the safety match. Sweden would become synonymous around the globe with matchmaking, thanks initially to the Lundström brothers—Johan Edvard and Carl Frans Lundström— who grew Pasch's invention into a network of giant factories churning out trillions of safety matches a year. Peter Edvard Kreuger's match holdings never rivalled the Lundströms, but he wisely bought himself a stake in this developing export and set the stage for his great-grandson, who would build an empire on the tiny wooden sticks.

That was years away, though. As the 19th century wound down, a teenaged Ivar maintained decent grades and caused no trouble; but he never distinguished himself. A magazine biography described the young man, pictured in his high-school graduation outfit, as "a lad of sixteen with a passion for cherries, a contempt for money, and no particular brilliance in the studies he had just completed." Ivar attended university in Stockholm, leaving an equally unremarkable impression on his surroundings.

In 1900, shortly after earning a degree in civil engineering, Ivar left Stockholm for New York City. He felt the urge, like many of those born to power and money, to strike out on his own. But the American metropolis did not instantly spark with the young engineer. He couldn't find any construction work, or any work at all. In weeks his money had run out. He was dependent on the kindness of some fellow Swedes who loaned him a few dollars, enough for food and shelter. But Ivar wasn't deterred. "Back home people talk about their love affairs," he wrote to his father. "Here they talk about their prospects. I can breathe here."

Ivar answered an ad for a group of real estate developers who catered especially to the immigrant buyer. It was a demanding and often crooked game. You were expected to give as dirty as you got. Young Ivar, primed to make his way as a businessman—ready for hard work and long hours, whatever it took—was ruffled when a man in the real estate office asked him, "What are you running from?"

"I beg your pardon," Ivar replied.

"Everybody who comes over, not only but especially we Swedes, is running from something. What are *you* running from?"

Ivar replied he just wanted to learn the business. "Then get to work," the man replied. Ivar leaped into the housing market, but nothing jumped back at him. He had a hard time working up a sales pitch. He strained to sound enthusiastic, but that was just it, he strained. All his exertions were eventually swamped by his earnest and somber tones. He was no salesman. After three months, he finally sold a piece of land, drew his $50 commission at the county clerk's office, and left town.

Ivar used part of the money to obtain a surveyor's permit and joined work crews moving down the East Coast. He made his way to New Orleans, where his luck promised to change. There Ivar at last found work in his profession—he and 14 other engineers were hired to manage a bridge-building project in Veracruz, Mexico. Ivar excitedly shipped his few belongings to Mexico and began reviewing the prints for the new bridge. Unfortunately, nobody had engineered for yellow fever. Before the materials for the project were even delivered, malaria killed all but two of Ivar's team.

Still Ivar was determined. After a few months' recuperation at his father's house, he returned to New York in the fall of 1901. As an employee of the Fuller Construction Company, Ivar helped build a number of New York City's noted landmarks, including the Plaza Hotel, R. H. Macy & Co., and the MetLife Tower. Ivar received 50 cents an hour to verify the calculations in structural plans. He also got a street-level education in how the construction business was conducted—through graft, bribery, embezzlement, guns, and secret ledger books.

For the next seven years Ivar chased construction projects around the world: Germany, South Africa, India, and finally back to the U.S. by way of Canada. In New York for the third time, he took a fateful job supervising the construction of Archibald Stadium at Syracuse University. His team built the stadium using reinforced concrete, or as it was called, trussed concrete. This recent innovation strengthened a building's frame and foundation by placing bars of iron inside the concrete forms.

Ivar immediately recognized an opportunity. He traveled to Detroit and met with Julius Kahn, who had invented trussed concrete and held the patents for it. By the time he had finished raising the monumental Archibald Stadium, Ivar had also become an entrepreneur. He borrowed 10,000 kroner (about $25,000) from his father and set up Kreuger & Toll, partnering with fellow engineer Paul Toll. Under a sign heralding "The Trussed Concrete Steel Company" Ivar and his partner introduced Sweden to a new age in construction. It was 1909. Kreuger & Toll were hired to build an electrical plant in the small town of Gullspang.

Local leaders were so impressed with trussed concrete that they immediately engaged the company to build a six-story department store in the center of town. Ivar accepted heartily and struck a bargain with the legislative council. Sweden was in the middle of a cold winter. Ivar promised that if downtown Gullspang couldn't boast its first "skyscraper" by the springtime, then he would pay the council $1,200 a day for each day the project went over schedule. On the other hand, if he beat the deadline—four months away—Ivar would collect $1,200 a day for every day he came in early.

Ivar had already arranged for the construction site to be outfitted with huge tarps. He installed floodlighting and heating equipment to keep the workers going day and night. The town square clanged 24 hours a day with the sounds of giant concrete mixers and laboring men driven to a frenzy. A reporter from Stockholm visited the work-in-progress, and worried in his column, "If this American method of building catches on, the Stockholmer will never have a quiet night again."

For the next few years, the people had plenty of occasion to lament the new-fangled construction. Ivar brought the Gullspang store to completion two months ahead of schedule, collecting more than $70,000 in bonus money for his and his workers' effort. Then Sweden's latest tycoon began populating the landscape with his handiwork. Never mind that others were actually putting their shoulders to the wheel, drawing the plans, stirring the concrete, installing the doors—in Ivar's mind, each new tower sprang whole from his will to power. He had less interest every day in the minutiae of construction; he was always turning to the next deal.

Paul Toll found himself distanced and stymied by his partner. He complained that Ivar spent too much time and energy schmoozing potential clients. Ivar had not yet developed the aloof, taciturn persona of the Match King. He had in fact worked at developing a warmer embrace for the men who sat across from him at the negotiating table. It was embarrassing, Toll finally blurted, the way Ivar flattered their backers.

"You can flatter so much that you're ashamed of yourself," Ivar answered, "but you can never make the person you're flattering feel ashamed."

Ivar put his tell-em-what-they-want-to-hear philosophy into major action when he publicly incorporated Kreuger & Toll. Besides its "contracting and building operations," the prospectus suggested the undertaking might, "in connection with its affairs, acquire shares in other concerns in investments." But not to worry, Ivar assured the endemically conservative Scandinavian investment community, "[Kreuger & Toll] may not carry on a regular trading business in securities." Two years later, in early 1914, the company began trading securities on the Stockholm Exchange without ever bothering to revise its corporate status. Ivar followed this simple rule his entire life: Say anything. Do what you will.

Ivar itched to get beyond the construction industry. It had served its purpose, but one could only go so far trussing concrete and bribing city hall. To his partner's irritation, Ivar's eye fell on match factories, including the two owned by his father and uncle. Paul Toll wasn't the only one concerned about this latest move. Ivar's brother, Torsten, warned him against the match business. Torsten helped run the family's various concerns. Yes, Torsten allowed, Sweden dominated the world market in matches because of the Jönköping Trust, which was the popular name for the conglomerate established by the Lundström brothers in the 1800s.

"That's the point," Torsten lectured Ivar, who was now just past 30 years old. Jönköping controlled everything except a few scattered operations in the country—those owned by old-line Swedish families, like the Kreugers—and some isolated factories in Eastern Europe and Japan which were run by competitors in those countries. No one can beat Jönköping, Torsten insisted.

Ivar persuaded several banks, if not his brother, to consolidate those factories that lay outside the Jönköping trust—11 different plants altogether, including the two run by the Kreuger family— into a gigantic United Match Factories (UMF). The merger would compete with the Jönköping trust and make lots of money for everyone concerned. What Ivar didn't say was that he had set his sights beyond Jönköping. As the United Match Factories deal got underway, Ivar ran into an old friend from his stay in South Africa. "In the last 24 hours," Ivar declared, "I've created a plan to consolidate the match business of the world under one control. It will require extremely large sums of money to build the structure, but the sums will be repaid with very handsome profits to every investor." With an initial loan of $1 million, Ivar's UMF went after the Jönköping trust, with all of Europe just around the bend.

World War I broke out soon afterward, causing shortages of raw materials, including wood for matches. Ivar persuaded the larger Jönköping trust, which was capitalized at more than $3 million, to share the aspen trees grown in northern Sweden with his UMF. Then he proceeded to betray his new partners by making a secret trading deal with Germany. Many nations weren't dealing with the Central powers, but Ivar stepped in before Jönköping could even scratch their heads and signed monopoly agreements with the Kaiser's government. With the resulting boost in UMF's production capacity, Ivar made big gains in his rivalry with Jönköping. He also seeded a number of startup companies to provide the UMF with supplies, saving the middleman costs, and he launched an aggressive sales organization.

Ivar was laying the foundation for a huge, closed system of companies. The new, expanded UMF was known as the Kalmar Trust, named for the city of its headquarters, in the manner of Jönköping. Kalmar lost money the first year. The second year it cleared $60,000. As Kreuger's expansion plans took effect, the venture thrived. For the fiscal year 1916, just three years into its business plan, the Kalmar trust reported $500,000 in profits and paid its investors a dividend of 17 percent.

The rival Jönköping trust was suffering doubly during the war years. Hostilities cut them off from one of their largest markets, the Far East. Besides this handicap, a Japanese producer stole Jönköping's secret formula for combining phosphorous, potash, and other materials into the match head. Previously, matches made in Asian plants were widely regarded as inferior, prone to flash burning or not igniting at all. According to Swedish lore, the Japanese company sent a chemical engineer to visit a Jönköping plant. While taking the courtesy tour, the spy accidentally dropped his hat into a vat of chemicals. Retrieving the hat, he brought it back to Japan, where it was analyzed and the secret formula was divined. (There are a lot of holes to this legend, besides the ones in the chemical-soaked hat. Suffice it to say that the Japanese got hold of the recipe and took a big chunk out of Jönköping's market share.) The fabled Jönköping trust was crumbling. Ivar was pounding them at home, with foreign competitors adding body blows.

When the war ended, Ivar threw the final punch. He assembled a funding syndicate of Sweden's largest banks and approached Jönköping with an offer to merge with the UMF. Ivar handled the negotiations personally. After holing up for a few days in his Stockholm office, he emerged with a phony balance sheet that inflated Kalmar's value by almost half, and proceeded to absorb his much larger rival. Merging virtually the entire Swedish match industry into his fold crowned young Mr. Kreuger's adventures to date and launched his career in fraudulent financial statements.

With Jönköping in hand, Ivar finally owned something worthy of the title *trust*. The Swedish Match Company, as he appropriately named his new baby, combined the United Match Factories with Jönköping's production lines, suppliers, paper mills, printing mills, machine-making facilities and, not least of all, 100,000 acres of prime Swedish woodland where some of the world's best aspen trees grew in abundance.

You wouldn't have known it to look at him—Ivar wasn't one for "celebration"—but the newly crowned Match King was tickled pink. As a reward for his endeavours, His Highness promptly transferred 120,000 shares of the Swedish Match Company to his Kreuger & Toll holding company. He planned to use the shares as collateral for a loan, should Kreuger & Toll find other "concerns" it wished to acquire. Ivar credited Swedish Match with $2 million for the stock sale, though he neglected to deduct any payment from the Kreuger & Toll books. In other words, he puffed his balance sheet with a stroke of his pen.

Ivar's *geldlust* grew in proportion to his power. In 1919, deploying his gifts of persuasion and gesturing to the string of hits behind him, Ivar convinced a group of Scandinavian banks they ought to loan him $150 million. He would use the money to invest in rebuilding Europe and, as an added benefit, boost the lagging Swedish economy. The bankers pointed out an obvious impediment to Ivar's plan: world markets were in disarray, and entire regions of Europe's industrial infrastructure had been blown to pieces. Economic hardship buffeted the world, from the Far East to downtown London, where poor families split their matches in two to conserve what they had.

But where Swedish financiers saw disorder and lack, Ivar saw opportunity. "If I move now," Ivar explained, "the Swedish Match Company can gobble up factories and grab monopoly rights throughout the world. That largesse, plundered from several continents in the midst of rebuilding themselves, will all come home to Sweden. Conquest takes lots of cash, it's true," Ivar admitted. But did the banks want to miss the big returns of a world monopoly because caution kept them from opening their eyes?

Ivar's boldness paid off handsomely. He snatched back the Asian markets that Jönköping had lost during the war and jumpstarted a string of faltering operations in the West. In Germany and Russia, where the local currencies staggered from one crisis to the next, Ivar found a dumping ground for billions of low-grade matches left over from wartime manufactories. Without firing a shot or suffering a single day in a muddy trench, the Match King turned the force of war to his advantage. An aching world trying to put itself back together was buying lots of matches.

Ivar's empire produced enormous wealth. It functioned with precision and efficiency. Working for him, however, wasn't much fun. Isaac Marcosson of the *Saturday Evening Post* observed the 150-person staff in action. "You scarcely ever see anyone as you move through the halls and never hear a sound," Marcosson wrote. Kreuger & Toll's palatial headquarters resembled a morgue more than a corporate command center.

Marcosson's profile confirmed the many rumors of Ivar's eccentricity. He was an inveterate smoker, for one thing, capable of puffing away a box of Turkish cigarettes in an afternoon. But, to the curiousity of those around him, he never carried a match. Asked why he above all people lacked for matches, Ivar fixed his questioner with a tense look and said, "I have a petty superstition that prevents me from it."

A paragraph of the Kreuger legend attributes another, more widely broadcast, superstition to Ivar. It's said that he invented the "three on a match" jinx, the belief that it's bad luck to light more than two cigarettes off the same match. Ivar supposedly made the whole thing up, a wicked bit of marketing to cause people to use more matches.

At least that's the kind of legend Ivar was inspiring, yet still no one knew how truly crafty Mr. Kreuger was. Maybe he plotted ways to enter the buying public's gestalt or maybe he didn't. Ivar had certainly developed the wily manner of one who'd gone down to the crossroads and taken the devil's turn.

****

Carl Bergman, a Swedish-born engineer, first met Ivar at the University of Stockholm and later went to work for him at Kreuger & Toll. Since both men were confirmed bachelors, they often spent evenings together, eating what Bergman called "a frugal dinner" at Kreuger's house—"too frugal if you ask me," Bergman groused.

"We never left the office before seven," Bergman recalled. "Ivar's whole life, as far as I could tell, was his work." When the two men discussed the prospect of marrying and raising a family, Ivar declared, "Swedish Match is my only child. Most people throw off their work at five o'clock, but I'm at my best after that. That's when I like to sit down and plan."

Bergman admired more than his friend's dedication. He saw in Ivar "an odd air of greatness":

> I think he could get people to do anything. They fell for him, they couldn't resist his peculiar charm and magnetism.... Above all there was a look about him that made a difference. I saw J.P. Morgan's eyes many times in New York. They were like fire coals. But Ivar's eyes were not like that. They had another quality. Though small and narrow, they seemed capable, if he desired, of looking right through you.

Dr. Charles Bove, who served Kreuger as his personal physician, said, "I knew him for an indefatigable worker who put in long hours at his business, keeping awake by plunging into ice-cold baths."

Not much held Ivar's attention besides his incessant scheming. When an employee—staggering through his 18th hour of work without so much as breaking for lunch—told Ivar they simply had to get something to eat, the boss feigned resentment. "Eating makes one lazy," he retorted. For his usual breakfast Ivar ate a bun, a few pieces of fruit, and a cup of tea; more or less the same for lunch; and a hearty dinner of a main course and a dessert. He thought the only thing more overrated than food was sleep. "Unfortunately, I can't rest, even if I wanted to," he said. "Something inside me goes on thinking all the time."

While his empire grew—by 1919 Ivar's personal wealth exceeded $5 million—he collected the trappings of a rich man, though with little noticeable passion. His 23-room duplex in the center of Stockholm gave off all the warmth and glow of a hotel. Ivar shipped in furniture from around the world, and stretched the best carpets on the floors and tapestries on the wall. But he either scattered the materials with no thought of how items might coordinate, or he constructed a room as if he were building a Noah's ark of collectibles, with pairs and groups of items stacked around the perimeter. A rigor dominated the furnishings of Villagatan 13, Stockholm. It wasn't exactly homey. A visitor said the place resembled "an exhibition hall.... The dining-room looked like it belonged in a clubhouse, and the salon as if Paris mannequins might suddenly appear."

Ivar owned other places—apartments in Berlin and Warsaw and a five-room flat near the Seine River in Paris. He kept a suite at the London Carlton on permanent reserve. None of these dwellings offered Ivar anything like a home, though in the last moments of his life he seemed to have deliberately made his way to the Paris flat.

Of all Ivar's living arrangements, he felt the most personally taken with his penthouse on 74th Street in New York City. Never mind the Rembrandt and the Reubens and the rest of the $200,000 worth of art. Ivar liked to play with the lighting board. The biographer Robert Shaplen describes the scene:

> *An intricate system of switches and rheostats...enabled him to bathe any of the nine rooms in white, red, blue, or amber light, or blendings of these colors. He especially liked red, and by a hidden button at the head of his bed could put out all the lights in the room except for four red ones left softly glowing in the corners. The walls were covered with expensive cloth, and the reception hall was paved with flagstones and lined with mirrors. The place was full of labor-saving devices. For his roof garden Ivar imported tons of soil from France, which he spread seven feet deep for elaborate beds of flowers, fruit trees that burgeoned, and a willow that spread its branches 20 feet high and extended out*

over Park Avenue. In the center was a Japanese rock garden where a blue light played on a nude, while a white stone Cupid spouted what looked like blood when a red spot shone on it at night.

Ivar's Xanadu surpassed the bounds of mere taste. If his color schemes leaped out of *Lurid Homes and Gardens*, his emotional visage completed the ensemble effect. During his youth, according to legend, Ivar had carried on an ill-fated and mainly one-sided love for a Norwegian girl. The girl hadn't returned Ivar's affection directly, or at any rate she died before he felt sufficiently "established" to ask for her hand. If Ivar truly loved this mist-shrouded waif, it was the first and last time he experienced anything approaching romantic devotion. He once announced, with a sardonic lilt to his voice, "Marriage is for my employees, not for me."

He made banal jokes: "I need at least eight days to get married, and I haven't got time." When a New York banker warned him how many foreign businessmen fell in love with American girls, Ivar smirked, "I prefer a Swedish match."

Ivar treated women with a strained indulgence. He kept a drawer in his Stockholm residence full of cigarette cases, brooches and other trinkets. "I know a lot of girls," he shrugged, when a friend asked him why he'd gathered up such a hoard. "I'll use them."

Make no mistake, Ivar came steeped in the misogyny of his day; he had no sympathy for women's emancipation. But he held his fellow men in little better regard. He told a female friend, "All human beings are reprehensible, especially those who can get everything they want."

Ivar knew precisely what he was talking about. "I am very unhappy when I have to be with people for a long time and talk to them unofficially, as it were," Ivar wrote to one of his courtesans, a German woman who used the alias Itta Sandt in her relations with Ivar.

> *I don't mind speaking to them when I can give orders, when I can say "do this" or "do that," "take such and such a post." But the things they call "worries" when they talk to me privately always bore me. None of them know what they are living for. At most they have an idée fixe—one is always talking about his dentist, another about his family's bad luck, and a third about the job he didn't get. When I compare our contemporaries with the people*

> *whose biographies I have read, I realize all the more how petty*
> *everything is nowadays.*

Ivar pictured himself an *übermensch*, a moral superman, standing outside the pale of merely human relations. Of course he won't have been the first social critic to brand his peers and his historical moment as inferior. But his fortune allowed Mr. Kreuger to put his curmudgeonliness into action.

Not that Ivar lacked feelings altogether. He occasionally allowed the curtain to drop on his somber visage, and could talk for hours about philosophy, art, or, his favorite topic, the lives of great men. His most admired figure? Napoleon, fittingly enough.

Ivar even deigned to play the game of romance. Society pages buzzed for a short time that the Match King had been spotted with, of all people, Greta Garbo. Apparently each was drawn to the enigma of the other.

Ivar's one extended affair, though, began earlier, in 1915, while he was busy laying the foundations of his career in trussed concrete. The woman, Inge Hässler, wrote a memoir after Ivar's death about their relationship. She characterized their early days as "lots of roses and shyness." Whatever his power in the boardroom, Ivar moved skittishly in the landscape of love. He signed his letters to Inge with a terse, "Greetings," but more than once he threw jealous fits, and occasionally stationed a guard outside Inge's door. When she left Stockholm for a while to attend a seaside resort, Ivar wrote her a typically convoluted set of greetings:

> *My dearest Nigger-baby: I suppose that you are now lying in the*
> *sun on some rock while I, poor boy, have to sit here and long for*
> *you. I'm sitting in the office all day and, like a good boy, go to*
> *bed at 9:30 every night, so I'm sorry I have nothing of interest to*
> *tell you.*

Inge knew her poor boy spent nights alone only when he chose to; fidelity for Ivar meant he still thought about Inge even if he had other women occupying his immediate attention. For her part, Inge also conducted herself in a "worldly" manner. She and Ivar had their understandings; they each got what they wanted from the other. He enjoyed female company without emotional obligation; she occupied her own furnished apartment, received a steady income, and made luxury jaunts around the world, both with Ivar and alone.

Still, even the cosmopolitan Mr. Kreuger couldn't resist adding a postcript to his vacationing lover: "I hope there are men enough out there so you can get all the dancing and flirting you need to be able to live." It was a typical Kreuger gesture, superficially nonchalant but with a petulant underbelly.

Inge and Ivar maintained their arrangements from 1915 into the middle 1920s, even after Inge married another man and subsequently divorced him. She probably achieved closer and more extended relations with Ivar than anyone else ever did, though she was only one of several women who lived in a Kreuger-furnished household and who spent money proffered her through the cold fingers of the Match King. After Ivar died suddenly in 1932, various ladies in Paris, Stockholm, and New York petitioned the executors of his will, hoping the estate would continue sending their pension checks.

In life, Kreuger gave many women money, but apparently kept his feelings to himself. As he wrote to an old friend:

> *You asked me once whether I could tie myself permanently to a woman. I believe I could, externally—because I should only see her occasionally anyhow. But spiritually, I must honestly say, no. I don't care about children. I don't know why, except that they always do things differently from what one would like, which must be so annoying. Nor do I wish to be burdened with love.*

Besides, Ivar told his fellow bachelor Carl Bergman, "I already have a child. An only son, named Swedish Match." To Inge Hässler he confided, "If my life's work were ever destroyed, I'll put a bullet through my heart."

High Priests and Crazy People

As Ivar was crossing Germany by train, having dominated the worldwide production of matches, he became uncharacteristically talkative. He said to his traveling companion, "You know, it's a curious thing how every period in history has its own gods, its own high priests and holy days. It's been true of politics and religion and war, and now it's true of economics. We've created something new. Instead of being fighting men, as in days of old, we're all in business, and we've chosen some new high priests and called them accountants. They too have a holy day—the 31st of December—on which we're supposed to confess. In olden times, everyone would go to confession because it was the thing to do, whether they believed or not. Today the world demands balance sheets, profit-and-loss statements once a year. But if you're really working on great ideas, you can't supply these on schedule and expose yourself to view. Yet you've got to tell the public something, and so long as it's satisfied and continues to have faith in you, it's really not important what you confess. The December ceremony isn't really a law of the gods—it's just something we've invented. All right, let's conform, but let's don't do it in a way that will spoil our plans. And some day people will realize that every balance sheet is wrong because it doesn't contain anything but figures. The real strengths and weaknesses of an enterprise lie in the plans."

Like many a sovereign before him, Ivar found the doctrinaire rantings of his own high priests—all those fussy bean counters and analysts—irksome. They only got in the way of the ideas twirling around in Ivar's head. He'd always treated finance as nothing but a means to an end. So when the directors of the Swedish Match Company approached Ivar in 1919, agitating him for a profit-and-loss statement, he obliged them, but on his own terms.

See, Ivar had a problem. He held substantial properties in Germany, but the country's economy had been reduced to rubble by the First World War. As he pondered how to represent his net worth to the directors, Ivar determined he simply couldn't let the worthlessness of the *Deutschmark* ruin his big show. So he wrote down the value of the properties in Swedish money—some 9 million *kroner*—as if the two currencies were trading at a normal rate. The actual value might have been half what Ivar reported. But, he reasoned amiably with the underling who helped him prepare the balance sheet, the directors were looking toward Swedish Match's *future*. The fudging actually represented a more accurate accounting than following the rules. Germany would no doubt recover from her injuries, Ivar reasoned, and then everything would fall in place.

A few years later, Ivar arranged for the German property to be transferred to a new company he called Union Industrie. He'd formed Union Industrie with his brother, Torsten Kreuger, and a stockbroker—with a typically muddy past—named Bror G. Bredberg. Ivar informed Bredberg, as Union Industrie's titular head, that the German property had been sold for $3.5 million. Ivar said he had financed the deal himself for 12.5 percent per annum. When the interest payments came due and no one could track down the buyer, purportedly one E.H. Lehmann, Ivar said he would tend to the matter himself. That ended the inquiry. Lehmann never turned up.

It was discovered, much later, that Ivar had "sold" the German property to several different shell companies he had set up, milking the "sale" each time he needed to draw on the net worth of this or that subsidiary. By passing the real estate from one hand to another, with a profit tacked on each time, Ivar transformed a piece of undervalued property into a gold mine. (This same method was used by Charles Keating, Jr. and others during the S & L boom of the 1980s.)

Ivar never hesitated to sweep aside bothersome details. "His essential philosophy of accounting...," according to biographer Robert Shaplen, "was that a balance sheet existed mainly to paint pretty pictures for the public. He had an almost poetic approach to annual reports—he usually wrote them himself—and he believed the function of figures was not to reproduce a situation as it existed but to create an impression of it as he wished to portray it."

Ivar operated his master plan on two fronts: tapping new markets for capital, and using that capital internationally to extend his influence. Each arm reinforced the other. As he acquired more capital, world leaders provided concessions and monopoly guarantees in exchange for bailout loans; as he called the tune in government chambers, his businesses grew richer from the ministers' blessings.

Ivar's outline for world conquest took shape in the early 1920s. He was already highly regarded as one of the most powerful businessmen in Sweden, but Ivar longed for greater vistas. For one thing, Swedish circles were growing suspicious. A secret government memorandum told insiders that Ivar wasn't doing nearly the volume of business he was reporting. While he claimed to have doubled his exports since the end of the war, he had really only increased his shipping by about 25 percent—still an impressive number, but only half again what Ivar was suggesting. A number of people knew that Ivar was supporting his securities to make them look more desireable. And Ivar's insatiable thirst for capital had incurred some phenomenal debt.

However, Ivar found that audiences, small private confabs of select investors were more than eager to throw their money his way. The American stock market was revving up for what would soon be the Roaring Twenties, and the moneymakers needed a way to hide their capital gains from the tax collector. Ivar's International Match Company (IMCO), officially a subsidiary of the Swedish Match Company, filled the bill by classifying the profits as overseas speculation. The foreign status also helped skirt what puny accounting regulations the U.S. government had in place.

Wall Street was begging someone to take it for a ride, and Ivar obliged.

Two of the most enthusiastic passengers on the good ship Ivar were Frederic Allen and Donald Durant. Allen held a partnership in the privately owned investment firm of Lee, Higginson & Co, where Durant served as head of the syndicating department. The two were charged with taking the reputation of the firm—which had helped launch General Motors, AT&T, and the General Electric Corporation—to new heights.

"Look," Ivar told Allen and Durant, "there are millions of matches being struck throughout the world. At this very moment, someone is raking a match across a box. Very likely I sold him that match. If I need larger profits, I put a few less matches in each box and I charge a penny more for the lot. But better than that, by securing monopoly rights to a region, to a nation, and—why think small?—to the European continent, for example, I have a guaranteed source of profits. I establish a trust based on an inconspicuous though absolutely necessary commodity."

Allen and Durant nodded approvingly, as did their peers up and down Wall Street. Ivar quickly became what one of his several biographers called "the tallest representative of the illusory belief that the more money was spent, the more there was to be made; that vast stock issues, pyramided one upon the other through holding companies, led to proliferated plenty, to an endless rush of dollars pouring out of a fabled cornucopia."

Ivar used his attachment with Lee, Higginson & Co. to issue $10 million worth of Swedish Match, doubling the common stock of the company. To sweeten the deal he let the Americans buy the issues for $20 a share, as opposed to the usual $30. When his accountants clamored that they had to do something with the difference on the discount, Ivar muttered, "Debit it to me, personally." It was a formula he repeated endlessly. A shortfall in revenues? "Debit it to me." Money missing from a transaction between governments and Kreuger subsidiaries? "Debit it to me, personally." When the Kreuger house finally came crashing down, auditors found that Ivar's books—covering a maze of subsidiaries and several "personal" accounts—had been perverted "into a confused mass of figures, the balance of which...is entirely meaningless."

Accounting deserves its reputation as an art—as opposed to a science—and Ivar well knew how to manipulate the medium. When he prepared to form the Continental Investment Corporation— which alone among Kreuger subsidiaries would separate

Americans from almost $100 million—Ivar recruited a man named Ernst Hoffman from a New York bank. Hoffman answered an ad Ivar placed in the paper and showed himself the ideal compatriot for the Match King. He spoke several languages and had no qualms about using his financial wits to his partner's advantage, damn any laws and regulations to the contrary.

Continental Investment was incorporated by Hoffman in Liechtenstein, Switzerland, and capitalized at 60 million francs. Its three-man board of directors was comprised of Hoffman, Ivar, and a third crony, "the bland and obliging Krister Littorin." Littorin first met Ivar when they were both in college at Stockholm and had worked for him since the early days of the Kalmar trust. Among Littorin's most desireable qualities were an unquestioning admiration for his boss and a sunny disposition that offset the mordant-faced Ivar. If he appointed Littorin as Director of the Trash Heap, Ivar would have received nothing but gratitude in response.

The 60 million francs for Continental's startup came in three parts: one million francs in cash, nine million in checks drawn on Kreuger concerns, and the remaining 50 million in a "personal guarantee" signed by Ivar Kreuger. In other words, Ivar persuaded Liechtenstein's Court of Commerce to give its blessing and protection to a 60-million franc enterprise, with only one million francs on the table.

Ivar excelled at pulling this sort of rabbit from his homburg. In November of 1923 he convinced Lee, Higginson & Co. to help him establish a special subsidiary. The International Match Corporation, or IMCO, was officially described as an equal partner with Ivar's beloved Swedish Match. But nobody really believed that. IMCO's real purpose was to siphon money out of America into the home office. The subsidiary carried a large portion of Swedish Match debt on its books; in turn it sent cash, millions of it, back to Sweden. The "joint" status of the two companies enabled Ivar to avoid taxes both at home and abroad, since he could shift assets either way if the publicans came calling.

Having hit on a winning formula for incorporation, Ivar followed suit with IMCO. The board consisted of himself and several dupes, including Donald Durant. As president Ivar retained "special powers to make and enter into all contracts on behalf of the corporation, to execute any and all instruments of transfer of any part of the personal property of the corporation." That is, Ivar could do what he damn well pleased.

And please he did. IMCO's first issue of $15 million in debentures sold out immediately. In 1925 Ivar used IMCO to raise $25 million for the Garanta company, which had supposedly acquired monopoly rights to sell matches in Poland. In 1926 IMCO received $22 million from investors. Ivar's cover story claimed the money went for "transactions in Greece, Portugal, Algiers, Norway, and Manila;" in fact, he shuffled the funds through various accounts, then skimmed them for personal use. All told, IMCO milked the American public for $150 million in its nine years of operation.

Still something kept worrying Ivar as he expanded. Taking investors' money was one thing. But when investors became shareholders, they wanted to poke around in their company. To keep his beloved mother corporation safe, Ivar turned to the idea of selling securities labeled "Swedish Match B," an anemic version of genuine stock. By Ivar's arrangement, Swedish Match A shares, which carried full voting rights, could only be held in Sweden. Swedish Match B shares paid the same dividends as A shares, but they could be held anywhere and—here came the crucial difference—they commanded only 1/1000 voting rights. This allowed Ivar to retain a nearly absolutist control over $600 million in resources, despite holding less than one percent of the total shares. Ivar believed investors ought to be seen, but not heard.

Ivar ran various deceptive schemes, but they all turned on one element: *subsidiaries*. There's no better way to hide financial chicanery than playing pass the peas between a handful of companies all under one's control. For example, about $12 million of IMCO's initial $15 million issue was transferred to Continental Investment in Liechtenstein. Continental, in turn, forwarded the money to an entity called A.B. Russia. Ivar was running A.B. Russia as a personal slush fund. As soon as the IMCO funds hit the A.B. Russia account, he issued checks to pay off several Swedish bankers who were badgering him about his debts there. In a move that was to become typical, Ivar never showed that A.B. Russia owed anything to Continental Investment, even though Continental carried the debt on its books and recorded interest payments on the account among its profits.

Besides shuffling subsidiaries with the cunning of a riverboat gambler, Ivar protected his empire by invoking the need for secrecy. He was dealing with international governments who couldn't agree on anything except wanting more money. To his credit, Ivar really did need to keep many details under wraps in order to negotiate amid post-war conditions. But he also knew how to make a virtue of necessity. When Lee, Higginson insisted in 1927 that they be allowed to inspect the ledgers of Swedish Match, comparing them to what they saw at IMCO in New York, Ivar readily obliged. But he didn't actually follow through on the invitation. For years he had kept accounts in his head—literally, in some cases—and settled any discrepancies by either transferring assets from one subsidiary to another or by making an "adjustment" to the accounts. Lee, Higginson wanted to see some paper.

Lesser operators might have folded at this point, but Ivar held steady. An accountant named F. Gordon Blackstone arrived in Stockholm to find Ivar waiting for him.

"Before we get down to business," Ivar suggested, "perhaps you'd like to join me on a tour of our Polish factories."

Blackstone declined, muttering to himself, "I'm not here to watch wheels go around." So Ivar made the trip alone, leaving Blackstone with a cadre of stonewalling sycophants who kept feeding the accountant the party line and showed him nothing of consequence. Every question of any weight had to be postponed until the boss finished making the rounds in Poland.

Ivar returned two months later, brandishing a sheaf of telegrams in the young man's face. "He said it was a request from some other outside accountants," Blackstone remembered. These men, too, wanted to audit Swedish Match, and Ivar was furious. "He insisted that this all implied a lack of confidence and that it would disturb the atmosphere around the company and in Sweden generally."

Because Ivar Kreuger represented Lee, Higginson's best hope in a turmoiled market, the brokerage headquarters telegrammed Blackstone, telling him to pack his bags. "He took the wind right out of my sails," Blackstone said. "Kreuger told me he would discuss the problem with the Lee, Higginson people in New York and that maybe a year later I could come back, but nothing more was ever done about the matter."

Donald Durant shrugged. "Kreuger & Toll was the leading company in Sweden; and Sweden did not relish having foreign accountants come in and look over its affairs."

Testifying in the receivership hearings following Ivar's death, Durant admitted that Ivar had kept very little money in the IMCO accounts. Almost as soon as funds were raised, they were deployed into other Kreuger concerns. Then, each year when dividends came due, Ivar deposited just enough to make the payments and no more—a little more than $2 million each year, like clockwork. "The reason, I understand," Durant intoned, "was not to bring into the parent corporation all the dividends and earnings from the subsidiaries. By not bringing the earnings into the parent corporation each time, but keeping them in the subsidiaries, it was not necessary to pay an income tax on earnings which were not brought into the country."

But, the attorney asked Durant, why didn't anyone ever check out Kreuger's operation? "Did you ever go back to the Ernst & Ernst quarterly reports?" [Ernst & Ernst handled all of Kreuger's U.S. accounting.]

Durant replied, "We relied on them."

"You accepted these without going to the original source?"

"Yes, we relied on Ernst & Ernst," Durant said.

"And you knew, of course, did you not, that Ernst & Ernst in turn relied blindly on what was cabled over from Europe?"

Durant admitted, "I don't know what Ernst & Ernst relied on."

This kind of casualness was the rule rather than the exception. Chief among the factors that allowed Ivar to perpetrate an unprecented worldwide fraud was "the loyalty or unquestioning obedience of officials," according to an analysis by the firm of Price, Waterhouse.

As auditor and writer Robert H. Montgomery reports, "At the beginning of this century, the public accountant's function was largely that of an adjunct to the accounting department of business. The chief service required of the public accountant by owner-managers was to furnish them with a competent outsider's check on the accuracy of the records and to furnish reasonable assurance that the bookkeeper had not misappropriated funds." An auditor existed to check the bookkeeper's math. Competence and assurance in auditing did *not* require verifying funds and physical assets. Those standards would not be enshrined in accounting regulations until the 1940s after one of Ivar's greatest admirers, another Frankenstein of Fraud calling himself Dr. Donald Coster, forced the issue.

****

Ivar played governments the same way he played businesspeople, like a harp from hell. He had always averred that the best way to compete was to eradicate the competition, and so, in 1925, he set out to establish a series of lucrative international agreements using his immense cash reserves. The first, in Poland, laid the groundwork. Ivar lent $6 million at seven percent interest to the ailing Polish Diet. The Poles turned over ten factories to Ivar on a 20-year rent agreement. Ivar's genius showed itself in the terms of the deal. Swedish Match (or IMCO, in this case) paid a royalty to the state treasury on the profits from the monopoly. The royalties secured the $6 million loan and, as Ivar had intended, covered the annual debt services due plus a healthy profit margin for the government of 25 percent to 50 percent. The catch was that the government couldn't take any profits until it had paid off its total debts to Ivar. As he remarked, "The loan itself is nothing but an advance of future royalty payments." By tying up royalty payments with the loan, one observer noted, Ivar "thus provided not only for a banker's profit on the loan and a match maker's profit on the concession, but also arranged for complete security for both."

Ivar bought up factories and secured monopoly agreements throughout the world. In England he merged with the largest producers, and in Japan he surreptitiously purchased the operations which had plagued Western competitors for decades. Throughout Europe he traded with cash-hungry governments for the concessions that would make him the world's most powerful entrepreneur. A Swedish diplomat described Ivar as "very much a *conquistadore*, the kind of man you had in rougher centuries." The New York-based *Journal of Commerce* thought Ivar's campaign recalled "the great merchant and trading companies of the Middle Ages and of early modern times which, in addition to their regular operations, financed wars and supported or overthrew dynasties."

The point wasn't lost on the Communist leaders in the Soviet Union. A number of Stalin's ministers were smitten with Ivar personally, and they argued, "We badly need his money." Despite his reputation as an exemplar of "those American circles" of capitalist greed, the Soviets dickered with Ivar over deals for $40 million and $80 million. However, neither side could come to terms. Ivar appears to have never taken the prospects very seriously. At one point he suggested he would raise $1 billion for the Soviet government if he in turn controlled all the sugar, tea, tobacco, and matches coming into the country. Stalin raged that he would never surrender to this poster-boy for capitalism. "It's not in our interest to encourage and favor the Swede," Stalin declared. "On the contrary we must bind him and make him harmless. He is a danger to us."

But Ivar, like many people in business, flattered himself that his gambits not only made him rich, they worked for the good all of humanity. And he was right. Greece used its $5-million loan to repatriate refugees stranded in Turkey, Macedonia, Bulgaria, and

Hungary. Poland was able to provide flood relief to victims in Upper Silesia. Hungary, Latvia, and Estonia initiated land reforms with $185 million of Ivar's money. Governments in France, Romania and Ecuador attained at least a temporary economic stability with Ivar's help. Both America and England had refused to give Romania a dime, but Ivar stepped in, yoking his own greedy desires with those of a nation in distress. The *Journal of Commerce* opined that conditions were tilting awry when cooperative ventures were "being farmed out to private capitalists." Meanwhile, France awarded Ivar the Grand Cross of the French Legion, and the self-satisfied savior of Europe continued his plans for world conquest.

By the end of the decade Ivar had 250 match factories under his thumb. Where he couldn't grab a state-sponsored monopoly, he would finagle the competition until he won a practical monopoly. He puppeted several companies in America, quietly acquiring their match factories or assuming a cloaked but nevertheless controlling interest in them. Worldwide, citizens were buying 40 billion boxes of matches a year, for about half a penny a box. Ivar enterprises provided 80 percent of those boxes—roughly $160 million annual gross. Able to draw about half of this in profits, Ivar had reason to feel cocky. Not to mention his "dabbling" in industries like paper-and-pulp, telephone service in 17 countries, several newspapers, and the much-touted Boliden gold mine.

"They're crazy, completely crazy," Ivar quipped about investors as he watched his shares climbing higher. "But they'll get more crazy."

Ivar ultimately fell prey to the same forces that had made him rich. He had built his vast estates on two dangerously slippery bases: the securities markets and government loans. Mistakenly, he had strategized that the one would cover the other, the securities providing huge short-term gains, the government loans maintaining a reliable profit over the long haul. If anyone should have recognized the volatility of the stock market—especially the giddy American market of the the so-called Jazz Age—it was Ivar. He just refused to believe that his stocks could fall. As for dealing with nations, Ivar remarked, "You know, I've come to the conclusion that government bonds are the safest thing to have because no government has failed on its obligations since 1815." This was a man who backed up his musings by loaning $400 million to 15 countries. He was forgetting how quickly and devastatingly Czarist Russia fell, of course, and the hordes of stakeholders wrecked by the October Revolution. That was no mean oversight. If anything, the odds of governmental default had increased in the decade since Stalin had taken control. And the Soviet Union was hardly alone in this respect. Ivar had seriously overestimated the resilience of a world devastated by a string of wars and industrial strife.

Forging Mussolini

Who's to say that Ivar wouldn't have survived a mere gutting of his stocks if he hadn't been tromping through the halls of politics? Ivar had started to believe his own press. He couldn't be persuaded to restrain the long arm of his ambition, not by his advisers or his enemies. He knew very well that his securities were the most widely held in the world. What he had never anticipated was that international stock markets might go to hell and take the wealth of nations with them.

Of course, the Swedish Match King didn't let on he was worried. It happened, coincidentally, that he graced the cover of *Time* magazine the week the great stock market crashed in October 1929. By the end of the month, while millions stood aghast, Ivar mounted an ad campaign for his latest issues, a large offering at $24 per certificate. Other conglomerates were shutting down projects and backing out of deals. Ivar announced he still had the same confidence he'd expressed to the editorial board at *Time*.

He was going ahead with his plan to loan Germany $125 million. "If I don't get control of the German markets, the Soviets will," Ivar warned the international community. Besides, he suggested, this fellow Hitler might actually set his war-beleaguered nation on firmer ground. A long-time Kreuger advisor, Gunnar Cederschïold, who had brokered deals in Paris and elsewhere, inquired, "Don't you think it will be difficult to get all the money for the German loan?" Cederschïold knew that Swedish Match was already seriously leveraged.

"There's plenty of time," Ivar replied, "a lot will happen before then."

Ivar arranged for his American bedfellows at Lee, Higginson & Co. to assume $50 million of the offering that would cover the German loan. Donning the mantle of Europe's Savior, he attended the second Hague Conference in early 1930 and helped settle arrangements between Germany and its creditors. If Ivar was worried, he never let on.

He should have been worried. "Nothing in Ivar's career was more amazing than this suicidal loan made in the shadow of the Great Depression to a nation with impaired credit by a man whose securities would not sell," the poet and author Archibald MacLeish remarked. At first, the old guy's luck seemed to be holding. France decided to pay off its $75 million debt early, sending some much-needed capital into the Kreuger & Toll coffers. Market watchers nodded approvingly, noting that Kreuger stock had never taken the big plunge suffered by other large corporations. Many people asserted that the great financial boom had only suffered a tiny nick. They required only a brief period for the self-regulating markets to adjust; then everyone would be flying high again.

"No one can examine the panorama of business and finance in America without realizing that we are living in a new era," John Moody, founder of the Moody credit ratings agency, had declared in 1927. Americans didn't need to fear the vicissitudes of the economic cycle any longer, thanks to advances in corporate planning, a strong Federal Reserve governing the money supply, and most especially thanks to "captains of industry" like Henry Ford and Ivar Kreuger who would point the way where mere mortals foundered.

But privately many insiders, and short-sellers, saw the sky beginning to fall. One man predicted that nothing would brake the international money disaster until three things occurred: (1) the banks in Austria and Germany failed; (2) England abandoned the gold standard; and (3) Ivar Kreuger filed for bankruptcy.

Jacob Wallenberg, a Kreuger skeptic for some time, remembered his feelings: "I had never quite understood where he made all his money anyway, but even though I hadn't been able to make sense out of his profit-and-loss statements, he apparently had been quite liquid around 1927, before the overlending and overborrowing began. By 1931, however, when it was pretty obvious he needed money, I was particularly puzzled by the fact that he still showed a big cash reserve in some of his companies and in some banks." Wallenberg's Nordic practicality smelled something rotten in Ivar's poetically phrased annual reports.

Ivar raised $25 million on the IMCO debentures, but that was like handing someone 50 cents to pay their house note. He needed much more. Germany's banks were indeed hemorrhaging; they had closed once, reopened a few days later, and were barely staggering through each day. Kreuger & Toll had also lost some of its characteristic footing, and people were starting to notice.

Ivar was so used to doing whatever he wanted, he felt slapped in the face when he was finally challenged by one of his employees. Sigurd Hennig, who served as chief accountant for Swedish Match, approached Ivar on a blustery spring day in 1931. Hennig broke the Kreugerite vow of acquiescence and told his boss something had to be done about the company's books. Too many items were being tossed from one ledger to another; assets were being duplicated; others had disappeared; interest payments due the Kreuger & Toll mother ship were not coming in; and Hennig couldn't locate the debtors. Ivar fixed Hennig with arched brow and said, "There must be something wrong here, Hennig. The money can't have run away, can it?"

Hennig wouldn't yield. "What about this 400 million francs?" he wanted to know. "What are they doing in this Dutch bank no one's ever heard of?"

"That bank is a good bank," Ivar retorted, which wasn't the question Hennig had asked. Ivar knew that many of the banks on his books were not *good*; they were not even banks. They were shells he had created for transferring money. When Hennig persisted in getting verifiable answers, Ivar exploded. "Is this a conspiracy against me? Have you all joined in an attack against me?"

Ivar had feared this might happen. Even he wouldn't be able to fend off inquiries forever, pleading secrecy agreements, or muttering, "Debit it to me personally." Being a resourceful man, Ivar had prepared for this eventuality with his own brand of insurance policy. Back when he was negotiating the bailout loan with Minister Pinochet in France, he had also been carrying on hush-hush talks with Mussolini's government in Italy. But the Italians weren't biting. They operated their own match-factory consortium under state control. What did they need with the arrogant Swedish megalomaniac? Fine, Ivar responded, and then quietly began buying shares in the Italian monopoly, so that by 1930 he owned a third of the conglomerate's shares.

In October of that year, Ivar again travelled undercover to Italy and met with Giovanni Boselli, the director of the monopoly administration, and Antonio Mosconi, the Italians' minister of finance. The Fascist government was clamoring for money to fuel its rearmament program, so they weren't so quick to rebuff Mr. Kreuger this time around. This time it was Ivar who demurred. He explained it would take a while, considering the state of international finance, for him to obtain the necessary funds for the loan. In the meantime, rumors soon reached the Italian ministry that Ivar was going to float his venture in Italy by issuing debentures in France. But the French were opposing Italy's rearmament at every turn. So as soon as Boselli got wind that France was involved in the deal—a contention that Ivar branded a "shameless lie," perpetrated by his enemies—he whipped off a Dear John letter to Ivar.

> *I note that you prefer to wait on account of the present financial situation. In view of this and also in view of the mendacious talk that has occurred [the rumored French connection] I am compelled to inform you that we do not wish to continue the negotiations. These are therefore terminated.*

Mussolini was later accused of taking Ivar's French-sponsored money under the table while he was spurning the Match King in public. *Il Duce* scoffed at the suggestion. He didn't have a problem with Ivar. To Mussolini, here was yet another of the historical moment's great men taking advantage of his natural advantages. But, Mussolini swore, "Even if we were dying of starvation, we'd never take a lira as a loan from France."

Ivar remained undeterred. If he had been the kind of man to get derailed by a breakdown in negotiations, he would never have gained his pseudo-royal status. Failing to make the Mussolini deal, he went ahead and acted as if he had. He arranged for the printer who usually prepared Kreuger & Toll's stock certificates to issue him a batch of counterfeit Italian bonds. Each of the 42 bonds carried a face value of 500,000 English pounds. Never one to overlook the details, Ivar handed the printer a letter bearing the Italian coat of arms to use in embossing the notes, and dictated the terms: According to the text, these were "treasury bills" worth six percent interest redeemable at Barclay's Bank, Ltd., in London. Each bond was stamped "Rome 15 August 1930" and bore signature lines for "G. Boselli, General Director," (his official title) and for "A. Mosconi, Minister of Finance," another of the Italian representatives. Ivar filled in the signatures on the bonds himself. Besides the bonds, he also forged five promissory notes representing interest payments of 1.5 million pounds a piece.

Altogether Ivar had created $142 million worth of phony government issues, some of which he used to placate his bothersome accountants who were growing more concerned by the day about "holes" in the Kreuger & Toll balance sheet. Ivar also pledged the bonds and promissory notes as collateral to borrow more money from his Swedish bankers. Even though many of these gentlemen had ridden Ivar's coattails to prominence, they were becoming alarmed. The directors of the Scandinaviska Bank at one point determined to call their most illlustrious debtor onto the carpet, but Ivar again set off a smoke screen. He told the Scandinaviska official that he had been invited by the German chancellor, Heinrich Brüning, to attend a closed-door conference on the country's financial trauma. "How was it possible to treat a man too harshly who in this way was permitted to take part in the big, decisive conferences of the world?" the official wondered. "The liquidity problems of the Kreuger group—and also those of our own, as far as that goes—were suddenly reduced in importance quite considerably."

While he labored to appear as sanguine as ever, Ivar was feeling the effects of the quakes in his empire. It was later discovered he had spelled *Boselli* three different ways on the Italian forgeries. His railing at the accountant Hennig about conspiracies was more than bluster, too. He was convinced a world-wide confederacy of dunces was allied against him. Ivar barged into an associate's office one morning, scowling and looking about. He said that the night before he had been dining at a restaurant when he ran into the nephew of Alfred Nobel, the famous Swede who had invented dynamite and established the Nobel Prizes. "He told me I was being followed by the police. What do you think it means?"

"It's probably just for your protection," the associate assured his boss. "Maybe they're afraid the Bolsheviks will kidnap you."

Ivar asked, hopefully, "Are you sure that's it?" (Supposedly he really was being "observed" by the French police, who were keeping tabs on many prominent internationals at the time. A second World War, once it arrived, made wise men of many paranoids.)

Whatever his private horrors, Ivar maintained his classic countenance in public. Traveling to America he met with President Herbert Hoover, also an engineer by training, and assured his host that the waves in the stock market would soon subside. Negotiating a potential merger of his telephone holdings in Sweden with International Telephone and Telegraph, Ivar commented about the proposal, "Yes, it's fine, but can I trust the ITT balance sheet?" He told Donald Durant at Lee, Higginson—in utmost secrecy—that he had just consummated a fabulous deal with the Italian government for almost $150 million and was setting up deals with two other countries. Ivar had earlier shared with Durant what he called the "XYZ Memorandum," which described deals in the works with three necessarily anonymous countries. Italy, he teased Durant, was country X.

Edwin Chinlund, an ITT vice president at the time, recalled how Ivar wowed his counterparts at the negotiating table. Usually focused and precise in his exchanges, Ivar would take advantage of a break in the conference and begin to talk "about some subject that he would unobtrusively bring up or pick up from what someone else had said and expound on it so thoroughly, and with such an obvious wealth of information, that we would be astonished at the knowledge he had in his head and his great memory for facts and statistics. I decided one day that I'd check him on details—I think it had to do with Hungary's economic and financial condition—and I was amazed to find out that he had been right about every last decimal point and conclusion. Less than a year later, in Stockholm, I discovered from one of his business associates how he did it. The night before an important meeting, he would look up a lot of information on a specific subject and then simply make sure the subject came up the next day. I'm positive he used the same trick when he spoke with President Hoover and other statesmen, as well as with his American banker friends."

Ivar's "friends" increasingly found themselves shoved against a wall. For one thing, his enemies were gaining momentum every day. Bearish market speculators, led by a vituperative anti-Kreuger constituency in France, were pummeling his stock price. By December 1931, Kreuger & Toll, once trading upwards of $30 a share, had sunk to $4.25.

Two of his critics' most dire predictions had come true. England had dropped off the gold standard in September, followed quickly by Sweden. The Austro-German banking crisis grew into a full-scale debacle that same month, when Germany was granted a moratorium on its debts, including the $200 million they owed to Ivar. All that remained now was for the third of the critic's dire predictions to come true: for Ivar Kreuger to admit his bankruptcy to the world.

Stock market bears in France—and sharks everywhere—were crowding Ivar. He fought back by supporting his securities himself, through various shadow companies, with the help of banking allies, and even by encouraging his friends to buy up Kreuger & Toll stock, promising them huge returns when he bounced back. Ivar's doctor, Charles Bove, personally lost $113,000, thinking he was helping a friend and getting rich in the process. In two trips to America, Ivar trumpeted his interest in Boliden, Incorporated, a gold mine whose potential he was naturally overstating. He denounced the fluctuations in Kreuger & Toll stock as the product of mercenary brokers, the stock market equivalent of vultures.

But the French bears, as they preferred to be called, were finding support around the world. Jackson Martindell, a Texas-born broker who, as it happened, owned one million of the 7.5 million shares of Kreuger stock certificates outstanding in America, claimed he had a gut feeling that Ivar was all wrong.

Martindell could never get any solid information from the company, or a straight answer. When he started dumping shares, various Kreuger sympathizers and stakeholders tried to talk Martindell out of it. Ivar himself sent a report—two typewritten pages—to Martindell, hoping to allay the broker's fears. But Martindell pronounced it "gobbledygook" and kept selling. Finally a prominent New York banker dropped in on Martindell and put the matter bluntly.

"You're trying to ruin the country," the banker accused Martindell. "As you well know, there is a brokerage syndicate buying up Kreuger & Toll shares as quickly as you throw them on the market. But we have no choice. We were formed to support the Stock Exchange itself, because we're all trying to save a very damaging situation."

Martindell replied, "If I see that the stock is really worth $9 a share, I'll stop my orders." But he never saw anything of the kind, and he kept on dumping.

Chinlund's Question

Herr Kreuger's fraud, though massive, followed the same law as the most routine scam. Once you're chasing bad money after good, and then bad money after more bad, it's an endgame. Sooner or later you're going to crumble. "Some of Kreuger's subsidiaries were real," wrote Archibald MacLeish, "some were a set of books, some were a name; but name, books, or reality, the entries spun back and forth, the debit and credit items tangled from roof to wall." And when the web started to knot and rip, the financial world went batty, shaking economic and political structures to their foundations. It was more than coincidence: business deals and treaties alike for the past ten years had been strung together with promises nobody really believed, and fueled by borrowed funds.

The forged Italian bonds saved Ivar's neck in 1930. He listed about $45 million of them directly on Kreuger & Toll's financial statement, and pledged the rest to Skandinaviska Kredit A.B. for a loan, the proceeds of which he passed to the German government as the first installment on his bailout. Archibald MacLeish later reported, "About 425 million kroner of assets shown on Kreuger & Toll's 1930 balance sheet were created by fictitious gains...and more than half the company's net profit for that year was the product of bookkeeping, not match selling." According to Price, Waterhouse, the firm whose auditors were charged with sweeping up Ivar's mess, actual profits would not have permitted annual dividends of more than 1-1/2 percent of capital, while Ivar was paying 20 percent.

Ivar's person was starting to show the effects of his position. An associate in Paris wondered, "Why are you not with us as before?"

Ivar replied, "I don't dare be with people anymore. I'm scared to be influenced by their wrong opinions." He grew testy and forgetful, switching moods as if he were taking off his hat. After dining with Ivar, Per Jacobsson felt disturbed. Jacobsson had worked for Ivar a few years before, and thought he was casually meeting an old associate. "He had been animated and optimistic while we ate and talked about the decline and what to do. Then, when lunch was over, I went with him to the hotel and saw him there alone. He fell suddenly into deep despair."

No wonder, since Ivar was performing his most daring act yet of financial dazzlery. In summer 1931, with July dividends due, Ivar at last settled a deal between his Ericsson Telephone company and International Telephone and Telegraph. With ITT's commitment for $11 million in hand, he borrowed $4 million from various American banks to meet his immediate obligations. Back in Stockholm, he scanned for options, considering which sources for funds might remain untapped, seeking any asset that he hadn't already pledged as collateral. With no other out, he again dipped into the Italian bonds.

What he really needed was to get at the stock of his Boliden gold mine, the last carrot with any power to make the moneychangers respond. But the Boliden stock was already held by the Skandinaviska Bank against a loan. Undeterred, Ivar replaced the Boliden stock at Skandinaviska with bonds from German match factories. He replaced the German bonds, which were listed on IMCO's books, with his faked Italian ones. Now that he'd freed up the Boliden stock, Ivar went to the Riksbank and prodded them into loaning him 40 million kroner, about $10 million. He offered the Boliden shares as collateral. Still the Riksbank directors resisted, until Ivar reminded them what kind of damage they and the bank would suffer if any of Ivar's enterprises were allowed to fail. He got the loan of course, but didn't stop there. He then listed the Boliden stock as "sold" to Kreuger & Toll for $20 million worth of debentures, even though it was supposed to be standing as security for the loan. He hoped to cash in the debentures on the New York stock exchanges.

If it's hard on a first reading to decipher Ivar's game of financial Twister, imagine the desperation which motivated this once imperturbable con, the man who had bluffed world leaders and brushed off competitors with a smirk. However he strained, Ivar couldn't stretch far enough. Late in 1931, Ivar left Sweden for the last time. He was traveling to New York, where the deal with ITT had begun to falter. Edwin Chinlund, leading the merger team, had gone from suspicious inquiries to demands. He threatened that if he didn't get answers he would advise the directors to pull the plug.

As Ivar prepared to leave his homeland, he decided to take an afternoon and visit Inge Häsller, his discreet lover from 1915. Despite their lengthy attachment—the closest thing to love that either, perhaps, would ever know—Ivar and Inge had grown distant. They hadn't met face to face in years, and they had only talked on the phone once in that time, in 1925, when Ivar was celebrating his German loan. He had called Inge and asked her to play the piano over the phone. While Russian melodies crackled down the phone lines, Ivar sat smoking a cigarette, momentarily lifted from his dour concentrations. Ivar had been calling that night from Berlin. Robert Shaplen reports that the next night Ivar travelled to Paris, where he "solemnized the event more tangibly with one of his newer girls there."

The man who came to visit Inge in the last days of November had none of the younger Ivar's power or charm. "I was scared when I saw how he had changed," Inge wrote in her memoirs. "He was nervous, there was a jerky movement in his shoulder, and I wondered if he had had a stroke. He smoked constantly, something he had seldom done before." He told Inge he had provided for her in his will and took his leave.

He arrived in New York a few days later. His housekeeper, Hilda Aberg, panicked when she saw her boss stepping into the Park Avenue apartment carrying a gun. Ivar set it in the umbrella stand near the front door. He lit one cigarette after another, puffing on them severally or not at all. Hilda said she woke up one night to find every light in the house burning and Ivar gone. The next morning, when she asked where he'd been, he coughed, "Out."

At the ITT negotiations, Ivar staunchly assured his associates, his creditors, and Edwin Chinlund's negotiating team that nothing was amiss in the merger. But he knew he was caught. Though there was no such moniker at the time, Chinlund worked what we would now call a classic fraud examination on the Ericsson books. Before Chinlund, everyone who dealt with Ivar Kreuger had followed the lead of Ernst & Ernst, the firm that nominally audited Ivar's International Match Corporation. Ernst & Ernst, of course, got their info from Kreuger & Toll. In a typical statement written by

E & E's lead accountant, one A.D. Berning, the auditors avowed, "We have examined the books of account and record of IMCO and its American subsidiary companies as of December 31, 1930, and have received statements from abroad with respect to the foreign constituent companies as of the same date." Chinlund knew crap when he saw it. And the more skeptically he held up Kreuger's balance sheet to the light, the crappier it looked.

Over the ensuing weeks, Chinlund began the process familiar to any fraud examiner, the crazy, boring hours required to verify assets and trace their use in various transactions. Not one item could be taken for granted. Chinlund found what he was looking for, fittingly enough, in one of Kreuger & Toll's "statements from abroad." About $6 million of Ericsson's assets, Chinlund discovered, had been listed as "cash in hand and in banks" on the English-language contract describing the merger. But, as Chinlund learned through his translator, the Swedish version said the money was held in "cash, bankings and *on deposit*." Chinlund traced the funds, discovering that the $6 million was *on deposit* at the central office of Kreuger & Toll.

The money, which should have remained at Ericsson, had been shifted into the parent company and "replaced" with bonds from a German match factory. However, the bonds were a liquid asset, like the cash they were standing in lieu of. And the continuing wilt of the *Deutschmark*'s value meant the bonds didn't cover the debt at the present exchange rate. Chinlund eventually made a list of discrepancies between what Ivar said about Ericsson and what an inquisitive reading of the details produced, and brought the grim news to the ITT board.

For the first time ever, someone was publicly challenging the way Ivar kicked his assets around like a football. Ivar claimed there was a translation problem with the "on deposit" section of the document.

Chinlund retorted, "You made the translation yourself."

On February 19, a Friday, the ITT directors told Ivar that if he couldn't show them Chinlund was wrong, the merger would be cancelled. Ivar waited and said nothing. Not only didn't he have the $11 million cash that ITT had put into the deal, he knew in his bones that his empire would never survive this news. Too many enemies, too many French bears, too many holes in the balance sheet. The Match King's silence bought him nothing this time, and the ITT deal was canned. He had until Tuesday to inform his various associates, the directors somberly decreed; a public announcement would follow.

Since he had the weekend to stall, Ivar thought he might be able to pull off another dazzler. Edwin Chinlund showed up at Ivar's apartment on Saturday to say that several interested parties were playing golf the next day, and asked if Ivar would object if Chinlund told these people that the merger had been cancelled.

"On my way up," Chinlund recalled, "I rehearsed what I'd do if Kreuger pulled his cigarette stunt on me." In addition to treating the ITT team to his feats of memory, Ivar had manipulated them with a version of the stalling trick he had used on the French in 1922. At ITT Ivar had not only tapped the cigarette, he had methodically shredded it into an ashtray at the conference table, waiting with Job's patience for someone else to break the silence.

"I resolved to grit my teeth and let him be the one to talk first," Chinlund said. "I put my question to him almost as soon as I got there. Out came the customary cigarette. He lit it, twirled it, squeezed it, broke it, as always, then he said: 'Well.' And stopped. And went through the whole procedure again. I sat tight."

Finally Kreuger said, "Well, Sunday or Monday or Tuesday, I don't suppose it makes any difference." There was another long pause, and Kreuger looked at Chinlund gravely and said, "Mr. Chinlund, you are committing the worst mistake anyone ever made. Up to now, you have had a fine career, and now you'll be ruined."

Chinlund replied, "If that is so, if a mistake has been made, I'm already ruined, and nothing I can do will alter that."

Kreuger said, "Think about it. You still have until tomorrow morning to change your mind."

As Chinlund recalled later, "He apparently meant the golf date, where I was to inform the others. I again said there was nothing I could do about it, the facts were all there. I started for the elevator and he accompanied me, asking about my relatives in Sweden. As I walked through the hall, I noticed the gun in the umbrella stand and asked him if he got any chance to do any shooting in this country."

Kreuger answered, "Yes, occasionally."

****

Ivar sailed back across the Atlantic on board the *Ile de France*. At his Paris apartment he met with several of his closest associates, including his longtime aide and business partner, Krister Littorin; Victor Holm, who headed the entity known as Dutch Kreuger & Toll; Anton Wendler, auditor for Swedish Match; and Kreuger's lead accountant, Sigurd Hennig. Besides their sad declarations of how unfairly they'd been treated by Chinlund and ITT, the men kept returning to one question: *What about the Italian bonds?*

Hennig went so far as to speak the question out loud: "Are they authentic?" he asked his boss, remembering well how Ivar had ranted about conspiracies.

"Yes!" Ivar snapped. "They're authentic." He would discuss the bonds no further. He couldn't use them as collateral without getting Mussolini's ministers to agree, Ivar told the assemblage, and for that he would have to go to Rome, and there wasn't, he insisted with a swipe of his hand in the air, enough time for shuttling off to Italy. The meeting broke up, and Krister Littorin promised to stop by and pick up Ivar for lunch the next day. "Everyone could use a rest," they all agreed.

After dismissing his associates, Ivar had a bath and then dined in with a young woman he had traveled with upon occasion. Unbeknownst to her, Ivar had written a Norwegian friend just a week before on the woman's behalf. "If you do not hear from her before three months from now," Ivar instructed his friend, "please write her a letter offering your help." (The woman's only comment, when she was told of M. Kreuger's passing, was, "Ivar was very happy that night.")

The next morning, Ivar met with Littorin briefly. Littorin was still upset, this time about some outrageous predictions of "cash forecasts" that Ivar had made to Donald Durant at Lee, Higginson. Ivar mused, "It was probably not so good to make that statement."

Littorin took Ivar by the shoulders—this man, he and at least a score of others, had pledged their lives and their personal fortunes too. Littorin told him, "Whatever you have done, whatever you have said, and whatever you have written, you must realize that you are surrounded only by friends who wish you well and who want to help set everything straight."

Ivar told Littorin he would meet him and the others for lunch at the restaurant in an hour, and Littorin departed. In the interim, Ivar met with his personal secretary, Karin Bökman, with whom he was very close. Ivar had sent Karin three $10,000 bills in an envelope from New York, accompanied by a farewell letter. Days later he'd cabled her from the *Ile de France* and told her to forget it. They hadn't talked about either of the messages since, and they didn't talk about them that morning. They pretended Miss Bökman was helping him plan an itinerary as normal. She felt afraid for Ivar, she revealed later, but she wouldn't speak it. Miss Bökman left just before 11 a.m. with orders to travel to Stockholm and await further word from her boss.

Ivar performed his final task as cleanly, and classically, as befitted his status. Like the fabled equestrians of Rome, he chose death over the indignity of being dragged before the vulgar masses. His housekeeper, Jeanette Barrault, was still at the open market gathering provisions; his associates were waiting in the restaurant, refusing to order until their boss arrived. Ivar took a 9-millimeter revolver he had bought the day before and squeezed a round into his heart.

His corpse was discovered lying neatly on the bed, as if Ivar had stretched out, leaving all his clothes on, for a late-morning nap. There was "a little blood, a very little blood, below his heart," Archibald MacLeish reported, but otherwise Ivar had left his life as he lived it: composed. In New York, over the long weekend before the ITT fracture became public, he'd scribbled a note which now sat on the dresser: "I'm too tired to continue."

At the restaurant, Krister Littorin and Karin Bökman became worried. They jumped into a taxi and rushed to Ivar's address. Jeanette answered the door, and told the worried visitors, "Monsieur is sleeping." She knew because when she returned from the market, she looked in on him; the phone had started ringing and she was surprised he hadn't answered it.

Littorin shoved past the housekeeper into Ivar's bedroom. In a moment, he returned, confirming what both women were fearing, "*Il est mort.*"

Headlines the next day echoed the declaration:

IVAR KREUGER DöD

MORT DE M. IVAR KREUGER

KREUGER'S LETZE TAGE

The *London Times* blamed politics. "Here is new evidence," the editorialist averred, "of the war which international indecision [regarding national debts and monetary policy] is waging against the interests of manufacture and commerce." The *Economist* compared Kreuger to "a hero in an Aeschylean tragedy."

Time magazine, who saw Ivar as "the self-made colossus of Scandinavian finance," headed its eulogy:

"POOR KREUGER"

On July 8, 1932, the Dow Jones hit its low point, 41.22, a 90-percent drop from its pre-Crash high. In the months following Ivar's suicide, worldwide grief had turned to anger. An audit by Price, Waterhouse exposed the Swedish Match King as a fake, his riches mostly sham, his victims wide-eyed and willing to see whatever he willed them to see.

Philip Musica
(1884 - 1938)

CHAPTER 4

Citizen Coster: Philip Musica

"I learned that the possessions most esteemed by your fellow creatures were 'high and unsullied descent' united with riches."
—*The Creature*

On December 16, 1938 Dr. Frank Donald Coster was pacing the floors of his mansion. A chronically inflamed ulcer usually kept him away from alcohol, but he'd been downing highballs since eight o'clock in the morning. And pacing. He'd skip up the winding staircase to the second floor, cracking the door to every room. Then, click-click, click-click, his shoes echoed throughout the vestibule as he mounted the steps to the third floor. At the top, he peered from the overlook window at his shrub-lined driveway. Seeing no one on the lawn, Dr. Coster turned back to the staircase, taking three steps at a time, calling his butler to bring another drink.

It was a little past 11 a.m. now. Coster flopped into an overstuffed velvet chair, just below a portrait of Theodore Roosevelt that dominated the eastern wall. His gaze settled for a moment on a Steckley table, to the photo of his wife in her white feather boa. On the wall behind the table hung a framed admonition, something Carol Coster gave her husband for his 54th birthday. The text was written by Harriet Beecher Stowe:

> *When you get into a tight place and everything goes against you till it seems as if you couldn't hold on a minute longer, never give up then, for that is just the place and time the tide will turn.*

Coster had squeezed through some tight spots. He'd steered the McKesson & Robbins corporation through the Depression, hadn't he? But this morning he feared the tide had turned against him.

Only one year before, Coster sat in the same chair, wearing the same blue suit, anxiously smoking a cigar while a gaggle of financiers, several congressmen, and select representatives of the Republican Party begged for his attention. His hands had been shaking that morning, too, when a bank president from New York City rose to his feet and began speaking in a stentorian tone. "Dr. Coster, we think you should be a candidate for President of the United States. We want to assure you of our complete support, both moral and financial. And we would like permission to use your name in our preliminary plans." The banker showed Coster a telegram from the Republican leadership in California, unanimously endorsing the "Coster for President" campaign.

Coster told his visitors he, too, was fed up with "that other Roosevelt," Franklin Delano, trouncing Republican candidates. He agreed they couldn't run another Alf Landon, as they'd done in '36. Fiddling with the round lenses of his eyeglasses, Coster turned his hoot-owl stare on the assemblage: "Gentlemen, I cannot tell you how much I appreciate your confidence in me. I wish I could find it possible to join with you in this important project. However, personal reasons, which I am sure you will understand, dictate my reluctant regrets."

Almost 12 months later to the day, Coster sat alone, his fingers twitching, his head slumped to his chest.

"Are you okay, Frank?"

Coster was startled when Leonard Jenkins called his name, then he realized it was his brother-in-law again, inquiring after Coster's health. Carol Coster had demanded that Leonard stay overnight, to help her watch her husband. She and Leonard had carried off every gun in the house and ordered the chef to remove his kitchen knives.

"Yes, I'm fine," Coster said to Leonard in a wispy voice. "I'm just going to the bathroom."

A half-hour later, the good doctor had not returned. Leonard went up and knocked on the bathroom door. For a moment there was no response. Then a sigh.

"I'll just be a few more minutes," Coster said in a muted voice. He was staring out the porthole window onto the front lawn. He could hear Carol's prize chows barking from their kennels. A car was turning off the main road onto the paved drive. He watched as the driver pulled next to the house and three men exited the vehicle. Two of the men he tagged as federal agents—they were wearing long jackets, officious expressions, and $2 hats. The agents accompanied George Dietrich, the assistant treasurer at McKesson & Robbins. Dietrich wasn't cuffed, but he was bookended by the agents as the trio strode across the manicured lawn, apparently in too much of a hurry to use the sidewalk.

Coster abruptly stepped away from the window and faced himself in the mirror. When he heard the doorbell chiming, he slipped a .38 revolver from his pocket, the one he kept in his safe. The shot, exploding just behind his right ear, spun Coster's body around and dropped him face first into the bathtub. His head snapped so furiously that his glasses jumped off his nose, landing in the sink. Both lenses were splattered in blood and the left one was cracked.

Dr. Frank Donald Coster never heard the men racing up the stairs behind Leonard. He didn't hear Leonard shout, "No!" He didn't hear his wife Carol emerge screaming from her room at the other end of the floor, her fur-lined house slippers scraping *chuh chuh chuh* against the marble tiles, her frightened eyes pleading for the men to do something. Leonard booted the bathroom door open, confirmed what they all knew, and turned to bar his sister's way. Carol gripped Leonard's arm in both her hands, shrieking at the crumpled figure in the tub, "My God, Daddy, why did you do it? Why did you do it? Why? Why didn't you face it? My God!"

Dr. Frank Donald Coster, CEO, Girard & Company

Though he was nowhere near the premises, the man who backed Coster into that bathtub was Julian Thompson. Until recently, Thompson had ranked among the foremost admirers of Dr. Frank Donald Coster. Thompson served as treasurer at McKesson & Robbins, the once floundering company that he and Coster built into the nation's leading wholesale pharmaceuticals distributor. The very embodiment of East Coast sophistication, Thompson studied the McKesson & Robbins books through his pince-nez, the instrument dwarfed by a nose that stretched from his forehead like an oil derrick. Deep lines around his mouth framed Thompson's speech in parentheses.

Thompson's speech was not only grammatical, it was dramatic. That is, he wrote plays. He found his greatest success in 1932 with the opening of *The Warrior's Husband*, a Broadway show that introduced a fiery young actress named Katherine Hepburn.

In the closing months of 1938, after 12 years of doing business with Frank Coster, Thompson didn't want to admit that his boss ("my friend") was a fake. But $20 million worth of raw pharmaceuticals was missing from a McKesson & Robbins subsidiary in Montreal. The more Thompson pressed Coster for an answer, the more Coster replied in riddles, *non sequiturs,* and, finally, with denunciations. When Thompson said he wanted to personally verify the assets, Coster sniped, "If you refuse to take my word, you are calling me a liar. I demand your resignation. Now. Before you leave this house."

Thompson urged Coster to come clean with the Securities and Exchange Commission: either produce the missing drugs or explain their disappearance. Failing to do so, Dr. Coster was charged with fraud, alongside two McKesson & Robbins officers—the assistant treasurer, George Dietrich, and George's brother, Robert Dietrich, who ran the firm's shipping department. When federal marshals went to Coster's house on the morning of December 16, 1938, they were under orders to revoke his bail. Coster decided a bullet behind the ear was a preferable alternative.

As the remains were prepared for the crematorium, Carol Coster and Julian Thompson weren't the only ones asking, "Why?" Six years earlier, when Coster learned that Ivar Kreuger (the Swedish Match King) had shot himself in the heart, Coster said, "It's terrible when a man like that goes back on himself. I am repelled by the notion that such a man should find his end in the tragedy of suicide." Now a phalanx of judges, lawyers, regulators, detectives, reporters and scandalmongers wanted to know why Coster had also pulled the trigger. Was there a Rosebud, perhaps, some lost talisman in Dr. Frank Donald Coster's past? Something that explained both the superhuman drive that propelled him to the heights of American life and the gloom that engulfed him at his zenith?

Julian Thompson told police he first met Coster in 1925. Coster wanted to sell shares in his pharmaceuticals concern, Girard & Company, and Thompson was assigned by a Boston firm to see if the offering made sense. It would take a couple of years to bring Girard to market, as Thompson determined during his week's stay in Mount Vernon, New York. But the sometime playwright effused compliments for Girard's management, especially its chief executive, "a charming, knowledgeable, intuitive, and efficient man of the world and man of affairs." Dr. Frank Donald Coster held a Ph.D. in chemistry from the University of Heidelberg, where he'd also been certified as an M.D. Thompson, a Princeton man, class of

1911, was impressed by Coster's aloofness and his confident intelligence, which Thompson regarded as a sign of the Germanic national temperament.

Julian Thompson spent the next 13 years swallowing Coster's line. Dr. Coster of Heidelberg was in fact a high-school dropout, and Italian, not German, by birth. Most recently he'd used the name *Frank Costa,* before switching accents and genealogies to become *Coster.* Girard was a concoction, too. Coster said he formed the company in 1923 with a "silent partner" named Horace Girard, his mother's rich brother. There was no such person. Horace Girard was a paper creation designed to shield Coster's mother, Marie Girard, the real silent partner in this and every aspect of Coster's life.

Girard & Company sold pharmaceuticals like *eau de quinine* and camphor spirits, a line of hair tonics, and bay-rum colognes. The firm made its reputation pushing a furniture polish called "Woodtone" and a high-powered hair tonic called "Dandrofuge." What the Julian Thompsons of the world didn't know was that the modest factory on North Washington Avenue was mainly pushing bootleg liquor.

Girard's tonics and tinctures were all "cleaned" before distribution, i.e., some guys in the factory cooked out the alcohol and bottled it for the speak-easy bars of Prohibition America. Dandrofuge hair tonic was especially easy to clean. A liniment called "Painophobe," on the other hand, had every bootlegger in Brooklyn stumped until Coster hired Dr. Emil Fanto, a chemist who really did have a degree from the University of Heidelberg. Fanto developed a way of using caustic soda to clean Painophobe into a more or less ingestible product.

Business was booming. George Dietrich, Coster's chief financial officer at Girard (and later at McKesson & Robbins), told investigators, "On paper, we sold enough shampoo to wash every head in the world. But 90 percent of it we sold to bootleggers." Dutch Schulz, known as the King of Needle Beer and one of the overlords of Brooklyn's numbers racket, provided a fleet of trucks and drivers. George Dietrich described 300-barrel truckloads of *eau de quinine* and *lilas végétal* which were sold the next day as "eight-year-old rye," "bottled-in-bond bourbon," or "Highland Scotch," depending on the customer's preference.

The sweetest piece of Girard's business was a permit from the U.S. government for 5,000 gallons of denatured alcohol a month. Instead of making spirits of camphor, which sold for $2 a gallon, Coster's lab yielded "Georgian vodka," which brought as high as $5 a gallon. Robert Dietrich, brother to CFO George Dietrich, oversaw the permit business. Robert explained the two-fold impact of bootlegging government alcohol: all profits above the market price for camphor spirits were tax free; and because Girard consistently sold out its quota, the company's alcohol allotment was boosted again and again. By the time Julian Thompson dropped by in 1925, Girard was handling 25,000 gallons of government alcohol a month.

In the spring of 1925, Julian Thompson persuaded the board of the Bridgeport City Trust to back Coster. Bridgeport's president, Clinton Barnum Seeley, started the ball rolling with $20,000 of his own money. Seeley told Dr. Coster that, yes, the Barnum in his name was from P.T. Barnum of the Barnum & Bailey circus. "My grandfather was first and foremost a businessman," Seeley averred. "And he never said, 'There's a sucker born every minute.' It's true enough as an observation, but it wasn't my grandfather who said it, one of his competitors did."

Following Seeley's lead, other Bridgeport officers invested in Girard. The board enthusiastically committed the bank to a $100,000 loan in May. By Christmas, Coster had paid them back with interest. When he asked for $400,000 more, the board was all smiles.

"He had a way of making you like him," Seeley explained. Not that Coster was exuberant or anything; he smiled only faintly and he didn't make small talk. "Don't ask me what it was that made you like him. It was something he turned on and off, like a radio set."

In November of 1926, Coster phoned Clinton Barnum Seeley to say he was going to take over McKesson & Robbins, a 100-year-old firm that had fallen on hard times but which offered a bargain to the right entrepreneur. "I want you to help me," Coster said. "I need a million dollars."

"Oh, I'm afraid you've exceeded the reach of our little bank," Seeley answered. Nevertheless, he heartily recommended the venture to his board, who as usual nodded, smiled, and signed. "We were impressed by the tremendous dynamic power of this man. He completely took our breath away. We country boys figured that we better let go the tail of the bear."

Soon as the McKesson & Robbins papers were inked, Coster slipped his copies into a briefcase and made for the door. His driver took him to Brooklyn, where Marie Girard kissed her eldest on his pale cheeks. She hoped he'd get more sun and exercise. Coster spread the acquistion papers across a lion-clawed coffee table and reviewed the deal for his mother. They talked in spirited Italian, evaluating point by point, for the better part of two hours.

By the time Marie was satisfied on the particulars, it was nightfall. She spoke in English. "And what of your...woman? How does she think of this?"

"I came straight here. I'll tell Carol at dinner tonight."

"If she's home."

If Carol Coster wasn't shopping, she was traipsing after the two dozen chows she kept as show dogs. Coster was lucky to get a kiss on the cheek and a "Hi Daddy!" before she went scurrying behind one of her dogs, dragging the furry edge of her dressing gown across the marble floors. Carol was nearly ten years junior to the 42-year-old Coster. The daughter of a policeman, Carol had always dreamed of landing a man who'd buy her diamonds from Cartier's and dresses from the Elsie de Wolfe boutique.

If Carol looked toyish next to her formidable mother-in-law, she nevertheless gave as good as she got. While her husband doled out his charisma in soundbites, Carol entertained the senators, local dignitaries, and foreign businessmen who sought Coster's attention. Carol picked out their 18-room mansion at 400 Mill Plain Road in Fairfield, Connecticut, and supervised the remodeling. In the library, oak cabinets boasted an array of books on chemistry, medicine, and economics. Though she indulged her husband with a life-size portrait of his hero, Theodore Roosevelt, Carol reserved the rest of the house for herself.

She chose an Asian theme. The powder walls were hung with Chinese silk paintings, original Hiroshiges and Utamaros. Dancing figures, carved in ivory and jade, swooned in various rooms. Bronze Buddhas grinned from their perches in front of sandalwood screens. Charles Keats, who reported on the Coster affair for the Bridgeport *Sunday Herald*, said the plush, richly colored divans in the sitting room, littered by mounds of pillows, "gave the appearance of an Oriental potentate's zenana," the tucked away portion of a Chinese nobleman's household reserved for his mistresses. In the second floor sunroom, Carol had installed rock gardens, rotating the flora with the seasons, and a fieldstone fountain to stir the air with the sounds of trickling water.

Coster kept the goods coming as long as Carol kept herself reasonably presentable and talked a little babytalk. If not, she wasn't above reminding Coster, "I know your real name, Daddy. Wouldn't they like to hear *that* at McKesson & Robbins? Seen Mary Brandino lately?"

Many a morning Coster glanced down from his fourth-floor office, watching a thousand employees come and go, and suddenly there'd be Mary Brandino, her jowls brushing the lapels of her coat. She'd be leaning against a rusted-out car, puffing on a hand-rolled cigarette and blowing the smoke skyward, as if she could spew the fumes directly into the executive suite. If Mary spotted Coster looking at her, she'd bump her ape-shouldered brother Guiseppe, who was dozing across the car's hood. "Wake up and wave, beast!" she'd order, and the two of them waved to the silhouette in the window.

You know who we are, Coster heard them saying, though they merely waved. *You know who we are.*

Frank D. Costa, Owner, Adelphi Pharmaceuticals

Guiseppe and Mary Brandino spent their lives hustling. A squat, brown-haired man with sleepy eyes, Guiseppe would do anything for a buck, provided his sister pointed the way. He'd beaten a murder rap in 1915, but Guiseppe enjoyed killing, especially using the stilleto Mary gave him for a Christmas present.

Mary's face looked twice normal size because of the dewlap that melded her chin and her neck. She wore a floppy man's hat to obscure her gender and to generally keep folks from staring at her. She nearly had to use Guiseppe's own knife on him to make her brother introduce her to Frank Costa. Guiseppe knew Costa from prison—though his name wasn't Costa back then—and Guiseppe didn't like him. Guiseppe was pretty sure Costa had been a stoolie for the guards. Mary Brandino figured a man like Frank Costa would keep her and Guiseppe in business. Costa feared his past might take a bite from the seat of his freshly pressed trousers.

The Adelphi Pharmaceuticals Company was named for its address on Adelphi Street, Brooklyn. Adelphi manufactured Golden Rod Extract and a few hair tonics—enough to draw 5,000 gallons of government alcohol a month. Adelphi formed the first stone as Frank Costa moved away from his scarred, criminal past into the promised land of big business and a life as Dr. Frank Donald Coster. He learned how to deploy dummy corporations and a closed circle of insiders to make his business look completely real. He manufactured just enough legit product to show around, dumping the rest of the alcohol into tanker trucks for the mob.

Coster's associates, George and Robert Dietrich, created every last piece of documentation—from raw materials and processing through packaging, shipping, and selling—which would be generated by a typical American business of the time. George suggested they pay their bills late now and then, and age their accounts receivable, so they'd imitate the struggles of a young company struggling to its feet. Robert Dietrich laundered all the company's receipts through a Montreal subsidiary called W.W. Smith, safely outside the jurisdiction of America's booze-busting Treasury agents.

Costa had no choice but to deal with the Brandino *Brothers*, as Mary and Guiseppe were snidely known. But he forbade them from entering Adelphi's office. He worried that Mary's floppy hat and coarse language, in tandem with Guiseppe's murderous glances, might give people the right idea. Mary ostentatiously called her new partner *Cost*-A, overemphasizing the *A*. She mocked the way he salivated after the Broadway set, how his eyes danced when some swell strolled by fingering his watch chain. Mary laughed, her jowls shaking, her mouth agape. She'd love to see him fall.

"Of course, if I go, you go as well."

"So I 'spose we're stuck together," Mary snorted, raking a wad of snot from her nose with an index finger.

****

The last person Costa wanted to bump into was Edward Hubbard. As the only son of a well-to-do family, Hubbard had grown up expecting to become a lawyer. But his father died of cancer and his mother squandered all their money in bad investments. So instead of entering Harvard, Hubbard entered the legal field as an investigator. He specialized in financial matters, snooping out the dirty details of business deals for law firms, investment banks, and rival corporations.

Hubbard and his wife were walking on 57th Street in New York City one afternoon when he saw an old colleague. "Johnson! Johnson! Hey, Johnson!" Hubbard called out repeatedly, until Costa had no choice but to stop and pass a few minutes of polite catch-up banter. Costa explained with some obvious satisfaction that he was now a successful businessman. "And I go by my *real* name now, Costa."

Turning to his wife, Hubbard explained that he and Johnson, that is, Costa, had worked together for the U.S. Attorney's office during the recent World War, chasing down draft dodgers and investigating suspected collaborators. Carol Jenkins Hubbard nodded politely.

She was a policeman's daughter, Hubbard told Costa by way of introduction. She had worked for Hubbard as a stenographer during an investigation on behalf of the Long Island Railroad. Carol's batting brown lashes and little-girl giggles had turned Edward into a marionette doll, his knees gone rubbery, his arms akimbo. Within weeks he proposed marriage, but Carol said they ought to wait and see if Hubbard's newfangled detective work panned out. The couple was married two years later, in the spring of 1912, when Hubbard's registry bulged with clients.

"You must be the luckiest man alive, Edward," Costa said, his eyes bouncing between Carol Hubbard's flirtatious smile and her strategically profiled bosom. Hubbard pretended not to notice. He suggested he and Costa meet for lunch the next day—to discuss a problem at Hubbard's brokerage.

At Delmonico's the following afternoon, Hubbard said his brokerage partner, Stanley Clarke, was trying to oust him. He was already getting short-changed on the profits, Hubbard knew, and though he'd admittedly been treated for paranoia before, he was sure Clarke was out to get him. "I'm going to Nevada for a few weeks," Hubbard said. "I'd hoped you could look at Stanley's affairs while I was gone. I know you're the best." He pushed the keys to the Hubbard & Clarke offices across the table, and a stack of notes on Stanley Clarke's personal habits.

In the space of three weeks, Costa assembled a feast for Hubbard's fears. He brandished a handful of checks that Stanley Clarke allegedly had drawn on the firm's bank account to pay for renovating his house. He played a recording of Clarke discussing how to cut Hubbard loose from the firm altogether. Audio technology in those days was less than high fidelity, so no one could've sworn it wasn't Clarke's voice. Hubbard moved immediately to dissolve the partnership.

Costa also struck at Hubbard on the personal front. He sent an anonymous letter to the father of a teenage girl, claiming that Edward Hubbard was having an affair with the man's daughter. Though the father hesitated to approach Hubbard directly, the Brooklyn rumor mill easily brought word of the accusation around to Carol. "My God, I sing in the choir with that girl!" she cried.

As his marriage followed his business into the abyss, Hubbard fell apart. He was given to fits of weeping. He wouldn't sleep for three or four nights in a row, then he'd refuse to get out of bed for a week.

For nearly a year, Hubbard sought "cures" for his depression in one locale or another. Carol moved back in with her parents. During this time, Frank Costa served as Carol's steadfast, though platonic, friend. He did admit, during a walk through Central Park, that he loved her. But he protested that he held both Carol and Edward in too high a regard to act on that love.

In the summer of 1923, Edward seemed to improve—he'd started trading stocks for a small firm, and was beginning to reconcile with Carol. Then fate struck again. Hubbard was arrested on a charge, two years old, that he'd used a customer's account for his own gain. Hubbard frantically told the court that he and this customer had settled the man's complaint by cashing out the man's account and giving back all the firm's commissions. But prosecutors came armed with documents and an array of incriminating statements supplied by "a concerned citizen."

Found guilty, Hubbard spent 90 days incarcerated on Blackwell's Island. Carol met him on the day of his release and presented him with a petition for divorce. As he collapsed in tears onto the sidewalk, Hubbard noticed Frank Costa looking on from a car, to which Carol returned.

By this time Costa had outgrown Adelphi Pharmaceuticals. He had amassed plenty of capital by manipulating Adelphi's books, and he'd arranged with his mother to set up Girard & Company, listing her non-existent brother as the firm's principal backer. All Costa needed was to erase Adelphi and start over.

It had taken some tricky maneuvers to unravel an 11-year-old "marriage," but Costa rid himself of Mary and Guiseppe Brandino effortlessly. Through an anonymous tip, a Treasury agent learned what Adelphi really did with its alcohol allotment. Within a week, the factory was padlocked, the assets seized, the alcohol permit revoked. Mary and Guiseppe were arrested for trafficking liquor. No charges were filed against Adelphi's owner, Frank Costa, who had disappeared.

Bill Johnson, Investigator, Office of the Special Deputy Attorney General

Harry Cohen was sentenced to the electric chair in Sing Sing for killing a man during New York City's Poultry Wars. Barnet Baff, the man Harry was supposed to have gunned down on the street, was the most powerful member of the Jewish-run Live Poultry Association. It didn't make sense for Cohen, who was himself well-connected in the Live Poultry Association, to kill Baff. More likely Baff's assassin came from the "Poultry Trust" in Little Italy.

In fact, Deputy William Johnson of the New York Attorney General's office had spoken with an eyewitness who said he'd seen two Italian gunmen make the hit. Johnson heard from another source that the order came from a Poultry Trust operator named Antonio Cardinale. Johnson, who was concealing his own Italian heritage, didn't like what he was hearing. Johnson convinced the Cardinale source that Harry Cohen of the Live Poultry Association had hired men to kill Barnett Baff. Harry and his brother, Joseph Cohen, "King of the Chicken Pullers," were plotting to take over the Live Poultry Association, so they had Baff knocked off and threw the blame onto Italian suspects.

That's the story Johnson fed the courts, and the courts ate it up. Harry Cohen was placed on Sing Sing's deathwatch seven times. One night he'd already been shaved, his shirtsleeves rolled back, and his pants split up the legs when the governor's notice of reprieve arrived. Cohen could be heard shrieking, "Johnson!" throughout death row. In his mind's eye he saw Johnson's plump cheeks and drain-plug eyes. Cohen was driven nearly mad by the image of Johnson's thin lips grinning ever so faintly while he lied and swore to it.

Johnson, who performed the state's dirty work for both money and pleasure, already had one execution under his belt. He'd befriended one Hans Schmidt in prison. Schmidt, a clergyman, was accused of raping a teenaged girl, then hacking her up with an axe and throwing the pieces into the East River. Pastor Schmidt confided in Johnson that he'd been having sex with the girl for several months when she told him she was pregnant. After a back-alley abortionist killed her, Schmidt was stuck with a bloody corpse. Panicky, Schmidt sawed the body in half so he could fit it into a burlap bag, which washed to shore several days afterward.

Johnson told Schmidt to forget the abortion story, and enter an insanity plea instead. He brought Schmidt a set of lawbooks, underlining the key points for achieving an insanity verdict. At Schmidt's trial, the prosecution suddenly produced the lawbooks, pointing to the underlinings as evidence Schmidt was shamming his defense. Had he pled guilty to manslaughter, Hans Schmidt might have served ten or 15 years for his grotesque error in judgment. Instead he was executed in early 1916.

Bill Johnson served the state of New York so well, he won himself a promotion into the U.S. Attorney's office in 1917. His days chasing gangsters and freaks were done. Special Investigator Bill Johnson now combed the streets for draft dodgers and seditionists. The German threat must be extinguished, certain parties whispered, even if the United States did not join the ongoing World War. Establishment America had turned rabid against everything German and anyone suspected of sympathizing with the Kraut was a threat as well.

Johnson served his country by slandering William Randolph Hearst, the newspaper mogul who had repeatedly rubbed the seats of power raw with his opposition to the Spanish-American War, and who now opposed America's entry into World War I. Johnson bribed chauffeurs and door attendants who testified that Hearst regularly received subversives at his home on Riverside Drive. Chief among these guests was one Bolo Pasha, a Frenchman by birth, known as publisher of the Paris-based *Le Journal* and as Germany's most vigorous propagandist. (Pasha was later executed by the French government for treason.) Several times, Johnson swore in his report, Pasha had been accompanied to the Hearst residence by the German ambassador, Count von Bernstorff.

Hearst fired back in 1918 with a call to his friend, Senator James Reed of Missouri, who headed the Judiciary Committee of the U.S. Senate. In the course of Reed's hearings, it became clear that a string of so-called "counter-espionage projects" had escalated into a domestic terror campaign. A prime example of the mercenaries drawing U.S. government paychecks, Senator Reed declared, was one William Johnson. Reed passed around a deposition in which one of Johnson's colleagues related Johnson telling a room full of investigators, "We might as well finish this bastard Hearst once and for all."

Calling Deputy U.S. Attorney General Alfred Becker to the stand, Senator Reed said he understood Johnson wasn't even the man's real name. "Is the real name of this man Bill Johnson?" Reed demanded. "Or is it Philip Musica?"

"I decline to answer," Becker answered, glaring at the dais.

The senator opined, "If this man Musica, alias Johnson, was employed in this business, and is a convict and notorious criminal, it bears upon the good faith of this whole transaction." When Becker demurred, Senator Reed brought up the murder of Barnet Baff. "Was it not the theory of this man Musica, during the Baff case, that a man named Cohen was the murderer, and not the men seen by eyewitnesses? And Cohen was convicted and is now under sentence of death—is that true?"

"The theory that Cohen was the man was proved!" Becker nearly shouted.

"Musica was in touch with Cardinale, the man who put the blame on Cohen. You and Musica succeeded in getting Cohen convicted, and the original defendants went scot-free," came the senator's rapid-fire response.

"That is about 50 percent right," Becker groused. He admitted that Johnson had a criminal background as Philip Musica. But, Becker argued, "I became convinced he had repented of his sins. He is and for some time past has been the intimate associate of my family. I have seen in this man the coming to life of a beautiful spirit, which convinces me there is such a thing as reform.... There is no man in the world I trust more than Philip Musica. I am his friend, and I shall continue to be."

Philip Musica, Owner, U.S. Hair Company
Partner, Musica & Son

Joseph Cohen, erstwhile chicken puller and convicted murderer, avoided the fate of Hans Schmidt. Seven times Cohen faced the electric chair before he finally attained a pardon from Governor Nathan Miller in 1921. The chief witness against Cohen, Joseph Sorro, admitted to the governor that he had never known Cohen and never overheard Cohen hatching a murder plot. Sorro said he had only mouthed the story forced on him by an investigator named Bill Johnson.

Cohen returned to his home in Brooklyn, swearing revenge if he ever found the man who had made him look death in its black eyes so many times. Ten years later, on April 9, 1932, Cohen sat on his porch at 240 Westminster Road playing pinochle with his wife, Mina. While Cohen spread a winning hand across the card table, two masked men walked onto the porch, drew their guns and fired nine bullets into his astounded body. Nine days later, Cohen's brother Joseph, King of the Chicken Pullers, was gunned down on the street in Jamaica, Queens. No one was charged for either murder.

The history of the Poultry Wars was briefly recounted following the death of the Cohen brothers. The incident became a hot item again in 1938, when Dr. Frank Donald Coster of McKesson & Robbins shot himself in his bathroom. One of Coster's staff members, Bill Simon, was a former "chicken czar" in the Live Poultry Association, and had been involved in Harry Cohen's frame-up. After serving a two-year sentence for fraud, investigators learned, Simon had joined his friend Coster at McKesson & Robbins.

Like Coster, Ben Simon was known by many names. On the McKesson & Robbins payroll, he drew salaries as Harold Redmond, George Goulet, and L. Hartman. Simon fronted several companies—Simon Brothers, Rameses Inc., the Woodtone Company, and Liberty Drug & Chemical Company—that Coster used to divert McKesson & Robbins alcohol to bootleggers.

One time Simon even impersonated Philip Musica, the "real name" behind the string of aliases that led to Dr. Frank Donald Coster. When an old debtor sued Philip Musica in a New Orleans bankruptcy court, Simon caught a train south and settled the matter. Soon after, the *Times-Picayune* reported that Philip Musica had been killed in an auto accident.

If Ben Simon had a job title at McKesson & Robbins, it would've been *Biographical Valet.* Whenever Coster spotted Mary and Guiseppe Brandino loitering below the executive suite, he dispatched Simon. The Brandinos had not done well after Coster (as Frank Costa) deserted them. When President Roosevelt repealed Prohibition, Mary and Guiseppe were washed up completely. Without bootlegging, they were two aging thugs ravaged by gout and years of sipping their inventory. At the McKesson & Robbins gates, Mary and Guiseppe complained to Simon about their doctor bills, their past due rent, their lack of grocery money, their empty coal box, their broken down truck. They didn't ask for much, $50 or $100 at a time, but they kept coming back.

Ben Simon built the Dr. Coster identity. In August of 1928, Coster listed shares of McKesson & Robbins on the Big Board, hoping to raise $250 million. To do so, he had to make Frank Donald Coster bullet-proof to SEC investigators. Simon prepared an affidavit from one Adele Vinard, a midwife, whose address was given as 1840 Grand Concourse, the Bronx. (This was Simon's own residence.) Taking the train to Washington, D.C., Simon filed the necessary papers with the Bureau of Vital Statistics, and had a birth certificate prepared. According to the document, Frank Donald Coster was born in the nation's capital on May 12, 1884. His father, Anthony Coster, was a chemist. His mother, Marie Girard Coster, was a homemaker who, like her husband, had been born and raised in Baltimore, Maryland. The couple had no other children.

Who's Who in America for 1937 contained the following entry:

> **Coster, Frank Donald,** *corpn. official; b. Washington, D.C., May 12, 1884; s. Anthony and Marie (Girard) C.; Ph.D., U. Of Heidelberg, 1909, M.D., 1911; m. Carol Jenkins Schiefflin, of Jamaica, L.I., N.Y., May 1, 1921. Practicing physician, N.Y. City, 1912-14; pres. Girard & Co., Inc. (succession to Girard Chem Co.), 1914-*

> 26; also pres. McKesson & Robbins, Ltd.; dir. Bridgeport City
> Trust Co., Fairfield (Conn.) Trust Co. Methodist. Clubs: New
> York Yacht, bankers, Lotos, Advertising (New York); University,
> Black Rock Yacht (Bridgeport); Brooklawn Country. Home: Fair-
> field, Conn. Office: McKesson & Robbins, Inc., Bridgeport,
> Conn.

It was true that Coster headed McKesson & Robbins, and that he belonged to a lot of social clubs—which, incidentally, he rarely visited. Everything else was a lie. Girard & Company was formed in 1920, not 1914. Carol's first husband was named Edward Hubbard, not Schiefflin; she and Coster were married in 1926, not 1921. And, of course, the man had never practiced medicine, nor held any degrees from Heidelberg. Later, the red-faced editors of *Who's Who* declared, "This is the only instance—during nearly five decades of continuous publication involving over 77,000 biographees—of a fictitious biographee foisting himself" on the annual.

In the wake of Coster's suicide, police officers joined the editors of *Who's Who* to find the real story. Ben Simon agreed to help, hoping for a walk on the charges against him. It seems that Simon had filed more than one birth certificate that day in Washington, D.C. He had carried three others, in fact: one for George Dietrich, the assistant treasurer for McKesson & Robbins; one for Robert Dietrich, the director of shipping; and one for George Vernard, who ran W.W. Smith, a distribution firm linked to a McKesson & Robbins subsidiary in Canada. Each man was an imposter, Simon revealed to his crestfallen audience in December 1938. "They're all fakes."

George Dietrich was actually George Musica. Robert Dietrich was Robert Musica. George Vernard was born Arthur Musica. They were brothers. That December, they were mourning the death of their eldest brother, Philip Musica.

****

Philip Mariano Fausto Musica was born on May 12, 1884. With the aid of a midwife, he first drew air in a cramped set of rooms shared with two other families at 377 Broome Street, on the Lower East Side of Manhattan. His mother, Assunta Mauro Musica, greeted her firstborn as a sign, if not from God, at least from the gods of circumstance, that her life would get better.

Mama Assunta, who eventually had four boys and four girls, stood a little more than four feet tall and weighed 300 pounds. In

Naples, she had married Antonio Musica only after he'd spent several years wooing her. Antonio, who was 12 years older than the teenage Assunta, was a barber by trade. Assunta meant to have more. Before she mouthed one syllable of her wedding vows, she told Antonio, "Show me the tickets to America." He would become a businessman there, Antonio agreed. No one, Assunta told her doting husband, ever got rich clipping hair and shaving men's chins.

As a teenager, Philip Musica stood five feet eight. He was described as plump, an inheritance from Mama Assunta, though he never quite crossed the line into fat. He kept his hair short and patted it down with his father's finest oils. Mama Assunta pointed out to neighbors how her oldest boy, with his prominent jawline and cocoa-colored eyes, emitted a natural air of aristocracy. To the neighbors, the boy's constantly wide eyes made him look surprised all the time.

Philip could be forgiven for a skittish nature, given his surroundings. Mulberry Bend, so named for a plow-like kink in Mulberry Street, hosted New York City's most vicious criminal gangs. According to *Nooks and Corners of Old New York,* "In this slum block the houses were three deep in places with scarcely the suggestion of a courtyard between them. Narrow alleys, hardly wide enough to permit the passage of a man, led between houses to beer cellars, stables and tumble-down tenements. Obscure passageways honeycombed the entire block—ways that lead beneath houses, over low sheds, through fragments of wall—ways that were known only to the thief and the tramp. There 'Bottle Alley,' 'Bandit's Roost' and 'Ragpicker's Row' were the scenes of many wild fights, and many a time the ready stiletto ended the lives of men, or the heavy club dashed out the brains."

Mulberry Bend's dark filthy streets were ruled by gangs: the *Dead Rabbits*, the *Slaughterhouse Gang*, the *Plug Uglies* (who filled their giant plug hats with rags and straw to protect them in battle), and the most vicious gang in the Five Points grid, the *Whyos*. Women scrapped right alongside their men in these quarters. At a saloon called The Morgue, the story was told how "Gentle Maggie" fought "Lizzie the Dove" for the affections of a Whyo leader who didn't care piss for either of them. After nearly an hour's struggle, Maggie rammed a knife in Lizzie's throat and settled the dispute.

Assunta cursed her husband for bringing her to this sewer. As she gave birth to one, two, three, four, five, six, seven, eight children, she cursed more furiously. It was only thanks to the dowry Assunta brought to the marriage, combined with the pittance Antonio saved at his barbershop, that the Musicas at last opened a small shop, selling pasta, sausages and dried fruit imported from the Continent. Antonio continued to cut hair on the side, while 14-year-old Philip, following Mama's orders, dropped out of school to run A. Musica & Son.

In 1901, as A. Musica & Son began to boost the family cash flow, Assunta moved her brood to a modest home in the Bay Ridge section of Brooklyn. Assunta began coaching Philip on how to branch out from shopkeeping into wholesaling. The cheese-and-sausage shop was located at 25 Water Street, within walking distance of the East River docks. Philip gradually made contacts on the waterfront that allowed him to import his own goods and sell to other retailers. By 1909, Philip's brothers George and Arthur ran the shop on Water Street, while Philip tended the wholesaling concern.

Late that year, waterfront detectives found that Philip had been bribing cheese inspectors, persuading them to write down his cheese at half its actual weight. Since cheese was taxed by the pound, the bribes allowed Philip to clear 2-1/2 cents a pound on his inventory, while his law-abiding compadres struggled to make a half-cent a pound. Philip was also keeping two sets of books, another technique he learned from Mama Assunta. One ledger accurately reflected his inventory, and one matched the falsified records of the shipping docks.

Philip told the anti-corruption task force, "I acted alone. My father and brothers knew nothing of my arrangements with dock inspectors." No one asked about Assunta. The court sent Philip, now 25 years old, to the Elmira Reformatory. He won a job in the warden's house by convincing his captors he held a degree in accounting. Philip's supervisor praised him as "bright, alert, aggressive, and sure of himself on all occasions."

Five months and 15 days into his sentence, Philip was suddenly, unexpectedly pardoned. The order came from William Howard Taft, President of the United States. No one in the New York system had seen this coming. U.S. Attorney Henry Wise protested:

> *Musica was sentenced to one year and has not served half that. The regular practice of the Justice Department, when an application for pardon is presented, is to refer the application to the prosecutor for his comment and recommendations. This young man, however, had sufficient influence to bypass this usual procedure. I declare the whole performance a travesty.*

It was rumored that the Italian ambassador had personally called the White House and secured Philip's release. To this day, it's not clear why men in such high positions concerned themselves with a small-time importer of Gorgonzola cheese and olive oil. But Philip had received the first of several favors from the U.S. government.

****

Philip next became involved in human hair. As they had since the end of the 19th century, most fashionable women in 1910 wore pompadoured hair styles, elaborately coiffed and supplemented by extensions known as *rats*. Italy, along with China, supplied most of the raw material for these creations. Despite her antipathy for Antonio's barbering, Assunta Musica argued that hair was the family's next big thing. Macaronis sold at A. Musica & Son for 16 cents a pound, she lectured. Good hair brought $80 a pound.

Mama Assunta took her youngest boy, Robert, and her four girls to Naples, where she held court with select Italian businessmen. In the space of a year, she'd raised more than $1 million (an impressive sum in 1910). U.S. Hair began trading on the New York Curb Exchange 18 months later. The company was capitalized at $2 million, with more than $600,000 in hair assets. From his headquarters on 67 Front Street, Philip managed satellite offices in London, Berlin, St. Petersburg, Hong Kong, and Yokohama. The family bought an estate in Bay Ridge, Brooklyn, complete with servants' quarters and stables in the rear.

Philip Musica, meanwhile, became *Phil*, a frequenter of Broadway shows and the Metropolitan Opera House. Phil kept his hands manicured, his hair pomaded, and his neck well-powdered. He dressed in the finest hand-sewn suits, checking to see that the spats on his shoes matched the clothes. Phil attended the gayest uptown soirées, and held standing reservations at the Waldorf's Peacock Alley, Rector's, and Delmonico's. He kept a room at the family's Bay Ridge compound but slept most nights in a king-sized bed at the Knickerbocker Hotel.

Phil's dreams of the swell life were dashed when U.S. Hair stock got sucked into a sell-off by rogue members of a Wall Street investment pool. The sudden attention got regulators asking about the firm's robust growth. From a few thousand dollars at its founding, U.S. Hair had become a $3-million corporation in just over two years' time.

Philip talked a lot about volume and resale arrangements. He asked the regulators to let him move the nine cases of hair currently sitting dockside on the ship *Germania*. The regulators said they'd need to inspect the cargo first. Inside each of the long wooden crates, the regulators found a layer of hair, far inferior to what the paperwork described; below that, barbershop sweepings and wads of newspaper.

Like most of U.S. Hair's business, the *Germania* cargo was faked. Philip and Assunta had used the phony shipments as a front for U.S. Hair's main function—laundering money through its fleet of international offices.

When federal deputies raided 67 Front Street early the following morning, they found the U.S. Hair offices deserted. No one had thought to dispatch a deputy to the Musica estate in Bay Ridge. When the delegation finally arrived, they found the place ransacked, all the furniture removed along with the paintings, rugs, linens, and silverware. The Musicas had even torn the velvet drapes from the windows.

Philip led the family—his brothers, George and Robert; two sisters, Louise and Lucy Grace; and a weary Papa Antonio—on a spectacular getaway. (Mama Assunta stayed in touch by telegram from Naples.) From Long Island they caught a train to Washington, D.C., and from there, they traveled in pairs to Atlanta.

Meanwhile a private detective named William Burns, hired by the American Bankers Association, was canvassing greater New York City. At the Knickerbocker Hotel, Burns talked with a valet who said he'd sold Phil a $12 trunk for $50 a week or so before. With a description of the trunk, Burns tracked his prey from the Long Island depot to Atlanta. Next stop: Mobile, Alabama, where a conductor had seen six people matching the Musica description as they left the train.

Burns arrived in Mobile only to find that the telltale trunk had gone back to Atlanta. He lost another day riding the train back up the coast, only to find the trunk had not been claimed in Atlanta. Sensing he'd just been played, Burns took a hammer to the trunk's latch and discovered...wads of newspaper.

The trail went cold. For several days Burns sat in an Atlanta hotel, wiring cities up and down the Gulf Coast. The dragnet eventually turned up a telegram, addressed "Assunta," cabled just before noon the day before, from the Hotel DeSoto on Canal Street, New Orleans, Louisiana.

> *DID YOU HIDE PISELLI [a code name for money]? SUSPEND*
> *COMMUNICATIONS. POLICEMEN ARE FOLLOWING*

ARRESTING US. LOOK OUT. BE CAREFUL. PROTECT YOURSELF.

A check of the shipping news showed only one southbound passenger ship in the next few days, the *Heredia*, sailing for Colón, Panama. Burns allowed the family to board the *Heredia*. Then, accompanied by New Orleans deputies and shipping authorities, he had the group ushered to the upper deck. Philip walked at the fore of the line, expressionless. He was professing complete ignorance as to why he, "William Weeks," ought to be rousted in such a manner, when his sister Lucy Grace ran toward the ship's railing. From beneath her blouse, she yanked a brown paper bag. She was heaving the package over the railing when a detective caught her hand.

"It's mine! It's all mine! Every cent of it!" Lucy Grace wailed. The detective found the package held $18,600 in large bills, mainly in $1,000 and $5,000 notes. Immediately Burns ordered the rest of the family patted down. He found Arthur Musica holding $50,000, partly American currency, partly Mexican. Both Lucy Grace and Louise Musica were carrying jewels, worth some $12,000. Neither George Musica nor Papa Antonio had anything but pocket change. The big score, of course, came from frisking Philip, who clutched an $8,000 uncut diamond in his coat pocket and $250,000 worth of insurance policies inside his vest.

What the friskers missed was Philip's pearl-handled revolver, the sort of thing you might expect to find on a riverboat gambler. Papa Antonio, sweating and shaking, jerked the gun from inside his son's coat and swept the circle of cops.

"I won't give up! I won't give up!" Antonio cried, holding the little pistol with both hands, sweeping its muzzle at the agents and his children.

Philip snatched the gun and put it to his own head. "Back off!" he warned. "I'll kill myself!" In careful language, as if they were all perched around a conference table, Philip explained, "The embarrassment we find ourselves in was due to the failure of three large human-hair exporting and importing firms—two in France and one in England. We intended remaining away until such time as matters could be adjusted."

The Great Human Hair Swindle marked a turning point in Philip's life. Antonio Musica suffered a heart attack as he was led into The Tombs prison and died a few months later in a state hospital. As he'd done in the Cheese Fraud, Philip claimed sole responsibility for the Great Human Hair Swindle. He couldn't say what had happened to the assets of U.S. Hair, or to the $600,000 he owed 22 banks, and he had no inkling about the destination of $209,000 he had dispatched to Naples just before the family went on the lam.

But Philip Musica had friends, and he suggested to his captors that he could make others. In exchange for letting Mama Assunta return with the rest of her children to the Bay Ridge estate in Brooklyn, Philip became a prison informant for the New York District Attorney's office.

He was never charged with a crime. But for three years Philip lived day and night in a dungeon called The Tombs, second only to Sing Sing as the most brutal prison in the East. A former inmate described how The Tombs got its name:

> *All the windows were 30 feet high, and you could not see out of them because they were made of non-transparent glass running from the bottom floor clear to the top of the building. Bars ran straight up, then across every few feet like a ladder. You could only look toward the window and see the sunlight filter through or watch the sun fade and the dark of night appear.*

In The Tombs, Philip Musica met Dutch Schulz and other future bootlegging legends, as well as small-timers like Guiseppe Brandino. Every so often, when the D.A.'s office needed info, Philip was led from The Tombs through an enclosed passageway connected to police headquarters on Centre Street.

"The astonishing thing is that he wasn't killed," said an assistant D.A. "A lot of men in The Tombs knew what he was up to and wouldn't talk to him, but he kept ingratiating himself with new inmates. There was a wave of silk-robbery cases in those days. Musica would suddenly show up with the names of the girlfriends of truck drivers who were being held, or with the identities of missing drivers, and before we knew it, we'd have broken another case. He was very helpful about telling us what sort of defense a man was going to put up, too."

Philip's relations with his captors were almost homey. The assistant D.A. recalled, "Judge Delehanty, who was supposed to sentence Musica, kept asking me, 'When are we going to get rid of this Musica fellow?' and I kept saying that there was no hurry, that he was being useful. As long as Musica was happy in The Tombs, it was all right with us."

The Short, Happy Life of Philip Musica
a.k.a. Dr. Coster, President, McKesson & Robbins

Julian Thompson noticed that whenever a McKesson & Robbins group did business in New York City, Dr. Coster walked a few steps behind. "At first we thought he was being standoffish, or just plain rude. Then we guessed he was absent-minded, or thinking of something else. He seemed to be absorbed in his thoughts. Often he was turning over a problem in his mind, or preparing the remarks he'd make at the meeting later." Actually, Coster was looking out for someone who might recognize the former president of U.S. Hair.

When Frank Coster set his sights on the McKesson & Robbins company, the wisdom of the move was not immediately apparent. The company dated to 1835, when Daniel Robbins partnered with John McKesson, who had opened his first drug store on Maiden Lane just two years before. By the spring of 1926, McKesson & Robbins was feeling its age. A single factory in Brooklyn employed 50 people. Its biggest seller was tooth powder. The McKesson family had pulled out of the operation a year earlier, taking a wad of cash and leaving the remains to Herbert Robbins, a grandson of co-founder Daniel Robbins.

The nugget Coster saw in McKesson & Robbins was its reputation among independent druggists, hundreds of businesspeople in small towns who owned their own stores and who were being crushed by chains like Walgreen's. Coster outlined for Julian Thompson his plan to organize the independents under the McKesson & Robbins umbrella. "We tell them the truth: either be swallowed up by Walgreen's or Liggett's, or ally with us and survive."

"A refurbished McKesson & Robbins factory will turn out a range of new products," Thompson told the wholesalers, "supplementing your own brands. Plus, a wholesaler in the alliance can replenish a low inventory or expand its product lines by activating the share agreements with other stores in the McKesson & Robbins alliance." The pitch almost sounded patriotic—instead of being colonized by imperialist chain stores, the independents could band together, forming a more perfect and lucrative union.

The independent owners exchanged their private, family-owned stock for stock in the McKesson & Robbins corporation. The owners of each house became salaried vice presidents of the parent company. To ally with McKesson & Robbins meant, in effect, being acquired by them, but that didn't appear to disturb the owners at the time. Dr. Coster and Julian Thompson raised $36 million in stocks and bonds for the alliance. In the first year, 15 wholesalers signed on. By 1929, the McKesson & Robbins umbrella covered 66 regional wholesalers, posting $140 million in annual sales.

Still, Coster supplemented the McKesson & Robbins financial statement by providing Dutch Schulz and other bootleggers with fresh products. Cleaning tincture of iodine was almost as easy as boiling water. Drivers in trucks marked "W.W. Smith" backed up to the McKesson & Robbins docks, acquired 50 barrels of tincture of iodine, and carried the load to a warehouse across town. In a matter of hours, the violet vapors of the iodine were driven off, yielding "imported cognac," "Jamaica rum," and "premium Scotch."

More cleverly, Coster and his brothers, shielded with bulletproof aliases, established a phantom arm of the McKesson & Robbins corporation. McKesson & Robbins Canada, chartered in October 1927, became Coster's "pet project." It was a boutique operation, controlled solely by the Brothers Musica, that dealt in "crude drugs," that is, the raw materials used to manufacture a retail pharmaceutical.

Dr. Frank Coster impressed the Fairfield board with his knowledge of crude-drug staples like Spanish saffron and balsam of Peru; an array of oils including dillseed, orange, peppermint, lime, ginger, juniper, geranium rose, sandalwood, and lavender; and other exotics like dragon's-blood, powder bright, Mexican vanilla beans, and benzoin of Siam. "Now is certainly the time to send someone to Chile to look into iodine," Coster told the board, because the Chilean iodine trust was throttling its American competitors with a cheaper product.

A board member later pleaded that Coster's ruse was impenetrable. "He seemed to know what he was talking about. The books balanced and showed a profit. We're talking about $20 million here. He'd have had to have an entire underground operation to simulate that much business."

He did. Say, for example, Dr. Coster mentioned during a board meeting that McKesson & Robbins Canada had spotted an opportunity in Mexican vanilla beans. George (Musica) Dietrich scanned the markets for quotations on vanilla beans, chose a price and a selling company, and told his brother Robert (Musica) Dietrich to place the order on behalf of McKesson & Robbins Canada. Robert, lead buyer in the Fairfield shipping division, supervised the nuts and bolts of each crude-drug transaction. Then, with the aid of a satellite printing office in nearby Stamford, Robert assembled documents for three separate companies. Not one gram of dragon's-blood ever changed hands, though. The massive bins of vanilla beans and the barrels of iodine existed only on paper and only in the fervid imagination of Philip Musica, Dr. Coster.

To satisfy any curious eyes, both W.W. Smith and the Manning Bank had offices in Brooklyn, at 1 Hanson Place. The companies shared the space and employed a pretty, young receptionist who sat in the immense lobby between the matching suites and gabbed to her friends all day on the phone. The executive office was occupied by George Vernard (née Arthur Musica), who did even less. Because his brothers kept him at arm's length, Vernard spent most of his time down the street from 1 Hanson Place at a bar called Jack's. In the early days of the fraud, Vernard handled the correspondence among the various sham companies. However, his drinking rendered him increasingly unreliable, so Vernard was cut out of the loop entirely. Occasionally he signed a voucher or a letter, but mostly he sat in the Brooklyn storefront and he drank at Jack's.

The "main" offices of W.W. Smith and Manning Bank were located in Montreal, Canada, 1396 St. Catherine Street West. Violet Quesnot, a petite, middle-aged brunette, earned $27 a week for her "secretarial services." Primarily she devised ways to keep from going mad. "I sit here waiting for a letter to come so I can send it on to someone else," Quesnot told investigators. Once in a great while, George Vernard (Arthur Musica) showed up at the Montreal office, but Quesnot said, "He never did any work, or held a meeting, or anything businesslike. He'd call back and forth to Brooklyn, some place called Jack's Bar, then excuse himself. I was relieved when he left."

Just down the street from the Manning Bank, 18-year-old Betty Whyte handled correspondence for W.W. Smith, which meant forwarding two letters a month to Brooklyn on behalf of the Montreal concern. Each day at noon, Betty Whyte walked the few blocks to the Manning Bank and sat at Violet Quesnot's desk while her boss took lunch. On December 2, 1938, Quesnot told her junior colleague they'd received their strangest orders yet. Vernard had called and instructed them to burn all the records in both offices. He didn't say why and Violet didn't ask. With permission from the building superintendent, the women dumped 11 years of W.W. Smith files into the basement furnace.

****

In 1937, McKesson & Robbins sales topped $174 million, for earnings of $3.6 million. Coster had weathered the Great Depression, thanks to his bootlegging and crude-drug operations. He had consolidated independent wholesalers and retailers into a mighty distribution network. He had been crowned a potentate of American business and courted for the Presidency. And it was all about to explode.

The bootlegging took care of itself. Anticipating that Prohibition couldn't last, Coster began setting up a liquor subsidiary of McKesson & Robbins in 1931. As Franklin Delano Roosevelt was announcing the repeal of the Volstead Act in 1933, Coster's trucks were already pulling away from the docks.

The notorious Dutch Schulz (born Arthur Flegenheimer) had moved the headquarters of his liquor and gambling racket to Bridgeport, Connecticut, not far from the Coster residence on Mill Plain Road in Fairfield. Schulz claimed he wanted to be near "influential friends in the area, men who carry a lot of weight even in Washington." He was gunned down by assassins in October 1935 while he was finishing dinner at the Palace Chop House in Newark, New Jersey. Two of the killers sprayed a torrent of revolver fire while two others blasted with 12-gauge shotguns.

Though his bodyguards died instantly, Schulz himself held on for 22 hours, talking out of his head in the grips of a 106-degree fever. Federal agents huddled around Schulz's bed, transcribing every syllable and grunt into a stenographer's notebook. Among the utterances: "Now listen, Phil, fun is fun," and "George, don't make no fool moves." At the time, no one knew who Dutch was talking about. Three years later, it became apparent he was addressing his friends, Philip and George Musica.

Schulz and his ilk were doomed; in the years following the Volstead repeal, they were all either jailed or killed. If a few smalltimers like the Brandinos hung around, they were easily hushed with a few bucks and a bag of groceries. Coster's transition from the bootlegging business to legitimate business couldn't have gone smoother.

Not so for Dr. Coster's "pet project" at McKesson & Robbins Canada. The Fairfield board voted in 1937 to institute a cost-cutting program. Julian Thompson had settled into his job as treasurer by this time, after a rollercoaster decade in which he'd made and lost a fortune in the stock market, authored a hit play for the Broadway stage, and played the good lieutenant for Dr. Coster. Each time Thompson asked Coster about the crude-drug operation in Canada, Coster brushed him off. But the ledgers showed McKesson & Robbins Canada holding $18 million worth of drug inventory, besides another $1 million in accounts receivable. Digging through the subsidiary's history, Thompson saw a steady profit of ten percent a year, but he noted that all those profits had remained in Canada. It only made sense to bring some of that largesse into the parent company.

In March 1938, Thompson was working on the annual report when he saw that McKesson & Robbins Canada had not reduced its inventory by $1 million, as the board had ordered the year before, but had, in fact, added $1 million worth of products. Coster said they'd deal with the issue after the annual report. When the annual report was done, Coster said let's wait until the fall.

Thompson was already curious, but now he was becoming furious. A Dun & Bradstreet report on McKesson & Robbins Canada described the facility as "a small space for the use of persons traveling from Liverpool." Though W.W. Smith had satellites in Brooklyn and Montreal, apparently its "real" headquarters was in England. But when Thompson called the Liverpool number, a secretary directed him to W.W. Smith's Montreal office. "There was no business done at those addresses that amounted to anything," Thompson concluded.

He was struggling with his conscience and his heart. "I felt that if I went to the president with a suspicion but with no knowledge and he just explained the whole thing to me, I would either have to accept it or say, 'I think you are lying to me.' I could not prove he was lying to me, and I decided that the thing for me to do was just inform myself outside in every way I possibly could.... My responsibility to the stockholders was simply tremendous if anything was wrong. I had helped put the thing together. I had helped sell securities in the beginning. It was inconceivable to me that there wouldn't be any assets. Mr. Coster was, in my opinion, too intelligent and too capable a man ever to let himself get into a position where he'd falsify books.... So I said to myself, 'There must be some assets there. For some reason that I don't know, he's kept this from me and masked this thing.'"

Thompson kept digging, but the things he found smelled worse all the time. Company records showed that the commission checks paid to W.W. Smith were by the McKesson & Robbins treasury in Fairfield. That meant that the subsidiary was not only withholding its profits from the parent company, it was billing the parent company for commissions. "I have enough evidence," Thompson decided. "I have to do something immediately."

When Thompson arrived at the Coster home with the D&B report and the other documents in hand, Coster promised a full disclosure at the earliest possible date. Coster then changed the subject to a major bond issue he was trying to float, a move requiring the treasurer's approval. "I left with the feeling I had been stalled," Thompson said. He and Coster agreed to meet for lunch the next day in New York.

Thompson came to the point as soon as he and Coster were seated in the restaurant. He thought Coster was intentionally holding back information. Why?

"I'm trying to smoke you out," Coster said.

"What do you mean?" Thompson asked.

"There's something back of this. It must be a conspiracy of people in the New York office or something." Coster was thinking of a consultant's report issued through the New York office in 1934 which had concluded, "There is no place in the future of this corporation for Frank Donald Coster."

Thompson retorted, "There *is* a conspiracy in the New York office. In fact, it's right in your treasurer—namely, me—and I will let you smoke me out."

"What's the matter?" Coster asked with his not-quite-a-grin. "Do you think there are no assets in Canada?"

"You're too smart not to have assets. But I must know what they are."

Thompson was crestfallen but he argued with himself, "This is all negative information, not proof positive. Coster has set up a screen to hide something, some other sort of business."

Coster skipped their next appointment, begging off with a chronic sore throat. On Tuesday the 29th of November, 1938, Thompson returned to Coster's home. Anyone could see, and hear, that Coster really was a sick man. He was dressed in a wrinkled shirt and slacks, no belt. His voice crackled as he wheezed a few words at a time. Thompson moved straight to the point: along with W.W. Smith and the Manning Bank, McKesson & Robbins Canada was bleeding the parent company for cash while hoarding millions in unverified assets.

"There is something wrong here," Coster consented, adding in his scratchy whisper, "something wrong at Dun & Bradstreet."

Thompson disagreed.

"What do you want, Thompson?" Coster asked.

"I want to visit the Canadian subsidiary."

Coster suggested that Thompson write down his questions, and the answers would be obtained directly. Thompson refused.

"If you've got such anxieties about the functioning of this company, perhaps you should step down as treasurer," Coster whispered.

"I prefer to have my concerns addressed."

"If you do anything to wreck the credit of McKesson & Robbins, you are going to regret it."

Thompson didn't reply. He couldn't figure out what Coster was getting at.

"If you're not careful, I'll throw the company into receivership myself and wipe out the common stockholders."

"You're the biggest common stockholder," Thompson reminded his boss, who held ten percent of the common stock. "You'd be the greatest sufferer." A silence fell between them, during which both men wished for a way to turn back their clocks.

Thompson said at last, "I have to personally verify the Canadian assets."

Coster's voice popped and wheezed like a busted radio. "If you refuse to take my word, you are calling me a liar. That's enough. I demand your resignation immediately. Now. Before you leave this house."

On Monday, December 5, Thompson was gathered in consultation with members of the McKesson & Robbins board when the group learned that Coster had been true to his word for once—he'd put McKesson & Robbins into receivership. The gates of the factory were chained; all bank accounts were frozen; all records were impounded.

On Tuesday Coster appeared at his office for the first time in a week. He had a clerk fetch him a bottle of Martin's V.O. Scotch from the warehouse and he opened the day with a stout glass. Unfortunately, there was no business for Coster to do. The receivers had everything under guard. Coster sat at his desk, glaring at the clerks, accountants, and attorneys scurrying past his door. "He was just sitting there, doing nothing," Julian Thompson observed. "No one spoke to him and he didn't speak to anybody."

The receivers were busy grilling Albert Ritts, a senior accountant at Price, Waterhouse, about the inventory of McKesson & Robbins Canada. Ritts, who'd led the audit team since Coster took the company over, explained that corporate auditors didn't inspect inventories, and they didn't verify sales. "Accountants are not competent to judge physical inventory," Ritts maintained. "They could show me a barrel of drugs and say it was thus and so, but I wouldn't know."

You didn't need a degree in pharmacy to see that McKesson & Robbins Canada was a sham. For example, the company owned very little warehouse space. An SEC investigator said, "We figured if they'd really had everything on hand that they claimed they had, they'd have needed a couple of buildings the size of the Empire State to hold it all." Coster's supply of ketone musk, which is a perfume fixative derived from a gland in the Himalyan musk deer, exceeded the combined lifetime production of every deer in Asia. With a passing knowledge of crude drugs, or for the price of a cursory consultation, the auditors could have spotted the exaggerations. George Vernard's sloppy paperwork offered other clues. Invoices listed shipments to absurd addresses like *Ceylon, Asia; Bavaria, Germany; and Tasmania, Australia.*

The Accounting Standards Board decided, in the wake of Coster's debacle, that all corporate auditors ought to physically verify the inventories they certified. This landmark decision promised a new era of corporate accountability.

Over the next week, a dozen federal, state and local agencies launched investigations into McKesson & Robbins. Coster's gig was up. He was arrested at his home in Fairfield on Wednesday, December 14. Though he was fingerprinted and photographed by federal agents, Coster wasn't taken into custody. While the dejected entrepreneur stood with a brown bathrobe over his trousers and shirt, his lawyer paid the $5,000 bail. Coster was told that George and Robert Dietrich had also been charged.

As the law enforcement retinue motored down the Coster driveway, Irving Kauffman, a young assistant U.S. Attorney, remarked, "That man has a weird look in his eye. He'll either die a natural death or kill himself before this is over."

Two days later, Kauffman's prediction came true. Dr. Coster's glasses fell into the sink, and Philip Musica was unmasked. The McKesson & Robbins board had gathered on the afternoon of December 16 and had just voted to fire Coster when a messenger burst in with news of the suicide. "Let's fire him anyway, for his sins," suggested director Sidney Weinberg of Goldman, Sachs. When it was revealed that Coster was only one of the president's several identities, a board member suggested that "perhaps he couldn't face the Musica."

Philip's brothers pled guilty to the charges against them. George was sentenced to two and a half years in prison, Robert to a year and a half, Arthur to three. Ben Simon, the biographical valet who maintained Coster's cover for a decade, was sentenced to three years after his guilty plea.

Julian Thompson, devastated by Coster's deceitfulness and by his unwitting complicity in the scheme, seemed to sleepwalk through the aftermath. He spent long days testifying before boards, special investigators, and judges. He sometimes spent entire nights weeping. Though no one ever suggested that Thompson was in on the fix, he saw himself as a fraud. He caught a cold in mid-April 1939 that straight away escalated into pneumonia. On the 29th of April, some four months after Coster put a bullet in his brain, Julian Thompson suffered a respiratory arrest and died in his home.

****

In a four-page letter, scrawled in frenetic handwriting, Philip Musica/Dr. Coster defended the McKesson & Robbins fraud.

> *If profits hadn't been maintained since 1929, the bankers and lawyers who wanted to milk the company through receivership would have succeeded. I tried to stop them. Let the world judge if the bankers, lawyers, auditors, and appraisers who got millions out of the company knew nothing....*

> *I was making a desperate effort to salvage something out of the wreck. All of a sudden the treasurer and inside shooters started a secret investigation...and ran to cover, making me and my underlings the goats and bringing shame and humiliation to my poor loving wife who was ignorant of the conditions.*

> *My poor wife is the innocent victim of my frantic operations to hold up this concern of McKesson's. My brother-in-law, Leonard Jenkins, did as I asked because he thought it was right and proper to do so and he trusted me. He received no material reward. George and Robert Dietrich took orders.*

Finally, Philip Musica/Dr. Coster summed up a wretched lifetime with an oath and a prayer:

> *As God is my judge, I am the victim of Wall Street plunder and blackmail in a struggle for honest existence.... Oh, merciful God, bring the truth to light.*

Stanley Goldblum

(1927 -)

CHAPTER 5

The Strong Man:
Stanley Goldblum

"To examine the causes of life, we must first have recourse to death."
—*Viktor Frankenstein*

Gordon McCormick had this Amazing Big Idea. In the summer of 1958, he was crammed into a booth at The Hut, a diner off the Santa Monica Freeway, telling a circle of life insurance salesmen he was going to change their lives. Gordon called his idea the "Equity Funding Concept." The salesmen were all ears. Their coffee sat cold on the tabletop and their cigarettes smoldered, unpuffed, while Gordon explained Equity Funding.

"Your life insurance policy pays three cents on the dollar every year," he said slowly, as if he were teaching schoolkids one-plus-one. "Three percent a year, that barely keeps pace with inflation. Some years, if inflation is four percent, and your policy pays three percent, you fall behind. The best years, you're just breaking even.

"Now invest that same money in a mutual fund, you draw eight or nine percent interest a year, triple what the life insurance offers. Nevertheless customers don't want to turn loose of their life insurance policy. It's like a security blanket for 'em to hold onto."

Gordon showed the men at The Hut how to get at people's life insurance money without disturbing the security blanket. "You have them move the cash value of their life insurance into a mutual fund. Then they borrow against the mutual fund to continue paying their life insurance premiums. The interest on the loan is covered by the three-percent annual returns of the life insurance policy. The nine or ten percent profit on the mutual fund makes the exchange worthwhile.

"You guys," Gordon McCormick told the salesmen, "draw double commissions, one on the mutual fund investment, and one on the life insurance policy."

"Won't the mutual fund charge management fees?" a man at the edge of the crowded booth asked. "Yeah," said another, "and there's still inflation." A third man carped, "What if the mutual fund dips? Maybe it only returns five percent. With the commission, fees, and inflation, the customer won't be any better off than when he just had the life insurance policy."

"Yes, but you'll be rich," Gordon pointed out, and everyone nodded, smiled, and headed for his car.

Assembling the Cast

Actually Gordon McCormick was one of many life insurance agents in the '50s who realized a mutual fund account could generate enough profits to pay for a life insurance policy and still have money left over. The agents didn't have a choice. Mutual funds were claiming a bigger share of Americans' savings every year, some $17 billion by 1958, much of it transferred out of life insurance policies.

To fight lagging sales, insurance companies offered sign-up promotionals. "Pay ten percent down today, and you pay no premiums for the first year. You pick up with your regular monthly payments the second year." The customer gave the salesperson a check for $20, against a $200 yearly premium. Back at the office, the salesperson collected a handsome commission—the first year's premium, plus ten percent, or $220.

By passing up $180 in income and paying out $220 in commission up front, the insurance company began the relationship with its new customer $400 in the hole. When the second year rolled around, about half these policies turned into "fence posts," i.e., the customer didn't renew the policy. The company got screwed while the salesperson—who wasn't above pointing out to a customer he'd never have to make that second year's payments—happily continued planting fence posts up and down America's brand-new interstate highways.

Another trick was known as "twisting" the customer. Targeting someone insured by a rival company, the salesperson offered a big discount, or the first year's premiums free—some enticement or another. Maybe the customer dropped out soon after signing—

twisted by a second salesperson, perhaps, the way some people jump phone companies today. The salesperson didn't care. He had his commission and the company wouldn't catch on for a while.

Fence-posting and twisting by insiders, combined with the damage inflicted by mutual funds, were threatening to topple the life insurance industry. Gordon McCormick and a few others suggested the way to beat mutual funds was to join them. Gordon was no rambler, though. He was a businessman at heart, and on March 31, 1960, he formed the Equity Funding Corporation.

Starting in modest offices on Wilshire Boulevard, Gordon turned his Amazing Big Idea into a phenomenon. First, he established a base in San Francisco by partnering with Ray Platt, a man known for two things: an unslakeable thirst for whiskey, and a knack for wielding his drunkenness in the service of a deal. Ray told his clients, "First, let's grab a *gazuguda*" (Ray's catch-all term for drinks) "and then we'll do business." He was the epitome of the cocktail era businessman, ready with a joke, a pitcher of martinis, and a pen to sign the contract.

As an Irish Dean Martin, Platt contrasted with the Equity Funding partner from Long Beach, California, a man named Eugene Cuthbertson. Gene had studied engineering at the University of Southern California, but he was drifting when he met Gordon McCormick. Thanks to his recent marriage into the Huntington Harbor set, Gene was testing the waters of the mutual fund industry. As he listened to Gordon talk, Gene's engineering mind warmed to the Equity Funding Concept: on the one hand, it was a straightforward use of financial instruments; on the other, the process depended on several disparate elements, including the rate of inflation, the stock market, and that mother of all variables, consumer confidence. To Gene, Equity Funding looked like the perfect marriage of the simple and the complex.

Gordon also recruited Stanley Goldblum into the Equity fold. Approaching 30, Stanley showed more promise than results. He'd sold insurance in the mid-'50s before launching a few private ventures that all failed. Stanley liked the insurance *industry*. But Stanley didn't like *selling* insurance. The typical agent subsisted on $5,000 or $10,000 policies, keeping a few hundred dollars for himself. Stanley preferred increments of $50,000 and $100,000.

"He was not the salesman type," a co-worker recalled. "To sell, you have to have a nice disposition and be able to ingratiate yourself. Goldblum was crisp, direct, and businesslike." Ralph Robbins, who partnered with Stanley for a short-lived foray into "executive planning," said, "He kept trying to generate capital. We'd have been better off if he had generated business."

A slight grin often played across Stanley's face. His eyes sparkled with curiosity, giving him an air of perpetual amusement. Standing 6' 2", Stanley liked to flex the shoulders of his big-man suits. Four afternoons a week you could find him at the Vic Tanny gym, lifting weights. On Saturdays, when he wore a sports shirt to the office, Stanley's forearms bulged from his sleeves. He was the Charles Atlas of the insurance world.

Stanley figured his strengths as a planner and motivator balanced any perceived weakness. Gordon McCormick, who wasn't so hot on the sales racket himself, acknowledged, "I trained Stanley, so I knew he wasn't a salesman. But he had a brilliant mind." Gordon put Stanley in charge of managing Equity Funding's sales force, which already numbered more than 1,000.

The Equity Funding Concept not only saved the life insurance industry, it provoked a boomlet in mutual funds, as people learned they didn't have to choose one means of saving over another. "I ought to be the number-one mutual fund salesman in this country," a voice on Gordon's phone said one bright afternoon in 1960, "but there's a guy on the West Coast who's beating me up." Mike Riordan was calling from Keystone Funding in Boston, where Equity Funding's high-dollar growth was commanding attention.

Gordon turned to Stanley Goldblum. "You remember Mike Riordan?"

Stanley had shaken hands with Mike Riordan a month before, when Mike dropped by Equity Funding's Wilshire headquarters. Stanley saw a man who expected to win and who therefore almost always won. No one drew more admiration in financial circles than Mike Riordan. Stanley heard that it took the long-jawed dealmaker an extra half-hour to get to his office every morning because so many people stopped him on the street to talk.

"Feel like a trip to New York?" Gordon asked when he hung up the phone. Mike Riordan wanted the Equity Funders to fly to New York and discuss a partnership. Stanley nodded and smiled.

Mike clicked with everyone at Equity Funding. Gordon admired the money swirling around the Riordan offices. Gene Cuthbertson was fascinated with the intricacies of the Keystone conglomerate. Stanley hit it off with Mike, too. When Mike took the group on a tour of New York City's entertainments, he and Stanley bookended the table.

Ray Platt made the scene by fulfilling the stereotype of the hard-drinking Irishman, a tradition Mike wasn't afraid to embrace himself. As the clock lolled past midnight, Mike burst into "Dream the Impossible Dream," the grandiloquent theme song from *Man of La Mancha*, a musical version of the Don Quixote story. Mike snatched off his clerk-style black glasses and swirled them in the air. His New York friends explained to the California guests this was Mike's signature song.

Mike would fight if he had to, but he preferred an alliance. "I can't figure how you're getting those numbers," he told Gordon. "Your second-year stats are beating everyone else by twice." Mike panted to know the secret. Gordon saw a chance to pull the East Coast into his territory.

Three months into his sojourn in New York, Stanley Goldblum was still training salespeople for Mike Riordan. The Equity Funding Concept was now owned by five men: Gordon McCormick, Ray Platt, Gene Cuthbertson, Stanley Goldblum, and Mike Riordan. Adding the East Coast people expanded the sales force to 2,500.

When they should've been toasting themselves, the partners were grousing. Gene thought they were growing too big too soon. Ray Platt hated living out of a New York hotel room. His drinking turned from social lubricant into high-octane resentment. Stanley nagged the others, telling them that Gordon wasn't playing fair. They'd all been promised shares in Equity Funding; instead, they'd received a few shares, far fewer than promised, in a holding company called Tongor Inc. (The title combined Tonya and Gordon McCormick's first names, Tonya being Mrs. McCormick.)

Over several late-evening dinners, Stanley whipped the others into a frenzy of suspicion. He showed them a stack of delinquent bills. "Gordon said these were paid. But he lied." Gordon had also sold stock to outsiders without telling his core group.

Smelling trouble, Gordon went to Mike Riordan. "Goldblum's trying to raise an attack against us," he complained. He murmured something about it being in Stanley's nature, meaning, *You have to watch those Jews*. Mike took offense, but he let the slur go. He pressed Gordon to settle the hubbub by giving everyone their fair shares. Gordon hemmed and hawed.

Stanley laid down a gauntlet. At Michael's Pub, which had become one of the Equity Funders' favorite New York hangouts, Stanley told Mike Riordan straight up, "You're Gordon's pigeon." Mike said that was ridiculous, but he knew it was time to fight or fly.

In a showdown at Equity Funding's temporary offices on 40 Wall Street, Gordon McCormick bellowed, "You're fired right now." He was pointing at Stanley, who stood near the doorway, shadowing the space with his frame and smiling, enjoying the spectacle.

Mike told Gordon to stop acting childish, but Gordon wouldn't relent. "You're a bunch of bastards," he griped, turning on the room. "Whatever else you do in life, you're not going to do it with me." He demanded the others buy him out. Since Gordon wouldn't accept a check, Mike agreed to pay cash for Gordon's share of the company, some $56,000 and change. Gordon counted the change.

Mike gave his brother, Bill Riordan, some astounding news in the spring of 1961. "I'm going to quit my job. I'm going out to California, and I'm going to make a hundred million dollars—and I'm going to make it with Jews. The only people who ever fucked me have been Gentiles. I've never been fucked by Jews."

****

First things first. The Securities and Exchange Commission decided in 1961 that yoking life insurance with mutual funds created a new product, one that henceforth needed to be registered with the SEC. So the Equity Funders sat out the next 18 months, waiting on the regulators' green light. The Equity Funding Corporation re-emerged in October 1963, leaping straight away into one of the most sustained growth spurts in history. Equity Funding shares were first offered to the public in 1964 at $6 a share.

In the interim, Stanley shed another partner. Ray Platt confessed, as the Equity Funders left New York in early 1961, he knew he'd gone too far with his drinking. Stanley agreed, adding that he was tired of Ray picking fights in the office. Ray said he'd be fine once they got back to L.A. Instead, he got worse—more belligerent and less reliable. A waking hour was cocktail hour. Ray made it to some meetings, he blew off others. He flew to Vegas and Tahoe a lot, where his losing streak was gaining momentum.

Stanley, Mike, and Gene gave Ray $51,000 for his stake in Equity Funding. A year later, Ray fell off a barstool at the Club Luau, clutching a half-full gazuguda with one hand, his chest with the other. The poor slob was dead of a heart attack at age 38.

Stanley said his conscience was clear. He'd done everything he could to help Ray. Now Gene Cuthbertson, Equity Funding's sad excuse for a sales manager, he was another matter. Gene's staid, overcautious style bugged Stanley. Stanley had once managed Equity's sales force himself and he didn't like sharing the house with a wimp. He pushed Gene constantly, lecturing how sales was no place for exercising restraint. Stanley needled Gene in meetings.

He mocked Gene's proposals, or he simply dismissed them—"It won't work"—and proceeded through the agenda.

Fed up, Gene demanded in October 1965 that Mike and Stanley buy him out. Gene netted $870,000 and counted himself lucky to be shut out of the Equity Funding Concept.

Five years into the company's life, just two founders remained. Mike Riordan lived on a spacious hillside estate in the Mandeville Canyon area of Brentwood. His voice pegged him as a New Yorker, but he moved gracefully in West Coast circles. Mike bounced between company mixers and community galas, racing down the Strip at 100 miles an hour before he pulled off to spend the rest of the night carousing with old football buddies. Among his celebrity friends Mike numbered comedian Jonathan Winters and the NFL's Vince Lombardi. Occasionally Mike found time for his wife Jackie and their two kids. But not that often.

Stanley Goldblum never kept pace with Mike's social exertions. Stanley liked to hang around "the house," a multi-dwelling affair in the Trousdale Estates of Beverly Hills. He lined the front and back walls of his poolhouse with beveled mirrors and populated the space with $100,000 worth of exercise machines. Entering the building you felt as if you'd stepped into a post-industrial torture chamber where the racks and pulleys gleamed.

"You live inside of your body," Stanley preached to his friend. "You should take care of your home." Mike asked what kept Stanley coming to the gym day after day, flexing rep after rep. Stanley said it was the same desire that kept him driving into Equity Funding every day: "To get big."

Stanley wasn't just a jock. Though infamously reticent and blunt, he had a romantic side. He'd dropped out of UCLA shortly after his 22nd birthday and married his girlfriend, Leah Cherry. For five years, Stanley labored in the Cherry family's Supreme Meat Packing Company. "I did everything," he boasted. "I hauled the meat, I ran the smokehouse, I made the sausage, I cut the meat, I rebuilt the plant to conform with USDA regs."

Later on, Stanley preferred to downplay his scrappy background. He resented the way certain people looked at him, like they thought he was "a cigar-chomping former sausagemaker."

Stanley's romantic flair hadn't diminished over the years, and he proved it in 1966. He'd been married to Leah for 17 years and she'd raised two of his children, but Stanley told her he was filing for divorce. He was in love with another woman. Not just any woman. Until recently Stanley's love, 30-year-old Marlene Cherry, had been married to Leah's brother, Joseph.

Things were looking up for the newlywed Goldblums. Equity Funding was among the most celebrated companies on Wall Street, leading a wave of so-called "concept stocks." It wasn't an insurance company, though it owned insurance subsidiaries and sold policies for other insurance companies. It wasn't a brokerage house or a mutual fund, though it owned brokerages and sold shares in other companies' mutual funds. Equity Funding wasn't in the cattle business, but its Ankony Angus subsidiary fed 90,000 head a day. The Equity Funding Corporation sold only itself, by selling shares to the public.

Using the Equity Funding holding company to dabble in the transactions of a bunch of smaller companies, Stanley could produce a balance sheet of pure *performance*, the byword of the go-go markets of the 1960s. Equity Funding was nothing but numbers. All Stanley needed was an upbeat quarterly report. Neither he nor the Wall Street herds gave a damn what happened with real steers and policyholders.

In 1968, Stanley addressed a meeting of the New York Society of Security Analysts, where a frumpy, contrarian analyst named Ray Dirks sat in the audience. Equity Funding's earnings per share had risen by at least 66 percent a year—every year—since 1962. Stanley remarked to the crowd, "Interestingly, 1967 showed an increase of 82 percent over 1966, and earnings for the first nine months of 1968 increased by 100 percent over the same 1967 period."

"We are pleased by that record," Stanley said, "primarily because it was not an accident. It was achieved as a result of careful analysis, planning, and execution. We continually recognize the necessity to not only realize results in each particular year, but to concurrently plan for the continuation of similar results in future years."

Simple Twist of Fate

"I feel as if I were walking on the edge of a precipice, towards which thousands are crowding and endeavouring to plunge me into the abyss."

—Elizabeth Frankenstein

"They felt they were on the threshold of this giant thing—they were going to shape the destiny of the universe." That's how a friend described Stanley Goldblum and Mike Riordan on New

Year's Eve, 1968. But those who court the universe must brave her bite, a lesson nobody learned like Mike Riordan.

With his personal fortune approaching nine digits, Mike was turning mellow. He pulled back on the drinking, he made cigars an occasional thing, he spent more time at home. He told his brother Bill, in one of their coast-to-coast telephone chats, he was through with the booze-and-broads crowd. "I haven't been good to Jackie," Mike said. Nor to yourself, Bill wanted to add. The kid was wising up, at the tender age of 41.

In mid-January 1969 it started to rain. For hours a day, every day, rain soaked Mandeville Canyon and the entire Brentwood area. Roads were flooded and blocked by mudslides, and still the drenching continued, unabated. Mike and Jackie escaped for a week to Miami, Florida, where they sat with the Lombardis to watch SuperBowl III. Mike won a few dollars and the stadium went nuts when a cocky young quarterback named Joe Namath led his New York Jets to victory over the highly favored Baltimore Colts, 16 to 7.

On the plane back to southern California, Mike was sneezing a lot. He told Jackie he'd caught the football bug. Their home remained shrouded in storms. Brentwood had suffered plague-level deluges of rain, according to the television. The death toll stood at 48.

On a Friday night, not yet a week since the Super Bowl, Mike called his brother Bill. It was still early at Mike's house, but past 11 p.m. in New York. Mike said he had this amazing Big Idea.

"I want to buy the Dolphins," Mike said.

"The *Miami* Dolphins?"

"Yes. For real."

Bill said he had never seen that one coming, but why not? Mike said he and Bill could run the team together. They talked for a while about the coaching staff. Bill started to think Mike was serious. Mike said, "I am." They hung up and agreed to talk in the morning. Mike called down the hallway to Jackie, but she was engrossed in the flood coverage on T.V. and couldn't hear him. He turned over and went to sleep.

A couple hours later, Jackie was dozing through the late movie when she heard a rumbling, like before a train—or a quake! Jackie thought—then the mud slammed *whoom!* into the house. It hit Mike's bedroom, throwing tons of brown gunk through the sliding glass doors. In the time it took Mike to open his eyes and draw a breath, the room was waist-high in gunk. The air tasted sour, gaseous. It was hard to breathe. Mike kept trying to stand up, but he couldn't feel his legs. He spat gunk from his mouth. He was panicky.

"Jackie!"

The firefighters explained to Jackie that they had no way to remove her husband other than to dig him out. The room had become a giant mud box. While Jackie showed Chief Paul Augustine to the house's main breaker, three firefighters climbed into the gunk with Mike. One man held Mike by the shoulders while the others shoveled mud from around his waist. They all heard the rumble before they felt it. Then the hillside wall collapsed and a second wave of muddy gunk, larger than the first, plowed through the room and burst through the opposite wall. The three firefighters were corked onto the Riordan lawn. Chief Augustine called for his men and each answered. But Mike Riordan lay beneath the mud, his lungs convulsing, his heart squeezed by the dark, unrelenting coils.

****

At Riordan's funeral mass in St. Martin's Cathedral, a soloist led a children's choir in singing, "Dream the Impossible Dream." Afterwards, more than 100 mourners gathered at Stanley's Trousdale mansion, where Jackie and the kids had been staying since the catastrophe. He had tears in his eyes when he told Jackie, "Mike was the greatest man I ever knew." But grief didn't bar Stanley from calling an emergency business meeting in his den.

"We need to play down the effects of Mike's death on the company," Stanley said. Stanley told Bill Riordan, "We need to know what's going to happen to Mike's 400,000 shares." Bill said the family would protect the stock price by selling in small parcels. He produced an agreement to that effect and had Stanley initial the pages.

From the front lawn a chorus of "aaahs" and a kid squealing penetrated the businessmen's sad assemblage. "The rain stopped," Stanley said, snapping the drapes apart with his massive hands. A gray light fell along the cobblestone drive.

Century City

When Stanley joined Equity Funding in 1959, Century City didn't exist. Back then, the 176 acres of the old Tom Mix Ranch belonged to Twentieth Century Fox. The studio ran a backlot operation there and housed a couple dozen support staff. The Alcoa Corporation bought the ranch in 1961 and began construction on a "new urban village." Every square foot of Century City was designed to serve America's business aristocracy, men like Stanley Goldblum, trafficking in insurance, finance, and computer technology.

By 1969, the town that Alcoa built was swinging and the Equity Funding Corporation of America (EFCA) had become a model corporate citizen. Each morning Stanley's tan Rolls whizzed past high-rise office parks, gleaming shopping centers, and manicured roadsides bursting with a rainbow of flowers and shrubs. It was Technicolor gone live. At the Equity Funding Tower, 1900 Avenue of the Stars, Stanley tossed his keys to the security guard, who parked the Rolls while the boss strode toward his private elevator.

Stanley's office on the 28th floor boasted fat leather chairs, hand-carved paneling, and a mahogany desk three yards wide. Stanley kept the desktop spotless and allowed only two items to rest there: a hand-sized memo pad and a $15,000 Mont Blanc pen. On the walls, original artworks, chosen by Stanley himself, horrified the tasteful. Two pieces were remarkably stinky: a free-form work composed of four garish swaths of paint—greenapple, screamred, yellowyellow, and neonlavender—the colors spread like cheese samples with a giant serving knife; and "Checkmate," a globby textured portrait in which a group of old men in Elizabethan robes leaned over a chessboard. The varnish lay so thick on "Checkmate" you couldn't tell a queen from a pawn in the glare.

From the window behind his slab of a desk, Stanley could watch members of the Los Angeles Country Club playing the fifth hole. If he wanted, he could peer through the vintage telescope, trimmed in brass, which stood near the window. There had never been a Goldblum at LACC, nor any other Jewish members. Stanley mused to a visitor one afternoon, "Someday I'm going to buy that place and send in the dozers."

With Mike gone, Stanley governed Equity Funding virtually alone, a condition he took to with gusto. His chief assistants were two obliging fellows named Fred Levin and Sam Lowell, known in executive-suite gossip as Tweedledum and Tweedledee. They were both stubby middle-aged men with more money than hair and more waist than taste.

Fred Levin came to the Equity Tower in 1968, when the life insurance company he was working for in Chicago was acquired by Equity Funding. Fred's father was a kosher butcher whom Fred remembered as "a weak man, harried by a disgusting business...."

He tried to overdose on pills. Another time, I found him in front of the oven with the gas on." Though Fred remained in the Orthodox synagogue as an adult, he couldn't put enough distance between himself and the slaughter business. Stanley, the former sausage maker, could relate.

Fred was known as one of the industry's sharpest lawyers. From 1961 to 1964 he'd worked for the Illinois Department of Insurance, monitoring the ways insurance companies recorded and handled their assets. At Equity Funding, Fred took charge of Equity Funding Life, an insurance subsidiary.

Fred did whatever Stanley told him to, and he ruled his own underlings the same way. Governing 4,000 salespeople in more than 100 offices across the country called for a firm hand. Others might have called it a sharp axe, including the 14 Bankers Life executives Fred terminated when Equity Funding took over the New Jersey firm. Fred did the act gleefully, after golly-joshing for four hours about the future of the firm.

He craved approval even when he was swinging the blade. As the Equity Funding limo pulled away from Bankers Life, Fred gushed, "They loved me! Didn't I wow them? Didn't I have them eating out of my hand?"

Stanley's other Tweedle, Sam Lowell, came to Equity Funding in April 1969, not long after Mike Riordan's death. As a staffer for Haskins & Sells, Sam had audited Equity's books until the contract shifted to Wolfson, Weiner. Stanley made Sam his executive vice-president in charge of finance, later praising him as "the financial architect of the corporation."

Sam certainly wasn't a cattleman, as evidenced by his visit to the Ankony Angus subsidiary. In photos passed around the home office, Lowell stood in a pen, grinning like Howdy Doody next to a row of stocky black cows, one hand on the nearest animal's back, the other waving a cowboy hat. His shoes were wrapped in plastic so he could stand next to the feed trough in the soupy soil. Sam hadn't been so excited since the fall tournament at the Wild Whist Bridge Club.

Sam Lowell's career in fraud began soon after he arrived in Century City. Reviewing Equity Funding's ledgers, he found a loan that had been delinquent for five years, kept out of the collections department by executive request. Sam told Stanley, "I know a funny loan when I see one."

"Well, Sam, you've got two choices," Stanley said. "You can leave. Or you can help me clear this up."

To clear the books, Sam created a shell company and stuffed its treasury with Equity Funding Life commission funds. This shell company acquired the shell that Stanley had used to front his phony loan, then paid off the loan with the commission funds. Consider it a corporate reach-around: Equity Funding paid out the funds to the company that paid off the loan.

Stanley kept Fred and Sam well fed. Both men drew $250,000 a year in salary and bonuses, plus each received $1,000 a month for local entertainment expenses. On the road, life was just as sweet. The Equity elite flew first-class and were shuttled by limousine to the best hotels. When Fred Levin went to fire everyone at Bankers Life, he refused to stay near the company's headquarters in Parsippany, New Jersey. Fred charged $300 a day to his corporate account for a chauffeur to drive him from the Central Park Regency in Manhattan to Parsippany; then he had the driver wait outside the building.

By contrast, the typical Equity Funding manager drew $28,000 a year and hoped he got a few hundred shares at bonus time. The managers knew that Fred Levin could mow them down on a whim. And many of them knew that the boys on the 28th floor were cooking the books.

****

Since 1964, some part of the Equity books had been diddled. That year, their first as a public corporation, Stanley and Mike Riordan didn't like the revenue numbers, so they agreed to include in the current year's report the profits they *expected* to make on an upcoming insurance deal. Over the next two years, they continued to record more policies than they sold. They figured how to offset their exaggerations later, by increasing sales and by merging profitable subsidiaries into the corporate umbrella.

EFCA's annual report in May 1967 claimed the company sold insurance policies on behalf of Penn Life worth $200 million. But Penn Life, in its annual report a month later, stated the company had underwritten $60 million worth of policies for Equity Funding.

Fred Levin turned up the heat with a little piece of financial magic called *reinsuring*. Let's say Equity Funding sells a life insurance policy worth $10,000 in premiums over ten years. Instead of collecting that money over time, Equity immediately *reinsures* the policy by selling it to another company. The other company pays Equity Funding $2,000 (the cash value of the first two years' premiums) and receives the customer's monthly premiums, amounting to $10,000 over ten years.

It was actually one of Fred's $28,000-a-year middle managers who saw that reinsurance could host a killer of a scam. This guy made up a bunch of fake policies and slipped them into a batch marked for reinsuring. Once the policies were sold to Penn Life, the manager collected a big commission. He kept up appearances and stepped up his cash flow by occasionally killing off one of the fake policyholders, causing Penn Life to mail a $25,000 death benefit to the manager's mail drop. "I use some of the cash to pay the premiums on the other fakes, and I keep the rest for daddy," the manager bragged when his supervisor noticed the scam.

Levin saw a way to boost his short-term earnings by recreating the manager's scam on a corporate scale. Thus did several Equity Life executives, including one Ronald Secrist, find themselves assigned to a forgery party. The executives each wrote a stack of phony policies. These policies were reinsured through other companies, producing large cash infusions. The gang called their products *Y* policies: you took a Xeroxed original (an *X* policy, for the first and last letters of *Xerox*), wrote the personal information onto a new form, and you'd made a *Y* policy.

Secrist said the forgery parties were tense and giddy. "It took a long time and you had to be careful about date stamps and other details. But I had fun being the doctor and giving the guy's blood pressure and all that."

Like Viktor Frankenstein, Stanley held the power to give life and to take it away. Having sold off 300 fake policies, the gang staged paper deaths for a handful of beneficiaries. Fred Levin salted the payoffs into the income report for Equity Funding Life.

Stanley's role in these proceedings was intentionally shaded. He never spoke about any of the scams directly except in closed-door sessions with Fred and Sam. He certainly never attended any forgery parties. Stanley gave his underlings one piece of advice: "A public company doesn't lose money." The rest was understood.

****

Stanley reigned supreme in the halls of Equity Funding and damn his detractors. When a stock analyst asked what Stanley would do if a member of his board opposed him, Stanley said, "Get a new director." He wasn't kidding.

Not everyone thought Stanley was cute. A report by the Argosy group acknowledged that Equity Funding's "accounting practices are seen by most as complicated, and by some as suspect, or 'creative'.... Equity Funding is perceived as a 'go-go' company rather than as a fiduciary institution.... More orthodox analysts are put off by the company's promotional flavor."

Stanley responded to the criticisms in his usual way: He got bigger. The forgery parties were moved to their own offices at 341 North Maple Drive, a squat piece of red brick plopped between an office supply company and a metaphysical institute. The scribbling execs were replaced by a dozen or so young women, dubbed "the Maple Street girls," between the ages of 17 and 22, each paid $2 an hour, whether there was work to do or not.

Most of the time the girls sat and talked in a wide rectangular room, unfurnished except for three folding tables and some metal chairs. They crocheted and talked about boyfriends. They sang along with the Top 40 squawking from a transistor radio, a silver nub where its antennae used to be. They assembled a handful of inside jokes that could send the whole room into laughter spasms. One girl laid across a table to demonstrate her IUD and referred three of her new friends to her gynecologist. The girls smoked marijuana and shared Qualuudes. On certain days they spent the morning cooking a lavish meal, the consuming of which lasted till mid-afternoon, when most of the crew headed home for a nap.

Every now and then a man named Bill Symonds brought over 200 or 300 files. He was often sweating, imploring the girls to write faster and to stay late, "just this one night." Symonds explained that auditors needed to see the files the following morning. The girls each took an *X* policy and copied the info, everything except the name, onto a *Y* policy. Fictitious names were filled in later by Equity Funding execs.

During 1970, the Maple Street girls rolled out more than 10,000 policies, establishing themselves as the company's most reliable profit center. While the rest of the insurance industry posted losses, Equity Funding claimed $11 million in earnings—in fact the company *lost* $7 million. For 1971, Equity reported earnings of $27 million when it actually *lost* $400,000. In 1972, earnings were predicted to top $30 million, disguising losses of equal magnitude.

Equity Funding Life carried "six-and-a-half billion dollars" worth of insurance on its books, Stanley bragged to the New York Society of Security Analysts in January 1973. "In the past year our insurance in force has been rising at an average of two percent a month, approximately three times the average for all other life insurance companies." Sales for 1972, "a record amount," totaled $2.5 billion. (At least $800 million was faked.)

Keeping the records straight on this massive illusion required constant attention and lots of computer work. With guidance from

Fred Levin and other VPs, a programmer named Bill Gootnick wrote software to track the phony policies by attaching to the file a secret *Department 99* code; the field was only visible if the user knew the proper keystroke to display the *Department 99* information. Gootnick also had to doctor the software to allow for the *Y* policies, because the fakes repeated blocks of information from other policies.

To prevent auditors from noting duplicate policy numbers, Gootnick altered the computer's *Print* function so the policies were listed by a three-digit prefix instead of the full five-digit policy number. An auditor looking at a scroll of computer paper who saw two policies both numbered 10234 might become suspicious. But since Gootnick's printouts only displayed each policy's three opening numbers, the auditor saw a range of policies beginning 102. If the auditor was curious, he could request to look at the corresponding paper files. Someone on Fred Levin's staff checked each file to be sure it was clean and passed it on.

None of the auditors verifying Equity's books ever examined any electronic files or inquired about the computing center's methods. According to Bill Gootnick, no auditor ever visited his floor, where rows of filing-cabinet sized mainframes—leased from IBM for $30,000 a month—crackled and whirred.

Despite Equity Funding's reliance on computer deception, the heart of the fraud remained analog. In late 1971, Stanley had Fred Levin and a few members of his staff counterfeit several batches of grade-A corporate bonds. The names came from the "Big Bidness" honor roll, including Dow Chemical, Firestone Tire & Rubber, Woolworth, and Southwestern Bell. All told, the boys printed $25 million worth of phony bonds, which Stanley used as collateral for a series of loans.

Twenty-eight-year-old Bob Ochoa, who managed Equity's in-house print shop, wasn't used to seeing suits in his hot, trash-strewn basement, and he'd never printed bonds before. The bosses said they needed "facsimiles" for a corporate presentation. But, they cautioned, the impressions had to be perfect.

Ochoa turned out several negatives for each bond until he got the right match. Once the plates were prepared, the suits, including Fred Levin, donned aprons and started making paper. The counterfeiting went on for three weeks. Ochoa was paid $20 cash for his work.

Enter: The Hippie Analyst

In March 1973, Ray Dirks was listening to another Equity Funding employee who'd been stiffed by Stanley Goldblum.

"My name is Ron Secrist," said the voice on Ray's phone. "Equity Funding is about to issue a bogus annual report."

How bogus? "Hundreds of millions. Maybe half a billion dollars. They're making up insurance policies. Whole segments of the business are fake."

Secrist didn't know the intricacies or dollar amounts. He didn't know for sure what was fake and what was right. But he wasn't guessing about the fake insurance policies. "I did a file," he told Dirks.

Why wasn't Secrist talking to the authorities? "If Goldblum and Levin found out there was an investigation, they would stonewall it. They're clever enough—they've probably got an evac plan for how to cover up what they've been doing. I'm calling you," Secrist told Dirks, "because you were recommended by Pat Hopper—he was a vice president at Bankers Life until about a year ago. He quit because Levin kept trying to siphon Bankers' assets into Equity Funding. Anyway, Hopper said you'd go after the dirt on a company and wouldn't let up."

Thirty-eight-year-old Ray Dirks liked it that people on Wall Street called him a "hippie analyst." His hair drooped around his ears and his bangs rested on the rims of his eyeglasses. He had babyfat cheeks and fancied himself the smartass of the financial circuit. Gray sideburns, like sew-on patches, trimmed his jawbone.

Educated at DePauw University in Indiana, this son of a career Army officer had tried to avoid a financial career. He dabbled in stocks a while after college, but then Ray followed his dream by opening a theatrical company. Inside of two years, when the money dried up, he was back on Wall Street where he and his brother, Lee Dirks, started a stock-picking firm. In 1970, Ray helped bust the intended merger of ITT with Hartford Fire Insurance through a skeptical reading of the Hartford balance sheet. The publicity sealed Ray's reputation for culling insurance stocks, one of the main reasons that Ronald Secrist came calling.

Secrist sent Ray to other ex-Equity men, including Pat Hopper of Bankers Life, and Frank Majerus, who'd served as comptroller for Equity Funding Life. Hopper said he had fended off at least five or six of Levin's attempts to transfer cash into the parent company, reminding Levin each time that Bankers Life was not allowed to transfer funds without approval from the state insurance commission.

Frank Majerus told Ray that he had "adjusted" the Accounts Receivable ledger with Levin's guidance, then quit because he felt guilty. Frank came back a few weeks later, then quit a second time. Hopper and Majerus both said they'd heard crazy rumors—about a policy factory, about a mysterious *Department 99* in the computer files, about the executive staff donning aprons and printing corporate securities in the basement.

Both men spoke of the "Y Business," as in the Y policies prepared by the Maple Street girls. Majerus said he'd heard Fred Levin remind his staff, "Don't forget, whatever we miss in the policy quota, we can make up with Y Business," which was also known by other names: "Stanley Goldblum's Friends," "the Employees' Franchise," and "the Telephone Directory."

Another story was breaking that March. Two reporters from *The Washington Post* were claiming that the Nixon White House served as headquarters for a vast shadow government. The story had emerged as the reporters investigated a break-in at the Watergate office complex. Ray Dirks told his A-list clients and friends, "Equity Funding is the Watergate of Wall Street."

When some of Ray's clients, including the Boston Company and Institutional Capital of Chicago, began dumping Equity Funding in blocks of 300,000 to 400,000 shares, market watchers snapped to. Stanley Goldblum nearly burst a neck vein as the numbers ticked across his desk. Somebody was yanking his chain and he wanted to know who.

Ray took his story to Bob Spencer at the accounting firm of Seidman & Seidman. Spencer headed the audit team that had just given the "cold comfort" signal on Equity Funding's 1972 annual report, meaning the audit was nearly done and everything looked ready to go. Ray said he'd been hearing a different story from former Equity employees. Spencer said the men had been fired in the recent layoffs and were yapping in the wind.

"I don't know," Ray said, "they're pretty convincing. They're backing each other up. Secrist and Majerus both said they'd done a file."

Spencer said he wanted to see details. Ray said he'd send over a copy of his notes, which by this time were an inch and a half thick.

The following afternoon, Ray caught an airplane to L.A., where he had scheduled a meeting with Stanley Goldblum. "I've been hearing amazing things about your next annual report," Ray said to Stanley's personal assistant, "and I'd like to get a closer look at the company." Stanley said he always had time for an analyst. He reminded Ray on the phone they'd met in 1971 at a brokers' and businessmen's lunch. The receptionist made Ray an appointment to meet Mr. Goldblum at the Equity Funding headquarters.

On the morning of March 23, not yet a month since he had first spoken with Ronald Secrist, Ray was eating a bowl of bananas and cream in the lobby of the Beverly Wilshire Hotel when Stanley Goldblum appeared. Fred Levin followed close behind. Ray nearly spat his bananas. How'd they know where I was staying, he wondered

Stanley and Fred declined when Ray offered to share his breakfast. They wanted to know why a 400,000 share block of Equity Funding had just passed through the New York Stock Exchange.

"That would be Institutional Investors," Ray guessed correctly.

Stanley leaned his massive forearms along his knees. He was seated directly across from Ray, who had wisely pushed aside the bowl of bananas. "Who else did you talk to?" Stanley demanded. "What have you been saying?"

Ray's heart surged. They knew! Bob Spencer at Seidman & Seidman must have sent the notes to Stanley.

"People have been telling me about fictitious policies," Ray said, trying to sound noncomittal, like maybe he didn't believe the rumors.

"Who?"

Ray said he couldn't tell who. Then he said Pat Hopper was one.

"Pat Hopper's a beach bum," Stanley blurted, repeating company lore that Pat had lost his marbles and moved to Fiji.

"These notes comprise the story of three individuals," Ray said, holding up his papers demonstratively. "They are saying you have a substantial amount of business on the books called *Y* Business."

"How do you spell that—*w-h-y* ?" Stanley asked.

"Just the alphabet, *Y*," Ray corrected.

"We've had some people stealing at the company," Stanley shrugged. "It must be them."

Stanley said Ray should come to Century City as planned. The two of them rode in Stanley's Rolls while Fred followed in a Cadillac. "We have some other guests today," Stanley warned. Examiners from the California and Illinois departments of insurance were in temporary offices near the executive suite. "It's nothing. It's like this stuff in your notes," Stanley said, pointing to Ray's lap. "Preposterous."

Inside Equity Funding headquarters, Stanley and Ray met up with Fred Levin at the executives' elevator. After a tense, silent ride up, Ray twitched when the doors opened onto a giant picture window.

"It's the 28th floor," Fred said, noting Ray's nerves. "Don't worry, the windows are locked."

"It Doesn't Hurt Me At All"

Stanley could have thought about unlocking those windows for himself. It never crossed his mind. He had a cadre of Equity Life executives file through an office and talk to Ray Dirks. Not one man had ever heard of the Y Business. Every few minutes Stanley strolled in, threw his bearish arm around the hippie analyst, and asked, "Well? What do you think now?"

The cover-up was an exercise in absurdity. Stanley's big problem wasn't Ray Dirks, but the insurance examiners who were closing in on the computer department. Fred Levin called in Bill Gootnick and asked the systems manager if he could destroy the *Department 99* codes and shuffle the Y Business into other parts of the record system. Bill said he couldn't erase tapes without risking the loss of other essential data. They were hung.

Stanley decided to set up a spy operation. It was his idea to put the visiting insurance examiners on the 28th floor instead of the sixth floor, where the Equity Life people worked. He had an electrician hide microphones in every office used by the examiners. The mics were wired to two tape recorders, one under Fred Levin's desk, and one in Stanley's private bathroom, behind the toilet.

Whatever Stanley heard on his tapes, it did him no good. First the insurance examiners verified that tens of thousands of policies were faked. Next the auditors discovered that $25 million in corporate bonds, supposedly held at the American National Bank & Trust Company in Chicago were actually at "American National Trust Company," apparently an empty storefront rented by Fred Levin.

Fred scoffed at the news. "These stories are bizarre. There's no credence, no truth, no believability to these bizarre accusations." A few days earlier, Fred had called Pat Hopper, one of the men who put Ray Dirks on the scent. Because he worried about spies outside his door, Fred was whispering. "I'm trapped into doing the things I'm doing. I wish I had met you before I started doing things under the table."

Sam Lowell swore, "I know nothing." Lowell hadn't been around much the last year or so. He'd spent his time at the Wild Whist

Club and in New York City, where he furnished an apartment for a 20-something female English professor.

Stanley, apparently amused by his lieutenants' anxiety, said the fraud rumor "might be true, it might not be true." After a long silent smirk he added, "I don't think it's true."

When Equity's general counsel, Ron Loeb, called an emergency board meeting the following week, Stanley brought an attorney with him. Frank Rothman informed the board that his client would have nothing to say. Stanley Goldblum sat poker-faced on a long black leather couch.

Herb Glaser, who'd been a member of the board since Stanley invited him in 1968, stood up. Most of the assembled thought of Herb as the grandfather of Equity Funding. The 70-year-old growler gave them hell for some of the company's wackier stunts with money, but he loved the business.

"I want everyone to give an affidavit, saying they know nothing about this mess," Herb told the room. Then he looked at Stanley. "Why can't you make an affidavit?" he asked. "I can make an affidavit."

"I can make an affidavit that you can make an affidavit," Stanley replied.

Glaser was stunned. Stanley was telling him to step back— you're innocent and you need to stay out of the way. Glaser wanted to slap Stanley.

Stanley, still seated, looked at Glaser. A panic-stricken Fred Levin thought he saw tears gathering in Stanley's eyes.

"You must think I'm a prick," Stanley said to the old man.

"Yes, you are a prick," Glaser answered.

"Herb, you have the right to call me anything you want, or think anything you want to. It doesn't hurt me at all."

"How could you do such a thing?" Glaser boomed, jittering the water glasses on the table with his pounding fist. "I have to believe you're guilty."

"You should be glad you don't know anything about it," Stanley answered.

****

If Herb Glaser felt glad, he was alone. Plenty of people knew about the fraud and chose not to say anything. Hundreds of them were grilled by investigators from the Securities and Exchange Commission, the IRS, and the various departments of insurance. Twenty-two of them were indicted alongside Stanley Goldblum and Fred Levin. Not that the regulatory agencies were taking a bow on this one. Stanley Goldblum was wearing cuffs because a rogue, "hippie" analyst played gossip games.

The IRS and the SEC had each bungled a chance to nab Stanley. In 1967, the IRS charged that Equity hadn't properly accounted for the stocks it exchanged with other brokerage houses. The company owed back taxes of $34 million. Stanley and his lawyers stalled for three years until the agency offered to settle for $9 million, no questions asked. Stanley rejected the offer. In August 1971, he settled the debt with a check for $165,000.

The SEC gave Equity a clean bill of health in early 1972, just a year before the bust. William Mercado, who'd been fired by Sam Lowell for insubordination, told investigators that Equity Funding had exaggerated its 1970 assets by at least $8 million. Mercado said he could prove it with a simple run on the company's computer tapes.

SEC attorney Ray Garrett talked to Sam Lowell and two other Equity employees about Mercado, then wrote his report. "The individuals were questioned and stated that there were no irregularities in the operations or accounting practices of Equity Funding." Basically, Garrett said, *We asked them, and they said nothing's wrong.*

"Earlier suggestions to the contrary resulted because the corporation had been founded by salesmen who were not qualified accountants...." Remember this defense the next time *you're* audited. Tell the agent you're an insurance salesperson, so you're not so good with numerical niceties. See if that line works as well for you as it did for Stanley's boys.

It's true there are complexities in auditing a company of Equity's size and nature. But, as Ray Dirks complained, "If routine auditing procedures can't detect 64,000 phony insurance policies, $25 million in counterfeit bonds, and $100 million in missing assets, what is the purpose of audits?"

Ray had reason to gripe. For all his meandering heroism, Ray got slammed. Early on, when he took his concerns to Bob Spencer at Seidman & Seidman, he was betrayed. "I went to them truly believing I was doing this nationally ranked auditing firm a favor," Ray said. "They were about to certify a report I believed was fraudulent. Instead of reporting the matter to the SEC, the auditor applied the most narrow interpretation to his role and went directly to Equity Funding."

After the SEC threw the company into receivership and began filing indictments against Seidman & Seidman along with the

Equity insiders, Ray called Bob Spencer. "Why'd you take my notes to Stanley Goldblum?"

Spencer replied, "They're clients of mine."

"Aren't you independent auditors?"

"Sure we're independent," Spencer said, "but we have an obligation to our clients."

Ray had even more pain coming. The very first charges filed by the SEC did not name Stanley Goldblum or Fred Levin or the host of company men like Ronald Secrist who admitted, "I did a file." The first indictment named Ray Dirks as defendant. He had committed insider trading, the SEC accused, by sharing the Equity Funding rumor with his clients. Much as the regulators appreciated Ray doing their job for them, he had no right to talk about his concerns with the people who paid him for investment advice.

Ray welcomed his martyr status. He appeared unshaven for his arraignment, declaring to reporters, "I'm growing a beard until I'm cleared." He had a long wait. Ray was convicted and lost several appeals. It took until 1983 and cost Ray $100,000 in attorney's fees for the Supreme Court to clear his name. In its landmark decision, the Court held that since Ray did not personally benefit from the rumors, he was not guilty of insider trading.

How Could It Happen?

Here's how Ray Dirks described the go-go financial markets of the late 1960s:

> Any company with "computer" in its name could sell for 20, 40, even 60 times earnings. The multiple of earnings—the ratio between what a company earns per share and the price of each share—became so high as to be all but irrelevant. Stocks sold not on the basis of present earnings but of future earnings. Even those stocks of companies that were losing money did well on the Street, on the thin assumption that the companies would earn money some day.

When Ray first heard about Y policies in March 1973, Dick Nixon was entering his second term. Peace had broken out in Vietnam. The Dow had just reached 1,000, its "greatest psychological barrier." In Nixon's wake, a sea of voices demanded political reform. In Stanley Goldblum's wake, the voices demanded reform in insurance and securities markets. Speaking at a conference on Equity Funding in 1975, a group of attorneys predicted the case "will serve as an incentive to make needed improvements in the regulatory, accounting, and securities marketing systems of insurance."

It appears, almost 30 years later, that the reformers went unanswered. If anything, the financial terrain is worse than ever, teeming with mob-run brokerages, billion-dollar Ponzi schemes, and Internet pickpockets. And there, in the midst of it all, the monster Stanley Goldblum is still pumping iron. He was convicted as the director of the Equity Funding conspiracy in 1975. After serving four years in prison, Stanley laid low throughout the 1980s. He emerged in 1990 with a company named Primedex, running a string of medical clinics. Five years later, Stanley and his partners were charged with phony invoicing, giving and receiving illegal kickbacks, and forging medical reports. In February 1999, when the 72-year-old Goldblum stepped into an L.A. courthouse for a hearing on Primedex, he was arrested again. He had allegedly faked $900,000 in assets as collateral for a loan. As if this writing, his fate hangs in the judicial balance.

Robert Vesco

(1935 -)

CHAPTER 6

The Outlaw:
Robert Vesco

"I am malicious because I am miserable."
—*The Creature*

Some 30 select shareholders were milling nervously around the conference room of the Regency Hotel. They were expecting to meet Robert Vesco, the man holding their company's future for ransom. But nobody had seen Vesco. Nobody had a clue where he was staying, or even if he was in Manhattan. He was known for a vulgar mouth and canine table manners. Someone joked he was probably driving from his house in New Jersey, snarling in traffic.

Then word came from the concierge, "The meeting has been relocated to the Holiday Inn in Wayne, New Jersey." Vesco didn't think the Regency was secure. "There are cars waiting outside," the hotel attendant shouted across the room. "If you gentlemen can make your way to the lobby..."

On that gray day in March of 1971, a hastily assembled procession of limousines shuttled across the George Washington Bridge. It looked like a state funeral. Several literary-minded riders pondered the line from *Julius Caesar*: "Beware the Ides of March." It wasn't clear, though—not yet—whether Vesco was Brutus or Marc Antony, since Vesco's loyalties and his next move remained in question.

One old guy got so worked up as the caravan started for New Jersey, he threw a fit. Fumbling with the window controls, the man yelled, "It's the Mafia! I don't need this!" As the limo driver slowed for a red light on Central Park West, the man flung his door open and stepped into the street. With some difficulty he was coaxed back into the car, and the driver sped off.

Arriving at the Wayne Holiday Inn, the shareholders were crammed into a hot room bounded by off-white temporary walls and cheap red carpet. Twenty minutes later Bob Vesco arrived, full of grins and hi-yas, leaning over a row of folding chairs to shake a friendly hand, nodding brusquely toward or ignoring the hostile glances of the majority.

"There's a rumor that I've stolen your company from you," he said at the room's tiny podium, flicking his thin black mustache with his thumb for effect. "Well, rest assured, it hasn't happened— yet." Vesco said he didn't know what business they had to conduct. He hadn't made up his mind how to pull off such a giant-sized heist. "Let's just say for now that I see the future of your company, Investors Overseas Services, in its becoming the major arm of a future conglomerate, which I am in the midst of establishing."

While Vesco fished eyeglasses from his pocket and began reading a ten-minute drone of legalese, an audience member cracked, "He doesn't exactly look like a New Englander's idea of capitalism." Vesco, the Detroit-born six-footer, wore a black suit with a white shirt. His necktie was black and untapered. He'd oiled his hair and combed it away from his brow, forming a small box on the crown of his head. The *Cosa Nostra* effect was completed by the stern, studiedly unexpressive faces of several assistants who were standing behind Vesco, their hands clasped over their belts like pallbearers. Among the entourage stood a particularly sneaky drunk known to many IOS shareholders as Norman the Burble.

Vesco folded the resentment of the room into his hand and gobbled it up. "As for our current cash-flow problems, well, the lending institutions—if we can get anyone who'll actually lend us some money—once they've come in, we're gonna give them a big con job and get them in permanently, which is the object of our maneuvers." He smiled, his lips puckering slightly.

"Once it was over," a shareholder remembered, "we were leaving the motel and checking to see if we still had our underwear." Vesco had dragged the businessmen out to New Jersey to tell them what he could've said in a two-word telegram, the first word beginning with *F* and the last word being *You.*

****

A few months later Bob Vesco was baring his teeth again, this time to a Swiss magistrate with the ominous name of Judge Robert

Pagan. Vesco offered legal opinions to justify his takeover of Investors Overseas Services (IOS), and he outlined for the judge his rank among international businesspeople. Judge Pagan swung his right hand toward the doorway of his chambers, to attract the gendarme's attention, then pointed to Vesco's chair. "Anybody can buy a legal opinion," Pagan snapped. "You have endangered the reputation of Swiss banking by your actions. I intend to set an example in your case, to illustrate that Swiss law knows no double standard." Outside chambers, Pagan would say he was sick of the "white-collar Mafia" who abused the hospitality and discretion of Switzerland's business-friendly banking laws.

Though he knew Vesco spoke no French, Pagan addressed his defendant directly. "*Il est dans votre propre interet, donc, que je décerne contre vous un mandat d'arret.*"

"What'd he say?" Vesco blurted to the interpreter.

"He said you and your colleagues are under arrest."

"What?"

"He says," the man said more slowly, "you're going to jail."

As Vesco was led from the room, his attorneys promised to contact the American embassy.

"No," Vesco barked, "call John Mitchell in Washington." He meant the U.S. Attorney General. "Make sure Nixon hears about this personally." He meant President Nixon.

A restless stay in Saint Antoine Prison did nothing for Bob Vesco's congeniality. "If they're going to treat me like a criminal, I'm going to act like a criminal," he complained. "I'm gonna steal everything that's not nailed down."

The Salesman

Robert Vesco's father, Donald Vesco, was lucky enough to ride out the Great Depression in the service of the Chrysler Corporation, welding car doors on the assembly line. Donald and his wife, Barbara, already had a girl when Bobby came along in 1935. Soon after, Donald was promoted to supervisor, with a title patch to sew on his coveralls and a few extra dollars in his pay envelope. The Vescos lived on Hastings Street in eastern Detroit, alongside other families who gauged their lives by the production cycles of the American auto industry. Donald lectured his children constantly to work hard in school so they wouldn't have to follow him to the line. Cynthia Vesco got the message and made the grades. She would grow up and become a professor of psychology at Michigan State University. Bobby required more care and feeding.

"He and his father hit the books night after night, at a table in the kitchen," a neighbor said. "Sometimes they were still poring over them, his father helping the boy, at two or three in the morning."

Twice Bobby dropped out of high school. The first time he threw in with a few older guys who were starting a body shop. "We took in cars that were wrecks and we put new fenders on, painted them— that was during the day. At night and on weekends I worked as a driver. Including the moonlighting, I made $50 a week."

In 1953, Donald Vesco talked his son into giving school one more try. Bobby didn't last through the spring. A new girl had arrived at Pershing High, a girl named Patricia Melzer. She was the perkiest, widest-eyed girl Bob had ever met. She talked with a hick accent, the sound of her vowels ringing like steel on steel when she told Bobby, "I grew up in Bad Axe, which is in northern Michigan, what they call 'The Thumb' of the state. My daddy's a farmer, like all the Melzers have been. I've got four brothers, all older than me. I'm the baby girl."

She might as well have been singing an aria, for that's what Bobby heard. When Pat became pregnant that summer, Bobby didn't hesitate. From the JP's office where they said their wedding vows he headed back to the body shop, promising he'd earn his diploma through night school.

Bobby only finished half his GED courses, but he cribbed enough reading technical books in the library of Wayne State University to pass himself off as a blueprint operator and trainee draftsman at the Packard Motor Company. Six months or so later, fed up with the demands put upon an "extrusion engineer"— basically, running a metal-shaping machine—Bobby talked a supervisor at the nearby Bohn Aluminum plant into hiring him as a production assistant. At Bohn, Bobby claimed, his bosses recognized his genius and almost immediately had him "physically designing tools, and then I moved into estimating costs."

However marvelous his services, Bobby was still only earning $55 a week at Bohn. And he saw right off, his gifts did not lie in the technical realm, though he persistently called himself an "engineer," exhaling the title with the clumsy gusto of a young man who just *had* to make it. "I decided I wanted to be president of a company. It was very much a planned thing. What I did was, I looked around, and whereas the presidents of other companies were typically engineering or manufacturing type people, I felt they should be more marketing and sales oriented."

Bobby's next step brought him to Reynolds Aluminum, where he worked as an administrative assistant, supporting the engineering staff. He was attached to a team charged with developing a new line of one-piece aluminum bumpers for the Oldsmobile division of General Motors. "The idea was to use more aluminum per car, because it would be lighter than the steel they were using. We found a good way to do that. We replaced the multi-paneled steel grill with a one-piece aluminum model." The technical achievement was a coup for the production team, but Bobby was most impressed by the economics built into the new product: "The one-piece construction meant you had to pull the whole damn thing out to put in a new one, and it ran the customer three times as much money."

Bobby was transferred in 1959 to Reynolds headquarters in New York City. At $10,500 a year he couldn't afford a Park Avenue apartment, so he commuted from Rowayton, Connecticut. Narrating his memoirs into a tape recorder during the late 1960s, Bobby told how he deliberately plotted his metamorphosis into a businessman. "The next thing I needed to do was to get into something like a staff function, so I could get experience as a general manager running something and being directly responsible for it, and also getting exposed to the financial community as such."

Bobby and Pat had three children now, Danny, Robert, Jr., and a girl, Dawn. As far as Pat was concerned, they were already the richest family in America. In a few years' span, the girl from Bad Axe had become the wife of a successful New York businessman, and she'd found her personal calling in motherhood. Pat seemed so lively, racing and squealing around the lawn with her kids, some neighbors mistook her for a teenaged babysitter. Bobby ran the career track, and Pat ran the house. When Bobby announced he was quitting his job at Reynolds to become a freelance manufacturer's rep, Pat hugged her husband, bathing him in her smile—*and what would hubby like for dinner?*

Bobby didn't see his little family much. "We'd moved to a house in New Jersey, in Denville, where it was a lot cheaper to live. I borrowed some money from a bank in New York—$2,000 or something like that. It carried me for a few months. I had a 1957 Plymouth. I used to hop in the car Monday morning and come back Saturday night after trying to sell and buy things. I lived in my car or hunched inside a telephone booth."

Bobby kept driving, hoping and scheming, covering New Jersey's shiny new highway system on a half-tank of gas and a prayer. "Fortunately, after not too many months I did make a few measly good put-togethers. I made a deal with a company by the name of Eagle Aluminum Products. Eagle had a plant in Dover, New Jersey. It had a press which was sitting dormant. So I made a deal with them that I would get selling for that press if they would put a crew on, and we would figure the cost of making the product. So they hired three or four guys to run the press and I trotted out and got business for it. And as a result I made quite a few dollars."

Thus was born Bobby's first business—Aluminum Services Incorporated. The holdings consisted of two boxes of business cards and a desk in a corner of the Eagle Aluminum office. Lucky for Bobby, a manufacturing boom was underway, spurred by a Cold War defense buildup and an unprecedented economic expansion. He kept Eagle's press running and gathered enough overflow business so that he started selling for other producers as well.

The big players in the manufacturing boom were building conglomerates of companies, snapping them together and taking them apart at will. It didn't matter if one company made U-bolts and the other made underwear. It didn't matter, for the most part, in which states the two companies were located, or which country. Even size didn't matter. You could pump up a little bitty $5-million company with some financial backing and take over a huge $100-million company. You could merge or shed businesses whenever you liked.

"The go-go years have hit the business world," financial journalists cheered. Young men whose lapels could pass for body armor, who sported sideburns and freeway-sized neckties, were challenging the old guard's buttoned-up ways. Doing business a-go-go depended only tangentially on production schedules and labor relations and the cost of goods sold. The days of the one-company man were done. Doing business, as Bobby Vesco saw to his pleasure, depended on how dexterously you hustled together contracts and articles of incorporation and shareholders' covenants—a dance Bobby felt in his bones.

The Seducer

His first big score was Captive Seal, a tiny concern that held a patent on a high-pressure gasket used in aircraft. The company had no machinery to produce the seals itself; there was only an assembly service, where 20 or so minimum-wage workers put together prefabbed fittings. Even this dwarf operation was about to fail from managerial neglect. But Bobby thought the company could survive—with $100,000 to launch a manufacturing arm and some refinancing, Captive Seal could be dressed up and sold to a conglomerateur, or used to incubate a brand new corporation of corporations.

Bobby was having a hard time persuading people to see the magic in Captive Seal when he met Malcolm Evans McAlpin. "He was a lot older than your average trendsetter, but Mac was a pretty fancy guy," said a friend. "He graduated from Princeton in the 1920s and quickly became a successful businessman. He was a broker, very well connected on Wall Street, with his own seat on the stock exchange, and always looking for a quick buck. He lived in a splendid home out in the country, with a swimming pool and a tennis court."

Bobby saw right off that Mac McAlpin had *the stuff*. It wasn't just his pedigree, the Ivy League credentials, the money, the house. Mac had the grace that comes from owning these as one's birthright and the experience of making his advantages count. As Mac whizzed into the Eagle Aluminum parking lot, Bobby noticed the license plate on the silver Mercedes said MAC-2. The Rolls, MAC-1, was being modified, Mac explained, and he reserved his Ferrari, MAC-3, for maneuvering the steep hills and hairpin turns around his estate in Morristown. Mac said he'd driven out to see Bobby on behalf of some clients who wanted to invest in American technology companies. "I hear you have this excellent property called Captive Seal."

Mac, approaching 60, leaped into the role of Bobby's mentor. "In the beginning, Bobby was the most attractive, most able, most interesting young man with an unlimited capacity for work," Mac recalled. Mac was soon spreading the word on his discovery to everyone he met. "Mac was very sold on Vesco," a friend said. "He told me to jump if I could get a piece of the action because he said I'd make a lot of money."

Mac connected Bobby to a New York doctor named Benjamin Payn, who was himself connected to the money-managing network of the famous London Rothschilds. With Mac and Benjamin Payn vouching for him, Bobby easily won the money to put Captive Seal back in action, and he wasn't sitting around waiting for the next song to start. Mac had spotted a failing company on the American Stock Exchange called Cryogenics Ltd. There was nothing left to Cryogenics but a "shell"—that is, a corporation that exists on paper and lists shares on the exchange but has no assets. By merging Captive Seal into the Cryogenics shell, Bobby could sell shares in his pet company without having to register Captive Seal with regulatory agencies. Captive Seal could dance using Cryogenics' name tag.

Bobby the aluminum salesman became Bob Vesco, corporate tycoon, by creating yet a third company, which he named International Controls Corporation (ICC) and merged into the Cryogenics shell. A press release announced that the company formerly known as Cryogenics would continue to trade under that stock symbol, but had changed its name to International Controls. "So we went public by the back door, so to speak," Bob recalled, wetting his lips before flattening them into a smirk, "though any old door will do."

By the summer of 1965, Bob had inked the documents on the International Controls Corporation. He had also spent all the money he and Mac had raised, and per SEC regulations he wouldn't be able to offer stock in ICC until the end of the year. Without cash, he wouldn't be able to build a Lego car, much less a conglomerate. He needed $500,000.

Mac McAlpin combed his Rolodex and came up with Ruth Axe, the 60-something chief of the Axe Science Corporation. Ruth was intrigued but skeptical. Bobby had good references. However, ICC's numbers weren't so impressive and the company had no track record. Ruth's flesh was willing, but her spirit kept nagging her with reasons to abstain.

Bob later recalled, "We had to have the money. Without that operating capital, we were through." So when Ruth said no, and kept saying no, Bob kept coming back until she finally said yes, though she couldn't promise the entire half-million. "Why did she do it?" Bob asked, shimmering his fingers in the air. He had scored $200,000. "Well, she fell in love, I guess." Presumably Bob was speaking metaphorically, but he pushed the figure of speech as far as he could. "I talked to her two or three times by myself. Her attorneys had told her not to do it. But she did it anyway. She actually—she tried to hire me. Well, I guess I did intrigue her with my financial agility. I guess that's really why she put the money in."

Bob wasn't forgetting about his chicks back home. He bought himself a Mercedes, which he licensed as RLV1, and got Pat a Buick, RLV2, for her birthday. With his personal proceeds from the past years' deals, he bought four-and-a-half acres about to be foreclosed. The property was secluded from Old Denville Road by a stand of spruce, and edged by a river. When Bob phoned his parents back in Detroit to tell them the news, he announced that "the company," his International Controls, had purchased a bungalow on the property's western edge. Though reserved for corporate visitors, Donald and Barbara Vesco were the only ones who ever stayed at the bungalow.

With momentum behind him, Bob resumed his conquests. In 1967, he picked up Century-Special, which produced machine parts for the aircraft industry, and Fairfield Aviation, in Fairfield, Connecticut. By the end of the year, he was constructing a new headquarters for ICC at the landing strip, which became known as the Fairfield Complex. The year 1968 was even better. ICC snatched up eight separate companies and was tagged as a rising star in the next generation of conglomerates.

"It's as easy to take on a large company as a small one," Bob reasoned with his friend Mac. "The steps are the same." The large company Bob had in mind was called Electronic Specialty, a California-based operation that was founded to produce electric razors and later shifted into aircraft manufacture. The price tag would run $10 million or $15 million.

As Bob saw it, Electronic Specialty was a pushover. "Top management was more interested in playing golf and chasing girls than running a business. And going off on safaris down to Africa. This was their idea of bigtime management. There was no harm in chasing girls. But you can do that on your own time."

William Burgess, chairman of Electronic Specialty, saw nothing but trouble in the Vesco crowd. "From what I knew of Vesco—and I had taken a prior look at International Controls—I concluded I was not interested in getting involved with him," Burgess said. Nevertheless Burgess invited Bob to drop by his home in Pasadena. "I'll show you my butterfly collection," the amateur lepidopterist offered. Bob forced a chuckle and pinned Burgess with his heavy-lidded eyes. "I'd like that."

Bob was making friends and influencing people all over. During 1967 Mac had fixed him up with a broker from Geneva named Henry Buhl III, a money manager for a collection of offshore mutual funds called Investors Overseas Services. As Bob crouched to make his move on Electronic Specialty, Buhl took him "on the circuit," introducing the upstart to New York's richest investment bankers: Lazard Freres, Salomon Brothers, Allen & Co., Loeb & Rhoades, Lehman Brothers, Smith Barney. Henry quaked as he watched his rube of a friend—who just two years before was sweettalking Ruth Axe for a couple hundred thousand dollars—give New York's financial elite the high hat. At Arthur Andersen, Bob interrupted the firm's executive vice president to tell the man, "You don't know what you're talking about."

"It was just bad manners," Henry fumed later. "He always acted haughtily and never conducted himself humbly with very successful men. I thought he should show a little bit of humility. They all called and asked me not to bring him back again." People also whispered behind their hands that Vesco exhibited atrocious table manners. He'd tear into a four-star meal with expulsions of breath and a noisy smacking of his chops, as if he were a riveter on break at the Chevy plant wolfing down a cheese sandwich and a bag of chips.

Bob wasn't wowing anyone with his "financial agility" this time around. At William Burgess' home in July of 1968, while the host prattled about the heraldic markings of his favorite butterflies, Bob referred obscurely to his intentions regarding Electronic Specialty. He wouldn't say exactly how much of the company's shares he'd picked up over the last couple of months, but he suggested five percent or so would probably constitute a substantial holding. Burgess sadly agreed it would. A five percent stake was a strong base. With a lucky alliance, Vesco could command enough votes to swing a takeover. A few days later, *The Wall Street Journal* quoted "anonymous ICC sources" who claimed the company had in fact achieved a five percent stake in Electronic Specialty.

Once more Burgess invited Bob for some informal discussion. "Bring your wife—Pat, isn't it? I'll bring my wife and we'll have dinner in New York City." By the night's end, Burgess thought he'd convinced Bob there was no future for ICC and Electronic Specialty. The next morning, both ICC and Electronic Specialty announced the merger was off. Bob put his 36,000 shares—a little more than two percent of Electronic Specialty's shares—up for sale.

Meanwhile Bob told his team to quietly finish assembling the offer. At some point during the week of August 5, one of the lawyers thought to ask how much stock ICC currently owned. Bob answered that he'd sold a few thousand shares over the past week, so he'd have to see how much he had left. The lawyer cried, "Jesus! No! You can't dump your stock like you're backing out of the deal when you're about to make a new offer." Bob didn't see why not. "Because," the man explained, "it looks like you're trying to depress the price."

"Oh," Bob responded, and cancelled the sale order.

Mac McAlpin and Henry Buhl had persuaded Bank of America to back the Electronic Specialty takeover, which was in full swing by mid-August. Bob arranged the underwriting through a contact at Orvis Brothers, a respectable second-tier firm that had underwritten stock and bond issues for ICC. He could go as high as $50 million. ICC began running ads, looking to buy back 500,000 shares of Electronic Specialty for $39 each (the stock was currently trading in the low 30s).

William Burgess telegrammed ELS stockholders:

> DON'T ACT IN HASTE. Electronic Specialty Co. is being raided by a small AMEX [American Stock Exchange] company called International Controls, financed by foreign investors. It is a much smaller company with sales in 1967 of $6.8 million, compared to our sales of $112 million.

Next Burgess filed for an immediate injunction through the district court. Bob had committed fraud, Burgess accused, when he had pretended to own five percent of Electronic Specialty's stock when he only owned two percent. Second, Bob had tried to manipulate the market price and investors' perceptions by pretending to back out of the merger and then selling his stock.

As a federal judge conducted a hasty review, the world of business turned its eyes to Bob Vesco. He looked a bit like Errol Flynn, whose suave profile gave Bob the idea for his swipe of a mustache. Vesco occasionally played the cocktail circuit, gossips reported, usually in a black mohair suit. He was especially fond of the race-track lounge, though he also enjoyed showing off his abilities in chess for $1,000 a game. One evening he appeared at a party wearing a red velvet smoking jacket and performed a Hugh Hefner impression for an adoring crowd of sycophants. He pretended to be a shy, delicate flower when one of the young women at the table flirted with him. His buddies noticed that Vesco's fingernails were glossed with clear polish.

And there was the family: now three boys and a girl. If Bob wasn't home much, you had a good idea what he was doing when he was there. The Vesco estate now encompassed 80 acres and three houses. They'd added a swimming pool and a riding stable. A set of tennis courts lay on a hill overlooking an artificial pond. For more than a year, Pat was occupied shuttling information between her husband and the platoon of renovation workers who added some $500,000 worth of materials to the main house.

"I never asked for anything," Pat said about those days. "I rarely used charge accounts at New York stores." She bought her dresses off the rack right there in New Jersey. She seemed to have little interest in money, as long as Bob kept the money coming. "I know we earned more than $10,000 a year," she said. "We spent more than $10,000 a year."

From admirers like Mac McAlpin, Bob had picked up a sobriquet, "The Bootstrap Kid," in honor of those early days he'd spent hunched in telephone booths, the days when Bobby Vesco filled out his own invoices and filed the carbons in a box at the Eagle Aluminum plant. Some of that charmed luck stayed with Bob as the verdict came back on Burgess' fraud charges in the Electronic Specialty deal. Judge Ed McLean held that:

(1) the initial tender offer by ICC was misleading;
(2) Burgess' charges met the standards for proceeding to trial;
(3) Burgess would probably win at trial.

But McLean floored his audience—including Bob Vesco—when he added that he would not prevent Bob from taking over Electronic Specialty. "A preliminary injunction here might do the stockholders more harm than good," wrote Judge McLean. Bob had won himself a company, taking down a corporate elephant with a popgun and some wily maneuvers.

He'd also secured himself a place on the dais. At that year's Alfred E. Smith Memorial Dinner, staged in the Waldorf Astoria and managed by Henry Buhl's mother, Bob sat immediately behind President Lyndon Johnson. One $10,000 plate over from Johnson sat the man about to claim the White House, Republican presidential hopeful Richard Nixon. The seating was terraced, allowing Bob to peer over Johnson's shoulder and across at Nixon. Afterward, Bob always kept a framed photo on his wall: in the shot, President Johnson is gesturing at the assemblage and braying a comment to Nixon. Nixon is straining to hear over the crowd noise, so he's also looking at the photographer while cocking his ear toward Johnson. With a third man, James Farley, pinned between them, the two presidents look like a pair of Marx Brothers, listening to Farley's heart without a clue what they're hearing. Just over Johnson's shoulder in the photograph sits Bob Vesco, his neck straight as a barber's pole. The collar of his tuxedo is crisp. He's pretending to be engrossed in the evening's printed program.

Mac McAlpin saw that his protégé was not adjusting gracefully to success. "Communications with him became increasingly difficult. He was always away or closeted in meetings and you couldn't reach him. It got worse and worse. His ambitions and designs eventually became overpowering."

After stifling his yawns for a couple hours' worth of speeches, Bob was relieved when the Smith dinner's formalities ended and the schmoozing began. In a transfiguring moment, he was introduced to Richard Nixon. Bob's political thinking had previously been limited to the observations broadcast nightly on the Chet Huntley-David Brinkley Report, but all that changed when he touched The Hand. "I decided Nixon was a good guy," Bob said. "Or, of the two, him and Hubert Humphrey, Nixon was the better."

While her husband made small talk with his destiny, Pat Vesco sat at home in Boonton, New Jersey, fuming. Bob's "sweet, friendly, long-suffering dumpling" had gained a few pounds over the years. But she'd strengthened her spine. She no longer revered him as the knight who would save her from the wilds of Michigan. Pat had learned exactly what men wearing red smoking jackets and fingernail polish were about. One evening at the Lutèce restaurant in Manhattan, Pat shoved back from the table and shouted, "Go fuck yourself, you son of a bitch." As she stomped toward the exit, Pat caught the eye of a couple she and Bob knew socially. "You know Bob," she blurted, as if that explained everything. Then she disappeared through the door, Bob trotting close behind.

The Schmuck

Way back in 1956, when Bobby Vesco was running a metal extrusion machine, Bernie Cornfeld was making financial history. Though not yet 30, Bernie projected an air of maturity as he talked to a group of young men in Paris. He flaunted his baldness, which he'd incorporated into a look along with silk jackets and Hathaway shirts and shiny Italian shoes that discreetly raised Bernie to about five and a half feet tall. Bernie's mother, who traced her descent from Russia's Tsarina Catherine the Great, assured her boy, "If you keep a good suit, and you're a gentleman, you cannot fail to make your way."

Bernie put Sophie Cassini Cornfeld's formula to the test when he started pushing mutual funds. Standing before an audience of salesmen who had answered his ad in the Paris *Herald Tribune*, Bernie said, "I have only one question for you, really. It's the only qualification necessary for this job. Other than being intelligent, of course, which you all obviously are, and being able to speak English reasonably well, since we are dealing with American clients who are living overseas for one reason or another."

Bernie was almost whispering, another of his trademark methods for getting people's attention. The scuff of his shoes caused a few listeners to miss a word here and there. Bernie pulled up short and cast his puffy-lidded eyes across the room. "My question is a simple question. Answer it honestly, and everything else will follow."

Perhaps the gathering would not have been surprised to learn that Bernie's father, Leon Cornfeld, had made a name for himself as an actor before he was driven from his native Romania by the Communists. Shaped by his father's instincts for stagecraft and his mother's hyper-consciousness of class, Bernie knew he did not need to shout to capture his audience's attention. He needed only to capture their desire.

"Do you sincerely want to be rich?" Bernie said at last. He clasped his hands, watching the faces around him. When he spoke again, his emphasis was clear. "Do you *sincerely* want to be rich? Does it mean everything to you? Do you want to be used by the capitalist system or do you want to use it?"

It wasn't a hard test. If you answered Bernie's ad and got suited up to hear the little man with the big round head talk about selling mutual funds, you damn well wanted to be rich. And if you listened for a minute, you began to feel the power of what Bernie Cornfeld was telling you. This wasn't just another sales manager pumping up his team. Bernie was shaping mutual funds into something of world-historical importance.

Bernie believed in the power of willpower because he'd used it himself to overcome a stutter that jumbled his speech if he got nervous or excited. In his college psychology class at Brooklyn College, Bernie learned that his stuttering was a kind of social defense mechanism. He was intentionally hesitating, which he masked through sputtering, because he feared participating directly in conversation with others. Stuttering was also, according to this school of thought, a childish plea for attention. "Look at yourself in the mirror when you start to stutter," Bernie's thesis adviser commanded. "See how you purse your mouth? The mouth purser is saying, 'Kiss me. Kiss me.'" Perhaps the shame alone was enough to untie Bernie's tongue.

Standing before his Paris recruits, Bernie spoke with absolute calm. "Write down the names of your nearest relatives. Then, write down your closest friends. Then, write down your doctor's name.... Then, write down your dentist's name, and the guy who fixes your car, and anyone else you can think of. Now tear up the list and throw it away. Because you're not going to be talking to your friends. You'll be talking with strangers you just met. And you'll be persuading them to give you their savings."

Bernie had staked his reputation on mutual funds, an investment vehicle that had been around since the 1920s. Since the end of the Second World War, mutual funds had been booming. By the late '50s, Americans were holding $17 billion in mutual funds. The concept was simple enough: instead of investing directly in the market, mutual fund investors bought shares in the fund. The managers of the fund invested the cash in a diversified portfolio and returned the profits to investors. Mutual funds remain popular today because they allow individuals with small amounts of capital to enjoy the security and benefits of diversification available to large-scale investors.

To hear Bernie tell it, mutual funds were the cannon fodder of a new social revolution, beating Karl Marx at his own game. "What I've done is to apply socialist ideas about redistributing wealth in a free-enterprise context. We're in the business of transforming the proletariat into a leisured class, painlessly. It's revolutionary and it's goddamn exciting." Bernie's capitalism-for-the-masses attracted enough young men, and even a few daring expatriate American women, for him to found his own mutual fund company, Investors Overseas Services (IOS).

The IOS sales team found a willing audience among the 800,000 American military personnel stationed abroad, the men and women busily waging a "cold war" on Communism. There were also some 2.5 million American civilians who sought work overseas during the early 1960s. Bernie's investment plan was convenient, and its earnings tax-free, since IOS was chartered in Geneva and Panama, but not in the U.S.

Even before Bernie rode these people's paychecks to riches and glory, he'd enjoyed a reputation as a swinger. "Did you ever see the penthouse in New York?" IOSers asked each other jealously. Bernie shared the condo, which was known as Bernie's Whorehouse, with eight other young men. Those legendary walls fairly burst with drugs, alcohol, and lewd dancing by sporting young ladies. Bernie himself stuck with mineral water. He never smoked, snorted, shot, or drank anything intoxicating; he spoke in a voice barely loud enough for his limo, much less a disco; but he mingled with the beautiful people till dawn. The profile was definitely part of the success: "I suppose a salesman might find it easier to identify with me, as a symbol of success, than with mousy Jacob Rothschild, fiddling with his pencil."

Bernie kept area gossips atwitter when he moved his headquarters to Geneva, Switzerland. Locals knew, when they heard helicopters buzzing the Bella Vista estate and saw tufts of cotton floating in the air, that the world's most famous pornographer was in town—one of Bernie's dearest friends and business associates was *Playboy* publisher Hugh Hefner.

Bernie wrote *his* name in the history books in 1962 when he created the mutual fund to end all mutual funds. It was a mutual fund that sold shares in itself and invested in—*other mutual funds.* "A Fund of Funds!" Bernie exclaimed. The master Fund would invest in the best performing individual funds. Bernie himself reaped most of the benefits. For starters, he put large stacks of the Fund of Funds money into mutual funds owned by Investors Overseas Services. That is, Bernie put the Fund of Funds cash into his own mutual funds. It's as twisted a practice as it sounds. Bernie charged fees for investing people's money in his own investment funds.

With the economic niceties obscured by 8,000 IOS sales professionals, Bernie's revolution spread. The Fund of Funds held about $1 million in October of 1962; a year later, there was $17 million. By 1965, FOF was booming with $200 million. Besides funneling money to other IOS funds, FOF bought stakes in all of America's premier mutual funds. Knowing that the money managers back home were dependent on IOS for tens of millions of dollars, Bernie negotiated deals in which the funds charged him no front-load fees; then he charged IOS customers the fee himself.

Bernie found his "champagne wishes and caviar dreams" were coming true. He was toasted wherever he went: his twin estates in Geneva, the *Villa Elma* and the *Bella Vista*; his chateau in Haute Savoie; his apartment in Paris; his London town house; his apartment on Park Avenue in Manhattan, and his penthouse downtown. Bernie lined the walls of his office at 119 Rue de Lausanne, Geneva, with raw silk. Ed Cowett, IOS vice president and Bernie's managerial right arm, followed suit by covering his walls in red velvet. It was said that Bernie kept leopards and cheetahs at Bella Vista, letting the big kitties run loose during week-long orgies. Nineteen-year-old Heidi Fleiss was bowled over. The woman later known as Hollywood's Madam said she first tasted luxury while riding around Europe in a Rolls Royce with Bernie Cornfeld. "I don't think Bernie could bear to be alone for more than two hours," Heidi said, explaining why a teetotaler would spend his considerable leisure surrounded by cokeheads and drunks. Bernie said he gave Heidi more than $1 million in cash, and lots of "tangible support."

In the world according to Bernie, "I really don't see why affluence should cause one to surround himself with ugly people and gloomy surroundings. I think that if the affluence didn't exist, I'd also strive to surround myself with amusing, creative—*beautiful* people, if you like—rather than gloomy, dreary people. And I really don't think it's a product of affluence, because I think that all of the same kind of people were around as far back as I can remember."

****

Bernie was particularly excited about making contacts among the local rich in the so-called Third World: Rio de Janeiro, Manila, Mexico City, and Nassau. He and Hugh Hefner were breaking ground on a chain of Playboy Hotels in Latin America. "People will always go to the Playboy Hotel," Bernie reasoned, "because they're hoping to get laid." In the summer of 1968, Bernie went scouting the Paradise Casino at Hog Island, the Bahamas, where a friend and IOS colleague named Henry Buhl III flagged him down. Buhl couldn't stop talking about this man he'd just met, a young guy, 33 years old, who had forcefully acquired a $100-million company with his $6-million-a-year corporate shell. Like Buhl himself, the man came from Detroit, though the Buhl estate in Grosse Pointe sat several notches above the Vescos' clapboard house on Hastings Street.

"He's a bit, I don't know...hoody, perhaps," Henry said to Bernie. "But he's got some real action going. He's going to make some money."

"What's the guy's name again?" Bernie asked.

"Vesco."

"Is that the company's name, or his? Vesco sounds like the name of a company."

Henry pointed across the room, where Bob sat with a middle-aged couple. Bernie didn't have time to go over, but he did have a few things he wanted to discuss with Henry. The two of them moved to stand at the edge of the bar.

Bob's hosts, the middle-aged couple, were drunk. Shirley Butler was badgering her husband again. How did Allan's "personal net worth" compare to that of the other men in the room? Shirley wondered aloud. Bob didn't venture a guess, and Allan kept silent too. Without Shirley's daddy's money, Shirley continued, there wouldn't be such a thing as Butlers Bank, and Allan Butler damned well knew it. Otherwise, he'd have shut Shirley up.

"Who's the little bald guy?" Bob asked, changing the subject by pretending he didn't recognize the man Henry was talking to.

"Oh, you don't know the great Bernie Cornfeld?" Allan Butler said in a swirled-tongue whine. "He's the richest man in the world. He uses other people's money, but he's awfully, awfully rich." When Bob proposed a toast to the richest man in the world, Allan rose from the table, a luger of champagne in his fist, and staggered toward Henry Buhl, who had turned his back on the table. Bernie saw Allan coming, but too late. Allan had already dumped a foamy stream of champagne on Bernie's head.

"What are you doing?" Henry scolded the drunken banker. Allan was pretending to laugh hysterically. Bernie was trying to curse, but his stutter clipped the words into short, guttural blasts. Henry pointed at his wet friend for Allan's benefit.

"That's Bernie Cornfeld!" Henry shouted.

The Player

May 1970. Henry Buhl called Bob from Geneva to say he'd found the "Big One." Bob had been casting about for a financial services company as a way to bring in some cash and power a new round of acquisitions at International Controls.

"How about IOS?" asked Henry Buhl. By all right thinking, Bernie Cornfeld's Investors Overseas Services shouldn't have been on the market. The company had just mounted a successful IPO on the London Exchange in late 1969. Sure, those shares had lost value over the past six months; but markets worldwide were slumping. The Dow Jones, which had become known as the *Down* Jones, had plummeted from its 1968 peak, just over 1000, into the 700s, and there might be lower lows ahead. But the new IOS investors weren't going to bail out so soon.

What Bob didn't know, and Henry proceeded to tell him, was that IOS was bust. There were still millions in the various funds, nearly $500 million in the Fund of Funds alone. But the IOS umbrella corporation was bust. The IPO money—more than $50-million—had been used to cover shortages and to pay off Bernie Cornfeld and his insiders. While the shares were sold explicitly for "the development of banking and insurance," some $8 million went directly into Bernie's pocket.

The April board meeting at IOS had turned nasty when Chairman Mel Lechner pointed out that Bernie promised

$25 million in profits for 1969, "when the goddamn number turned out to be $17.8 million." Those numbers might be revised further, the board had learned, perhaps to $10 million. And early reports on the first half of 1970 looked as if IOS was going to report a loss.

"How bad?" Lechner demanded. Perhaps $13 million or $14 million. The board also learned at this time that the company had no cash, despite its recent $50 million stock sale. At a special meeting to discuss possible rescue efforts, all eyes turned to Bernie Cornfeld. Bernie stood at the head of the table, brushing his beard with his twitching right hand, waiting for his stutter urge to pass. When he started speaking at last, he launched into a spiel on a project he called Cinema City. Bernie dreamed of building his own movie studio on some 500 acres of presently worthless land in New Mexico.

John Templeton, who'd founded the revered Templeton Funds in 1954 and would later be knighted for his financial services to the British empire, sat on the IOS board. (This is the same Templeton who cozied up to Jack Bennett and his New Era Philanthropy scam in the 1990s.) As Bernie got worked up and began to purse his lips, fighting back the urge to stutter, Templeton interrupted him. "Be reasonable," Templeton said. Templeton didn't have to remind anyone at the table that Bernie had lost $200 million since 1968, trying to buy a moviemaking company from Paramount Studios called Players. "Be reasonable," Templeton pleaded.

"How can I...be reasonable?" Bernie shouted, clipping his speech when he felt his stutter coming on. "How...can I be reasonable...? When these maniacs are trying to...take my... company away from me?"

Bernie was right, of course. "There's an opportunity for you here, Bob," Henry was saying to Bob Vesco a few days after the board meeting. Henry thought Bob ought to approach the IOS board offering a bridge loan to avert the cash crisis. If IOS pulled out of the crisis, Bob would profit on the loan and secure himself a favored seat at the Fund of Funds, which was approaching the $1-billion mark. If the company was broken up into individual mutual funds, Bob could pick up any of these at a bargain. Bob won either way.

Bob needed the IOS cash because he was feeling the pinch of his rapid growth at ICC. Besides his huge loan obligations, Bob found that his track record, now that he had one, was putting the lie to his reputation. The young Turk who had wowed investors with his "financial agility" had picked up a bevy of loser companies. "He made bad mistakes with high technology companies, like

Captive Seal and Datron, for example, one mistake after another," said Larry Richardson, who headed one of the few successful companies in Bob's stable. "He became enchanted with the products they made, which he thought he could use as the basis for a stock promotion deal."

Bob was itching for a hold inside the aeronautics and space exploration industry. If the United States was putting men on the moon, Bob, like every other businessperson alive, figured he ought to share in the glory and profits. Richardson said, "In technical areas, he was easy to con into an oversold position. The advanced technology deals became promotional devices in his mind. But they never got airborne."

In Geneva, Bob told the IOS board he would extend them a $20-million line of credit, with $5-million up front. "It is not our intent to assume control of IOS," he said, reading from a prepared statement, "but simply to benefit by what may be an attractive investment opportunity.... To this end, we do not insist upon control of the board of directors or principal officers of IOS.... We do, however, expect to have representation and to be in a position to understand proposed office alignments, as would any major institutional lender under the prevailing circumstances." Translated, Bob was telling the board: You can keep some of your people in place, but I'm calling the shots. Bob also demanded assurance that the present directors would fix what ailed the company. Unless a full reorganization was effected by July 1971, Bob would receive cash payments worth $3.5 million, plus stock warrants representing one-third of the company. Practically, the agreement meant that if the board didn't make a move, Bob would become a major stockholder as well as the leading debt holder. He would have a very good chance of taking over the company.

Bernie Cornfeld, still a major shareholder, was madder than ever. "Who does this small-timer think he is?" ICC had reported a puny $100 million in sales, and profits of $4.5 million for 1969. Even with its numbers revised downward, IOS was producing three times anything Bob Vesco owned. Bernie reminded anyone who would listen that IOS still controlled assets approaching $2 billion. "This Vesco is an interloper," Bernie said.

Bob had been called worse. He agreed to meet with Bernie, though he didn't expect to make a good impression. On August 7, Bob spent a couple hours having dinner at Bella Vista. The following morning, Bob told a group of reporters, "The conversation in the evening was not on the kind of business level we were accustomed to dealing with. It was not as conclusive as we'd hoped."

Bernie was more explicit. "I discovered exactly what his interest in our situation was. Namely, he wanted to control our company based on a $5 million, uncollateralized loan. I said I wouldn't support him. In fact, when I learned just what he had in mind, I told him to pick up his marbles and get the fuck out of my house. I said, 'I don't want to see you around here again.'" On a roll, just a click ahead of his stutter, Bernie continued, "Robert Vesco indicated to me last night that as long as he had complete control, he wouldn't care that much if he had Adolf Eichmann in as chairman."

Bob had only one comment in reply. "Bernie has to go."

The Dude

On December 21, 1970, guards in front of the White House were approached by a 30-something man who said he was carrying a letter for President Richard Nixon. The guards laughed at first. The man was wearing black velvet pants, festooned with a 4-by-6-inch gold buckle, and he dangled a purple cape off his shoulders. The five-page note was written in pencil on an American Airlines notepad. But when the guards realized the man was really who he said he was, they sent the note straight to the Oval Office.

"Dear Mr. President," it began,

> First, I would like to introduce myself. I am Elvis Presley and admire you and have great respect for your office. I talked to Vice President Agnew in Palm Springs three weeks ago and expressed my concern for our country. The drug culture, the hippie elements, the SDS, Black Panthers, etc. do NOT consider me as their enemy or as they call it The Establishment. I call it America and I love it. Sir, I can and will be of any service that I can to help The Country out. I have no concern or Motives other than helping the country out.

Elvis and Dick Nixon talked for an hour that afternoon. According to the official record, written by presidential aide Bud Krough, "The President indicated that he was aware how difficult it is to perform in Las Vegas."

The King urged the President to enlist him as a domestic spy. Elvis confided, "I have done an in-depth study of drug abuse and Communist brainwashing techniques and I am right in the middle of the whole thing where I can and will do the most good." Nixon expressed his belief, "that Presley could reach young people," and said it was important that Presley retain his credibility.

****

Bob Vesco didn't have the $5 million he'd promised to loan IOS. But his banker friend in the Bahamas, Allan Butler, did. Allan could only let the money out for a short time, he worriedly told Bob, or the Butlers Bank would go under. And Shirley would kill him. Bob kept Allan alive by convincing the IOS board to place $10 million in "cash reserves" with the Butlers Bank. Bernie Cornfeld had almost been right: Bob did intend to take control of IOS with a $5 million loan, only Bob didn't make the loan, Allan Butler did. Then, by transferring $10 million into Butlers Bank, Bob effectively repaid the loan and built up a surplus. IOS was funding its own takeover! And Bob Vesco was becoming a Frankenstein of Fraud.

His abrasive performance at the Wayne, New Jersey, Holiday Inn in March 1971 was nothing compared to what Bob held in store for the annual conference in Ontario that April. A showdown vote for control of the company pitted Bob and his current management team against Cornfeld loyalists and a generally hostile crowd whom Bob called the "dissidents." Bob had rigged the vote slightly in his favor by secretly buying up Bernie Cornfeld's shares. Using a company called Linkink Progressive, chartered in Panama, he'd snapped up 15 percent of the company for 95 cents a share—total cost, $5.5 million. No one knew that Bob had bought the shares, though Bernie bruited his suspicions in nightclubs and spas across the world. "It's a Panamanian company with a Chinese sounding name. Its shares are supposedly held by six different banks, one of them Swiss, the proprietor unknown, and it'll probably turn out to be Bob Vesco's grandmama."

Even with this advantage, Bob nearly lost the vote. In fact, six hours into the count, his insider on the election committee snuck a message to Bob that his management team was running behind. Bob mounted the dais and announced that the meeting would be suspended while the voting process was reviewed. The hall roared in protest. An army of men in suits yelled and shoved. They stood on chairs; they threw paper and pens at the dais. Bob leaned behind the podium for cover and quipped, "It's like the Vietnam War in here."

Retiring to his suite in the Royal York, Bob told his team, "We'll have to vote the stock-option shares." An Ontario judge had forbidden Bob's team to vote the 3.6 million shares held in the employees' stock-option program. But he'd lose without them, so Bob wrote a check for the shares, and voted them anyway.

"What about the Geneva loan shares?" Bob asked. He was referring to a block of 135,000 shares which were held by an IOS bank in Geneva, held as collateral against loans made to IOS employees. Bob knew the shares had been intentionally placed outside management's control, but he instructed one of his attorneys to write a legal justification for voting them anyway. While the brief was prepared, a Vesco lieutenant named Ulrich Strickler was dispatched to physically retrieve the shares. In Geneva, Strickler butted heads with the bank's director, who refused to give up the key to the safety deposit box where the bundle of shares lay.

When Strickler called Bob to let him know they'd failed, Bob growled, "Get me those shares!" Thus, on Sunday morning Ulrich Strickler was ushered into the safe of the Overseas Development Bank by two deputy managers, their hands trembling as they pushed back the steel door, each man reminding Strickler they still didn't have the key to the box. Once inside, Strickler set his briefcase on a tabletop and pulled out a crowbar.

Using every share in his arsenal, legally acquired and otherwise, Bob squeaked out a victory:

> *17,202,483 FOR Vesco Management*
>
> *17,104,316 AGAINST Vesco Management*

Bob had won by a 100,000-vote margin out of 34 million shares voted. "With that behind us," he told the room, "we are now addressing ourselves to the income side of the ledger."

****

Boonton, New Jersey was also in an uproar. Pat Vesco was being doubly assaulted: by the construction crews building the helipad on the family estate, and by her Boonton neighbors, who didn't want the concrete slab or the helicopter traffic it was designed to service invading their rural haven. When Bob called in—from Geneva or Nassau or Paris—Pat relayed the troubles, and Bob shrugged them off.

The Boonton zoning regulations were the least of Bob's concerns. A man named Stanley Sporkin, assistant director of enforcement at the SEC, was threatening to shut down both International Controls and IOS if Bob didn't make amends.

Sporkin was waving around a 1967 order that prohibited IOS from dealing with companies or mutual funds based in America. The order had declared IOS off limits until Bernie registered his company with the SEC, which he refused to do. Bernie dodged the order by arranging for a brokerage in London to move money into American funds based on IOS "suggestions." He had also moved his American-based IOS mutual funds across the border into Canada and restyled them as "proprietary funds." Though technically independent and open to the public, these funds each had only one investor, the Fund of Funds. While the FOF couldn't invest directly in American companies, the proprietary funds *could*. By 1971, Sporkin was ready to challenge Bernie Cornfeld's artful dodging. Whoever controlled IOS, Sporkin warned, would have to pick up part of the tab.

Sporkin also noted that the 1967 order had declared any company acquiring more than one percent of IOS stock became "a legal subsidiary" of IOS, and so was also subject to the American ban. Since Bob had purchased 3.6 million shares of IOS from the employees' Stock-Option plan, he'd placed himself under the 1967 order. As far as the SEC was concerned, International Controls Corporation was now a legal subsidiary of IOS and was no longer allowed to trade its shares in American markets or to hold direct interest in American companies.

For good measure, Stanley Sporkin had one more gripe. As part of Bob's $5-million loan to IOS, he had acquired IOS stock warrants worth $3.5 million. The company had promised that unless a reorganization plan was instituted by July 1971, Bob would be paid the cash value of the warrants. Sporkin's analysts noticed that, although the deadline hadn't expired yet, the International Controls financial statements for the first half of 1971 had already claimed the warrant money as income. The ICC cupboard was nearly bare, so Bob had slipped the money into his first- and second-quarter earnings. The move also signaled that Bob had no intention of reorganizing Investors Overseas Services. He was gonna loot her for everything she had.

The Other Dude

In August, an unassuming American-in-Paris type named David Tucker attended a party at a Swiss villa. Tucker drew lots of attention that night from IOS loyalists—the *dissidents*, as Bob Vesco called them—because Tucker had filed criminal charges against Bob Vesco. Among the 135,000 shares which Ulrich

Strickler had crowbarred from an IOS safe deposit box the previous April were 60,000 shares owned free and clear by Tucker. One of Bob's team had noticed the Tucker shares at the last minute, and held them back from the voting, but Tucker filed theft charges anyway.

A few weeks later, while he proceeded happily through a terraced garden, Tucker was approached by a youngish-looking man wearing silver-framed eyeglasses with smoky lenses. The man scratched his sideburns and spoke to Tucker in a low register, conspiratorially, scanning the garden paths while he mumbled from the corner of his mouth. He wore a white leisure suit with kite-sized collars.

"I'm traveling incognito, but you know who I am, don't you?" the man asked Tucker.

Elvis, maybe, Tucker thought, only this guy was too young and thin.

"I'm Don-Don Nixon," the man said when Tucker wouldn't venture a guess.

Don-Don was President Nixon's nephew, the wild-and-wooly son of Dick's brother, Donald. Don-Don had spent his early 20s at the Great Lakes Naval Training Center, preparing other young men for overseas combat. As soon as his military time was done, he had "run off into the hills" of northern California. Don-Don's Uncle Dick, who was mounting a fierce re-election campaign, ordered that something be done about Don-Don. The President of the United States couldn't be fighting hippie Communist rebels while his own nephew lived in a hippie commune. "A lot of people suggested I leave the United States," Don-Don said. "I'd been doing things I'd rather not discuss, so I wasn't surprised when I got a visit from the Special Investigations Unit." Federal deputies brought Don-Don to the office known as Dick Nixon's San Clemente White House, where chief of staff John Erlichman announced, "Congratulations, son. You're going to work for a man named Bob Vesco."

Just six weeks later, a very pumped Don-Don was negotiating with David Tucker on behalf of his new employer. Whoever ended up running IOS would have to deal with the SEC, Don-Don pointed out. With the stateside contacts he and Bob had together, the Vesco team was the only one with a real chance of turning back the regulators and saving IOS.

"So you're on Vesco's payroll?" Tucker asked.

"I'm a managerial consultant," said Don-Don, nodding his head to the thump of "Viva Las Vegas" in the background.

"How long have you been in Switzerland?" Tucker asked. He was intrigued by Don-Don's situation, and Don-Don, who loved to talk about himself, told the whole story.

As the two men parted with a handshake, Tucker said he'd think about what Don-Don had told him. The next day Don-Don was deported by Swiss authorities. Seems the First Nephew had never filed for a work permit, and "someone" had turned him in.

****

Bob spent only one night in Saint Antoine prison, Geneva, for lifting David Tucker's shares. Judge Pagan had no legal authority over the IOS parent corporation, which was chartered in Canada, and he knew it. The Tucker shares had never been voted anyway. But Pagan railed, "You have endangered the reputation of Swiss banking by your actions." Pagan made his point by locking Bob up. Bob was out in a day, thanks to a phone conversation between U.S. Attorney General John Mitchell and Judge Pagan's superiors.

Back home, Stanley Sporkin at the SEC was publicly accusing Bob of draining $224 million from various funds under the IOS umbrella "to further personal interests and pursuits." In Washington that spring, Bob lunched with Maurice Stans. As the financial leader of CREEP—the creepy acronym for the Committee to Re-Elect the President, Stans said he and President Nixon could sympathize with Bob's special problems. Bob needed someone to remove the SEC number-crunchers who were blocking his path. CREEP needed cash to hire some "plumbers."

Bob made at least two payments to CREEP: $200,000 in cash, which was omitted from the campaign's legal disclosure forms, and a check for $50,000 that made it on record. Bob's in-kind contribution—two yellow-and-brown helicopters at CREEP's disposal 24/7—was also gratefully acknowledged.

The cash was ultimately delivered to a man named G. Gordon Liddy. This self-styled political mercenary accented his stern features with a hairless dome of a head and a horsetail mustache. Liddy had been hired to break into The Watergate building, home of CREEP's campaign rival, the Democratic National Committee. Vesco legend says that Liddy and his plumbers—so-called because they wore maintenance worker's coveralls—received a second $250,000 from Bob. The money was never traced, however, and G. Gordon Liddy ain't telling what happened to it.

Maybe Bob felt the doom encircling himself and the President. While the SEC proceedings dragged on, Bob was using money from Investors Overseas Services to buy himself a Boeing 707 at a price tag of $5 million, including a five-year maintenance plan. On board, Bob customized air vehicle N11RV with a high-frequency phone system, allowing him to talk on the phone while riding in the plane—which in 1972 sounded like science fiction to most people. He built a dining room for 14 in the forward cabin. Bob's office included a roomy conference area and two secretarial desks in addition to his own. The master suite sported a sauna and exercise area. But the gem of this flying pleasure dome was its disco. That's right, the boy put a disco in his airplane: leather lounge chairs, a mahogany bar, a hardwood dance floor, and beat-sensitive lighting that flickered in time to the music. To boost the boogie factor, "flying playgirls" occasionally came along for the ride.

Given Bob's progress before the SEC, it looked as if he would be needing his wings. The official complaint, released in November 1972, sought the $224 million missing from IOS and also mentioned "other large sums of cash," a veiled reference to the money Bob gave to CREEP, which was also the target of a federal investigation. Bob was taking the 5th Amendment on all Sporkin's questions at this point.

In early 1973, Maurice Stans became the first of the Nixon loyalists indicted and Bob Vesco became a fugitive. With Don-Don Nixon at his side, Bob emptied out the contents of his New Jersey office. Pat and the kids had already been flown to Costa Rica, where Bob and Don-Don would soon join them. The two men, who had become like father and son, spent an afternoon burning files and cramming necessary items into moving boxes. In a memo to Don-Don's father, who was expected to show the document to the President, Bob once more mounted a self-defense. If cash wouldn't swing Bob a deal, he offered his diplomatic services. He referred to himself in the text as RLV, Robert Louis Vesco.

> *It is in the best interest of the U.S. to cause the SEC to drop the entire action, since RLV can uniquely assist U.S. objectives in Morocco, Spain, Costa Rica, the Bahamas, the Dominican Republic, Haiti, and many South American countries. This capability is available for official use by the U.S. on a clandestine basis.... It should be appreciated that since these countries view RLV as an independent international person and not a representative of the U.S. that intimate real views are necessarily disclosed.*

First Elvis, and now Bob Vesco, offering to help the President fix things. As Tricky Dick himself might have put it, the entire U.S. government was convulsing, and Bob Vesco was volunteering to share pillow talk with dictators and drug lords.

The Burble

Norman LeBlanc was burbling again, sloshing over the sides, and it wasn't noon yet. Just another day in the life of the man in charge of Kilmorey, a shell corporation that had bought up all but $150 million of Bernie Cornfeld's IOS funds. Bob Vesco had sold all his interests in IOS too. If anyone was asking, only Bob called the shots. The pressures of playing hatchet man for Bob Vesco kept Norman so wired that he usually began splashing gin into his water glass around 10 a.m. He became known as "Norman the Burble" because he wouldn't stop talking just because he had stopped making sense, or even to take his next drink.

Bob had learned to live with the Burble's habits. Not just because the keys to the IOS kingdom were in the Burble's name, but because the Burble made financial statements and articles of incorporation sing. Moving an IOS company named Vector into the Vesco holdings for a $1-million corporate credit, the Burble magically boosted those assets into $3 million cash.

The Burble's other talent was for making chunks of cash disappear into offshore shell corporations. "I have some 40 shell companies that I keep putting on top of one another to keep people from finding out what's going on," he said, candidly describing his feats to Robert Hutchison, author of *Vesco*. "Of course they are only good for so long, then I put another on top."

The Burble magic kept Bob's inner staff on salaries between $75,000 and $100,000 apiece, plus luxury apartments in the Bahamas, Costa Rica, and select sites in Europe. He kept a special pad of stationery with transfer orders and his signature already written. If he was away, Norman phoned the office and, provided his secretary could understand him, she filled in the cash amounts he dictated.

And there were the planes to attend to. Bob ruled the skies in his blue-and-white Boeing 707, named the *Silver Phyllis* because he said they were all going to catch *syphilis* from the party girls bumping and grinding in the disco cabin. Norman the Burble and five other Vesco assistants rode either in a Sabrejet or a Gulfstream. The gang was especially enamored of the Gulfstream because it had once belonged to Frank Sinatra. The Burble had gotten the bird for cheap from the Teamsters union.

"I wonder if I'll become a second Howard Hughes," Bob said to the Burble, who was barely listening.

The Don

Not since the days of Papa Hemingway had an American commanded such attention in the Caribbean. The name *Don Roberto* drifted through Costa Rica, the Bahamas, and Cuba. A restaurant owner in San Jose, Costa Rica, said, "From the first day when Mr. Robert Vesco ate here, I have had a fantastic number of clients. They come and ask where Robert Vesco sits. Sometimes I say inside, sometimes I say outside. Little old ladies come from San Ramón to see if he is here."

José Figueres Ferrer, the beloved Costa Rican president, embraced the fugitive like a brother of the revolution. "I admire the regulatory work of the American government," said Figueres, who was affectionately known throughout the country as *Don Pepe*. "But with Vesco they overdid it. I think he offended their vanity because he was able to stay out of jail."

To receive the love of Don Pepe Figueres opened doors. Born to rich parents, Don Pepe came of age in the 1920s and 1930s. He put his socialist ideas into action with a farm collective that raised hemp and with a handful of factories. He named this estate *La Lucha Sin Fin*, "the struggle without end." Don Pepe personally taught his 2,000 workers how to make rope, which he considered an ancient and honorable art. During the 1940s, he was arrested for criticizing the dictatorial government of President Calderón Guardia. In 1948, after Guardia rigged an election, Don Pepe led a bloody uprising and took control of the government.

After the revolution, Don Pepe broke with Latin American tradition—instead of slaughtering his foes, he welcomed them back into the country. Costa Ricans ought to concentrate on building a strong, modernized economy, Don Pepe believed. Soon after taking power, Don Pepe shut down the Costa Rican military. He said he had gotten the idea reading the social critic and science fiction writer H.G. Wells. "When I found myself with two armies on my hands—one, my victorious rebel army, the other, the government's defeated army—I decided to abolish them both." For his truly amazing statesmanship, Don Pepe was awarded the Nobel Peace Prize during the 1950s.

By the time Don Roberto Vesco arrived in 1972, President Figueres spent more time reading balance sheets than he did loading bullets. He'd had hair transplants and a face lift; he wore elevator shoes to compensate for his height, winning him yet another pet name, "Pepe Tacones," Little High Heels. But when Sandinista rebels from Nicaragua tried to hijack a plane in San José, 66-year-old Don Pepe ordered explosives experts to blow out the wheels of the plane. Ripping a machine gun from a SWAT officer, he turned to charge across the tarmac, but was restrained by cooler heads. A few hours later, when a terrorist walked cockily onto the plane's exit ramp, Don Pepe drew his revolver and plugged the man in the stomach from 30 yards away.

Don Pepe publicly praised and defended his guest, Don Roberto, but they had little in common besides their vanity and love of money. Bob obviously wasn't the SWAT type, and he didn't share Don Pepe's literary interests either. Don Pepe said, "I realized after he decided to stay, we didn't have much to talk about. I wanted to upgrade him culturally, and so I finally decided that O. Henry was about on his level, so we got him a volume of *The World of O. Henry*."

Don Pepe also presented his friend with a legislative security blanket—that is, he pushed a law through the Costa Rican parliament that allowed the president to grant political asylum to anyone he chose. The country would still extradite coke dealers and throat slashers; but if you won Don Pepe's love, you could stay. Thousands of Costa Rican nationals took to the streets, shouting against the "Vesco Law." Their signs demanded,

VESCO LAW NO!
CUÁNTO $$$$ [HOW MANY DOLLARS?]

In return for the Vesco law, Bob arranged for one of the IOS mutual funds—now controlled by the Burble—to invest $2 million in Don Pepe's ranch, *La Lucha Sin Fin*. Throughout Bob's stay, he kept Don Pepe, his son Martí, and a battalion of Figueres cronies flush with no-payment loans and unsupervised investments.

Bob read business correspondence and legal documents from his office, near his 1,000-acre ranch, *Lomas de Ayarco*. The main house was split into two sections, with a swimming pool on either side. Further into the property was a lake stocked with fish. A boat dock held cigarette boats and played home to the yachts christened *Patricia I, II,* and *III*. Because none of the three servants could produce satisfactory American pancakes, Pat cooked breakfast for the Vesco brood herself, who numbered five now, with the arrival in 1974 of a boy, Patrick. It wasn't easy, trailing an outlaw father through the Caribbean; and the longer Bob dragged things out, the more the family would suffer.

****

In mid-1974, a showdown with the U.S. government looming over his head, Bob fell sick. He'd been suffering from a chronic infection of his urinary tract and had to undergo an operation. For the rest of his life, Bob would need what he called "a Roto-Rooter job" every few months. Otherwise the infection would spread and ultimately kill him.

Stanley Sporkin at the SEC had passed off Vesco to the Justice Department which had decided to go after Bob in Bahamian court so they could avoid a nasty set of arguments about extradition. Paul Curran fronted a phalanx of five U.S. attorneys, seven outside counsels, and two Bahamian lawyers. When Bob arrived in Nassau, Curran met him with deputies and announced he was placing Bob under arrest. Bob smirked and asked to place a courtesy call to a friend on the island. But Arthur Hanna, the Bahamian Minister of Finance, said there was nothing he could do. Bob reminded Hanna of a recent $200,000 donation to the Progressive Liberal Party. Bob had also sunk $3 million into a catering business linked to the Prime Minister Lynden Pindling, and some $11 million into the Bahamas World Airways, $2 million of which kept a Lear jet at Pindling's constant disposal.

"I feel as if my friends are deserting me," Bob told Arthur Hanna.

"Call your friends," Hanna advised, meaning Pindling himself. When at last the prime minister took Bob's call, Pindling offered his regrets and suggested, "Get yourself a good lawyer." Pindling recommended the most prestigious lawyers in Nassau, two Bahamas-born locals named Orville Turnquest and Etienne DuPuch. Bob hired both men and assigned nine Americans to advise.

The Vesco defense squad faced three charges: *wire fraud*, because Norman the Burble had transferred IOS monies by wire; *obstruction of justice*, for the CREEP cash; and *mail fraud*, due to a $50,000 payment mailed to the address of Henry Buhl III, the man who'd introduced Bob to New York's financial firms. While other stockholders went begging, Norman the Burble had cashed out Henry Buhl's shares.

When he wasn't in court, Bob stayed in the commando-like headquarters that Norman the Burble had constructed for them in central Nassau. The facilities were located on the top, seventh floor of the Charlotte House, an elegant building Bob picked up cheap when Allan and Shirley Butler filed for bankruptcy. Arriving at Charlotte House, Bob was ushered into the lobby by uniformed guards. Wendy Kenyon, Norman's secretary, recognized the boss in her desktop security monitor and buzzed him through the front door, which was armed with motion sensors. The communications room, located in the heart of the building, was stacked floor to ceiling with the most sophisticated radio equipment money could buy. Bahamian authorities forced Bob to reduce his signal after it knocked out all other communications to the island. You were able to enter the communications room through only two doors: one located behind a false wall in Norman the Burble's adjoining bedroom, the other located behind a false wall in Bob's bedroom. The boys could stay up all night talking and nobody would ever know the difference.

Monitoring his shortwave one night during his trial, Bob heard the voice of an old friend. He pretended at first like he didn't recognize the man.

"Bernie who?" he asked.

"Look Bob, I've come all the way down here to see you and I would appreciate your cutting out this screwing around and getting together with me."

Bob and Bernie Cornfeld were reunited at the Paradise Island Casino, a store they'd both tried to buy at one time. Bernie spoke first. "Bob, I get the impression you're involved in something kind of crazy. Do you want to spend the rest of your life as a fugitive?"

"I'm going to be a rich fugitive."

"Doesn't it trouble you that it's other people's money?"

Bob shrugged off the thought.

"What about all those widows and orphans you're robbing?"

"They have their problems and I have mine."

"They'll blow your brains out," Bernie said, meaning the chorus line of lawyers chasing the IOS money trail.

"It's you they're going to get, Bernie."

Bob was right again. After a few weeks of hearing arguments, Judge Emmanuel Osadebay sided with Bob. Osadebay found all three charges lay outside the Bahamian government's jurisdiction. The *wire fraud* statute required crossing state lines and the Bahamas had none; bribing an American official violated American laws, not Bahamian laws; *mail fraud* was also a crime left unmentioned in the Bahamian books. If Curran and his prosecutors wanted Bob, they'd have to round him up and take him home.

Bernie Cornfled wasn't as lucky as Bob. Shortly after Bernie returned from Paradise Island, police officers knocked at his Nassau hotel room and led him away in handcuffs. He was immediately extradited to Geneva, Switzerland, where he was jailed for 11 months. When IOS crashed, the members of the legendary sales force were instantly transformed from paper princes into bankrupt frogs. All their millions lay in IOS stock options, which were rendered worthless by Bob's looting and plundering. After holding Bernie nearly a year in jail, a Swiss judge dismissed the charges for lack of evidence. Poor Bernie schlepped back to America, where he shared the Douglas Fairbanks mansion with an organ grinder's monkey named Sam and a parrot named Alfonse who spoke only two words, the first beginning with *F* and the last one being *You*.

Old and New Friends

Bob eluded the U.S. government one more time, but he lost his right arm in the process. Norman the Burble spent the first months of 1975 recovering from a ruptured pancreas. The doctors in Panama City told him he was lucky to be alive and suffering. A diabetic who covers the stress of 18-hour days with a stream of gin-and-tonics should expect to collapse. While he recovered from surgery, Norman spent time talking with his wife for the first time in a while. He held their child, a son born in the summer of 1974 while Norman had been holed up in the Nassau command center. "Hell, I'm 38 years old," the Burble decided. "I'm ill. My marriage is on the rocks. I've made no dough. Fuck it. I'm not going back to the Bahamas."

It would take a while to liquidate the shells and stuff the money into accounts controlled by "Bill Lee," one of Bob's aliases. But Norman had ceased to burble. From that point, he and Bob did business at arm's length; Norman returned to his native Canada. We're shed of Bob Vesco, he promised Karen and their son, and he hoped it was true.

Bob was playing it cool. He had a safe-house apartment on the island of New Providence; he had money stashed all over the Caribbean; he carried a suitcase bearing an array of wallets, one for each of several aliases, each with $5,000 pin money. He kept a four-wheel drive truck and a small fleet of boats fueled and stocked for travel, and he kept an extra briefcase, containing $100,000 bail money, with him at all times.

With the kind of friends Bob was making, he couldn't be too careful. A young man named Skip Wilson called Bob's secretary in San José, Costa Rica during the spring of 1976. "I have information concerning a spy operation targeting Robert Vesco," Wilson said to María Ermida Ulate. Wilson himself was that spy, having been converted to the spook life by an unlikely alliance of the CIA, the FBI, and the Drug Enforcement Agency (DEA). Wilson said he would take Bob down physically if he had to. "If you look at my record, it speaks for itself," the 27-year-old told a federal inquiry later. Wilson meant his record for kicking ass in prison, where he'd fended off three attackers, "and I wound up being charged with aggravated assault and battery, and they wound up in the hospital." Wilson had little else going for him as a spy. His crimes ranged from grand larceny and altering a motor vehicle title to counterfeiting checks. He had become a stoolie in prison and somehow, by a logic known only to himself and the agencies who hired him, won a shot at bagging an international fugitive.

Bob arranged a meeting with Wilson on a dark road that ran behind a disco club on the edge of San José. Wilson sat in the front seat of a Mercedes. Bob sat in the back. When Wilson tried to turn around, Bob told him to face forward. Right off, Wilson volunteered he had been sent by the CIA and others; but he was prepared to act as a double agent, twisting the feds to Bob's advantage. By Wilson's own account, he did everything but lick Bob's Topsiders.

"I have never had the honor of being in the company of someone with such stature as you," Wilson said he told his back-seat host.

"Well, I am sure that you have," Bob answered.

For several hours after the two parted, Wilson sat in his hotel room, where Bob had ordered him to await further instructions. Word came at last from a Costa Rican immigration officer and a policeman, who handcuffed the agitated ex-con and carried him to jail for violating his parole. The facilities received low marks from Wilson in his exit interview.

"The first three or four days I wasn't fed anything," Wilson complained to his American handlers. "I was lucky to get water occasionally. There was human manure in places, human urine standing an inch thick on the floor in spots. You could hardly breathe. I was allowed cigarettes, but no matches. I finally got one lit from a guard and went through four or five packs on a chain, lighting one off the other. Some I didn't smoke, I just let them burn to keep the light going."

Don Pepe was also calling on Bob these days. The old rabble-rouser had lost his lock on Costa Rican politics. He had taught his people the lessons of democracy so well that they turned the process against him. Don Pepe's handpicked successor, Daniel Oduber, was launching a move to roll back the Vesco Law. Don Pepe himself had been investigated by the American government for money flowing through several of his New York bank accounts, money the Americans said came from Bob Vesco.

"When I make a friend, I go all the way," Don Pepe said, and steadfastly refused to give Bob up. But a new round of demonstrations made the future clear, the crowd waving signs that demanded, "*VESCO FUERA*" (Vesco Go Home).

Don-Don Nixon told Bob he wished he could go all the way, but he couldn't. He was in love, Don-Don explained to his mentor. The girl's name was Helena. They were going to be married. Her father was throwing a traditional Jewish wedding in the States. The last of his wild oats sown, Don-Don was converting to Judaism and starting a family. For the huge California wedding, Danny Vesco, Bob's oldest son, stood in his dad's place as Don-Don's best man. That same year, when Danny married a Costa Rican woman, Don Pepe Figueres acted as the groom's father in Bob's stead.

By the time the Costa Rican parliament repealed the Vesco Law in 1977, Bob already had a spectacular hideaway set up for his family. Pat and the kids were shuttled to Cistern Cay on a yacht named the *Salude*. Just south of Nassau, the entire 200-acre spread of Cistern Cay belonged to the Vescos, who could see for miles from their house atop a steep bluff.

Bob spent lots of time in the Bahamas talking with their new neighbor, Carlos Lehder-Rivas, who owned the next island over, called Norman Cay. Perhaps the nastiest drug-lord of the Caribbean cartel, Carlos once forced his own mother to sneak a bag of cocaine into Los Angeles with her luggage. "She wanted a free trip, to see Disneyland," Carlos explained. "Everybody works in this business."

Carlos styled himself a modern-day revolutionary, growing his hair long and curly, wearing combat boots, "like Che Guevara," according to a former henchman. Carlos believed that his father's German blood had offset the racial liabilities of his Colombian mother, and he promoted this view through a group he called the National Latin Movement. The 15,000 strong NLM praised the misunderstood genius of Adolf Hitler and offered neo-Nazi solutions to restore the greatness of Latin America.

Carlos moved 70 percent of America's cocaine supply through his headquarters on Norman Cay. A massive runway system hopped at odd times of the day and night. A jet landed; lieutenants from the National Latin Movement removed the cocaine from the appliances which were listed on the plane's official cargo list. Then the packages were ferried to the American mainland using several smaller planes and speedboats. This scattershot approach to smuggling guaranteed that while a single batch might be intercepted, the bulk of the shipment made it through.

When Carlos Lehder encountered a rival, an informant, or an idealistic judge, he didn't insult them or make cracks about how he was going to steal their company; he shot them dead in the street. And this man represented Bob's future. Legitimate businesspeople, even those firmly entrenched in the scummy world of offshore finance, wanted nothing to do with him. "I had a dream we slept together on a cold night," a potential partner told Bob. "In the morning you had all the covers."

Supposedly Bob saw himself acting as a financial adviser to men like Lehder-Rivas. He'd show the drug bosses what to do with their cash, taking a cut like any agent. Bob could also arrange for the protective services of politicians like Bahamas Prime Minister Pindling. The husband and father of five chose to ignore the finer points of where the money came from.

Danny Vesco has recalled, "My dad's decisions brought a lot of suffering on the family." After the Vescos relocated to Cistern Cay, Danny took up permanent residence in the U.S., changed his last name to Adams, and refused to speak with his father. The other children remained loyal, tromping off like good soldiers when Bob hustled them onto a yacht and sailed off to nowhere. During the hotter phases of Carlos Lehder's business, or when Bob thought the CIA was back on his tail, he took his chickies on mini-cruises. One trip in 1979 lasted two months, during which time Bob and Pat lived on a 60-foot yacht along with their youngest boy, Patrick, their daughter Dawn, Dawn's infant child, and the child's nanny. The captain Bob hired said, "They were the worst people I ever had on the boat—and I told him so. Nobody ever smiled. Vesco stayed by himself reading and doing book work. Dawnie pouted. Pat and Patrick walked on the beach gathering shells. The nanny was grumpy."

The Beard

Ronald Reagan reclaimed the White House for Republicans in 1980, promising to heal the wounds of Watergate with some good old-fashioned sabre rattling. Soon after the inauguration, American "advisers" were arming guerilla soldiers across Latin America, battling Communist-supported movements like the Sandanistas in Nicaragua. The Drug Enforcement Agency complemented this assault by declaring war on the region's cocaine dealers.

In 1982, as Carlos Lehder-Rivas began moving his operation into Colombia, U.S. Senator John Kerry was questioning witnesses about Robert Vesco. Kerry suspected Vesco had tried to pay off members of former President Jimmy Carter's administration in exchange for a pardon. Vesco was accused of trying to sell Libya's Mohammar Khaddaffi some American airplanes, though the deal fell through. And, witnesses told the Senator's commission, Vesco was financing the drug trade.

If anything, the political charges helped Vesco charm the last of his several hosts, the one Bob called "The Beard." Fidel Castro said he wouldn't stand for drug scandals in The People's Revolutionary Republic of Cuba. Bob vowed he didn't touch the stuff. He did have some expertise in smuggling, though, and perhaps he could be of service to the Revolution. Castro offered Bob asylum with the understanding that Bob could help the Cubans dodge the trade embargo that kept American goods from entering the island country.

"Latin America is a powder keg," Castro warned Americans in a news conference. The keg would explode, Castro said, if one people continued to go hungry while another people grew fat and smug. When reporters pressed Castro about rumors that Cuba sheltered drug runners, he grumbled those were "filthy lies."

Next the reporters asked about Rober Vesco. Yes, Castro admitted, the fugitive Robert Vesco had visited Cuba. "Medical assistance was requested—he was treated for his urinary tract condition in Cuban hospitals—and we gave it. We would do the same for anybody else. I don't know that individual. I know people say he has money. We are not at all interested in him. We would say no to a billion-dollar offer." Castro scolded the American government for hunting Vesco "like a deer through the world.... They're persecuting a man that's living with his wife and family. What do they want to do, take his eyes out, or turn him into ground meat?"

Privately, Castro didn't think so much of his brown-eyed boy, who at the time—August 1985—had been living in Cuba for several years. *"Puta cono!"* Castro raged, after the reporters had gone. *"Puta cono!"*

The dirty whore, as Castro dubbed Bob, wasn't even putting out. Vesco had brokered a few black-market deals for the Cubans, but he'd never brought anything major to fruition. Bob owed Cuban authorities $1 million for the losses on a single deal, some food-processing equipment that was nabbed by U.S. customs. His enemies whispered that Don Roberto had staged the raid himself, diverting the merchandise and profits elsewhere.

Bob again disappointed his host in 1986 when he promised to publish a tell-all exposé of America's corrupt financial services industry. Castro even hired a writer to put Bob's memories into prose. Norberto Fuentes, who'd written a book on Hemingway's life in Cuba, was told that Father Fidel himself wished for the American's story to be told. Fuentes afterward described his meeting with "a big-boned character, dressed in oversized khaki Bermuda shorts, sockless in leather sandals. He was surrounded by a complement of security agents led by an ever-present Cuban mastodon named Junco."

Bob spoke to Fuentes about the writing project at length, but only in obscure terms. The story involved "a series of personalities," prominent men with whom he had done business. "A lot of these people are still hunting me. Or else they refuse to work with me. They're in it up to their asses, just the way I am. I'd like to call attention to the fact. And say, while I'm at it, 'Hey, I haven't forgotten you guys.'"

Bob said the dirt he had on these guys went so deep, and the players were placed so high up, that he didn't want to publish the stories all at once. Bob suggested to Fuentes they start off slow. First publish a round of relatively tame stuff. Then prepare a second volume with the really explosive material. Then make the rounds, visiting the "personalities," offering to drop each one from the book for a price.

Fuentes sent word to Castro that the famous Don Roberto was a common blackmailer and perhaps a little kooky.

****

Somehow, though, Bob held on. He curried favor with The Beard by maintaining investments in Cuba's sugar, tobacco, and coffee farms. He is said to have directed a money-laundering operation at Cayo Largo. It was also said that Bob earned brownie points by ratting out the popular general and revolutionary hero, Albert Ochoa. Castro publicly executed Ochoa and three other men in 1984 after learning that Ochoa had helped Carlos Lehder-Rivas fly cocaine through Cuban airspace. Bob Vesco remained alive and free, although it was he who first introduced the drug lord and the general.

In 1989, when Lehder was captured and sentenced to life in prison, he agreed to testify against his former associates, including Bob. A U.S. grand jury indicted Bob on charges of aiding and abetting the bloodthirsty Hitlerite. But The Beard pretended not to notice.

Over the years, Bob lost many of his special privileges in Cuba, like free long distance. He had to give up his second home. He and Pat lived in a plain white two-story home in the Havana suburb called Atabey. Bob drove a 10-year-old Russian Lada, and Pat did her shopping in a used Honda Civic. Most ordinary Cubans shrugged at the subject of their notorious guest. "He did not talk much," said a caddie at the Country Golf Club where Bob occasionally played the nine-hole course. "He did not leave many tips, and his Spanish was not very good." Bob was left alone for the most part and might have lived poshly into his dotage, except he still had the itch. He was looking for a deal.

****

Don-Don Nixon returned to the Vesco household packing the deal of their lifetimes. No, scratch that, baby. Not their lifetimes, not their children's lifetimes. This was history-making stuff. Don-Don had discovered a wonder drug, he told Bob. "It will wipe out 90 percent of the pharmaceutical companies, leave 50 percent of the hospitals empty, and change the political, social and economic structure of the world."

Don-Don's wife, Helene, had been diagnosed with breast cancer in 1985. After enduring chemotherapy for several years and having a breast removed, Helene still suffered. She had also been afflicted with arthritis. Don-Don scoured the world, looking for a way to help his beloved, but the odds remained in favor of the diseases. Then in 1989, an L.A. doctor started treating Helene Nixon with an experimental drug which the doctor called Trioxidal. Dubbed TX for short, the drug is obtained by cooking down the citronella plant, whose extract is used as an insect repellent in outdoor candles. Weeks after going on TX, Helene found her joints freer, her movements less pained. Her strength returned, and her cheeks showed color again. By the end of the year, the arthritis was gone. The following year, Helene's cancer went into remission.

Don-Don flew to Havana, where the Castro government had built state-of-the-art operations in biotechnology. Leading the world's medical advances brightened Father Fidel's image and reaped millions in funding. Don-Don figured with his old friend Bob working the business angles, they couldn't lose. Something about the citronella's makeup allowed it to act as a kind of universal neutralizer. TX could turn back any disease. Don-Don knew the drug cured arthritis and cancer, and who knows, maybe AIDS, too.

In short order, Bob assembled a select group of Cuban backers, including members of the Castro household. "Me and Bob went over to talk to Ramón, Fidel's farmer brother," Don-Don recalled. "Ramón's pet pig had a foot infection and it would have died. They put some of the ointment on there, and the stuff got rid of the infection immediately. The whole family started using it."

First at the Health Ministry, and later at Labiofam, Cuba's premier research facility, scientists began performing clinical trials on TX. Meanwhile Don-Don and Bob were rounding up foreign investors, passing samples from Labiofam around as finished product, telling their backers the drug was already approved and endorsed by the Cuban government.

Though they gathered funds wherever they found them, Don said he and Bob steered clear of the darker elements in the Latin American financial community. "We were approached by heavy drug money from wherever—old Nazi money from Brazil. But I am anti- all that stuff. So is Bob. It goes against everything I know about him."

Pat Vesco was happy to see Don-Don and glad for Helene's good luck. But as she approached 50, Pat wasn't eager to see her husband revving up the Big-Deal machine again. Pat wore her hair, which was streaked with gray, in a pageboy cut and donned tortoiseshell glasses for reading. For her, the more spartan aspects of Cuban life held the most charm. "The pace is so quiet and easy," she said.

Word came from Miami in 1992 that Bob's mother, Barbara, was in declining health. Pat volunteered to return to the mainland and care for her mother-in-law. (Bob's father Donald Vesco died of a heart attack in 1984.) Truth be known, Pat had longed for a way out. Though she yet recalled "the early days" her of marriage as a Cinderella story, she admitted, "More money didn't make it better." No one would accuse her of disloyalty, having spent nearly 30 years faithfully dragging five kids through the tropics at the behest of their outlaw father. When asked by a *Fortune* reporter to describe life with Bob, Pat said, "He was demanding. Maybe that's the way to put it."

Soon after Pat's departure, Bob began openly courting a Cuban woman named Lydia Alfonso. A 40-something mother who lived in the town of Playa with her teenage son, Lydia knew her paramour under his assumed name, Tom Adams. When they had become sufficiently intimate, he told her his real name.

"I said, 'Who's Robert Vesco?'" Lydia recounted. "I had no idea. He showed me some books written about him, but I never read them. I love him. I love everything about him." Besides wielding her more voluptuous charms, Lydia proved herself an able business partner. She was no Norman the Burble, perhaps, but Lydia knew no fear. A Vesco contact in the Bahamas said, "She came to Nassau and picked up more than $100,000 in cash to take back to Cuba. She has guts, that she has. She did things only a Cuban with her connections would do."

Maybe Lydia would've acted more cautiously if she had read the books "Tom" gave her and learned how many of Robert Vesco's associates ended up broke or in jail. Even Pat had been locked up in 1986 when she and Norman the Burble were caught in Panama City with a satchel full of cash. Though Pat and Norman were released the following morning, they never saw their cash again.

"I'll just say life with Bob was difficult," Don-Don Nixon opined, echoing the prevailing sentiment of the outlaw's women. Bob still threw fits as he'd done during the wild years in San José. He was as likely to call Don-Don "you stupid fucking idiot" as he was to call him "son." If anything, the paunchy Vesco, who'd traded in his gangsterish black suits for guayabera shirts and jeans, had grown more paranoid, his manners more strident. The backers of TX complained that Vesco was shorting them, deliberately keeping them in the dark, that he didn't have the support among Castroites he claimed.

There was a more vicious rumor, too. Don-Don prayed it wasn't true.

The End

A little past noon on May 31, 1995, Don-Don sat upstairs in Bob's house in Atabey. His friend was meeting with a delegation of Cuban officials on the lower level. Per their usual arrangement, Don-Don stayed out of sight during the discussion. For nearly an hour, Don-Don fiddled with paper clips at Bob's desk and strained to make sense of the murmurs drifting from below. Then one of the officials called for Senór Nixon.

Treading the stairs like a cat approaching a pack of hounds, Don-Don saw right off the situation wasn't good. "They've got Bob standing there—everybody's surrounding him—and I come around and pass him. Bob doesn't say anything. Not a word. He looks totally stunned. I said, 'What the hell is going on?' They said, 'We're taking Tom away.'"

Don-Don was asked to bring his things to the BioCaribe hotel, where he spent a month being interrogated by Cuban authorities. "We know you are CIA, Nixon!" the men shouted in Don-Don's face. "You're CIA.... You're laundering money for the drug cartels."

Don-Don replied, "You're out of your mind."

"Fine," said his captors, "You're not telling the truth, so you can go to jail." The Cubans also commanded Don-Don to sign a statement denouncing Vesco, who was accused of acting as "a provocateur" and "an agent for foreign special services."

Don-Don swore the charges were trumped up, and he refused to sign the statement denouncing Bob, so the Cubans made the choice a bit clearer: "Sign this, or you're not leaving."

"Where do I sign?" asked Don-Don.

****

Over his three decades as a fugitive, Bob made offers to people in the Nixon, Carter, and Reagan administrations to inform on his Latin American hosts. There's no record he ever passed on anything useful; and if he was employed by the CIA, it did him no good once The Beard decided to pull the plug. Cuban Prosecutor Edelmira Pedris charged Bob with endangering the Cuban government and its state-run biotechnology infrastructure by pretending the TX drug was fully approved and endorsed by the government when it was not. The initial reports on TX from the Health Ministry had, in fact, been negative. TX was no wonder drug. Pedris also accused Bob of filching money from the TX scheme to spend on the woman known as "Vesco's Cuban wife," Lydia Alfonso.

During the summer of 1996 Bob appeared before a tribunal of three judges. He wore standard issue prison coveralls, dinghy and gray. He seemed lethargic and weak. A scruffy growth of facial hair made him look a bit like Fidel. The judges sentenced Bob to 13 years in prison. Lydia Alfonso, convicted as "Tom's" accomplice, got nine years. Since the verdicts, there has been no word on Bob's condition. But to an ailing man approaching 70, spending more than a decade in a Cuban jail sounds like a death sentence. Perhaps this outlaw monster has been subdued at last.

Eddie "Crazy Eddie" Antar

(1947 -)

CHAPTER 7

The Antar Complex:
Eddie Antar

"All men hate the wretched; how, then, must I be hated, whom am miserable beyond all living things!"
—*The Creature*

There's a scene in the movie *Splash* when the mermaid, played like a fish out of water by Darryl Hannah, wanders into Bloomingdale's. Unsure about her new surroundings, the winsome blonde parks herself in front of a wall of television sets. A man's face on 20 screens is raging while the mermaid tests the glass with her long, white fingers. "I'M INSANE!" the man yells. He rends his clothes. "HOW CAN I OFFER THESE PRICES?" His cheeks are inflamed. He's gyrating his hands and whiplashing his neck. "BECAUSE I'M CRAZY EDDIE! I'M TOTALLY NUTS! I'M INSA-A-A-A-A-ANE!" The mermaid is frightened.

In his heyday Crazy Eddie became a fixture of the tri-state area, rivaled only by Lady Liberty herself for instant recognition. Everybody knew Crazy Eddie. Crazy Eddie's Electronics Emporia commanded the market for stereos, CB radios, telephones, televisions, not to mention appliances and jewelry, plus the very latest in trendy gadgets, such as personal computers with 512 kilobytes of internal memory. Crazy Eddie's Record and Tape Asylums housed acres of entertainment choices. If it ran electronically Eddie sold it for the cheapest prices known to man.

But Crazy Eddie was a fake. Literally. That face in the pixels belonged to a balding Irish actor named Jerry Carroll. The Eddie Antar monster was someone else entirely, a black-bearded misanthrope with an ego as large as his bankroll. Not to malign Carroll's performance, but there was always a bit too much in Crazy Eddie's histrionics. Somehow you knew that this guy wasn't just some storeowner with a frustrated artist inside. Crazy Eddie commercials were more campy than *Batman* reruns. He wasn't insane, he was just goofy.

Eddie Antar, on the other hand, the *real* Eddie....

From Aleppo to Flatbush

At 13 Eddie was cutting classes and spending his afternoons in shops around the Manhattan Port Authority Terminal hawking T-shirts, home appliances, and cheap audio equipment. It was 1961. The air on 42nd Street hummed with traffic and herds of people shouting, laughing, going places, looking for kitchen gadgets, love, and a decent knish for 15 cents. New Yorkers, and Americans in general, had never known such wealth as they were enjoying in the post-war boom, and Eddie plugged into this noisy energy. Every exchange sizzled in his hands. He saw each person stepping his way as his next chance to shine, the opening strains of a show in which Eddie danced, dazzled and, if necessary, harangued his customer into a purchase. If little Eddie Antar didn't sell you something, you weren't buying.

Eddie was hell-bent to conquer the world, or at least the strip of it running from Brooklyn to Manhattan. He styled himself a Lord of Flatbush, donning a black leather jacket and oiling his hair to make the thick locks shine like ebony. "Eddie was like...the Fonz," a companion recalled. After a good quarter-hour's worth of combing, his head appeared to be crowned by rows of insulated wire. Like his father, Eddie wasn't very tall; in fact, none of the Antar family stands above 5' 10". But Eddie lifted weights, talked tough, and backed it up with his fists if he had to. A swollen eye, puffed and purple, he displayed like a trophy. He gained a reputation for arranging back-alley deals and handling merchandise of questionable conveyance. One of the lawyers who later helped put Eddie in jail, a man named Howard Sirota, recalled, "I grew up in the same neighborhood as Eddie Antar, and I knew that he was a crook. I had friends who worked for him and who had done business with him. I knew who Eddie's friends were. They were the guys in the neighborhood whom I tried to avoid."

If Eddie sparked fear and loathing on certain corners, others saw him as the inspired scion of an honorable clan. Eddie's father, Sam M. Antar, had opened his first store at the age of 19. With a sandy complexion and a thick head of dark, curly hair, Sam was known for his rambunctious disposition. He stood about 5' 7", which combined with his ready smile to project a boyish air, a quality Sam would carry into his dotage.

Sam was the first Antar born in the U.S., after Murad and Terah Antar, Eddie's grandparents, moved here from Aleppo, Syria. One of the world's oldest cities, Aleppo was known for ages as the most important trading link between the Far and Middle East, a place where Jews like Murad and Terah worked in their market stalls alongside Arabs, Turks, and Egyptians. Murad Antar liked to remind his sons of a proverb: "An Aleppine can sell even a dried donkey skin."

It was no accident, then, that Sam Antar became a retailer and expected for his sons to follow him into the trade. New York's Syrian community, which spread from 20th Avenue and 60th Street throughout the Bensonhurst area of Brooklyn, was filled with families who made their living in wholesaling, retailing, or reselling. Eventually the neighborhood became known as Aleppo-in-Flatbush, and its citizens were called *S-Ys* (pronounced ess-wie) for the first two letters in the word *Syrian*.

Syrian Jews were often treated harshly by New York's Ashkenazi Jews. The Ashkenazis, who came mainly from Germany and Eastern Europe, looked askance at the darker skinned *S-Ys*. Some Ashkenazis called the Syrians dirty *Arabsche Yidden* (Arab Jews). "We had a name for the Ashkenazi, too," Sam Antar remembers. "We called them *Yids*, or more usually, we called them *Jay-Dubs*, for the first and last letter of the word *JeW*. To mock them like." *S-Ys* maintained a strict Talmudic religious observance and brought their sons into the family business, usually some type of retail operation, such as linen shops or gift shops, or wholesaling inventory to these shops.

After a stint in the Combat Engineers during World War II, Sam returned to Brooklyn and married Rose Tawil, whose father owned several clothing stores. He and Rose bought a beauty of a four bedroom home on East Third Street, between Avenues T and U. Economically the neighborhood ran the gamut from the very rich to the just-getting-by. A $5,000 house sat next to a $150,000 house. In later years, the better-off families, including the Antars, would move to the Jersey coast. But in those days, a former resident recalls, "It was more important to be near the community, regardless of how much money you were making."

The families of Aleppo-in-Flatbush centered their lives around the *Shar'aree Zion* (Portals of Zion) Congregation, a massive rotunda auditorium whose grandeur spoke to the Aleppine Jews' religious devotion. Though Sam Antar was constantly on the go, tending retail concerns in Detroit, Kansas City, Charlotte, Tucson and Bakersfield, he never began a day without first giving prayers at shul. Besides the gift shops he started with, Sam eventually owned discount department stores, costume jewelry concessions, and clothing stores across the country. Even so, Sam kept the Sabbath in whatever town he happened to find himself, ceasing work of every sort from Friday sundown until Saturday night, refusing to perform simple calculations or to flip on a light switch because of the Talmud's commandments not to work and to "light no fires" during Sabbath.

Sam and Rose began their family in 1948 with a son, Eddie, who was named after Rose's father. A growing household didn't change things much for Sam. He continued his nomadic life, chain-smoking Chesterfields and downing barrels full of coffee. After Eddie, Rose brought a girl, Ellen, and two more boys, Mitchell and Allen, into Sam's house. The kids saw their father only sporadically. But they had no doubt they still were part of a family. As the most successful of Murad's offspring, Sam was *de facto* head of the extended Antar network. Adjmis, Tawils, Gindis, and Shaloms tramped through Sam and Rose's Brooklyn home, which became a kind of headquarters for family business. "You had your business connections with your own people," one Antar remembers. "Often we got into retail and different ventures because we couldn't get jobs elsewhere. Other business people, other Jews even, wouldn't work with us. So we took care of our own."

Doing business with "your own" made it easier to fudge receipts, taking advantage of all the cash that rolls each day through a retail operation. Sam has freely admitted, with a gleam in his eye and a *whatever* roll of his shoulders, "I skimmed millions and millions of dollars. But I never lied, I never cheated anybody. I cheated the government maybe, but not anybody. I always worked hard." No one ever accused an Antar of dragging his feet. The entire family bounces with the energy of people born to sell. They've pushed everything from trinkets to air conditioners, and if they could buy a donkey skin at wholesale, chances are they would send you home with one.

As Sam's boy Eddie became a young man, he more than fulfilled the family tradition. Neighborhood admirers nicknamed him "Kelso," after a famous race horse. Eddie made it his business to live up to the name, strutting his stuff from Ocean Parkway straight into Times Square. He was pocketing several hundred dollars a week, real wages in the early 1960s, especially for a high school kid. As soon as he turned 16, Eddie left Abraham Lincoln High School altogether. No use pretending, everybody knew where this boy's future lay, and it wasn't in a book.

"By the time I was 15," Eddie remembered with a grin, "I was out of school officially. I mean, there was no keeping me in. My parents did try. But what was school gonna do for me? It's not like I wanted to go hang out on the streets. I wanted to work. I liked the sense of independence I got from buying my own pair of pants with my own money."

He got a lot more than pants. A natural salesman, Eddie was soon bringing home $700 to $1,000 a week, first at his Uncle Zookie's handbag shop, and later by selling appliances on commission at a department store called Crawford's, owned jointly by Sam M. and one of Eddie's cousins. Eddie's peculiar version of charisma gained him his second nickname. *Kelso* became *Crazy Eddie* when some teenage girls from his high school cut class to spend an afternoon browsing the aisles at Crawford's. Eddie was trying to sell a 30-something housewife a deep fryer. He flattered her, teased her, he darted up and down the aisle grabbing for display models, he cupped his heart with his hands and bounced on his toes, as if unloading this particular fryer meant the difference between living and dying. When the woman said she'd think about it, Eddie blocked her exit with a tall shelf. The woman had to either buy the fryer or set up housekeeping.

"Hey, Crazy Eddie!" the girls squealed when the woman finally squeezed down the aisle and out the door.

Eddie had a blast working sales but he dreamed of something larger. "If I'm getting $600 or $700 a week, my boss, he's getting a lot more," Eddie complained to his brothers, Mitchell and Allen. "Before I'm 20," he bragged, "I'm gonna be running my own store. Just like Pop."

He missed his mark by just a few months. Eddie had recently turned 20 when Sam agreed to stake him in a small electronics outlet. All the family turned out to stretch the banner—*Sights and Sounds*—across the door at 1119 Kings Highway, Brooklyn, near Coney Island Avenue. The full name of the store was Sights & Sounds ERS, a letter for each of its partners: Eddie, his cousin Ronnie Gindi, and Sam M.: ERS. Like all Antar ventures, the stereo store—"a 12-by-12-foot hole in the wall"—was a family affair. The only problem at Sights and Sounds was that nobody bothered to come to the party. They got plenty of traffic from friends and relatives, but not enough paying customers from outside the circle. A year and half after their grand opening, Eddie and Ronnie were about to go bankrupt. They owed $400,000 to trade creditors alone. Ronnie decided he'd had enough and left to join another relative's wholesaling business.

Eddie wasn't through. "Nobody knows we're here because they don't expect us here. They'll go to Cortlandt Street in Manhattan for high-fidelity components; if they're thinking affordable, but still nicer than the department store, they'll visit Audio Exchange on Flatbush Avenue or Davega's on Fulton Street." Eddie said they needed some promotions to get people's attention. "It's part of the culture," he explained to his father, "It's rock and roll."

"We were the greatest combination in the world," Sam M. said later. "I had an idea and he was a fantastic executor. I would come up with beautiful ideas but I could never execute them. But Eddie, he was able to execute them. I had an eye, and he had a way for making it happen." Sam bought Ronnie Gindi's half of Sights and Sounds and put the whole thing in Eddie's hands. Sam would retain a one-third partnership, technically, but he had his own affairs to look after. Eddie would run the business alone.

"Listen, Eddie," Sam lectured, "I'm giving this to you, but it's not *for* you. You can grow this business for the entire family. All these years, I've been going here, going there, pouring yo-yos and squirt guns into display bins, kicking shins under the table, passing envelopes. This is our chance, the family's chance, to have more than a few retail stores with cash income. We can have everything."

Eddie was barely listening. He found a space for lease on King's Highway, just a few blocks from the old Sights and Sounds and within sight of the Portals of Zion rotunda. With a flair befitting Arthur Fonzarelli, the man from Avenue T strutted onto the Brooklyn stage. For starters, he renamed the store. Sights and Sounds sounded like it came out of *Life* magazine. Eddie was looking for *Rolling Stone.* Remembering the squeals of his teeny-bopper fan club, he decided to call his store "Crazy Eddie's Ultra Linear Sound Experience."

A visit to Crazy Eddie's wasn't just shopping, it was a ride on a fast train. If Eddie let a customer out the door without selling them something, he felt miserable. At the least, he'd talk them into leaving a few dollars on the layaway counter. Eddie's flashiest maneuver, a holdover from his days pushing deep fryers at Crawford's, was to simply block a person's way—he'd walk over, lock the door, and announce, "Now you have to buy. We're all staying until we can make a deal." He talked one customer into taking off his shoes, then grabbed the shoes and put them under the counter. "Now," Eddie mocked, "You want your shoes back, we're gonna make a deal."

Behind the store, hunched over in a 12-by-12 inventory room with no ventilation, one of Eddie's cousins was busy uncrating turntables. Wearing short pants, chewing on his fingernails, his buck teeth and chubby cheeks marking him for life, the boy lacked Eddie's natural charm. The boy's name was Sam. His father was Uncle Eddy, Sam M.'s brother. They called the boy *Sam E.*, which came out sounding like *Sammy*, to distinguish him from the patriarch. To Eddie the boy was just another cousin on the payroll. But this little boy, this Sammy, so nervous he made others start to fidget in response, would bring down the mighty Antars without ever making a fist.

I'M INSA-A-A-A-A-ANE!

Sammy Antar remembers coming home from school one afternoon and finding out he'd be working in Eddie's store. "I had a job for $5 a day with Ronnie Gindi, working at Crawford's. Eddie offered me $10. Off the books, $10 cash. I would be making more money, but not just that, I would also be training to come into the business when I was a man. I was 14 years old in 1971. My father's business was not that much a successful business that I'd go into his business as his son. So I went into Crazy Eddie's. It was like Eddie saying I was going to come along. Though of course he didn't say it in so many words. If he spoke to me, it was like, 'Hey kid, clean the fucking bathroom, will ya?'" Sammy said they used him "as a maintenance boy, a janitor."

While Eddie swaggered in his leather jackets, Sammy talked hardly at all. He was shy, draped with a pot belly, and he walked in zig-zags. Sammy was prone to say something stupid if he could think of anything stupid. He knew he'd never be as charismatic and confident as Eddie. But he studied hard and made good grades. Sammy was a good kid. "I remember when I was in camp, about six or seven years old, Mitchell, Eddie's brother, he helped me out. Eddie didn't want anything to do with me. Mitchell, he took me out and taught me how to play...baseball. He gave me some kind of dignity." As for Eddie, Sammy remembers, "Eddie was a godlike figure to me. We all looked up to him like a leader. He worked out with weights, he carried himself like a prince or something, he was just so charismatic."

Life at Crazy Eddie's was good, even for the Antar family dork. "The first year, for a holiday bonus, Eddie gave me $1,500. In 1971, when you're a 14-year-old boy, that's a lot of money. Of course I idolized him. He didn't have to hug and kiss me. The next year, I was making $30 a day and I got a $5,000 bonus."

"Our families revolved around the businesses," Sammy remembers. "When we got together for dinner or a holiday, nobody talked up the football game or political bullshit. They talked business. When I got married in 1979, at the age of 22, I moved onto the block. Eddie lived there, so did Mitchell and Allen, his brothers. So did Sam M., all of them, on East Second between T and U. When Eddie's sister got married, she and her husband, Benjamin Kuser, they moved in next to her father. So that area, between T and U streets, it was called the *Antar Complex*."

****

One night in 1972, just after midnight, a deejay billing himself "Doctor Jerry" came on the air at station WPIX. Rattling his way through a spot for a local stereo store, Doctor Jerry Carroll ended the ad with a peculiar tag line. "Crazy Eddie," he sang in a *basso profondo* windup, "His prices are IN-SA-A-A-A-ANE!" Carroll's "A-A-A" ratcheted into the laugh of a cartoon crazy.

During the next song, a listener called to say he loved the way the Doctor yelled, "IN-SA-A-A-A-ANE!" The caller was Eddie Antar. He told Doctor Jerry to say the line that way every time. Soon, Jerry Carroll had become Crazy Eddie, and listeners followed his call—*I'M IN-SA-A-A-A-ANE!*—straight into the Antars' cash registers. By 1973, Eddie was opening a second store. Two years later, he'd placed a third Crazy Eddie operation in Manhattan and established a corporate headquarters to supervise further expansion.

Jerry Carroll put a face on the audio insanity in 1975, when he barged onto greater New York's television screens, blazing new trails in just how hard you could push a product. Eddie gave Carroll a wad of money and told him, go crazy. So, during a volcanic heat wave, viewers watched Crazy Eddie swabbing his perspiring face with a soaked rag, wailing in pain, his only relief the cool, cool prices available on Panasonic stacks. Crazy Eddie cavorted with baby ducks, bathing beauties, and dancing midgets. Crazy Eddie modeled Santa suits, leisure suits, and his birthday suit. In a movie-style scene, shot in a men's bathroom, a gang of Brooklyn hoods pranced around, working pocket combs through their greasy pompadours, humping their shoulders to look tough. Suddenly, they burst into song, doo-wop style,

> *When you think you're ready,*
> *Come to Crazy Eddie.*
> *He's got the cheapest prices,*
> *You know 'cause you been told.*

The chorus built to its hook:

> *Cra-zy Ed-die Won't-Be Under-Sold.*

As Jerry Carroll took on the public role of Crazy Eddie, Eddie himself became a sharp-tongued drunkard and braggart. He'd once ranked among Brooklyn's greatest salesmen, but Eddie was becoming a Dealmaker. He'd still do anything to get your cash. But he wasn't nice and his techniques weren't limited to stealing your shoes. A full black beard accented Eddie's thick lips, which were often scowling unless he was laughing at his own jokes. He lived on fast food and Stolichnaya. If he slept three hours in a night, he considered it a quiet evening. He'd show up late for a meeting, grouchy, lurking behind dark glasses, with Sugar, his 100-pound German shepherd, in tow. Sugar's sharp snout and serious eyes contributed to Eddie's negotiating power. He'd raised the dog himself, wrapping his forearm in a towel and teaching it to fight.

"What he did to that dog was a shame," Sammy says ruefully. "He took a fine animal, this little puppy that wanted only to run and play, and he made it a monster, always mean, always tense."

****

Sugar wasn't the only one feeling mean after a few outings with Eddie. His high school sweetheart, who became his wife in 1969 just as he was breaking into the electronics business, was finding that life with lover boy had turned into a serious drag. Her name was Deborah Rosen, a lovely blonde woman admired for having a bounty of good sense as well as a cheetah-sleek figure. She wasn't exactly the woman anyone expected Eddie to marry. Debbie was soft-spoken, reserved, gentle. Eddie was a maniac, constantly working his angles. She was a *Jay-Dub*, Jewish but not Syrian, from the shinier side of the ethnic tracks.

As soon as Debbie graduated from Brooklyn College, she and Eddie got married in a lavish ceremony at the Congregation Shaare Zion. They moved into a three-bedroom brick house on East Second Street, across from Sam and Rose. Debbie took a job teaching second grade in **Borough Park**. Two years later she quit, after she learned she was **pregnant**. Twin girls, Danielle and Gabrielle, were born in January of 1973. She never worked again.

Debbie's husband was in the process of making retail history, but Debbie was unimpressed. She hardly saw Eddie, who spent 14-hour days in his stores and then hit the town for long evenings "talking business," which naturally occurred in crowded uptown clubs. Debbie and Eddie's fights, which had become legendary for their duration and ferocity, eventually dissipated into a black wall of estrangement. The more stores he opened, the more Eddie had better things to do. He'd married her, given her kids, given her money. The rest she could do herself.

Sammy says, "He'd started drinking hard by this time. He'd always liked to party, but as he got more successful and the stakes got bigger he drank a lot more. It made him mean. He'd get drunk and spew his venom. He'd tell Debbie she wanted him to fail. He accused her of using him for his money, because she liked to spend a lot. One night she tore into him. She said that he took her career and her life from her, that he threw her in a house, impregnated her, and abandoned her. She told him she knew he slept around, and she'd kill him if she ever got proof. At this point in the conversation, Eddie was about to pass out. All he could hear was Debbie raving at him, not her words."

Eddie drew payback on a snowy Friday night in February 1977. About 2:30 in the morning, he stepped out of a discotheque called Hurrah's and was grabbed by two men. Each man knifed Eddie several times in the stomach, then dropped him to the sidewalk. Doctors at Roosevelt Hospital feared he wouldn't live through the night. It would take six operations to repair the slashers' damage.

Sam M. took a train to the hospital early Saturday morning, as soon as he got the phone call about the stabbing. It was over a woman, the caller informed Sam. Eddie wasn't going to say anything, but he knew well and good where the hit came from. Stalking to his son's bedside, Sam hissed, "What were you doing out there? What were you thinking? Aren't you a married man? You're behaving like a kid, Eddie.... And besides," Sam shrieked, his voice echoing down the hospital corridors, "It's the Sabbath! What are you doing out on a Friday night?"

Recovering from the assault, Eddie never looked back. He began remodeling his private office at Crazy Eddie headquarters. Besides a massive marble desk and leather furniture, the room contained a full bar and a workout area. Eddie, clad in his trademark sweatsuit *noir*, pumped weights during business meetings. His phone rang constantly, about a quarter of the time for business, the rest a stream of inquiries from drinking buddies and the women he met at clubs. The Fonz was morphing into Mr. Saturday Night.

A supplier's representative remembered that Eddie didn't look at him the entire time they were negotiating. "He was lying on his back on the weight bench when we got there. He talked with his head leaned back or just at the ceiling. After a while he got up and fixed himself a drink and motioned for us to help ourselves. Then he went back to the weights." The tough-guy act was aided by Sugar, who took a notion to sit on the couch next to the nervous rep. The man left with a deal to everyone's satisfaction, but the terms were strictly Eddie's.

Another Part of Life

Bob Marmon, who took over the Crazy Eddie operations after the Antars were ousted, feels a mixture of disdain and admiration for his erstwhile opponents. "There was everything wrong with how the family ran the company. But the sad thing is, Eddie Antar had the right idea. He proved that a free-standing electronics store could happen. Everybody thought electronics had to be part of a department store, where you could expand and contract the walls depending on what's hot. Eddie had the idea that a free-standing electronics store, all hyped up and promoted, could make it alone. He was right.... But he was stealing from the first day."

Sammy Antar admits the Antars always ran parts of their business underground. "We didn't think of it as fraud, just as part of our experience. Committing fraud was just like another part of life.

"For example, we paid some of our employees off the books. It's not uncommon, you know. No different than paying a babysitter cash. You just don't show everything to the government."

One of the people paid off-book was Allen Antar, Eddie's brother. As Judge Harold Ackerman later recounted during Eddie's trial, "Allen claimed that his entire compensation when he worked as a store manager was a weekly paycheck of $300.... Yet he drove a Jaguar..., was married with three children, two of whom were in private school with a tuition of approximately $25,000. Moreover, on a purported $21,000 annual salary, Allen was also able to take a three-day trip to Las Vegas where he proceeded to lose $19,000 playing keno."

The malfeasance became bolder as the company grew. Sam learned by watching his father, who directed a plan to skim cash out of the store receipts. "In 1973 my father started handling all the financial duties for Crazy Eddie's. The store managers would drop off cash to the house after they closed at 10 o'clock, or someone would pick it up." At least $2,000 to $3,000 of each day's purchases were paid for with cash, which Eddie's managers dutifully separated from the checks and credit card slips, hauling the sorted receipts to Uncle Eddy's house.

Sammy tells how, "My father would talk with Eddie and Sam M., and then he'd make the money into bundles: one bundle was deposited as store receipts, one bundle was to pay employees working off the books, the other bundle would be skimmed." Uncle Eddy kept $200 to $250,000 in rubberbanded bills hidden in his floorboards beneath an old radiator. When the stacks got too thick, Sam M. took the money to his house, where he stashed part in a padlocked file cabinet and the rest in a false compartment he'd constructed in his ceiling. Eddie had better than $200,000 lying in boxes underneath his bed. "This is fraud the old-fashioned way," Sammy says, "using strictly cash. That way there's no paper trail. At least a quarter of the merchandise that came through, we bought with cash, through independent jobbers, then we sold for cash." For every $5 reported as company earnings, the Antars took $1 for themselves.

After a while the radiators and phony ceilings were overflowing with cash. In October of 1979 Sam M. and his brother, Uncle Eddy, took their wives to Israel. Each member of the party carried $5,000 cash in their bags, which they used to open accounts at the Bank Leumi. Once the accounts were in place, a parade of Antars kept the cash machine running, carting several hundred thousand dollars a piece per trip. Eddie made several trips himself. According to Antar lore, he insisted on strapping stacks of large bills across his body and then hopping his plane. Presumably he had reason to believe he would never be patted down by a customs officer.

In April of 1980 Eddie's brother Mitchell and their sister's husband, Benjamin Kuszer, flew into Tel Aviv. Also accompanying them was an attorney named Solomon Antar, one of Murad Antar's nephews, who'd recently been named Crazy Eddie's corporate counsel. The three were carrying $600,000 in their suitcases. Hauling cash in increments this large required several participants because, as Sam M. pointed out to an unamused federal judge, "A million dollars is too much in one suitcase."

The family skimmed some $3 million to $4 million a year. No one knows the totals for sure. In a single Israeli account, Number 31332, the Antars deposited more than $6 million between 1980 and 1983. Later this money would provide the key to Crazy Eddie's finest hour, but for the moment it was tax-free, lying comfortably offshore, soaking up interest dividends by the ten-thousands. Sammy says, "Now we were going from kindergarten to the first grade in the school of fraud."

The New Year's Eve Massacre

By the early 1980s, Eddie was itching to list his company on the stock exchange. Jerry Carroll, who served Eddie as an armchair adviser as well as pitchman, told his boss, "Going public is the wrong thing. It's a different world, and it's run in particular ways. You're the wrong guy to go public." Carroll might as well have been talking to Sugar, the German shepherd. "Eddie always did what he wanted," Carroll shrugs.

As part of his IPO strategy, starting in 1979, Eddie skimmed a little less cash each year. So even if his sales had been flat (they weren't), the financial statement showed growth, because now more of the actual receipts were being reported. The strategy became known as the 3-2-1 method: fewer dollars skimmed each year boosted profits until the Initial Public Offering cashed everybody out. "Who knew," Sammy wonders aloud, "that telling the truth was so lucrative?"

By the end of the decade, the Antars promised, we'll run 50 stores. Some $8 million of the IPO funds, according to the CRZY prospectus, would be used to move the company into a new 110,000-square-foot headquarters in Edison, New Jersey. The flagship building would carry the Antars into a billion-dollar future.

But not everyone was convinced. The family had never let anyone get a look at their organization. No one from the company had spoken to the press in more than a decade. Even now, as they prepared to mount a public offering, the family wasn't talking. According to scuttlebutt and police records, Eddie's contempt for his wife and kids had circled back and slapped him in the face. Eddie and Debbie had five daughters by the winter of 1983, and they had little else. Both routinely threatened divorce.

Sam M. cornered Eddie in his office. He said, "Son, your womanizing, drinking, and carousing brings shame on everyone in the family, but most especially on five little girls: Simone, Nicole, Danielle, Gabrielle, and Noelle." Sam named each girl in a Mosaic voice and held five accusing fingers in front of Eddie's heavy-lidded eyes.

Eddie replied, "I am a big boy. I am over 21, you know. You can't tell me what to do."

"Tell him you're through," Sam M. told his daughter-in-law. "Either he acts right, or you're going to divorce him. Tell him I'll throw him out, just like I did Allen." In the mid-70s, when Eddie's younger brother Allen divorced his wife for another, (non-Jewish) woman, Sam barred Allen from family gatherings and had him fired from the company. Allen despaired. After a year and a half of unreturned calls and no luck finding any new business partners, he gave in, divorced his new wife, and remarried his first wife. Sam M. was taking the same stance against Eddie. If he couldn't make Eddie back down with a direct confrontation, he'd use Debbie as a lever.

Sam knew to expect a tougher fight from Eddie than he'd gotten from Allen. Mr. Saturday Night was getting loud these days. He'd limited himself to only one lover, but he was fiercely loyal to her. She played the ingenue to his strutting Little General. She lived rent-free in a Manhattan apartment building and drew a salary from a Crazy Eddie subsidiary.

Debbie Antar, who supervised the new Antar Complex in Oakhurst, New Jersey (where Sam and Rose had also moved), knew everything about Eddie's secret life with his new woman—her phone number, address, and how often Eddie visited her each week. And Debbie knew the woman's name: "Debbie." The other woman also had blonde hair. But where *Debbie 1* (as she's still called to this day by the Antars) dressed like a well-to-do mother of five girls—the very picture of Oakhurst wholesomeness—*Debbie 2* (Debra Ehrlich in legal documents) liked her makeup punchy and her hair with body.

Such are the vagaries of love (and the intricacies of divorce court) that Debbie 1, after ten years of battling Eddie, still hoped she and her husband could reconcile. He promised her, on the morning of December 31, 1983, that he loved her. He wanted them to stay together. He suggested that she leave the girls at his father's house for the night, and join him in the city to celebrate New Year's Eve. Debbie said okay, but sure enough, Eddie called a little after 3 p.m., as the girls were being dropped off from school, to say he had to meet with some investment people about the Crazy Eddie IPO.

And the Antar Complex exploded. Robin Antar, who was married to Eddie's brother Mitchell, quizzed her husband until Mitchell admitted that Eddie was spending New Year's Eve with Debbie 2. Robin called Ellen Kuszer, Eddie's sister, who offered to help. Ellen said she felt guilty because it was *her* husband, Benjamin Kuszer, who paid for the Manhattan apartment and Debbie 2's salary. Benjamin ran the Crazy Eddie Record and Tape Asylums on behalf of the family.

With so many tangled fuses lying about, Eddie's holiday was gonna show up with a bang. Debbie 1 asked Sam M. and Rose to keep the girls. Debbie arrived at the grandparents' house trailing overnight bags and dolls for five. Her sisters-in-law, Robin and Ellen, were waiting inside, smoking a train of cigarettes and cursing everyone's least favorite son.

Debbie didn't say where she was going because she didn't have to. The three women piled into the Lincoln with her, and while the clock climbed toward midnight they motored across the Williamsburg bridge. Knife-wielding assailants had failed to get Eddie's attention; perhaps the Antar women could. As they pulled into the parking lot, Debbie saw a limo idling in front of the building on 80th Street and First Avenue. Eddie was sitting inside, waiting for Debbie 2.

Slamming her car into "Park" while the wheels were still rolling, Debbie threw open her door and ran to the limo, beating her fists on the rear window for Eddie to get out. She screamed he was a coward. Nothing stirred behind the blacked out glass. Debbie cupped her hands and pressed them against the window trying to see inside. She kicked the car doors, raging in obscenities. Eddie wouldn't budge. Then the limo was moving, headed out of the driveway, and Debbie was climbing onto the car, hanging on with one hand while she yanked off one of her red spike heels with the other and began pounding dents into the roof.

When the door opened, Debbie jumped onto the pavement. Face to face, she and Eddie railed. The only sound rivaling their shrieks, even on a Manhattan New Year's Eve, were the howls and epithets emitted by Robin and Ellen, who were also letting Eddie have it. Debbie 2 looked on from her balcony.

As Ellen Antar Kuzer shoved between him and Debbie 1, Eddie slapped his sister across the face. Ellen recoiled in horror and searched for an appropriately vicious comeback. Eddie spat at her that she'd caused the whole thing. "Just like Pop, you're always stirring in something!" he accused. A doorman called the police, but before the patrol car arrived, Eddie leaped back into his limo and sped off.

The next day, Eddie freaked. On the 1th of January, he stalked into the company's Brooklyn headquarters, gripping Sugar's leash with clenched fists. He burst into Mitchell's office, loudly accusing his brother of fomenting the "attack" on him. When Benjamin Kuszer stepped into the office and told Eddie, "Calm down," Eddie shoved him away. "You're both out of the business," he threatened. "You can count your days."

Later that afternoon Eddie had a nasty encounter with his mother, whom he regarded as a traitor for siding with Debbie 1 against him. While they argued, Rose became so agitated she passed out. Sam M. flew into a rage, incredulous that his beloved first-born would treat his mother so. Sam raged so intensely and unrelievedly that he suffered a heart attack the 2nd of January 1984. Who could blame Ellen for exclaiming, "He's killing us! One by one, he's killing us all."

Sam M.'s heart attack was serious business. Murad Antar had died from a heart attack; Uncle Eddy had nearly died from a heart attack; now, Sam. His doctor insisted that Sam had to stop smoking. He'd gone to as much as five packs a day. "I could keep the Chesterfields or I could keep on living," Sam shrugs. The Vegas veteran knew it was time to fold. Even Eddie seemed to be braced by the threat of his father's death. When Sam was released from the hospital, Eddie was there to bring him home.

"We still have a business to run," Eddie said. No rift stretched so widely it couldn't be bridged by a few dollars, preferably in six-figure increments. "Everything is forgiven, everything is forgotten," father and son agreed. Sam M. spent his recuperation at Eddie's house, under constant care from Debbie 1 and his doting granddaughters. Eddie came by nearly every day, though he spent his nights in Manhattan with Debbie 2.

Sam recalled that in the days following his illness, "Everything was hunky-dory. Eddie was very civil to Debbie and he treated her very well and he gave her his whole salary, $700,000 a year, and everything like that." Sam personally watched Eddie give Debbie $1 million in cash.

Eddie promised to make everything okay. Sam hoped so, but just in case he'd taken precautions. Eddie didn't know it yet, but Sam and Rose had transferred $3 million out of the cash-skimming account they owned jointly with their son at Bank Leumi. Eddie discovered the transfer while Sam was recuperating from his heart attack. Standing over the old man's sickbed, Eddie swore he'd see his father in hell unless he put the money back, pronto.

"We own Crazy Eddie's together," Sam M. replied.

"You own one third only," Eddie said, "I own the other two thirds. Here you are trying to take half the money." (The account had contained a little more than $6 million.)

Sam said, "Okay, I'll return a million dollars." Sam told a judge later, "We said, 'Everything is forgiven,' but down in the heart it wasn't forgiven. It was forgiven because we had to be in business. I couldn't just stop the business like that. But I didn't like what he was doing. I didn't like his morals."

Going Public: Crazy Eddie as Rocky Balboa

Electronics retailers were doing $35 billion a year in 1985, and growing by 12 percent to 14 percent every year. By 1990, the National Retail Merchants Association predicted the industry would double its business to $77 billion a year, maybe $90 billion. Most of this boost occurred thanks to one hot-rod item: the videocassette recorder, or VCR, the very latest item on the American bourgeoisie's must-have list.

Crazy Eddie, grabbing a respectable share of the greater New York market, posted an increase in sales by 55 percent, from $29 million to $46 million in just the company's first year as a public corporation. What really wowed investors were the *earnings* Eddie was posting on those sales. Net income for 1985 rang up at $1.141 million (compared with $538,000 the year before), paying dividends of 17 cents a share. The Antars' price/earnings ratio was the highest in the industry.

"Crazy Eddie has never had a down year," Eddie bragged in his first annual report. Not in 15 years, not in one single store, had the company ever shown a loss. "Crow served here," Eddie told his critics. The company was building a giant 110,000-square-foot headquarters/warehouse in Edison, New Jersey. There, Eddie announced, "I'll be opening my own personal store."

Eddie had somehow transplanted his indigenous talents as a salesman into the richest ranks of American business. "He was such a charismatic figure," an observer remembers. "At annual meetings—not, historically, the sexiest event on the social calendar—the employees in the audience would chant, 'Ed-die! Ed-die! Ed-die!' Then he would come in raising his arms like Stallone in *Rocky*. It was like a cult."

Crazy Eddie's was part of a new breed of electronics *superstores*. Once upon a few years ago, manufacturers like Pioneer sponsored *company stores*. An entrepreneur set up shop as a "licensed dealer," carrying a respectable brand of merchandise. You visited your local Pioneer dealer, or Bose dealer, or whoever. But in the age of the superstore, every possible brand name is arrayed under one warehouse-sized roof. It's the Day of Pentecost for retailer shoppers.

At Crazy Eddie stores, the prices were affordable and the aisles, chock-full of electronics, roared like a circus. Balloons waved from the top of entertainment centers, music pulsed, greeters handed out prizes, stuck name tags to shirts, and served food, all opening the way for hordes of salespeople, emerging one after another from the stockroom like clowns crawling out of a car, men trained to talk people *away* from the model they thought they wanted and *into* what the purchasing department said to push.

Market watchers loved CRZY stock as much as shoppers loved the stores. Soon, Eddie announced in his 1984 report, we'll be launching a home-shopping network on New York television. The idea seemed outrageous at the time, but why not? Eddie's own TV channel. All Eddie, all the time. Sell people a telephone to make the call, then sell them something else.

Sammy Finds His Calling

His whole life, Sammy had lived in his cousin's shadow. Eddie made the big splashes. Eddie expanded the family into a conglomerate. Eddie got the girls. Sammy cleaned the bathrooms, totalled receipts, and banded skimmed cash into bricks for Eddie to haul to Tel Aviv. Whatever Eddie wanted, Sammy obliged.

"We need an accountant," Eddie announced when Sammy finished high school. "I'm gonna send you to college."

Sammy attended Baruch City College from 1979 to 1983 and earned an accounting degree. For his professional apprenticeship Sammy worked—where else?—at Penn and Harwood, the firm that performed Crazy Eddie's audits and who owed a third of their business to Crazy Eddie fees.

Sammy wasn't the only one helping Eddie fudge his numbers. David Neiderbach, the company's warehouse manager, said Eddie approached him near the end of the fiscal year 1985. "Eddie asked me to make changes to the inventory figures to show more inventory than was being counted. He said he wanted to do this to make the company look better and I never questioned that." Neiderbach boosted total inventory by $2 million in 1985 and $6 million in 1986.

When the auditors came to make their counts, Neiderbach climbed onto the product stacks himself, and called the numbers down to the person below. If the auditor insisted on climbing up, Neiderbach held the auditor's notebook and marked the counts himself. Neiderbach said he used a range of inflationary strategies: counting empty boxes as merchandise; listing cheap merchandise at premium prices; building tall "dummy" columns at the edge of a large shelf and claiming the containers were stacked three or four deep when the rear area was in fact empty.

Besides overstating the inventory ready for shipping to stores, the warehouse also fiddled with what retail people call their "reeps." Reeps is short for repossessions, i.e., products that have to be returned to the manufacturer, who then refunds the wholesale cost of the merchandise to the store. Crazy Eddie's reeps were inflated with $1 million of phony returns in fiscal 1985.

And as the saying goes, a million here, a million there—after a while you're talking real fraud.

"How easy was it do all this?" Sammy asks. "Pulling this stuff off is like playing with kids. The big firms use their audit detail as a training ground. It's not their fault, but these auditors, they're kids just out of college. The firm recruits them out of college with their nice 3.5 to 4.0 GPAs.

"The person who served as our primary auditor had only been at his firm for eight months. He had never participated in a retail audit. The kid who came in and worked on the Accounts Payable he was going to testify to—he worked on our books about three days. His supervisor reviewed the papers for less than a day." Besides being unprepared, the auditors "only took inventories of about a third of the stores anyway. And I helped them decide which stores to look at. We had, at the height, about 30 stores; I showed them a list of ten stores, and they chose eight of those and added two more that they picked on their own."

Sammy and his cousins also found ways to spy on the auditors. "This one guy in 1986, he hands one of our warehouse clerks a sheet of paper and says, 'Make me a copy of this, will you?' The paper listed the test counts, showing which parts of the inventory the auditors planned to do tests on and which parts they'd just take rough counts. Of course we made a copy for ourselves. We knew where they were counting and where we could do what we pleased."

****

When Eddie made Sammy his Chief Financial Officer in 1986, he wasn't exactly doing his cousin a favor. There was a $3-million deficit from the previous year's inventory fraud that needed covering up. Plus, Eddie said they were going to need a $10-million bump for the coming year. Growth in new sales had slowed from

20 percent to just four percent, but Crazy Eddie had never had a down year, and he wasn't going to start now. Eddie told Sammy to make the books look profitable. "He asked me about how to commit certain frauds. It wasn't like I was surprised or thinking, 'Wow-wee, how dare we do this thing?' It was a casual thing. He said, 'We need to do this and this.' And I said, okay, I'll show you how I would do it."

"Now, we commanded a lot of respect," Sammy muses, "Some people might call it fear, with a lot of businesses in the market. So it was easy to convince a couple of our large vendors to ship us a bunch of merchandise right as the fiscal year was ending. Privately, the vendor agreed to hold the bill for the merchandise until after the end of the fiscal year. Then we'd either pay for the merchandise in the new year, or we'd send it back after the audit was over. We basically borrowed inventory."

Sammy also brought new blood to the reeps fraud. The year before, Eddie and his lieutenants had simply claimed to handle more returned merchandise than they actually had, collecting about $1 million in reimbursement from manufacturers. Again with the year-end visit from the auditors in mind, Sammy suggested they produce documents saying that large lots of merchandise had been shipped off as reeps. In fact they kept the reeps merchandise stacked in the warehouse, and counted it as inventory.

Sammy's stroke hit full bore when he created his *Panama Pump*. That's the name prosecutors used to describe Sam's plan for manipulating the family's international banking connections. "I was surprised, really, that nobody had thought of doing it before," Sammy admits. "We had been gradually moving the money we skimmed into Israeli banks. So then I learned how to bring the money back using what's called a double secrecy jurisdiction transaction. Panama today has one of the strictest bank secrecy laws in the world. The country has no currency of its own. Panama uses U.S. currency. And some of the biggest banks in Panama are owned by Israelis. Since the banks are in the same network, you can request that both the withdrawal and the new deposit be kept secret. So we opened accounts in Panama using false names. Using the secrecy laws we transferred a million and a half dollars from Bank Leumi Israel to the Leumi bank in Panama. Then we had the alias-owned Panama account write drafts payable to Crazy Eddie. Now we had successfully brought the money into the company. The worst that happens is we have to pay some taxes."

Sammy broke up the million-five into smaller checks, ranging from $75,000 to $150,000. The funds helped stoke a figure known in retail lingo as *comparable store sales*. Comparable store sales, or *comps*, break down a retail chain's revenue store by store. Each location's present-year sales are compared to its sales for the prior year. To really see if a chain-store operation is growing you have to check to see if their comps are growing. Sammy puts it this way: "If I have one store and I go from $100,000 in sales to $200,000, then great. I just doubled my business. But say I open up ten new stores and, again, I go from $100,000 to $200,000. I'm only making 100,000 extra dollars off ten new stores, only about $10,000 a store. Now my numbers don't look so impressive. The comps tell you the real performance of the company."

By salting individual stores with the Panama drafts, Sammy pumped their comps by two or three-fold. It was a simple ruse that anyone attentively looking at the Crazy Eddie books should have seen in a flash. For one thing, Sammy listed each Panama check as a single transaction. "Suppose you're looking at the store's books, and you see this draft from an Israeli bank operating in Panama that says $116,000. Wouldn't you raise a question? Regular John Smith doesn't walk off the street and buy $116,000 of audio equipment. What kind of retail receipt totals $116,000? Also, you might ask, why are other checks, equally large, drawn from this same bank, showing up in other stores' receipts? Why are the drafts, deposited in different stores, consecutively numbered? And if you noticed several large checks, all from the same account name, deposited into different stores, you would ask, why are these checks all being deposited at comp stores?"

Like most Antar tricks, the Panama Pump didn't require a lot of brains, just balls. "During the year [1986], our comps were down, around four percent, where they'd been 20 percent the year before. This money from Israel, it brings our comp stores up from four percent to ten percent for that last quarter. Over the year, we got a 13- or 14-percent growth in comps. On March 5th, we announce our comps. Everybody cheers. March 7th is the new public offering. The stock shoots to $22 a share. Eddie and the old man cash in for millions."

Basking in his success, Sammy carried himself with more confidence than he'd ever known. "I had basically taken charge of all the frauds by this time. I didn't have a nameplate, I mean fraud wasn't in my job description, but that would have been my major occupation now."

On Wall Street the market's best and brightest danced to Sammy's tune. Drexel Burnham Lambert's "BUY" recommendation for 1986 was explicitly "based on 35 percent EPS [earnings per share] growth" and *"comparable store sales growth in the low double-digit range"* (emphasis added). CRZY stock prices, the report predicted, would double and more during the next year. As if they were working from an Antar script, DBL declared, "Crazy Eddie is the only retailer in our universe that has not reported a disappointing quarter in the last two years. We do not believe that is an accident.... We believe Crazy Eddie is becoming the kind of company that can continually produce above-average comparable store sales growth." The encomium singled out the chain's elusive but fascinating leader: "Mr. Antar has created a strong organization beneath him that is close-knit and directed.... Despite the boisterous (less charitable commentators would say obnoxious) quality of the commercials, Crazy Eddie management is quite conservative."

The Mountain Comes to Muhammed

Sammy used the company's relationship with its suppliers to run an alternative version of the Panama Pump. A small midwestern electronics distributor named Zazy needed merchandise. Zazy agreed to buy shipments from Crazy Eddie's, at prices just above Eddie's discount. Key to Sammy's plan, Zazy would pay for the merchandise with checks in small amounts. For a $200,000 truckload of components, Zazy handed over 15 checks, ranging from $10,000 to $15,000 each. Sam salted the checks into his comparable store sales, once again making the numbers sing.

But Sammy learned that fraud was a cruel and demanding master. "Crazy Eddie's was falling so fast we needed to create a fraud in 1987 that would make four times the money we had faked in the first couple years. We weren't going to make the company profitable. We'd given up on that. We just needed to cover our previous frauds."

Sammy made it through the first two quarters using a generous supply of Tagamet and $700,000 in wholesale receipts from pumping up the store comps. His reports showed a ten percent gain in comparable sales for the first quarter and an impressive 15 percent for the second quarter. The real numbers were hovering around three percent to five percent, but only Sammy and Eddie knew that. In the third quarter (Sept. – Nov.) the squeeze got worse. Companywide, store sales fell into the negatives—nine percent lower than the previous year. Sammy figured he had to scrape up several million dollars somewhere. He went for help to his old friend, Mitchell, the cousin who'd taught him to play baseball, and the one level-headed Antar in Sam M.'s brood.

Mitchell suggested they approach the Zazy company, which was already shipping merchandise to Eddie's without filing an invoice. "Only we need to borrow cash money this time," Sammy cautioned. "An extremely short-term loan, and we guarantee them dibs on anything in our warehouse—whatever's hot this Christmas, they got it in triplicate." Mitchell reminded the Zazy reps that Crazy Eddie provided a third of their product. Up against the wall, Zazy agreed to give Sammy $3 million in checks, provided the checks wouldn't actually be submitted for payment. Sammy would hold the checks, listing them in the third-quarter report as "deposits in transit." Once the quarterly reports came out, Sammy gave back the uncashed checks and returned to ponder his troublesome ledgers.

By October 1986 the stock's share price had fallen to $17.50. Even that was 6.5 times book value. A *Fortune* magazine prognosticator worried, "If Crazy Eddie has anything less than a terrific Christmas quarter, the stock will tumble." The writer recommended covering at $12.

But before the stock tumbled, Eddie did. He'd already cashed in between $25 million and $30 million of his holdings. Then, just before Halloween, Eddie told Mitchell to come to his office. Just a few years younger than Eddie, Mitchell looked like he was from somewhere else entirely. Unlike Eddie and Allen, who shared their father's bandyish looks, Mitchell looked like a Tawil, his mother's side of the family. He was lanky with a hatchet-head nose. His spectacles were thick as a windshield. Mitchell shared Rose's no-nonsense approach to life and business. He had little patience with his brother's half-drunk histrionics. Mitchell wanted to make a living. "You're taking over Crazy Eddie's," Eddie said to his brother. When Mitchell demanded to know what was going on, Eddie barked, "None of your goddamn business."

A terse announcement came in December: Eddie was resigning as president, effective the end of the year. Soon after, he resigned as chief executive officer. Even inside the family, there was little word from Eddie. Then he popped up in April 1987, announcing that since he still retained the title of Crazy Eddie president, he was firing his father (Sam M.), his brother Allen, and his mother-in-law, Lillian Rosen.

"Our father!" Mitchell raged. When Mitchell found out Eddie had fired Sam, he stormed the hallways of the Edison headquarters, bellowing, "Let the mountain come to Muhammed! Let the mountain come to Muhammed!"

"Pop has always been jealous of me," Eddie said to Sammy over drinks. "Because I've been successful where he wasn't. He does window dressings; he collects money from his little circle of stores. I own 30 stores. There's no comparison. It kills him to know that I'm more successful than him. Mitchell needs to face reality."

To replace the irreplaceable Eddie, the remaining board members formed an "office of the president." Mitchell, Sammy, and Dr. Isaac Kairey would together serve as a composite president. Kairey had joined the Antar fold in 1979, when he persuaded Eddie to help fund the shady, soon-to-be-bankrupt University of St. Lucia Medical School, located in the Bahamas. But the boys were losing ground by the day. During spring 1987, CRZY stock tumbled past $10 a share. It didn't stop until it hit $6.

Eddie's personal life sucked just as bad. Debbie 1 was threatening to haul him back into divorce court. In her confusion during the initial split, Debbie had mistaken Eddie for someone with a conscience. She'd allowed Crazy Eddie's general counsel, Solomon Antar, to handle both sides of the divorce suit. Under the terms (which Eddie dictated) she received $35,000 a year, plus $1000 a month in support payments for each of the five girls. Of course this didn't count Deborah's salary from Crazy Eddie's of $75,000 a year, pocket money for a woman of the former Ms. Rosen's caliber, or the $700,000 salary Eddie had been giving her, or the millions in the girls' names stashed in Cayman Island accounts.

But Eddie walked away from the divorce in pretty sweet circumstances. Figure his net worth at about $100 million. A regular Joe is worth about $100,000. So for Eddie to pay $95,000 a year in alimony and child support is tantamount to a regular Joe paying $95 a year.

Debbie was demanding Eddie turn over half the proceeds from his stock sales to her and the girls. She knew that Eddie had been siphoning money, almost $5 million, from the Cayman Island accounts they'd established in the girls' names. She wanted that back, too.

Eddie pointed out that while he'd dipped into the offshore "trust funds," he'd since built them back to almost $10 million. He said he and Debbie should work something out. Debbie laughed, humorlessly, in his face.

Sammy says, "Debbie plays the sweetheart game but she's as dirty as the rest of them. She knew there was plenty of money lying around, and she was set on getting some for herself. As much as she could lay her hands on."

When it became apparent there would be no peace with Debbie 1, Eddie struck again: he withdrew $1.5 million from his children's accounts, followed by $8 million in July, leaving a few hundred thousand in crumbs.

A day after Eddie's last withdrawal, Debbie filed a new claim against his estate, asking for $200 million.

****

Coda: The original divorce settlement was vacated in 1990, a legal ricochet in the ongoing Antar family wars. Back in 1984, Eddie and Sam M. arranged for the divorce to be handled by one Solomon Antar, a cousin to Sam M., 15 years younger than the patriarch. Solomon had given the family legal advice since the 1970s; he served as Crazy Eddie's general counsel starting in 1979, as the company was preparing to go public; and he helped smuggle money into Israel during the 1980s. Debbie maintained in her suit for a new hearing that Solomon had forged her name on the divorce papers.

Sam M., as usual in the thick of the proceedings, proved the accusation when he noticed something odd about the phone number listed in the header of the original settlement agreement: (718) 943-0100. Sam remembered that the New York Telephone Company had added a batch of new area codes in 1984, and that 718 was one of these new codes. The area code change didn't take effect until late that summer. But the letterhead, supposedly signed in April, at least three months prior to the change, listed the new area code. So the document must have been signed later. Set down one for truth, justice, and the harvest of a conniving mind.

In early 1999, Debbie won her civil suit against Solomon Antar for forging the papers. Solomon was ordered to pay Debbie's attorney's fees, but no damages were assessed. Though he had violated the rules of the Bar, and the judge called Solomon's actions reprehensible, no complaint was filed against Solomon's license to practice law. It turns out Solomon Antar had found ways to dodge the slings and arrows of the judicial system, and he proved just as adept at keeping his cousins and their internecine quarrels from staining his pinstriped lapels. Solomon took care of himself before he took care of his own.

Debbie found her victory against Eddie was made even more hollow by the fact that by the time the decision was rendered, her ex-husband had been forced by government attorneys to disgorge all his assets. She has yet to recover a penny.

Fraud in Plain Sight

Fraud was no fun. With the fiscal year-end careening down the pike, and the stock in single digits, Sammy had no time to fool around with inventory. "We needed 40 million dollars, and we found about half of it in the form of debit memos." The debit memo is an invoice retailers use to charge part of their advertising expense to manufacturers' accounts. Sony, for example, had helped finance a series of Crazy Eddie ads that prominently featured Sony products. Any kind of volume discounts or promotional discounts would also find their way into a retailer's books as debit memos. In the right hands a debit memo was as good as cash. "Worse comes to worse," Sammy figured, "we'll have to give an allowance if some of the memos are challenged. No big deal. The thing about debit memo fraud"—the aspect that Sam unapologetically relishes—"is that you can't hide the debit memo from the auditor. It has to be there in order to be part of your accounting system. It's fraud in plain sight. Right in front of their eyes."

While analysts read the Crazy Eddie annual report with their fingernails in their teeth, Sammy and Mitchell Antar counted their blessings. Earnings were down by 20 percent from 1986 and falling. However, the chain was showing a pretax profit of $10.6 million. Sales were still healthy, with a 34-percent rise approaching $300 million. But the sales jump came from 13 new stores. The important comparable store numbers—the ones Sammy had been so desperately subsidizing all year long—were lagging by 19 percent in the fourth quarter and down two percent for the year. Oh well, Sammy thought, on to the next hole in the road....

The BIG Time

Could there have been a better challenger to the rowdy Eddie Antar than Elias Zinn, a consumer electronics overlord from Houston? In 1974, a born-and-bred-in-Texas entrepreneur named Elias Zinn decided he'd rather run a business than study business at the University of Texas at Austin. In partnership with his father and two brothers, Zinn built a chain called "Custom Hi-Fi Shops" with 72 stores strong across the Southwest. But a family feud erupted in 1981 and Custom Hi-Fi was thrown onto the bankruptcy altar. Zinn's determined, some said blustering, approach to business had occasioned disaster and triumph in various degrees. In 1989, as he revved up once more, Zinn certainly had some stories to share with Eddie Antar.

Entertainment Marketing Inc. (EMI), the company Zinn created in the wake of his family debacle, had zoomed from $747,000 in 1984 sales to almost $90 million by early 1987. Still Zinn could not turn a profit. That was because he'd blown millions on a television venture called the Consumer Discount Network. Zinn, an ample-gutted braggart with enough money to pursue his goofiest ideas, envisioned a new form of programming: soap operas and sitcoms in which the principal characters also hawked some product or another. CDN would be like the Home Shopping Network, but with skits, little stories, built around each sale. The idea bombed, though in these days of product placement and movies starring toys, it's hard to know why.

Zinn's EMI was headquartered in Houston, occupying a 315,000-square-foot building that had once belonged to a Toyota dealership. Zinn himself lived in Manhattan, mainly because his wife, a dentist he met on a blind date in the mid-70s, despised the Gulf Coast. Itching to get into the Manhattan retail scene, Zinn flipped when he realized that Crazy Eddie's was a takeover waiting to happen. The family turmoil and anemic stock prices made the Antars an irresistible target for an economic poacher. "Before I made my move on Crazy Eddie, I visited everyone except my rabbi," Zinn joked. On the list of visits, he included a friend at the Palmieri-Oppenheimer fund. Victor Palmieri's management consultants were known as "turnaround artists," famous for coaxing Penn Central out of a financial coma, rebuilding Levitt Homes, and for handling a $600-million chunk of the Teamsters fund. The Oppenheimers were also known for underwriting the initial public offering of the stock called CRZY. Victor Palmieri's new venture was flush with $100 million in cash and, like Elias Zinn, Victor was aching to deal.

"Look," Zinn told Victor Palmieri, "these Antars are in trouble and they want to take the company private again. If we get in now, we make some cash on their move. Worst comes to worst, we've got a hot property for the turnaround department. I'll feed the stores with my warehousing connections." With Oppenheimer-Palmieri's backing, Zinn bought 450,000 shares of Crazy Eddie stock, 7-1/2 percent of the outstanding shares, for $17.5 million. The partnership also tendered an offer to take over the company at $7 a share.

Eddie invited Victor Palmieri and Elias Zinn to Crazy Eddie headquarters for a sitdown. It was a tense, hot afternoon in July. Elias Zinn arrived sweating profusely, tieless, awkwardly smoothing his plaid shirt over a substantial belly. While they waited for Eddie, Zinn jokingly called the meeting "a showdown." Eddie, in prime business-ninja mode, shook hands with Palmieri, nodded to Zinn, and announced, "Mr. Palmieri, I don't think you know what you're getting into."

The scent of a takeover deal drove stock analysts to start digging at the CRZY financials. It didn't take much exertion to uncover Eddie's doings. Wall Streeters learned that just before Eddie disappeared in the fall of 1986, he had quietly sold 1.5 million shares of his stock. Eddie pocketed $21 million in cash on the sale. Over the three years since the company went public, Eddie had sold 6.5 million shares, hauling away more than $74 million in investor funds. Most shareholders, by contrast, had spent the same time period watching their paper fortunes crumple into losses.

A slew of shareholder suits was filed against the Antar family. Meanwhile, Elias Zinn was gathering proxy votes by the thousands. Eddie and Sammy tried to shoot back. With tentative backing from the Canadian-based Belzberg Brothers, they mounted a counter-offer to Zinn's greenmail: $8 a share. Zinn promptly matched the offer.

As August steamed the streets of Manhattan and the word on Eddie turned more ill by the day, Sammy withdrew the takeover bid. The Crazy Eddie board told Elias Zinn to proceed; he had himself a company. Zinn's chuckles couldn't have lasted long, though. October 1987 reports showed Crazy Eddie posting losses of $8 million, 26 cents a share.

Eddie was doomed because he had nothing to fight with. He'd cashed in most of his stock and alienated all his natural allies. Like the hapless villains in *Creepshow* and *Tales from the Crypt*, Eddie Antar fell victim to his own scheming—he had become incredibly rich, but he was losing everything in the process. Sooner or later, he knew, somebody was going to try and put him in jail.

10 Cents on the Dollar

Meanwhile Sammy and the boys had to move. They spent days rearranging, misarranging, and editing—that is, shredding—files. After a while, if Sammy thought something in a file might raise questions he unceremoniously chunked it into the giant gray can beside his desk. He wasn't even looking at most files, just chucking them. "About nine days after they won the proxy fight," Sammy says, "Zinn sent his people to the office. They took over the company at three o'clock. I got my pink slip at six o'clock. I was out on my backside. That was after 16 years I'd worked there. My adult life. I was devastated. From the age of 14 to the age of 30, that was my entire life."

Bob Marmon, a cocky, fast-talking turnaround artist who'd been with the Palmieri Group for about ten years, arrived from Rhode Island with one day's notice of his new assignment. Marmon was tapped as the new CFO, taking Sammy's place in the financial driver's seat. He'd been hastily scanning Crazy Eddie annual reports on the plane and still clutched a stack of them when he was nearly knocked down in the Edison headquarters lobby by Sammy Antar. Sammy was weebling toward the door, dragging a suitcase on rollers. "I recognized Sammy from the files," Marmon says, "so I stepped over to introduce myself. He said to me, 'When the investors start yelling, you tell 'em fuck off. Give 'em 10 cents on the dollar.' Then he was out the door." Marmon had worked on some of Palmieri's most fabled turnarounds, including Penn Central. In short order, the feisty cost-cutter went to counting his toys.

In a couple of weeks the preliminary audit team came back with word—the company is not only in bad condition, it's in terrible condition. Offhand the reviewers guessed, from their brief glance, inventory was short by $40 million to $50 million. The official numbers finally came in at $65 million, which was later revised to $80 million. Victor Palmieri, the new and increasingly uneasy chairman of Crazy Eddie's, explained, "We inherited the worst-managed company in the U.S., due to both incompetence and corruption within the organization. All of the old management's figures are suspect."

Palmieri went calling on every banker he'd ever done business with, pleading for help. He secured new lines of credit and consulted with Zinn and Marmon on "getting the company lean." Corporate headquarters was moved to a smaller warehouse, and Eddie's palatial digs in Edison were put up for sale. More than 2,500 workers were laid off. Salespeople were placed completely on commission. The 80-car Antar auto fleet, including Jaguars, BMWs and limousines, was sold off. (There were three cars registered to Sam M., who has never driven a car.) Zinn held morning pep talks in an open end of the warehouse, and passed out "rah-rah" buttons, emblazoned with cheery motivational slogans like *I Can, You Can, We Can.* "When you get up in the morning," Zinn told the turnaround team, "I want you to wear your attitude."

To Victor Palmieri and the business press, Zinn crowed, "We're going to make money next year. Not much, but we'll turn a small profit in 1989. And after that, we'll see." But everybody knew they were just holding the patient's hand. The Crazy Eddie work force was not only losing morale; since many of them were stockholders, they were losing their shirts, their savings, their dreams. Howard Sirota, who led the fight to recover shareholders' losses, says Eddie as usual bullied his way into riches, often hurting those who could least absorb the hit. "The company encouraged clerks who worked in the stores to buy stock with their retirement funds, while Eddie was selling his," Sirota laments. "It was already a $200-million fraud and they (the Antars) also took some poor schnook's $5,000."

Next, as Sammy remembers it, "All of a sudden on a Friday afternoon I get this fax. It's addressed to our general counsel, Solomon Antar. From the SEC. 'Thank you for the conversation that we had,' it says. 'We now require these documents'—and they list off a bunch of them. And I know from looking, it's the right ones they're asking us for. They were looking at the debit memos and also at the Zazy deals. So I called Solomon, who is my uncle Sam's cousin, and Solomon says he doesn't know what the hell is going on. He says this new SEC lawyer named Ric Simpson called him up out of the blue. Then he says, 'Arnie Spindler's been talking.'

"See, the papers the SEC wanted were all part of our working with this one buyer, Arnie Spindler. And I said, 'Oh God! This guy has ratted us out to the SEC.' Arnie had been under some investigation himself. So he says to the SEC, 'I can point some people out to you who are doing things much worse.' I wasn't completely surprised. Arnie had approached me just before we lost the company to Palmieri. He'd been with us since the first days, when there were two or three stores. He'd helped work on the inventory numbers in the past, and he was worried about his future. Arnie was good friends with Mitchell and Allen, and so he was worried that with the feud going on, Eddie would try to force him out, too."

Arnie said, "I want $100,000 in severance to leave the company. Otherwise I have plenty of stories to tell should the right people come knocking." Sammy tried to get Eddie to make the payoff. "I said, 'Arnie's gonna rat us out,' but Eddie, he said, 'Arnie ain't ratting us out. He can't do that unless he rats out his best friends Mitchell and Allen too. He's never gonna do that.'"

But Eddie was wrong. Arnie ratted. With some notion he could pick and choose the people he would squeal on, Arnie Spindler told the SEC that Sammy and Eddie were running a racket. "But not the rest of the family. No one else knows." Arnie assured the SEC prosecutor, Ric Simpson, "Mitchell doesn't know. Allen doesn't know. Sam M. doesn't know. There's no reason to go after them." However, Simpson wasn't going to have the bounds of his inquiry set by an informant. He promptly served notice on the entire family. The old man confirms, "Arnie went and talked to the feds because he thought he was doing us—me and Mitchell and Allen—a favor. He thought the SEC would sweep out the bad guys, we'd take the company back, and everything would be settled."

****

Bob Marmon was furiously tapping numbers into his computer. "I finally determined that we could make this operation work with eight stores or with 75 stores. But not with 25 or 30 stores. Either you have to be small, direct and simple, or you have to go huge, attain full coverage of your territory, grow tons of volume. It won't work in between."

Crazy Eddie's was through. The Antars had handed Elias Zinn yet another defeat and made Palmieri-Oppenheimer's maiden investment a wreck. By June 1988 suppliers were demanding that the company liquidate itself so it could pay the $860,000 it owed for merchandise and services. Jerry Carroll, closing a 17-year chapter in his career, roared his insanity one last time between reruns of *M.A.S.H.* and the nightly news, announcing that the king of discount electronics had hit *ROCKBOTTOM!* There wasn't much left in the stores besides demo models and random accessories, but folks came to paw over the refuse and wonder what had happened to their store.

Discount Store News struck an elegiac note: "So the chain that virtually invented electronics discounting died an ignoble death, with creditors hovering over the remains, only to find that there was even less left than had been imagined."

Bob Marmon shipped off to his next Palmieri-sponsored turnaround. Elias Zinn went back to Texas. Crazy Eddie's now sat beside the Consumer Discount Network and Custom Hi-Fi as the third multimillion dollar disaster occasioned by a man who claimed he was a profit-pinching genius.

Sam M. and Mitchell kept telling the SEC that if somebody was phonying the financials, it was probably the Chief Financial Officer, Sam E. "Sammy" Antar.

Eddie Antar told his cousin, "You're on your own."

The Pitiful One

Members of the Antar inner circle—Sam M., Eddie, Mitchell, Allen, and Sammy—were spending lots of time with lawyers and investigators. Ric Simpson, who had just joined the Commission's legal department and had drawn a doozy of a first case, hoped if he kept stirring something would float up. Using Arnie Spindler's info on the warehouse frauds, Simpson asked, *Did you ever alter your inventory? Did you ever make an arrangement with another company to "borrow inventory"? Did you use money from wholesale transactions to boost your retail sales reports?* The Antars answered, "No, no, no."

When Sam, the old man, was forced to admit his repeated untruths in federal court, he declared, "You are 1,000 percent right. You can show me 29 books of depositions. I did lie, I did lie...," adding with vehemence and balled fists, "But I am not lying now." Sam M. huffed that he'd skimmed millions of dollars in five decades of business, but never took one cent from Crazy Eddie's after 1976, so that he could take the family legit. However much he'd sinned in the past, Sam swore he was clean now. "I lied, I lied, I lied, I lied, I lied, I lied. But then I rescinded the lies and told them the truth. That is all I did."

As New Year's 1990 approached, Bob Marmon was throwing out the last boxes from the chain's warehouse and the SEC was charging Eddie with fraud, specifically for falsifying financial reports and insider trading. A federal judgment demanded that Eddie bring back $50 million he was keeping in Israeli banks until an official inquiry could determine what had happened to his investors' money. After several months of fruitless haggling with this inveterate haggler, U.S. Attorney Dan Gibbons ordered Eddie to appear in court on February 10, 1990 and explain why he shouldn't be charged with contempt.

Eddie didn't show up for the court date, so a warrant was issued for his arrest. After a couple of days he surrendered to the federal marshal and was brought before the court. But the judge assigned to his case was away on vacation, so Eddie was released—

on his own recognizance —until after the judge's holiday. The judge returned promptly but Eddie never did.

Eddie shaved the dense black beard he'd worn virtually his entire adult life and picked up a passport in the name of David Jacob Levi Cohen. He'd been using an alias passport for several years, under the name Alexander Stewart, but the alias wasn't enough. An Israeli passport by law lists every known identity of the holder. So the name "Eddie Antar" was right there on the document. In planning for his rainy day, Eddie had traveled to Brazil a few years before and picked up a black market passport in the name of David Cohen. Next, he'd obtained his Israeli passport, with David Cohen as his "real" name. So when the time came, David Cohen casually boarded a plane to Israel while federal agents scoured New York and the Jersey coast for Eddie Antar.

In the town of Yavne, near Tel Aviv, Eddie set himself up in a luxury townhouse. Thanks to several decades of seeding, Mr. David Cohen had plenty of money to draw on. Besides Israeli banks, there were funds in shell companies around the world, and the requisite numbered accounts in Switzerland. Eddie could access more than 20 sources for cash: through coded accounts, business accounts registered in Liberia or Gibraltar, personal accounts in the names of his several aliases, including those in other (real) people's names, like his uncle Murray Tawil, and his friend Harry Shalom. Prosecutors later observed that while on the run, "Eddie Antar played bank accounts the way Heifitz plays the violin." Besides David Cohen, Eddie impersonated an army of alter-egos, including Alexander Stewart Israel, Shalom Harry Page, David Boris Levy, Carl M. Kabbani, Eddie Sam, and Jake Levi.

Eddie wasn't exactly partying during his run. He was angry, depressed, scared. For the first time ever, the swaggerer couldn't hide that he was scared to death. He slouched around a dirty apartment, stepping over soiled clothes and crumpled bags of takeout food, drinking a quart of vodka a day. An old friend who ran into Eddie in Jerusalem said, "He was presenting himself like the Pitiful One, like a character from the Yiddish theater, the slumped, round-shouldered lost little man. He was looking for sympathy, but as far as I'm concerned, he was just playing a role."

****

When Eddie disappeared, Sammy panicked. He told his lawyer, Anthony Mautone, "I cannot go to jail." Mautone approached U.S. Attorney Dan Gibbons and offered Sammy's cooperation in exchange for immunity. Gibbons, a harsh, unbending prosecutor, said no way. He had little use for a witness who wanted to recant two years' worth of lying and join the good guys, expecting a free ride. Gibbons said Arnie Spindler, the first Antar insider to jump ship, was telling him a completely different story. Arnie said Sammy and Eddie were running the fraud on their own, keeping the rest of the family in the dark.

"He didn't believe me," Sammy says, "and besides, he still thought he was gonna make the case with no deals, take down the whole dirty bunch of us."

****

On June 21, 1991, Sam M. Antar received a fax at his home. The text, all caps, read:

> TO SAM M. ANTAR, FAMILY PATRIARCH, BULLSHIT PHILOSOPHER, RELIGIOUS HYPOCRITE, FRAUD, CHEAT, CO-FOUNDER, EXECUTIVE VICE-PRESIDENT, MEMBER OF THE BOARD, MAJOR STOCKHOLDER, DEFENDANT, PRIME TARGET OF FEDERAL INVESTIGA-TION, AND GENERALLY ALL-AROUND SCUMBAG.

Salutations aside, the writer got to the point, still ranting in capital letters.

> YOU OLD GOAT! YOU TRIED TO DESTROY OTHERS TO COVER UP YOUR OWN FRAUD! BUT YOUR CORRUP-TION TURNED RIGHT AROUND AND BIT YOU IN THE ASS. THE BIGGEST SURPRISES ARE YET TO COME. YOU ARE ALL ABOUT TO GET YOUR "EQUITABLE DISTRIBU-TION." A NEW PITCHER IS COMING TO THE MOUND. SO, ALL GET READY FOR YOUR THIRD STRIKE. HAVE A HAPPY SUMMER. THE FORECAST IS THAT THERE WILL BE PLENTY OF HEAT, SO BE PREPARED TO SWEAT A LOT.

There was no signature. A phone number showed the message was transmitted from a store in the capital city of Panama, where the Bank Leumi held several cash accounts in various Antar names.

****

Shortly after the old goat received his fax, Dan Gibbons was replaced by Paul Weissman as the Crazy Eddie prosecutor. The

Mad Faxer obviously knew what he was talking about when he said a new pitcher was stepping to the mound. Weissman was ready to talk. No promises, Weissman said to Sammy, just a talk. After an hour's bantering in the U.S. Attorney's office, Weissman liked what he heard. Their meetings went on for two years—Sammy explaining the frauds, Weissman and FBI Agent Paul Hayes shaking their heads.

Thanks to this beautiful friendship, Weissman had a few documents and plenty of expert accounting analysis, but he hadn't achieved legal proof yet. Because Sammy had shred large holes in the paper trail, he did penance by filling in those holes with convincing testimony. Gesticulating wildly, careening from one thread to another in his tale, the Antar nerd let loose on his crooked family during hours of testimony and cross-examination.

As his official punishment, Weissman offered Sammy six months house arrest. For his 1200 hours of community service, Sammy decided to work as a tutor for children with attention deficit disorder (ADD). He still does the tutoring nearly ten years after fulfilling his sentence. "I have a son with ADD. It's some good I can do. After 30 years of being a son of a bitch."

He sounds impressively remorseful, but even so, squealing wasn't Sammy's first choice. He says he could've easily been swayed if his uncle had not behaved so cluelessly. "With all that money he was sitting on, why didn't he take care of me? It would've been simple. And cheap, relatively speaking. A couple million dollars. But he never did. The only time I heard from him was after I'd made my deal to testify. He called me up at two in the morning, and said he had a bone to pick with me. I told him to get fucked, because I was having a fight with my wife. I had better things to do."

Sam M. thought his ratting nephew was the Mad Faxer. It was keeping him up nights, so he'd called for a confrontation. As Sammy recounts, "The phone rang again, and he said, 'Do you want to keep on living?' I told him, 'You're pathetic. Find something better to do with your time.' The third time he called back, I said, 'Take these threats to the FBI. I got no time for you.'"

****

Two years after Eddie jumped bail, Israeli police waited for him at his favorite convenience store in Yavne. When he drove up to get his morning paper, three men surrounded him and put him in cuffs. He was taken to a jail in Tel Aviv to await extradition. As Eddie was ushered to his quarters, inmates craned their necks to get a look at the infamous American criminal. Someone who'd spent time in New York began clapping his hands and singing the old doo-wop commercial:

When you think you're ready,
Come to Crazy Eddie...

Rounding up Eddie didn't qualify as Mosaad-worthy detective work. He'd moved freely about Tel Aviv and made several trips to Europe during his time on the lam. The lease for his apartment was signed in the name of Alexander Stewart, whose passport listed "Eddie Antar" as his given name. Perhaps Eddie hadn't been so hard to find after all. The U.S. government was only waiting for Sammy Antar to build their case.

****

Sam M., meanwhile, was becoming more cooperative with Weissman's team. But only to a point. The old man now admitted that, yes, he and Eddie had skimmed money from the Crazy Eddie stores and smuggled that money to Israel. "But only until 1976," he swore. "After that we never took a penny, because we wanted to be straight so we could take the company public." All of his nephew's stories of skimming less each year to build up the IPO were "malarkey," Sam M. complained, wincing. He even produced an amended 1040, showing that he'd declared the skimmed income and paid taxes on it. "The IRS can't touch me!"

The Mad Faxer soon rang Sam M.'s number again:

I JUST READ THE GOAT'S AFFIDAVIT AND NEARLY
FELL OFF MY CHAIR. YOU STUPID MORON. EVERY-
BODY KNOWS THE HYPOCRITE YOU REALLY ARE.
YOU'VE GRADUATED FROM RELIGIS HIPOCRATE TO
ALLROUND HYPOCRITE. HOW DOES IT FEEL TO EAT
YOUR OWN SHIT AFTER YOU GAVE IT TO EVERYONE
ELSE FOR SO LONG TO EAT?...

YOU WERE SO FUCKING ARROGANT THAT YOU LET A
DROOLING CHERA RETARD STOCKBOY FORCE YOU
OUT OF YOUR FOXHOLE.

"Chera," according to a family member, "is a person with no class, kind of trashy. It wouldn't be a very nice thing to put in a book." It's an Egyptian surname, like Smith, or Jones, or Snopes. It's usually spelled *Chira*.

Sammy wasn't the Mad Faxer. Who then? Eddie? The charming dispatch, awash in images of excrement and vomit, continued with references to the divorce suit which Debbie 1 was pressing against Eddie:

> EACH AND EVERY ONE OF YOU WHO OPENED YOUR MOUTHS AND TESTIFIED AGAINST ME TO HURT ME WENT RIGHT DOWN THE TUBES OUT OF YOUR OWN MOUTHS. YES, RIGHT OUT OF THE BIBLE JUST LIKE PHAROAH. THEY CALL IT LOSHON HORAH [the evil tongue], RIGHT? IF ANYONE SHOULD KNOW ITS YOU.

A third fax arrived soon after.

> MOVE OVER LEONA [Helmsley] AND MAKE ROOM FOR SAM. SO YOU'VE FINALLY DECIDED TO TRY TO BULLSHIT YOUR WAY OUT. WHAT A JOKE. I'D GIVE ANYTHING TO WATCH THIS FARCE. WELL MISTER WAKE UP AND LET ME TELL YOU SOMETHING, NOBODY IS GOING TO BELIEVE WHATEVER YOU HAVE TO SAY.

That all sounded like Eddie. But then:

> I JUST READ A GOOD STORY BY FRANZ KAFKA. IT'S CALLED THE PENAL COLONY. FOR THERE TO BE ANY JUSTICE AT ALL IN THE WORLD YOU MUST REALIZE WHY YOU ARE SUFFERING.

Eddie most definitely wasn't a reader. Or a moral philosopher. So, Sam decided, Eddie isn't the Mad Faxer. Nevertheless, somebody had a hold on the old goat's harness and was yanking hard.

Liar's Poker

At trial in 1993, defense attorney Jack Arsenault explained to the jury that Eddie Antar's family took advantage of a troubled man's alcoholism and depression and turned the company criminal. "A family business became a corporate battlefield with boardroom intrigues, duplicity, hostility and distrust among family members," Arsenault said.

The courtroom was packed with spectators and with an appropriately bizarre cast of litigants striding the stage. U.S. Attorney Michael Chertoff, assigned to prosecute the case alongside Paul Weissman, was known in the Antar corner as "The Wraith" and "Count Chertoff," for the way his long arms raked the floor and for the bruise-colored hollows in his cheeks.

"Obviously the Antars have fought internecinely for decades," Chertoff argued, "but that hadn't stopped them from opening businesses together, loaning each other money, and defending one another from outside attacks." When Eddie was returned from Israel in shackles, Sam M. sent a message: "He is my son.... All he has to do is pick up the phone and say, 'Ma, Pa, help me.'" In time, and lacking money badly, Eddie did pick up that phone. Sam M. paid at least $5 million for Eddie's defense.

Chertoff said once Eddie started inflating his earnings, he couldn't stop. The Antar fiscal year always began in the red because of the previous year's defalcations. "It's like the high jump. Each year they had to raise the bar a little higher." Chertoff hauled in charts, graphs and family trees, anything to help the jury track the diverse cast and their devious turns in this soap opera of a scam. Bob Marmon, who ran the Crazy Eddie turnaround on Palmieri's behalf, told the court what he *didn't* find when he arrived—namely $80 million in missing inventory—and what he *did* find—a firebombed set of business records. The prosecution compensated for its documentary handicap with first-hand testimony from co-conspirators. A slew of former Crazy Eddie employees—Arnie Spindler, Abe Grienberg, David Neiderbach, Isaac Kairey, and of course, batting cleanup, Sammy Antar—told how they had personally altered documents and shifted inventories. The key point, Chertoff stressed with each witness, is that these people were operating at Eddie's behest. Maybe the boss' pen never smudged a 1 into a 4 on the audit reports, but Eddie directed and approved.

From his raised seat overlooking the litigants sat Judge Nicholas Politan, infamous in the New Jersey district for his unbending rule of the courtroom. Politan struck an imposing figure, with his heavy jowls and hard-bitten demeanor. He waded into Eddie with a vengeance. Several times, frustrated by the defendant's belligerence and his lawyers' legal sidestepping, Politan shouted down objections from the defendant's table.

In June of 1993, the jury retired and spent six days reviewing what they'd seen. When they came back, they pronounced Eddie guilty of 17 counts of fraud. Mitchell was found guilty of three counts, and acquitted on two. Allen, always the most distanced from the Crazy Eddie mess, was acquitted of all the counts against him.

Arsenault said they'd immediately file an appeal, targeting Judge Politan for the belligerent way he'd governed the proceedings. At the sentencing hearing, Politan played into Arsenault's hands. Crowning his trial-long impersonation of Judge Roy Bean, Politan took a final swipe at the Antar Complex:

> My object in this case from day one has always been to get back
> to the public that which was taken from it as a result of the fraud-
> ulent activities of this defendant and others. We will work the best
> possible formula we can to be as fair as possible to the public. If
> we can get the 120 million back [the estimated losses to inves-
> tors], we would have accomplished a great deal in this case.

Eddie's defense team pounced. They chose to take the judge's statements literally. "From day one," they argued in their briefs, underlining Politan's remarks for the appellate court. "He admits here that he had decided the defendant's guilt at the outset."

The appeal, as promised, revisited *day one* to show Politan's tendentious state of mind. In early 1993 Eddie had appeared before Politan requesting that he be allowed to post bail. Never mind that Eddie had been hopping nations the last two years; never mind his several contempt of court citations. He wanted out. But Politan was hell-bent on one issue: $60 million he knew Eddie had bundled in offshore accounts. Politan told defense attorney Jack Arsenault straight up, "I want your client's money."

As if tearing a page from Dickens, the defense revealed not only Politan's mammonism, but his utter lack of compassion. While Eddie was on the run, Eddie's middle daughter—Danielle, just short of her 19th birthday—was stricken with cancer. Eddie didn't learn about the disease until he was already jailed. Politan had agreed to let Eddie visit Danielle in the hospital during pre-trial motions, but only for 30 minutes at a time. For transport to the hospital Eddie was shackled and led by deputies to his daughter's bedside; the deputies unlocked the cuffs but stayed with him in the room. The visits were tense. Eddie tried to speak reassuringly. He told her he loved her, and tried not to cry until after the deputy led him from the room. Danielle replied in monosyllables, because of the pain and because she was furious at her father.

"We'd always been so close," Eddie said later. "When we'd go on trips as a family, to Europe several times, and to Israel, Danielle always wanted to stay in the room I stayed in. To her, my being in jail was an abandonment." Eddie wiped his eyes, and sobbed at the memory. "Here she was dying of cancer, and I was in jail. I couldn't do anything about it. I couldn't help her to die. That's the worst part of it."

On the second day of her father's trial, Danielle died. Dropping his pugilistic regard for once, Eddie pleaded with Judge Politan to be allowed to attend the girl's last rites. The Antars were observing a traditional period of mourning called *shivah* ("the seven days") and Eddie wanted to be with the family at this most intense, private time. By custom the family retreats from social exchanges during the week of *shivah*.

Eddie appeared before Judge Politan, asking for a week's recess of the trial and permission to stay in his father's house during that time. Judge Politan replied that "certain members" of the Antar family were suggesting Eddie's presence might disrupt the proceedings. "Besides," Politan announced, "I still want to see that $60 million. Putting up the money as a sign of good faith might sway an old judge's heart. There is $60 million laying out there.... I won't have any *hondling* in my courtroom," Politan said, using a Yiddish word for bargaining. "There is $60 million out there that I'm aware of that your client has refused to sign over to the trustee. So we're not talking about surety. Come on. Does he want to sign the 60 million over?"

"The price of my daughter is 60 million dollars?" Eddie shouted at Politan.

"Please sir," Politan urged.

"Please sir nothing," Eddie shot back.

"Please, sir," Politan repeated, "You're out of order. It's not a question of the price of your daughter. It is a question of the price of your flight, sir." Eddie refused to pay, so Politan denied his request. However, Eddie was allowed to attend Danielle's funeral, where Debbie 1 met him with a hug and offered him a chair beside her and the four girls.

Eddie marked *shivah* alone in his cell. His rabbi arrived the day after the funeral to perform the ritual *Qerriah*. Eddie bowed his head while the rabbi ripped a piece of fabric from the sleeve of his prison coveralls. Together the men uttered, *Barukh Dayan ha-emmet* ("Blessed is He, the Judge of Truth"). Truly now Eddie looked like the Pitiful One, his eyes swollen and ashamed, his face taut, suffering. His beard bloomed thick and nappy from neglect.

Meanwhile, the proceedings veered into absurdities. During the prosecution's closing, Michael Chertoff interrupted his own remarks and asked for a sidebar with Judge Politan. At the bench,

Chertoff complained that Jack Arsenault, seated at the defendant's table, was "mugging for the jury." While Chertoff was making his case, he said, Arsenault "conducted a kind of pantomime of eye-rolling, head shaking, grimacing, et cetera.... I would ask the court to tell Mr. Arsenault not to eye-roll, head shake or otherwise gesture.... just to keep a poker face and—"

"Judge—," Arsenault interrupted.

"Liar's poker," Judge Politan muttered under his breath.

All mugging for the jury aside, the appeals court bought defense counsel's argument. Judge Politan's remarks had given "the appearance of impartiality," the court ruled. In April 1995 the Third U.S. Appeals Court in Philadelphia overturned Eddie and Mitchell's convictions. After tracking Eddie Antar across the world, spending years and thousands of dollars on his prosecution, the U.S. government was losing its man.

Unmasking the Mad Faxer

Both Eddie and Mitchell felt they had the wind behind them. They might actually see this through. One of Judge Politan's last acts in the case was to forbid the Crazy Eddie jurors from talking to reporters. When the gag ruling was appealed and struck down, court records revealed that the Antar jury room had not been a warm, cuddly place to spend a week. In their first days of deliberation, the jury's foreman sent a message to Judge Politan asking him to rebuke a member of their group, who'd become "nasty and screaming," refusing to cooperate with the others. After returning the guilty verdict, two jurors seemed to regret their decision. A woman called Politan's office to say she hadn't really been clear on the federal racketeering law and the judge's instructions in that regard.

The Antar brothers told themselves they'd surely go free. But Weissman and Chertoff said, no way, we're going back to trial. Eddie needed to realize that he had snubbed New York Money, he'd jumped bail on the U.S. government, he'd harassed Swiss banking authorities, and he'd held shouting matches with a federal judge. Michael Chertoff told reporters Eddie was "the Darth Vader of capitalism." The Count promised he'd haul Eddie and Mitchell back into court, and win, unless their lawyers anted up. Eddie would get credit for the time he'd served since his return from Israel. Mitchell would probably draw about ten months, the same amount of time he'd spent in jail since the first trial.

Finally, in the closing days of summer 1996, ten years after he resigned from his company and consigned it to a tailspin from which it never recovered, Eddie admitted he defrauded his investors. He was led from the courtroom owing $150 million in fines and restitution, not counting the judgments mounting against him in civil decisions, which would eventually exceed $1 billion. In February of 1997, Judge Harold A. Ackerman of the New Jersey District Court sentenced Eddie to six years and 10 months in the federal penitentiary. At the Otisville prison, Eddie often worked 11 hours a day, helping to prepare kosher meals for the facility's Muslim and Jewish inmates.

Mitchell was appalled to hear Judge Ackerman remand him into state custody for 20 extra months, despite Chertoff's assurances he'd go free. Mitchell had already turned over $1.7 million, basically all his assets, and served nearly a year in jail. He says his prison time wasn't the country club experience of white-collar lore. "It was filthy, miserable, boring as hell."

Into 1999, the SEC team, led by Ric Simpson, and the class-action filers, led by Howard Sirota, continued to scour the world for Antar assets. Losses were set at $145.9 million. So far Simpson and Sirota have recovered about $135 million from bank accounts Eddie kept around the world, plus assorted change from Mitchell and various "unindicted co-conspirators."

More dollars might be arriving soon. A civil judgment against Sam M., his son Allen, and his grandchildren was decided in July 1998. Ric Simpson, whose very first case for the SEC (in 1988) was chasing down Crazy Eddie, asked for the old man to repay the money he made from selling CRZY stock, about $15 million. Plus, Simpson wanted the $3 million Allen Antar made on stock sales, and half a million from each of several grandkids. Then there's the matter of interest. Altogether Sam M. owes $75 million, by Simpson's accounting.

However, the crux of the Crazy Eddie case doesn't lie in accounting. It shows itself in the person of the Mad Faxer. The faxer's last dispatch came through U.S. mail, actually, and was handwritten. This one addressed Rose Antar.

> *Dear Rose,*
>
> *Well, it was only a matter of time before they caught your crooked son and gave him the prison term he deserves.*
>
> *And to dampen your spirits, you miserable bitch, the Newark FBI has been investigating into your Atlantic City Caesars Casino*

gambling, matching your income with what you spend on the high roller machines. Better be prepared for a court date. We all know you were spending the Crazy Eddie empire.

What goes around, comes around.

With the handwriting staring him in the face, Sam finally knew who the Mad Faxer was: the shadowy Solomon Antar. Not his nephew Sammy. Not Eddie. *Solomon.* The Faxer had complained of Sam M.'s *loshon horah* (evil tongue) and suggested Sam could benefit from reading Kafka. Those weren't words the book-shy Eddie was likely to choose. But Solomon.... He was Sam's cousin, some 15 years younger, Crazy Eddie's general counsel since 1979, and a key player in the family's currency smuggling. Like his cousin, Solomon is wiry framed and energetic. Like his cousin, he's got one hell of a temper. Unlike Sam M., Solomon skated through 12 years of federal prosecutions without a scratch. Solomon was never charged with any crime, though the FBI had documents and testimony implicating him in various acts. He was never called to testify in Eddie's trial. He was never charged for signing ersatz SEC reports as general counsel. He was never made to repay a single dime of his Crazy Eddie stock profits.

"Why not?" Sam M. asks, his eyebrows raising like twin bridges. He repeats, "Why not?" Solomon played foxy once the long arm of the federal law hit the Antar fold. When SEC prosecutors were stuck with lying family members and a few scattered documents, Solomon arranged for the papers from Debbie 1's divorce suit to show up in pink ribbons on Howard Sirota's porch. The class-action lawyer wasted no time sharing his gift with the SEC. In those papers, Debbie talked about how Eddie had secretly stashed millions in Israeli bank accounts, something no one at the Department of Justice had figured out yet. She wanted a piece of that money, even if it meant endangering the family's secret deals.

Solomon had kept the papers with the incriminating testimony sealed as part of the settlement. But whatever loyalty he felt to the family was worn down by their constant striving. When Debbie sued him for forging her name to the original divorce—and won in 1990—Solomon had had enough. She'd known and accepted the terms at the time, but under Sam M.'s prodding, had used a technicality to reopen the case, trying to grub a few dollars as usual.

When the Mad Faxer railed, at all-caps volume, against "YOU WHO OPENED YOUR MOUTHS AND TESTIFIED AGAINST ME TO HURT ME," Sam had thought the missive came from Eddie, who stood to lose millions in the divorce suit. Instead, it was Solomon, who stood to lose his license for forging a client's signature. In Sam's telling, Solomon extracted his revenge by coaching Sammy's testimony. Everyone knew, from Zinn-Palmieri's audit, how much was supposed to be missing—some $80 million. All Solomon and Sammy needed was a convincing tale for how things got so bad.

Sam avers, "For two years, Sammy sat in the U.S. Attorney's office, listening and talking. He attended 21 depositions to get his story straight. But Sammy never knew none of my business. Never. He tells stories, about trucks pulling up at his father's house in the middle of the night, but do you think I'd have a teenage boy helping me skim money? No. The only one who knew about the money in Israel and the divorce papers and all the rest was Solomon Antar."

According to Sam's "merry-go-round" theory, a host of legal types—including Ric Simpson, Howard Sirota, U.S. Attorney Paul Weissman, Judges Politan and Ackerman, and the FBI's Paul Hayes—went hounding for defendants to avenge the losses suffered by the Oppenheimer-Palmieri fund. Insiders protecting insiders. Solomon Antar pointed the way, by providing federal officials with documents, by fashioning a story to explain how the millions disappeared, and by bringing in Sammy, the government's prime witness, thoroughly rehearsed to deliver the dialogue. In exchange Solomon kept his stock profits and walked.

So, the lawyer did it. The family barrister teamed with the family accountant to bring a legendary family to ruin. It could happen.

****

"Whatever!" Sam M. interjects in a loud voice. "They can sue me for $75 million, or $175 million. I don't have it." Sam was diagnosed with prostate cancer in 1997. He's been doing some estate planning since then, transferring his assets to Rose's name. Ric Simpson countered by adding Rose to the judgment.

Sam laments, "I sold that stock to cash in on my golden years. Instead I'm spending my golden years in courtrooms. They're not going to stop until I'm dead. But that's okay, because that's when I'll give up. I will not admit to something I didn't do, and I will never give them a penny. They will have to come and take it from me."

Ric Simpson says, fine, we'll take it from you. If your business partner phonies the books and you make 15 million dollars as a result, you don't get to keep your proceeds. That's just the way public trading works.

The monster Eddie Antar is free, after slinging hash in a prison kitchen and sleeping nearly eight years in lockup. He clerks at Computer World by day. He spends his evenings and weekends with his wife, Debbie 2, and their son, named Sam, born through the miracles of *in vitro* fertilization while his father was in jail.

Debbie 1 and the girls live in New Jersey, near Sam and Rose.

Sammy Antar works with his father-in-law, selling real estate. He divides his time between a Manhattan headquarters and a satellite office in San Antonio, Texas. In his spare time, Sammy continues tutoring children with attention deficit disorder, which he began as part of his community service.

Allen Antar has declared bankruptcy. He and Mitchell help run a 3,500-square-foot electronics store, set in a strip mall just off the highway in Wayne, New Jersey. The store is called Crazy Eddie's. If you're not in the New York-New Jersey corridor, you can browse *crazyeddieonline.com*, then call "for a free price quote" from one of several Antar grandsons.

The new Crazy Eddie's is run by a kid named Sam, who looks a lot like his Uncle Eddie, especially with his hair slicked back and puffing on a Marlboro Light. Sam has a decidedly sweeter disposition than his uncle. His eyes are a deep stained walnut, like Eddie's, but they're lively, curious eyes, without Eddie's grudges and hurt. He's got Eddie's sensual lips. Sam is Allen Antar's son, a kid just past 20 years old, about to get married and start a family while he's learning the retail trade, tending the store, working the counter.... It's still a small operation right now, but who knows? It could be big.

Sam, young Sam, *Sammy the A*, the family calls him—he says, "I'd love to get our old spot back along King's Highway. That's the one that made us famous."

John Bennett
(1938 -)

CHAPTER 8

Loaves and Fishes:
John Bennett

"When I run over the frightful catalogue of my sins, I cannot believe that I am the same creature whose thoughts were once filled with sublime and transcendent visions.... But it is even so; the fallen angel becomes a malignant devil."
—*The Creature*

Jack

When I was a boy, my mother came into my bedroom one night. It was 3 a.m. I heard her steps creaking across the kitchen, turning down the hallway, passing Joan and Nancy's room before pausing at my door. My little brother Bruce wheezed on the bunk underneath mine, as usual all but comatose. I'd been lying awake since midnight, listening to Mother scrubbing the counters and crying softly. Whenever my father stayed out drinking, Mother cleaned. Sometimes she cried, sometimes she prayed. Sometimes she just sponged the Formica tops in circles and hummed her favorite hymn, "Living by Faith." The tones encircled my ears like the cottony folds of her nightgown.

"Jack?" she called from the half-lit hallway. "Jack? I need you, son."

Mother said he was sick again. He was out on the sidewalk. The snow was piling up with the storm, and she said she was sorry but please would I come and help her get him up. We lived in the Olney section of Philadelphia, in a rowhouse on Wellens Avenue. There were several parks for him to sleep in, if he couldn't make it home. But usually I went looking for him because Mother worried so. Sometimes I found him over near Germantown; and since it was too far to try and steer him home, I'd take him to the

Whosoever Mission and they'd give him a cot. When he slumped back the next morning, I couldn't tell whether he remembered I had been with him or not. He'd wash himself and go directly to his truck, without breakfast or a word.

This night, he was just a block or two over, but he was in the worst way. Vomit had dribbled along his cheeks. His head was leaning backwards off the stoop where he had collapsed, tilting a string of the puke to just beneath his right eyelid. His breath came in quick, sharp gasps. He held the gnawed butt of a cigar in his right hand. He remained unconscious and only grunted when we tried to wake him. When I touched his unshaven cheek, it felt like rubbing my hand across the concrete stair. The wind had blown his coat back and the snow was piling up in his belly button.

He drove a laundry truck for a company called Suburban Laundry. He picked up dirty clothes at rich people's homes—the Longstreths and the Bauers and the Van Eycks—and he took the clothes back when they had been cleaned, folded, and pressed. As soon as he'd run his route, he and his Teamster pals headed to the taps. There they sat drinking into the wee hours, talking about life back in Glasgow, where my father was born, singing songs with clucky rhythms and high trilling melodies. I loved to hear him sing, even when he staggered home in a mess and couldn't remember the words. But he scared me when he'd growl, "Jyne me boy!" and try to make me sing along. When I shrank back, he would start jabbering in Gaelic, his ever present cigar butt wagging in his clenched teeth like a stubby finger. Even after I had bolted to my room and locked the door, I could hear him, singing a while and jabbering a while, sing and jabber, sing and jabber.

I was distracted a lot. Not only by my father's drinking and the troubles that brought on, but I'd also discovered girls. One in particular.

I met Joyce Cowdrick at Olney High. She was 13, a freshman. I had seen her at church but I had never talked to her. She had dancing blue eyes. That day at school, I was on the verge of a panic attack. I couldn't find my band class. I'd been walking around and around, in this endless maze of cinder-block walls.

Joyce just came up to me and said, "You're Jack Bennett, aren't you? Are you lost?" I think I fell in love right there. She glowed along her cheekbones when she talked to me. Her blonde ponytail flicked across her shoulder when she pointed me toward the music room.

Joyce and I dated all through high school, though I didn't have much time to hang around playing beau. I worked a paper route after school, and on the weekends I delivered prescriptions for a pharmacy. I played baseball in the springtime and at summer camp, but my main activity, my heart's most burning desire was to sing. I was a soloist at First Presbyterian, and a standout tenor in the A Capella Choir at Olney High. When I tiptoed into my high A, it could bring down a house. Audience members grabbed for their spectacles, afraid for I'd shatter the lenses.

I confess, though, I never loved singing in choirs so much as I did with my little combo. We were a quartet, three of my classmates from Olney and I, called King's Court. Besides the religious standards like "How Great Thou Art," we played old-time gospel songs like "Victory in Jesus" and "He's Gonna Be Here Soon." Everyone loved King's Court, especially the younger people. That's how I first began my ministry, singing at camp meetings and fundays for elementary and junior-high aged kids.

Joyce made every step I did. She went to all my concerts and helped with the hauling and setup for King's Court. She seemed to relish the way everyone smiled and congratulated me almost as much as I did.

I always knew Joyce and I were meant for each other, and that both of us were meant by God to play a fantastic role in His kingdom. For one thing, my mother adored Joyce. The first time Joyce came to our house, she read the plaque Mother kept above the kitchen doorway out loud:

Lord if there is one good thing I can do today,
Let me do it today,
For I may not pass this way again.

Mother walked across the room and hugged her and said, "You precious child of mine."

Joyce and I always knew we were fated, in the way that kids think they know. Then we learned it was true. We were driving one rainy night. It was late, and all of sudden our car died. I had graduated from high school the year before and gone to work for United Airlines, carrying luggage. Joyce would graduate in June. We'd been to a banquet at the Methodist Church in Society Hill that evening, where I'd sung. (King's Court had broken up when two of our members left for college. I was strictly solo those days.)

Joyce and I hung around after the show to talk with some of the other young people. We'd had a lovely time, but we grew nervous on the drive back. We were both staying for the weekend as counselors in a children's camp called Camp Saginack. The rain started hammering down as soon as we left the city. We shouldn't have been out driving at all, but there was an 11 o'clock curfew at the camp. If we were late, the administrators would call Joyce's parents, and the Cowdricks were going to have a fit. They had told me more than once that I too often kept Joyce out past bedtime. So I was driving fast, sliding like a snake on the curvy roads outside of Pottstown, praying to get back before Saginack called lights out. Then the car just stopped.

I got out, drenched immediately in the downpour, and lifted the hood. I didn't know anything about cars; but it's just what you do, right? You see if a wire's hanging loose, or if something's cracked, and of course all you see is a wad of hoses and baffling iron things. I yelled to Joyce that I would try to find some help. She yelled back at me, but I couldn't hear her, because I had already walked up the road. I must have gone about a quarter-mile, which took some time because the water was backed up a foot or so high. My wet shoes were chafing blisters on my ankles. I could hear, somewhere ahead of me, the creek that ran down the hill from Camp Saginack. I knew I must be near the bridge, but it was hard to make out anything.

A flash of lightning spotted on something to the side of the road. I walked over and found a gas lantern lashed to a post, its wick drowned in the storm. A second lightning bolt showed me why the lantern had been hung there: the bridge was washed out. The timbers were wrecked; I could see parts of the railing snagged in a treetop a few yards away. I grabbed the lantern and slogged my way back as quickly as I could to Joyce. She yelped when I told her what had nearly happened to us.

"We would've run off the bridge, Jackie! My God! My God! Jackie, we woulda died!"

I hugged her as hard as I could, even wet to the gills like I was, and told her I loved her. I thought I'd never let her go, but Joyce noticed the lantern.

"There's something on it," she said.

I tilted the lantern to find a paper stuck to the bottom. It was a religious tract. It told the story of salvation, and gave a number to call at Camp Saginack, for prayer or assistance. And someone had circled a Bible Quote: *Because I live, you shall live also.*

We prayed together and thanked God for stopping the car. I knew then He had a plan for me. When I turned the key, the motor fired to life and we drove back to town.

Working for Nothing

"He's a father who is loyal and faithful, loving, prayerful, a gentleman, respectful, high morals, who wouldn't even think of words like *scheme* or *fraud*."
—*Joyce Bennett*

The bloom of Jack Bennett's youth had not produced any fruit. He took seven years at Temple University to earn his bachelor's degree and teaching certificate. He spent a few terms teaching science at the Agnes Irwin Girls' School. The one promise of the early days he'd followed through on was marrying his high-school sweetheart.

Joyce nearly went spastic with joy when he brought home his exciting news in the summer of 1967. The recommendations from Agnes Irwin had worked—despite a less than stellar undergraduate record, Jack had been admitted to the Medical School at Temple. He was gonna be a doctor after all. Joyce insisted they call Jack's mother, Evelyn, who'd been helping the young couple with $25 a week from her job as an LPN at the Central Baptist Old Folks Home. Evelyn matched her daughter-in-law squeal for squeal, and when Jack came on the line, she nearly wept. "Your father's proud of you, Jack," she told him, as if she'd read her son's mind. "He may not say so, but he is."

The other students at Temple admired Jack for signing up to run the med school gauntlet at the hoary age of 30. They called him "Old Iron Butt" for his amazing feats of sitting—Jack would spread his books on a table in the library, sit down, and stay there for hours, from after lunch until sundown, into the night, reading, reading reading. Some of the younger students swore Old Iron Butt only pushed back to stretch once every hour. He never took bathroom breaks. He just sat there reading.

"The experience of medical school is just pressure-packed," one of Jack's classmates explained later, discussing the future Frankenstein with reporters. "It's a nightmare for even the best students. You're in class nine hours a day, and then you're back in the section lab at night for another four or five hours. You have an assignment for each day, and you never have enough time to finish it.... To get through it, Jack relied on doggedness, rather than a brilliance he didn't possess."

In his first year, Jack flunked Anatomy. That's not so unusual, Joyce and everyone else told him. The gray wall of Anatomy has turned back legions of first-timers. Jack gamely signed up for a second year, but he still couldn't cut it. He was made especially miserable when he was assigned to share a cadaver with the top three students of that year's class. Next to the go-getters Jack looked fumbling, not to say dumb.

Near the end of the fall semester, he began complaining he was ill. "I'm suffering from labyrinthitis, which has become Menière's Disease," he told Temple officials. Menière's Disease attacks the membranes of the inner ear, prompting bout of dizziness, nausea, and deafness. It is treatable with medication and a prepared diet; in serious cases, doctors operate to remove the lesions from the inner ear.

Jack reported, "In my third year of medical school I weighed 92 pounds. I lost 80 percent of my hearing, especially on the right side. I was given an ultimatum that if I didn't take a medical leave of absence, I would be kicked out of the medical school. It was a devastating time of my life." Jack was formerly a robust man, 180 pounds or so, just more than six feet tall. You can't blame the Temple administrators for telling him to leave. If he shrunk to 92 pounds in the passing of a single semester, he had no business in the cadaver room.

Miraculously, you might say, Jack returned to his chunky, happy self soon after he left med school. The man had no time to malinger. Joyce was due to have a baby sometime in the fall of 1970 and Jack needed a job. On a visit to a Dr. Polk, who was handling Joyce's pregnancy, the couple found their prayers answered.

"There was a job opening to be a drug coordinator," Jack recalled with a self-satisfied gleam in his eyes, "and Dr. Polk asked me if I wanted the job. I told him I didn't know anything about drug abuse, *per se*, but you know, I knew about alcoholism. So I took the job and became very committed to the field of substance abuse."

Make no mistake. Jack had picked up a few things in medical school. He took a course in "doctor's deportment," according to a former associate. "That training—developing a bedside manner and such—taught him how to project an authoritative and commanding personality. He developed a resonant voice, slow enough to convey emphasis or warnings; and he acquired enough use of technical jargon to demonstrate superior knowledge and information."

Jack saw that Philadelphia, like every large American city, was infested. Heroin junkies and coke fiends staggered through middle-class streets at dawn looking for an angry fix. And these weren't just working-class zombies, or Negro boys from the riverside. A lot of kids from respectable families, bearing Mayflower credentials, were discovering the pleasures of drugs.

Jack said, "I had an ability to communicate with these young people, to talk to them and help them. Not really knowing a whole lot about drug abuse, but at least listening, and, you know, being there, and meeting with them."

Jack didn't spend much time actually listening to heroin addicts. He was an office man. Jack and a few of his colleagues formed a non-profit corporation called CODAC, Community Organization for Drug Abuse Control. They had no offices of their own; and most of the principals, like Jack, had only a year or so experience in the drug prevention field. But in a brand-new sector of social work, the CODAC crew were practically seasoned experts. Jack bragged, "I walked the streets of Washington and got $100,000 from the Department of Justice."

Well, he didn't pound the pavement exactly. "Not knowing anything about the government, I would kind of walk [that is, he'd call] each federal agency and just simply say, 'How do I get money for a drug abuse program?'"

CODAC decided instead of spending their $100,000 on junkies, they'd use the money to educate people about drugs. Jack said, "We began to implement drug prevention and coordination programs in our community. I traveled around Montgomery County helping other communities create these programs similar to the one we'd started in Merion."

Once CODAC had populated Montgomery County with seven drug prevention programs, they needed someone to supervise the sub-chapters. Jack was tickled to accept the position. The following year Governor Milton Shapp, a native of Montgomery County himself, asked Jack to join the statewide Council on Drug Abuse. Jack was constantly on the go, and agog at his luck. Here he was, a med-school dropout and son of a drunk, lunching with people he knew from the newspapers, talking politics over steak and tea with Pennsylvania's top legislators.

Problem was, Jack and Joyce were trying to raise two girls. Keri arrived in 1970, Kristin in 1972. The young family lived in Philadelphia, while the Governor's Council was located at the state capitol in Harrisburg. Jack decided to commute the 220-mile round trip. With some luck and a reasonable agenda, he could be home by 9:30, just in time to kiss Keri and Kristin before they were tucked into bed. On bad days, he was caught in late meetings and sometimes had to stay over.

Keri and Kristin took their first steps without Daddy. They learned to talk without Daddy. They knew Daddy as the big man who brought them whistles from Allentown's new mental health clinic, or dolls from the children's ward in Johnstown. As Jack tells it, he was snapped out of his pinball tour of Pennsylvania by a Hallmark moment with his little girls. "This particular week I left home on Monday and went to Allentown. I was supposed to go right back home. But the governor said, 'Jack, I need you to go to Pittsburgh,' so I didn't return home until Friday. I came home and opened the door, and my wife, who's so supportive, said to me, 'You know, Jack, for the first time, the kids haven't asked for you.' I went upstairs and I looked at them in their beds. Then I called the governor and resigned."

****

Jack began with a company he called Nova Institute International. He would help non-profit agencies raise money in exchange for a small cut of the proceeds. Despite its grandiose name, Nova's staff was limited to Jack, a physician named Hillary Oliver, and Jack's secretary from his days in the governor's office, Linda Forte.

Jack had no idea where his next paycheck was coming from, and now others were counting on him. The consulting brought in a few dollars for Jack, but Nova wasn't doing so well. They were finding plenty of clients; they just couldn't produce any significant funds. For one thing the agencies with money to give away didn't like Jack's funding structure—he insisted that donations be made directly to Nova Institute International, and he'd pass the money on. Respectable grant-making agencies preferred to send their funds to the intended recipient, and have the group pay the middleman from its treasury. It was just cleaner that way.

"In many cases," Jack admitted, "I was unable to deliver specific dollars to the degree I said I would to specific non-profit organizations." When it came down to *specifics*, Jack suffered a cognitive deficit. On the larger vision thing, however, he was flush. "I was concerned, but I felt that if I could keep Nova going, then certainly the funds would be found. It was just a question of time."

A doctor from the Medical College of Pennsylvania, one of Nova's clients, put it more bluntly. "Bennett was always talking about how he was well connected with local foundations and wealthy individuals, this person he knew, or that foundation. But he raised little or no money."

Bennett's creditors were filing judgments left and right. His office supply company was closing Nova's account. And the IRS was anxious to know why Nova Institute had never paid any taxes. Six federal liens were entered against Nova between 1981 and 1983. Jack slipped past most of those, but in 1984, the IRS hit Bennett and his wife with a personal bill for $30,000 in unpaid taxes.

"Oh, Jack, you work so hard, and you've helped so many groups," Joyce said. "But listen, honey. You put in 80 or 90 hours this week...but the only thing is, see, not one hour of that time was billable. You can't work for nothing, honey, or you're going to end up with nothing."

They were shifting from credit card to credit card, grasping for every dollar they could find. Joyce remembered, "There were times when three or four different people from the community would bring bags of groceries to our door. Our parents would send $25 here or there."

As Nova was burning out, Jack made his first lifelong enemy. He had aggressively courted a group known as Teen Challenge, run by the Wilkerson brothers, David and Don. David Wilkerson had made a huge splash in the world of Christian philanthropy with his 1963 memoir, *The Cross and the Switchblade*. A self-described "country preacher," David Wilkerson was pastoring a congregation in western Pennsylvania when he saw a story in *Life* magazine about four black youths on trial for murder. He decided to go to New York City and establish a youth ministry there. Besides preaching to Black and Hispanic gang members, Teen Challenge built safe houses and crisis centers. The best way to soothe a wounded man's spirit, Wilkerson preached, was to minister to his physical needs first.

Wilkerson's early success was crowned when *The Cross and the Switchblade* became a national bestseller. In 1970, the book was made into a film starring Pat Boone as David Wilkerson.

If Jack got his foot in the Teen Challenge door, he'd be set. The organization was 25 years old in 1983, and still growing. Don Wilkerson, who handled Teen Challenge's finances, was pleased at Jack's proposal, but he got antsy waiting for Jack to raise any money. After two years of promises, Don made some calls and learned that Jack hadn't contacted half the people he claimed were on his list.

"Why the lies?" Don asked.

"You don't understand, Don. I'm operating by faith here. If I've done anything to mislead you, or hurt you, I'm sorry; but everything I've done here and said here was for the greater good. I just believe so fully in myself that I'm giving you the same assurances I feel in my deepest heart."

Wilkerson knew the squishy sound of bullshit when he heard it. "You have lied to us for over two years," he wrote in a Dear John letter to Jack. "Now you are lying to yourself as the reason behind it all. I have never seen more deception and lying in all my years. And remember, I work with drug addicts and con artists."

A Kingdom Focus

In early 1982, as the Nova Institute sputtered to bankruptcy, John Bennett Sr. suffered a cerebral hemorrhage. Jack told his many well-wishers that even though he had been unable to intervene in his father's drinking, ill health had forced the old man to give up alcohol for the last ten years of his life. "Those were wonderful years," Jack smiled through wet eyes, though Jack hadn't been around much, and the old man had not become any warmer with age and a deteriorating body. Jack said his father was better off in Heaven.

Jack hadn't attended any church regularly in 15 years. But with his company failing and the family practically destitute, he agreed to accompany Joyce and the girls to the Church of Our Savior in the nearby township of Wayne. Pastor Raymond van Pletsen led a progressive-minded congregation for '80s professionals. His exotic South African accent and commanding personality attracted thousands of admirers, among them a sprinkling of Philadelphia's elite. The community at Our Savior brought food to Jack's house, donated dresses to Joyce and the girls, and raised cash for the picturesque all-American family. Our Savior's congregation fed and clothed the Bennetts and helped them pay off the $30,000 they owed to the IRS.

Jack was gaining momentum again. He had made important contacts at Our Savior, and started to link these with the people he knew at federal agencies and state offices. He needed the contacts because Jack had been inspired to launch a new business. "We realized at Nova that we weren't going to be able to get any monies by working for the non-profits. The last thing non-profits will put the money out for is fees for fundraising.... Then I thought, well, maybe I won't be able to help these groups directly. But I can help them by working for the organizations that give the money away."

The fruit of Jack's analysis was called Human Services Systems. By now he was gaining ground socially, even though his businesses were losing money and his family was itself a charity case. His partners at HSS included Richard Ohman, CEO of Colonial Penn Insurance, and William Thatcher Longstreth, five-time Philadelphia city councilmember and author of *Main Line Wasp*, a memoir about growing up in one of the city's most hoity-toity neighborhoods. John Salveson, another prominent area businessman, was tapped as executive vice president for the venture. HSS contracted with large corporations, including Bell Telephone, Playtex Products, and the Federal Reserve Bank of Philadelphia, to provide their employees with mental health services. The companies paid a subscription fee; then any time an employee needed mental health care—say for a drug or alcohol problem—HSS found the person a provider and picked up the tab. At this time, Jack also set up a non-profit operation he called the Center for New Era Philanthropy, to raise and distribute grant monies.

As usual, money was in short supply. Utility bills went past due, and vendors harassed the HSS staff for payment. Jack's employees—who included his wife, Joyce, and six or eight others—often found their paychecks denied at the bank. Jack hired William Bennington, a former senior vice president at Colonial Penn, to do public relations work for HSS, but Bennington also had trouble getting paid. Jack left him as much as $80,000 in arrears. Bennington, like so many of Jack's cohorts and disciples, took the slight in stride. It was all God's work and Jack always came up with another angle.

With a $350,000 grant from Bell Telephone, Jack established the Bell Institutes for Non-Profit Excellence, a series of short courses preparing people to work in the charity world. Jack and Bill Bennington lectured on business planning, organizational development, board development, and fundraising. "You're only as good as your board of directors," Jack admonished. "If you don't have a good strong board in place from the beginning, you're sunk." On the subject of finances, Jack was unequivocal: "You've got to have a board willing to stand up, be tough, and hold directors accountable for every cent."

He wasn't so tough on himself. He constantly shifted funds between Human Service Systems and the Center for New Era Philanthropy, pinching several hundred thousand dollars in the process. Meanwhile, the employees were paid in hot checks and the bills weren't paid at all. No one dared challenge Jack until 1987, when John Salveson blew up. Salveson, in charge of HSS finances, waved a handful of checks in Jack's face, all marked "NSF."

"You said the check you wrote from New Era would cover the HSS expenses, Jack, but the New Era check bounced. That made all the HSS checks bounce. What's going on here?" Salveson asked.

Jack said, "I deposited the check from New Era expecting funds to come into that account very soon. The money came late."

Jack admitted he'd had no idea where the New Era money might be coming *from*; he'd written the check to HSS *on faith*, he told Salveson, confident God would provide.

"Jack, that's not faith, that's called check kiting. You can't just move checks from one account to another hoping some real money will arrive. It's illegal."

"What's check kiting?" Jack asked. He later confessed, "I knew what I was doing. But it wasn't an issue of it being illegal; it was an issue of keeping alive components that needed to be kept alive. Sooner or later, money would come in from other things to cover that. To me it was an acceptable procedure because the bigger goal was to change the world. The higher goal was to remove pain and suffering."

In the spring of 1989, with his check-kiting debts pushing $200,000, Jack got word his mother had suffered a heart attack. She died a few days later on the operating table. For three weeks after the funeral, no one at HSS heard from Jack. On his first day back, he gave a long speech about his mother's love and how she had inspired him to a life of service. The staff burst into tears and hugs.

Later John Salveson came by Jack's office. Salveson had discovered a $300,000 transfer from New Era to HSS—money earmarked for the Bell Institute—which had been shifted a second time into Jack's personal account.

"Bell Atlantic gave that money for the Institute, Jack. Why was it transferred?"

"Oh, the money was spent on HSS business. It covered my consulting time, for my teaching and fundraising work."

Salveson was unconvinced. He showed Jack a page of handwritten calculations. "When you do the math, looking at the period of time covered and your daily rate, it would have required an almost impossible amount of time for the amount to be that high. You'd have to work well over 300 days a year just on the Bell Institute."

"That's none of your business," Jack blurted. Salveson remained still, gripping the paper of calculations so tightly his fingertips turned purple.

"Well," Jack said, grinning, "I don't mean to overreact. Look, I have my daily logs at home. If you really need to see them, I can get them for you."

"They should be here, with the rest of our records," Salveson noted testily. "I tell you what, bring them in, let me organize them, and I'll verify the amounts, just to be sure we're in line." Jack promised he'd gather the materials over the weekend. When Salveson arrived on Monday, a locksmith was installing new locks on the office file cabinet. Salveson resigned soon after.

****

Meanwhile Jack was worming his way further into the circles of the high and mighty. In 1988, he met John Templeton, Jr., the chief of pediatrics at Philadelphia Children's Hospital. Templeton said he'd be glad to help Jack bring his Bell Institutes into the religious world. Where Bell Atlantic's charter restricted its programs to secular materials, the Templeton Institutes were designed to teach Christian groups about money—how to raise it, what to do with it, how to keep more of it for the ministry and ministers. Dr. Templeton put even brighter stars in Jack's eyes when he introduced him to John Templeton, Sr., who'd founded the Templeton Investment Funds in 1954. *Sir* John became a British citizen in the 1960s after a tax dispute with the U.S. government. He was later knighted for his service as a financial pioneer and philanthropist *par excellence*.

Jack taught a course in the Templeton Institutes on Bible-based fundraising. Pulling quotes from the Old and New Testaments, Jack shared scriptural hot-tips on how to convert faith into funds. He ended every session with his favorite adage: "Don't give a hungry man a fish, teach him *how* to fish." Jack, for example, was not just doling out money to people, he was teaching them how to fish for dollars themselves.

Jack was better at raising money than handling it. He was known around the office for charming malapropisms like, "This amount will triple by 40 percent by 1987," and "There are only three months left in the quarter." It depressed him to think about balancing accounts and covering his obligations, so he didn't. By August 1989, his check-kiting habit was pushing him into crisis mode. He needed to cover $466,133 in his Philadelphia National Bank accounts and another $413,195 at Merrill Lynch.

No problem. What Christ did with a few loaves and fishes, Jack could do with dollar bills. He approached young Dr. Templeton with a new proposition. "I've talked with a wealthy member of our community, who doesn't want to give his name, but who's interested in a pilot project for giving. This person says if I can get 20 people to put up $5,000 a piece, he'll match the donations dollar for dollar."

"So we're essentially doubling our gifts with the match," Dr. Templeton responded. He couldn't have been more thrilled. Jack's pasty cheeks flamed infectiously whenever he talked of the millions, all the outreach ministries they could fund, the children's programs, the foundations, the institutes.

And his enthusiasm was catching. "Dear Jack," wrote Dr. Templeton in September of 1989,

> *I have enclosed a check for the exciting new program I have dubbed "New Concepts in Philanthropy." I am sure you and the originator have a much better term for this very imaginative and promising program.*

The Jack Bennett Doll

"The people who have described the Foundation as a fraud, I would say they're very ignorant and can't understand a good thing when they see it or hear it. They have focused their minds on what they have made it to be. They have focused their minds on the money part of it, on the getting, on the greed, and have lost track of the giving."
—*Joyce Bennett*

By now Jack's hair had turned white, perhaps an outward sign of his secret financial anguish. He used the $100,000 he raised in the "New Concepts" fund to plug the dike at PNB and Merrill Lynch. But he still had to account for several hundred thousand dollars, and he was expected to double the New Concepts money by January. Faith alone wasn't going to get him out of this one. Jack had friends who would.

One friend in particular turned the Foundation for New Era Philanthropy from another of Jack Bennett's small-time flops into a financial terror. That man was Doug Holladay. In 1984, Holladay was serving in the Reagan White House as a liaison to Protestant groups, the "moral majority" that gave Reagan a second term by herding religious conservatives out of their churchhouses and into voting booths. At a dinner for Christian businesspeople, a minister introduced Jack to Doug Holladay as someone who also understood how to bed down religious folks with politicos.

Holladay served stints in the Department of Education and the State Department before leaving government work for a cushy position at Goldman, Sachs. He billed himself as an "investment banker," but his nameplate said "administrative assistant." Doug met up with Jack Bennett again when he persuaded Goldman, Sachs to back him in establishing a charity. The firm kept paying Holladay's salary while they "loaned" his services to One-to-One, a group that matched disadvantaged youths with adult mentors and provided the kids with jobs. The only problem, Doug confided to Jack, was that nobody at One-to-One had run a charity before. Jack said he'd work for nothing. One-to-One's board members— New Jersey Governor Tom Kean, Vivian Weyerhauser Piasecki of the paper-mill Weyerhausers, and Matilda Cuomo, wife of New York Governor Mario Cuomo—made the time worthwhile. This was Rolodex gold.

Doug Holladay also ushered Jack into the prayer breakfasts held at the exclusive Links Club in Manhattan. Every month a group of evangelical-minded businesspeople met for prayer and croissants, with a healthy dose of networking to wash down the experience and make the cost tax deductible. Regulars included ABC anchor Peter Jennings; the philanthropist Laurance S. Rockefeller; William S. Kanaga, former chairman of Arthur Young & Co.; John C. Whitehead, former co-chairman of Goldman, Sachs & Co.; leveraged-buyout pioneer Raymond G. Chambers; and Julian Robertson, who managed a hedge fund. Everyone on the list, with the exception of Mr. Jennings, ended up slipping millions into Jack Bennett's coat pocket.

Jack felt a vision coming on. He owed $250,000 to John Templeton and the other "New Concepts" donors who had each put up $5,000 the previous fall. Lo! A check cometh in that amount, from Bell Atlantic. Jack paid off the donors and threw out a bigger chunk of bait. His "friend of significant wealth" was opening a new fund, matching contributions dollar for dollar, this time with a minimum ante of $50,000. "This gentleman has donated in excess of 60 percent of his income every year to worthwhile causes," Jack revealed. "His love of giving is what has driven him over the last 50 years of his life." Everyone who read the pitch knew who Jack was referring to: Sir John Templeton, Sr., one of the few men with the cash reserves and generosity Jack was talking about.

Jack let people believe whatever they liked. Each New Era convert spread the bug, swelling receipts from $366,000 in 1990 to

$1.3 million the following year. For 1992, Jack snagged more than $9 million, and in 1993, some $41 million. The pitch remained the same—we hold your money for six months, then we match it dollar for dollar. The enormous volume required expanding to six the number of "Anonymous Benefactors," who were paying the matches.

Jack still favored the standard preacher's garb, a starched white shirt, sweater, and slacks. But in this new era his collars were lined with designer labels. His shoes were cut from the finest Italian leather. He had his nails done once a week, spent a half-hour each morning with his blow dryer, and donned leather suspenders in place of a belt. Jack rolled up to New Era's office at the wheel of his new Sterling automobile, grinning behind dark shades, the very slyest of silver foxes.

Jack and Joyce bought a $225,000 house on Valley View Road in Narboreth, and they moved New Era's offices from Wynnewood into a roomy building in the more upscale town of Radnor. "His place in Radnor was decorated with Jack," said a friend of 25 years. "Everywhere you looked, there were pictures of him with the powerful and wealthy of this country. The Reagans, Nixon, Billy Graham, Sir John Templeton, of course. Jack made a point of letting you know two things: He was well-connected in the religious and political worlds, and his religious feelings were very important to him. He wore his religion on his sleeve. And he dropped names."

Jack's best publicity often came from people outside his organization. John Whitehead of Goldman, Sachs, said the quality of the participants told the story. New Era was for real. "We're not naive dupes, I don't think," Whitehead offered. "It may sound too good to be true, but nonetheless it is true." When the Billy Graham Crusade came to Philadelphia, Jack spoke to the throngs about Christian giving. In return Jack donated $21,000 to the Crusade corporation.

Doug Holladay upped his stake in New Era by corroborating the existence of Jack's mysterious "benefactors." The leader of an Atlanta foundation wrote his board in 1992, "I talked with a friend of mine, Doug Holladay, who is a personal friend of some of the six mega-wealthy donors to New Era. He said these men are very legitimate, very wealthy, and are very serious about putting up these matching funds.... I have a great deal of respect for Doug's integrity and do not feel he would be in on a scam."

On a trip to the Holy Land with a group of Christian philanthropists, Jack basked in their admiration. A businessman who counted a doll company among his holdings told the group,

"I've just come up with a new idea for my next doll. We'll call it the Jack Bennett doll. You wind him up and he gives you money."

Joyce averred, "Oftentimes in jokes is revealed what someone is really thinking." Mrs. Bennett swore that the family's quantum social leaps had not altered the fundamental decency she and her husband shared. "Jack would not be any more impressed with seeing a large Rockefeller come in this room than seeing a worker who stands at the door. He would give you the same respect.... And whatever a Rockefeller, whatever, they're human beings. The last thing that Mrs. Rockefeller and I said when we parted, the time we were up there, was, we can't wait to get together again to talk about Jesus Christ. And that had nothing to do with money."

That was a trip...

"They could just taste the money. I've never seen anything like it. The weakness around the mouth, the desire in the eyes. I'd always heard the expression, "you can see greed written," but now I've seen the reality."
—*Tony Carnes, an early New Era skeptic*

The Foundation for New Era Philanthropy wasn't really a foundation. By definition, a foundation uses the proceeds from an endowment to fund good works. New Era had no endowment; Jack spent money as fast as he could get it. Donations skyrocketed in 1993 after an official from Philadelphia's Academy of Natural Sciences asked if Jack could match a $250,000 offering and Jack heartily agreed. With the gate open, managers from non-profits throughout the nation sent millions: the Nature Conservancy, the Howard Butt Foundation, the American Jewish History Museum.

Jack knew the best way to lead, and the best bait for victims, was to give a little himself. When he met with Colonel Todd Bassett, a regional commander for the Salvation Army, Jack slipped a $250,000 check across the table. Then the group got down to business. William Schofield, a Salvation Army fundraising consultant, was itching so bad to join Jack's game, he said, "I'll put up my house for collateral." Bassett waved off Schofield's offer, but the commander did turn over $500,000 to New Era. When the first six-month term expired, instead of taking Jack's preferred check for $1 million Bassett left the money in.

Jack always claimed (he still does) he was so busy reeling in new money he never paid much attention to exactly how the Foundation handled that money. Not true. Jack persuaded a Prudential broker in Kenosha, Stuart Bianchi, to list New Era's funds as a "quasi-escrow" account. In a normal situation, a non-profit group places its money in an escrow account which is only accessible by one or two of the non-profit's own officers. Under Jack's *quasi*-escrow terms, the non-profit didn't control the funds at all, New Era did. "There's no such thing as *quasi-escrow*," assistant U.S. Attorney Rich Goldberg quipped during the New Era investigation. "It's like being *quasi-pregnant*. Either you retain control of the funds or you don't."

In 1993, Jack wrote to Pam Brothen, an administrative assistant at Prudential Kenosha, threatening to have her fired for discussing the *quasi*-escrow arrangement with a worried New Era client. From now on, Jack said, clients were allowed to know just two things: the type of investment vehicle their money was held in (a Treasury Bill, a certificate of deposit, etc.), and the date the money matured. Twice in the letter, Jack warned, "No further information is to be provided."

Ms. Brothen wrote back to say she was often asked for the names of New Era's board of directors. Jack said she could also divulge this information, and sent over a list of names, including John Templeton Jr., Vivian Weyerhauser Piasecki, and two other local philanthropists.

In fact, New Era didn't have a board of directors. This troubled Bill Bennington to no end because he regularly scolded non-profits for lax oversight. "Jack," he finally said, "it's embarrassing. We're teaching that you need a strong board, so we have to have a board ourselves." Bill said he'd serve, but Jack avoided the offer.

Jack's troubles were mounting with his receipts. The IRS came around, wanting to know why the Foundation had never filed income reports. And why, agents asked, was New Era calling itself a foundation when it had no endowment? Jack claimed his accountants at McCarthy & Company were scurrying to correct that oversight.

Though he was feeling the pinch of a $100-million con, Jack kept a happy face for the New Era family. His offices buzzed with young people like Tracy Ryan, Jack's 20-something personal assistant, and his daughter Kristin Bennett, 23, who had just graduated from Bucknell College with a double major in psychology and English. Kristin's fiancée, Mark Staples, also drew a New Era salary. The staff adored Jack, who loved the role of silver-haired father figure. Workdays in Radnor included lots of hugs and joking and long goodbyes ending with, "I love you, too." Joyce dropped by with stories of the people she and Jack were meeting—the Reagans and Bushes and Grahams and several large Rockefellers—clucking to her chicks.

With the kind of money Jack was throwing around, he couldn't help but inspire admiration. New Era receipts for 1994 hit $160 million. This more than matched the $41 million Jack had to cover in beneficiary payments for the year before. Jack treated the rest, as he did every unclaimed dollar, as discretionary funds. Jack transferred $9 million in New Era donations to Human Service Systems, which was just barely alive. Jack couldn't let HSS go down because a bankruptcy might attract predators to his fold.

New Era donated $1.1 million to Jack's friend Richard Ohman, an early HSS investor, to help Ohman launch Multi-Media Publishing. The company published religious-themed books by some of the biggest names in Christianity, including Billy Graham and former National Security Adviser Robert McFarlane. Their titles ranged from Andy Young's *Black Bible Chronicles,* telling Bible stories in Black English, to *My Prostate and Me,* in which sociologist William Martin discussed his bout with cancer. Those titles did okay, but the company took a beating on other issues, like a sequel to the *Wizard of Oz.* As Multi-Media faltered, Jack provided three separate cash infusions, totaling $1.65 million. At the same time, Jack kept Ohman on the New Era payroll as a $200,000-a-year consultant.

Besides propping up HSS, Jack kept a slice of the New Era largesse for himself. Between 1993 and 1995, he diverted $2.5 million into Bennett Group International, a shell corporation that paid the salary and expenses of its one employee, John G. Bennett, Jr. Meanwhile, Jack modestly said to anyone who cared to listen that he took no salary for his labors at New Era. He bought homes for his daughter, Keri, who lived in nearby Wayne, Pennsylvania, and for the soon-to-be-marrieds, Kristin and Mark. As a Christmas present, Jack paid off his future son-in-law's $30,000 student loan.

Joyce and Jack sold their house in Narboreth and bought a $675,000 place in the rarefied environs of Main Line. Jack traded in his Sterling for a Lexus. The Bennetts and their band of philanthropic consultants flew first-class and stayed in the world's most palatial hotels—the Waldorf Astoria, the Inn on the Park, London's Four Seasons, and the Regent in Hong Kong, where Jack was hoping to spur "the developing Chinese philanthropic community" with a new series of Bell Institutes, including a course on "ethics in business and philanthropy."

Joyce later said the people who criticized their lifestyle as "lavish" were as ignorant as those who couldn't see the miracles of New Era financing. "It's a figment of someone's imagination, what you want to call lavish.... The house, what it was sold for, at the time we bought it, was at an all-time high kind of price for that area. It was a development-type home."

As for the jaunts to New Zealand and Hong Kong, the five-star hotels, the entourage of 10 and 12 people in the New Era traveling party: "I wouldn't call that lifestyle," Joyce snorted. "That was a trip."

Jack and Andy, Jack and Albert, Jack and Steve

"There is so much widespread cynicism in the world that people cannot accept that there's a wealthy philanthropist who has a net worth in the hundreds of millions who is willing to give away substantial amounts and get no credit for it."
—*Andy Cunningham, New Era accountant, co-defendant*

Jack's demise came in three installments, three encounters with three men who challenged what Jack called his "kingdom focus." He stayed so focused on God's kingdom, he'd get blurry on financial details.

Jack received a call in mid-1994 from Andy Cunningham of McCarthy & Company. The McCarthy firm had been doing New Era's books since 1991, when Jack donated $15,000 to the *John McCarthy for Assemblyman* campaign. McCarthy lost the race, but he won himself a hell of a client. Soon, a third of his business was coming from New Era. He assigned Andy, a 30-year-old accountant, to prepare Jack's financial statements.

Andy told Jack he was concerned to find $100,000 on New Era's books for "personal loans." Jack promised to write a check immediately if Andy would wipe the debt away. Call it a deposit in transit, Jack said, and the cash account will balance for the time being. Jack asked for two other things—let's omit any mention of these loans as related-party transactions in the audit report, and can we just skip the board-meeting minutes for this year's report? Andy said sure.

But Andy wanted to know one thing: Why was the $41 million received from New Era's beneficiaries (the people waiting for their money to double) listed as "charitable contributions"? Jack was counting the money as income. But the money belonged to the beneficiaries, not to New Era, and besides, in six months New Era had to match those funds dollar for dollar. "And there ought to be a liability somewhere for the $41-million match," Andy said.

Jack said the matches for the past year had already been made. The $41 million belonged to New Era free and clear. Andy decided not to think about that answer. His boss, John McCarthy, had been clear: keep this guy happy.

How was Andy to know there had ever lived a man like Albert Meyer? Forty-four years old, with fleshy cheeks and sleepy eyes, the mild-mannered accounting professor first visited America in the 1980s, playing in the U.S. Open Chess Tournament. A few years later Albert persuaded his wife to leave their native South Africa and settle in Spring Arbor, Michigan. Albert taught at Spring Arbor College by day and helped out evenings by keeping the school's books. As usual, he was thinking several moves ahead when he noticed a $294,000 payment from Spring Arbor College to something called the Heritage of Values Foundation. He thought, "Is this Jim and Tammy Faye Bakker? Those religious nuts? Didn't they build something called the Heritage Theme Park?"

"We have no affiliation with Jim and Tammy Faye," Frederick Veit told Albert. The director of the Heritage of Values Foundation explained that, among other things, he—that is, the Heritage of Values Foundation—acted as a conduit for groups who wanted to participate in the New Era Philanthropy Foundation, matching non-profit's cash dollar for dollar every six months.

The next day, Albert tracked down the whole board of Spring Arbor College. There's some funny business going on in your investment portfolio, he warned. The board members told Albert to mind his own business.

But Albert couldn't stop thinking about New Era Philanthropy. On the phone with Andy Cunningham—and anyone remotely connected to New Era—Albert kept asking questions.

- *Why is Jack Bennett circulating an audit report when the notes clearly say his accountants have only conducted a review of the New Era books?*

- *Why is there a $1.1-million transfer to "non-marketable equity securities" [the startup money for Ohman's Multi-Media Publishing] with no other documentation?*

- *Why is there another transfer in excess of $1 million to something called Bennett Group International? [Jack's salary]*

- *Why aren't the beneficiaries' donations listed as a liability, since they have to be matched every six months?*

> • *Finally, why does an organization claiming to handle $100 million a year earn just $33,000 in interest dividends during 1993? [If the account balance averaged $10 million at any one time, yearly dividends would have run from $600,000 to $1 million.]*

Albert talked funny, and he seemed a little disconnected from the rest of the folks at Spring Arbor, but he saw Jack Bennett's game clearly enough. "He is not holding the money to earn interest," he told his bosses. "He has to pay it out because he is robbing Peter to pay Paul."

Since no one else could explain this New Era to him, Albert sent a fax directly to "Dr. Jack Bennett." He pointed out, "Your CPA firm uses the word *audit* in your financial statement, when they mean *review*.... I have a problem with the fact that you are not submitting your operations to a full audit.... Other than that I applaud you for your efforts." Also, would Jack mind if Albert posted New Era's audit report, along with commentary, on the Internet?

Jack minded. He found the fax on a Sunday afternoon and immediately fired back. In his fat-lined handwriting, part cursive and part print, Jack wrote, "Am completely confused re: your Fax. We are extremely public in our activities and uphold the highest standards." On the phone that afternoon, Jack suggested Albert discuss his Internet posting with New Era's attorney. Albert noted the threat and kept his files to himself.

Since neither Andy Cunningham nor Jack himself had satisfied Albert's worries, the crusading accountant took his case to the *Philadelphia Inquirer*, *The Wall Street Journal*, the FBI, the Securities & Exchange Commission, the Department of Justice, and the American Institute for Certified Public Accountants. He became obsessed. He carried a binder labeled:

> *Ponzi-File: If it quacks like a duck, walks like a duck, and looks like a duck, could it really be a duck?*

Many of the people faced with Albert's pressing questions wondered what sort of quack *he* was.

Meanwhile, at the Marriott in Conshohocken, Andy Cunningham explained to Jack that he was getting a lot of tough questions. "And these are hard times, Jack. I've been married 11 years, though I may not still be married this time next year. I haven't filed my tax returns since 1989. I have some personal loans that have gone bad."

"How bad is it?" Jack asked.

"Fifty thousand dollars."

Jack offered to spot Andy the $50,000 in the spirit of Christian giving. As Jack signed the lunch bill, he also wrote out a check. When they rose, he patted his young friend on the shoulder. "I know you appreciate it, Andy. I don't want to hear any more about it." At the door Jack paused. "I guess this means we won't have any more tough questions."

Andy's check was denied at the bank, but Jack transferred funds from New Era into his personal account and wrote a replacement. In December he gave Andy $1,000 to buy Christmas presents for his wife and two kids. In January, Jack offered another $25,000. And there were no more tough questions.

****

Albert Meyer knew how John the Baptist felt, shouting himself hoarse in the wilderness. It was the spring of 1995 before he convinced the SEC and the IRS to look at New Era. In the meantime, Albert had gained the ear of Steve Stecklow, a reporter at *The Wall Street Journal*. While regulators fiddled, Stecklow persistently squeezed Jack Bennett for answers.

Stecklow saw right off that Albert had every reason to worry. "Nothing about the financials adds up," Stecklow told Andy Cunningham. Stecklow had also learned that the 1993 board of directors' list was false. Andy explained that Jack had written "a kind of wish list" of names, which Jack's assistant Tracy Ryan had passed along to him.

Stecklow asked how New Era documented the anonymous donors' contributions. The philanthropists would need some kind of receipt in order to claim their tax deductions, wouldn't they? Andy said, "You need to talk to Jack."

When Stecklow at last convinced Jack to meet with him, Jack brought Bill Bennington and three lawyers into the New Era conference room. He then refused to answer Stecklow's questions. He did explain that the Foundation had never issued receipts to the anonymous donors—because the people were so wealthy they didn't need to claim the tax deductions.

Stecklow was floored. Who's too rich for tax deductions? The reporter told Jack straight up, "This looks like a Ponzi scheme."

"What's a Ponzi scheme?" Jack asked.

Stecklow said his story would be in next Monday's *Journal*.

God Called

"It kind of reminded me of the Good Samaritan, the man who, the person who fell off the horse. Well, Jack has fallen off the horse."
—*Joyce Bennett*

Prudential Kenosha, tipped off to the *Journal* article, called in a $65-million loan that Jack had drawn against his New Era account. Scraping together every cent he had, Jack still fell $44 million short. Prudential filed suit on Friday, May 12, 1995.

The next morning Jack dropped Joyce off at the airport to attend a bridal shower for their oldest daughter, Keri, in Boston. Joyce was worried. Twice, she turned back from her plane to ask, "Jack, are you going to be all right?"

He might not have been all right—Jack had decided to kill himself—but a miracle occurred on the way back from the airport. Jack said, "Route 95 kind of takes you up a hill; and when I hit the top of the hill, the whole sky opened up. I saw so much pain and how so many people would suffer. I saw children who were going to starve, and everybody would be hurt. I couldn't take it. I headed to the Delaware River to kill myself. But somehow my elbow hit the car phone and I heard a voice say, 'Hello?' I thought it was God. It sounds humorous, but I thought it was God talking to me in the car. When He said, 'Who is this?' I said, 'Obviously, God, you know who I am.' But it turned out to be Russ Caddell, a minister and a friend. I guess I'd talked to him the night before and hit the 'recall' button."

Skipping the Delaware, Jack drove into Radnor to meet his staff. They were all very worried. Kristin Bennett and Tracy Ryan in particular raged at the viciousness of Stecklow's worldly minded *Wall Street Journal* and this crazy accounting professor from Michigan out to destroy God's leading fundraiser. Bill Bennington was questioned by several lawyers, and kept telling them they'd have to talk to Jack, who had assured his friend, "This is a cash-flow thing."

Before a grand jury a year or so later, Bill recounted the final moments of New Era. "It must have been about nine o'clock, and Tracy's phone rang. It was Jack. He said, 'Tracy, I love you,' and hung up the phone. A few minutes later, he called Mary Sinclair, New Era's treasurer, and said, 'Mary, I just want you to know I love you,' and he hung up the phone. Mary and Tracy came to me and they said, 'We think he's going to try and kill himself.' I said, 'I've been sitting here thinking the same thing.'"

Jack arrived bearing dark circles for eyes and a sagging smirk for a smile. He asked Bill to bring the staff into his office. "Jack sat on his desk, with his arms crossed. I went over and stood by the window. Most of the staff, about six of them, sat on the couch at one end of the office, opposite Jack. He was crying. He said he was ashamed. He said he had seriously considered taking his own life that morning."

Shaking off his tears, Jack took a deep breath, then, whispering, said, "I've betrayed you all. I'm so ashamed of myself. All I ever wanted to do was help people. There are no anonymous donors."

As he spoke the last words, his eye fell on Bill Bennington, the only other senior man in the room. "There are no anonymous donors," Jack whispered, his eyes quivering and hurt, like he could hardly believe the words himself.

Bill walked over to him. "Jack held up his hands. He said, 'I don't want anybody to touch me.' I threw my arms around him. I put him in a bear hug. I said, 'Jack, I love you, and I'll be praying for you.'"

****

In an October 1995 videotaped address, sent to 500 former participants, Jack said, "Like Martin Luther King I also had a dream...I was a vision person—about the larger picture—a visionary not involved in the nuts and bolts of the organization. My dream became a nightmare for thousands this past May. Jobs were lost, relationships destroyed, charities suddenly in financial chaos, anonymous philanthropists exposed, family and friends badgered and harassed."

Judy Smith and Rich Goldberg at the U.S. Attorney's office noted a peculiar phrase in Jack's spiel: *anonymous philanthropists exposed*. After repeating his Saturday confession several times over, Jack had reverted to his story. At one point in the video, he addressed the nonexistent anonymous philanthropists directly, dabbing crocodile tears with a white handkerchief: "I apologize for the effect this will have on your anonymity and for the invasion of your privacy."

Jack had good reason to keep the snowjob rolling. Judge Anita Brady had evicted the Bennetts from their home and frozen New Era's assets. Jack's supporters, still believing he knew a hawk from a handsaw, had made the down payment on a new place and paid the monthly mortgage note. "We have two walls in the house covered in pictures," Joyce told the court. "One we call the wall of the angels. It's not exactly what it sounds like. These are the pictures of the people who kindly gave some money so that we can live in this townhouse. And the other wall is called the wall of the faithful. These are lots of pictures of those who didn't rush to judgment."

Kristin Bennett, despite hearing her father's confession from his own mouth, told the grand jury she wasn't sure whether or not there had been anonymous donors. She had blacked out that fateful Saturday morning. Maybe there were only one or two donors, she said, and Daddy had exaggerated them to six.

Joyce Bennett also had difficulties comprehending the liar she lived with. She bounced into a court-appointed psychiatrist's office a year after New Era's failure and asked, "So tell me, are there anonymous donors or not?"

The answer was NOT. Jack said that he had once believed in the donors, but now he knew he was just cuckoo for Cocoa Puffs. Planning to mount an insanity defense, Jack told how he met the figmentary philanthropists on Sunday afternoons, between 2 p.m. and 4 p.m. In one version, Jack said he laid out pencils and paper in the New Era conference room, then took his seat and twisted his pencil, at which point, "The donors appeared." In another telling, he claimed that when his hand touched the office door knob, "The donors appeared."

Jack persuaded two psychiatrists and a psychologist to support his insanity contention. Dr. Robert L. Sadoff of the University of Pennsylvania Medical School said Jack had been talking to God himself. "Jack has heard God's voice," Dr. Sadoff wrote, "especially once, on his dictating machine (but his wife was not able to hear that voice). He states he has never seen God, but wants to." Sadoff praised his patient's commitment to God's work and diagnosed "hypomania, brain dysfunction, and personality disorders."

Mary Anne Layden, a Ph.D. in psychology, went even further. Layden's impressionistic analysis related how "Jack would go into the office; and as he turned the doorknob to enter, it would propel him into the world of benefactors who could finally completely manifest the kingdom of God." Jack feared being crazy "more than anything, more than prison," Dr. Layden declared, but he really believed he had attended these meetings, and "could still see the donors in his mind's eye."

If it's true, as she claimed, that Layden never met Jack before he visited her office in the summer of 1995, then he quickly worked his magic on her. In a climactic judgment, Layden wrote, "Jack's belief system has undergone a psychological revolution. He appears now more like the psychotherapist who is in burnout from compassion overload and disillusionment. About the world and its peoples."

Layden acknowledged, "Jack Bennett is a smaller man now. His relationship with God is still personal but more tender. I hope the rest of us who are involved in recommending and deciding his future are willing to walk an equally long path and listen, as Jack has, to the better angles of our nature." Yes, that's right, she wrote "angles." Somehow with these psychotherapy types it all comes back to Freud.

Dr. Daniel Martell, hired by Assistant U.S. Attorney Judy Smith, had ways to prove a patient was faking mental illness. "On a short battery of tests designed to detect efforts to simulate or malinger symptoms of brain damage, Mr. Bennett failed at simple tasks that are so easy even persons with true brain damage can perform them adequately," Martell reported.

The delusional meetings with anonymous donors? Also fake, according to Martell. "His description of encapsulated, repeated, pre-announced, time-limited, psychotic experiences, integrating florid auditory and visual hallucinations with delusional beliefs that occur only on certain Sunday afternoons is frankly psychiatrically impossible."

****

Jack decided to plead no contest to the charges against him. "I would be lying before my God," he wrote to his last straggling loyalists, "by plea-bargaining to the charges, because I would have to admit I intended to defraud. There was never any intent, never a preconceived scheme, never a thought of devising a way to defraud anyone." Because Jack kept flip-flopping on the donor story, and because he refused to take responsibility for his crimes, Judge Brody sentenced him to 12 years. There's no parole in the federal system, prosecutors reminded Jack, so this creature would indeed serve the next 12 years behind bars in Fort Dix, New Jersey.

Mark Whitacre
(1957 -)

CHAPTER 9

It's a Wonderful Life:
Mark Whitacre

"Listen, therefore, to the deposition that I have to make.... The story is too connected to be mistaken for a dream, and I have no motive for falsehood."
—*Viktor Frankenstein*

Mark Whitacre took his seat, shoved his cup-shaped glasses to the crown of his nose, and began his story. Ronald Henkoff, a writer for *Fortune* magazine, tapped furiously on his laptop.

I SPIED ON MY COMPANY FOR THE FBI.

"That first evening I talked with Agent Brian Shepard, he was real easygoing. We talked about price-fixing meetings until two in the morning. ADM wasn't fixing prices yet, but we were heading there. He was taking notes like crazy. He would say things like 'Wow!' and 'You're kidding me.' You could tell he felt like he had hit a gold mine."

Mark said life was rough inside Archer Daniels Midland, the agri-chemical giant known to viewers of Sunday morning television as the "Supermarket to the World." For the past two years Mark had been secretly filming ADM's leading executives while they formed an illegal cartel with their Japanese competitors. As he rattled off details of barred-door summit meetings and industrial saboteurs, Mark's red mustache bounced to the teletype rhythms of his speech.

The key components driving a federal investigation? Fear and loathing. "The FBI gave me a little microcassette recorder you could put in your jacket pocket; it had a wire with a mike on it. I had nightmares people would see the mike.... I never felt like a secret agent man. But I did feel pumped. I felt I was doing a good thing. Brian told me I was going to be doing the country a great service, that I was taking heroic action."

But the government treated its hero like a rat. "Early on, about February 1993, the Japanese were wanting to set up the next meeting on price fixing. But the scheduling problem was me, and Brian knew that. One night we were in a room at the Holiday Inn in Decatur, and Brian heard the tapes saying that the Japanese wanted to meet. And he knew I was holding up the dates for another price-fixing meeting, and he was really pissed off. He took a briefcase, a hard-sided briefcase, and he took it by the handle, swung it around and hit me on the right arm. He said, 'You've got to make this investigation your Number-One priority, Mark.' That night I went home and told my wife, showed her my arm. It was red. It was bruised by the next day. I went over to my in-laws' house and showed them too...."

"The people who knew what I was doing, my wife, some of my relatives, a few good friends, sometimes they would ask: 'Hey, who are the good guys here?' It came to the point, after four or five months, where I wasn't sure who was dirtier, ADM or the FBI.... I was getting very depressed. I was realizing the FBI was not much different than ADM. They all had their own conspiracies. And I was just stuck in the middle. For the first time in my life I was very, very depressed. My wife noticed it. My in-laws noticed it...."

No one heeded Mark's cries for help. "In the spring of 1993, I told Brian Shepard and another FBI agent that I was considering killing myself. And I've got this conversation on tape too. I'll never forget this. They asked me how I would kill myself if I did. And I told them I would do it with sodium cyanide. I'd take some and swallow it...."

"I kept putting pressure on Brian Shepard. I said, 'What if ADM finds out and my great career opportunity disintegrates?' You can't just find another job like this in Decatur, Illinois. So he said they would work something out where they would buy our house and they would pay my same big salary, which was $320,000 at the time, for a year or two, until I found another job...."

The Department of Justice filed charges against Archer Daniels Midland in 1995 and told Mark the gig was up. "Justice Department attorney Robin Mann said, 'You've done a fantastic job. Now you should think about getting an attorney.'"

Mark had a problem brewing. While he was spying on his colleagues, he'd also been skimming money from ADM's construction budget. He didn't steal much, relatively speaking. From a $1.5 *billion* coffer Mark took $2 or $3 million, or it might be closer to $6 million, or, Mark confessed, maybe $9 million, or so.

"By early August, I knew ADM was going to bring up the embezzlement stuff to Justice. So I told the FBI agents myself. The next day, August 3, they told me the Justice Department prosecutors weren't happy. They told me the deal to buy our house and pay my salary was off. ADM was dumping me onto the street. And now the FBI and Justice were dumping me onto the street too. The world was falling through.

"By Sunday, August 6, I started writing suicide letters. I wrote a lot of them. We had all our stuff packed up in boxes. We were planning to move to Tennessee. But we had to back out. Justice canceled the deal to buy our house, and I had agreed to freeze the money in my overseas accounts. Everything was crumbling. I was thinking, 'This case is going to drag on before the price-fixing case gets to trial. And now there's going to be a whole new investigation on the money stuff. And I'm more of a crutch to my family than an asset.' So I decided to kill myself. One of the letters I wrote was to Brian Shepard. I said: 'You're the one who got me into this. You promised you'd protect me all the way through and told me I was doing the right thing. You told me I was going to be a hero'....

"My gardener found me slumped in my car, unconscious."

Spinning Corn into Gold

In 1965, Mark Whitacre stood on the back porch of his parents' house in Morrow, Ohio, and huffed out eight candles on his birthday cake. A few hundred miles to the south, in Minneapolis, a man named Dwayne Orville Andreas was changing the world. Dwayne had just bought himself a $3-million stake in a grain mill, an ailing concern owned by the Archer and Daniels families. Everyone in the grain business knew Dwayne Andreas. His bandy-legged energy kept him constantly on the go, while the Mediterranean tint of his skin and his bushy black eyebrows made him stand out from the industry's Scandi-featured crowd. Dwayne focused obsessively on making his businesses run. When other traders were celebrating their deals over steak and beer, Dwayne went jogging or swam a couple hundred laps in the nearest hotel swimming pool. Over the previous 20 years, Dwayne and his brother Lowell Andreas had rescued two other bankrupt mills, selling out for a big profit after they worked their magic. But when Dwayne joined Archer-Daniels, he wasn't looking for money and he wasn't playing the turnaround-fairy. He was building his legacy.

From the raw corn, wheat, and soybeans that swelled the company bins, Dwayne spun a bounty of new products: vegetable oil, animal feed, vodka, flour, caramel coloring, sorbitol (used to make vitamin C), and corn syrup. The company began to generate its own steam and electricity through a clean-burning technology Dwayne found in Scandinavia. In Minneapolis, Dwayne Andreas was called "the rain maker."

He said he learned everything he needed to know on his father's farm in Lisbon, Iowa. "Some people would say we were poor," Dwayne reflected, "but we didn't think so. We canned our own vegetables, grew oats for our horses, hay for our cows, corn for our chickens and pigs." Reuben and Lydia Andreas had no indoor plumbing and heated their bath water over a fire, but then again so did everyone else digging their livelihood out of the ground.

The family practiced the Mennonite religion, raising Dwayne, his four brothers, and their sister in the traditional ways. No newspapers or games on Sunday, no flashy clothes or jewelry, certainly no moving pictures. Mennonite tradition emphasized that the path to righteousness was cut with the sinner's own labor.

The way Dwayne labored at Archer-Daniels, sin didn't have a chance. In his first few years, he tripled sales, from $320 million a year to more than $1 billion. He pushed the sales force into lucrative international markets, "filling in the pieces of the puzzle," as he put it. He moved the company to Decatur, Illinois, in 1969, and was named CEO in 1971, the same year he hired his son Michael—known to everyone as Mick—to work in the purchasing department. An Andreas dynasty served ADM shareholders on a palatial scale. By the 1990s, ADM counted among its inventory 146 factories, 139 grain elevators, 2,000 barges, 9,000 railcars, and 100 chartered ships. Sales for 1998 topped $16 billion. ADM's market value, about $78 million in 1966, exceeds $15 billion today.

All this from a company that doesn't market a single product of its own. It doesn't have to. Writing for *Mother Jones*, Dan Carney reported, "ADM products are present in literally thousands of items found in supermarkets, liquor stores, even gas stations. In addition to milling much of the country's flour and manufacturing margarines and oils for such big-name brands as Crisco and Mazola, ADM processes ingredients found in products such as Nabisco Cheese Nips, Life cereal, and Reese's Peanut Butter Cups. ADM's protein enhancers are common in pet foods and its texturized vegetable protein is the stuff burritos and meatless burgers are made of. If you look at the side of a can of Coca-Cola you will see that ADM corn sweetener is the second ingredient listed, after water. If you tank up on gasohol, the odds are 60 percent that the ethanol in the blend is made by ADM. And if you decide to get tanked on martinis, you will find that ADM is also the nation's largest producer of the grain alcohol used to make gin, vodka, and liqueurs."

Carney called it "the whale theory" of public life: "combining a low profile above the surface with a hulking presence that looms beneath." No one in America is untouched by this colossus of production. Even the most ardent anti-tech militia member has to shake the ADM hand as he stockpiles foodstuffs for the nuclear winter.

That pervasiveness is just what Dwayne aimed at in 1965 when he spurred his modest little company into new lines of production. But Dwayne's *coup de grace* was to treat politicians like hothouse flowers. Dwayne didn't create "the farm program," but he did plenty to keep its dollars flowing. "We're the biggest agriculture company in the world," he has declared with characteristic bluntness. "How is the government going to run without people like us? We make 35 percent of the bread in this country, and that much of the margarine, and cooking oil, and all the other things.... Did somebody dream there is some way that the government doesn't need us? What in the hell would they do with the farm program without us?"

Hubert Humphrey, the well-known Minnesota senator, U.S. vice president, and one-time candidate for the presidency, counted Dwayne as a close friend and a leading supporter. The Humphreys and the Andreas families lived near each other in Minneapolis during the '40s and '50s. Their wives, Muriel Humphrey and Inez Andreas, socialized together. Their kids played together. They shared ideas, pleasantries, and cash. When Lyndon Johnson named Humphrey his vice president, Humphrey put his assets into a blind trust—managed by Dwayne Andreas. He took Dwayne on virtually all his junkets to foreign countries where the duo promoted food-aid programs.

Dwayne Andreas was already a political veteran when he met Hubert Humphrey. President Harry Truman asked Dwayne's advice on international trade in the early 1950s. In October 1960 Dwayne wrote to John F. Kennedy, "I think the next President of the United States...should inaugurate a program of buying soybean oil and cottonseed oil and lard for relief feeding abroad, and I would do this before harvest time, when the farmers have soybeans to sell." Kennedy thought it was a grand suggestion, and appointed Dwayne to the American Food for Peace Council. In their turn Presidents Richard Nixon, Ronald Reagan and George Bush all sought Dwayne's council. Former House Speaker Tip O'Neil once said about his golfing buddy, "He's a real gentleman, although he's not much of a golfer," adding, "He's one of the most knowledgeable men on foreign affairs, especially Russia, that I know of." When Tip was introduced to Mikhail Gorbachev he growled to the Russian leader, "Oh yeah, Dwayne Andreas told me about you."

Dwayne has kept his political friends happy with some $2 million in campaign funds per election cycle, and he doesn't discriminate on the basis of party. In the 1998 presidential election, Dwayne Andreas bankrolled Bill Clinton and Bob Dole both.

Working both sides of the congressional aisle has paid off big for ADM. "There is an agricultural mafia in this town, and Dwayne Andreas is its kingpin." So says Frederick Potter, a Washington consultant on motor fuels and former officer in the Department of Energy. Potter's sentiment is echoed by Andreas supporters like Robert Strauss, former head of the Democratic National Committee. "Dwayne Andreas just owns me," Strauss gushed. "He captures the imagination of everybody he touches. My God, he's the ablest man in America."

ADM critics allege that what Dwayne calls smart business is really an old-fashioned robber baron plundering the public coffers. For example, ADM controls 70 percent of the American market for ethanol, a clean-burning but costly motor fuel distilled from corn starch. Making ethanol is so expensive there wouldn't be an ethanol market if it weren't for government subsidies. Worldwide, industrialized countries spend more than $250 billion a year supporting ethanol producers. The U.S. exempts gasahol (90 percent gasoline, ten percent ethanol) from two-thirds of the federal excise tax, a privilege valued at between $450 and $600 million a year.

ADM also makes big profits feeding America's sweet tooth. The Department of Agriculture sets prices, limits production and installs prohibitive tariffs against foreign-grown sugar. This artificially raises the cost of domestic sugar by about $1.5 billion a year. ADM benefits from the sugar program because they make a cheap sugar substitute called high-fructose corn syrup. HFCS, as insiders call it, is the sweetener of choice for the soft-drink industry. It serves more than 40 percent of the entire sweetener market. Analysts for Common Cause, a liberal watchdog group, claim that every dollar of ADM's profit from corn sweeteners costs taxpayers $10 in sugar subsidies.

Dwayne has reaped plenty from his political contributions, but he has faced some tough calls, too. He was indicted for funneling $100,000 into Humphrey's bid for president in 1968, though he was later acquitted. In 1973, with the Humphrey charges still hanging over his head, a $25,000 check from Dwayne Andreas showed up in the bank account of Dick Nixon's "plumbers." The check to the Nixon re-election campaign was perfectly legal, but it did help tie the Watergate burglars to the White House. And in 1972, Nixon's secretary Rose Mary Woods testified that Dwayne personally carried $100,000 in cash—$100 bills in an unmarked envelope—to the Oval Office. Nixon supposedly kept the money in a White House safe for more than a year until, his removal from office all but certain, he decided to give it back.

Dwayne was never charged in the Nixon incidents. But his company pleaded no contest in 1976 to accusations it had short-weighted and misgraded grain being exported through a federal aid program. In 1978, ADM and two other corporations admitted they conspired to fix prices in the JFK-founded Food for Peace program. Also in 1978, Dwayne and his daughter, Sandra McMurtrie, were chastised for donating $72,000 to a trust fund in the name of Humphrey's adviser, David Gartner. At the time of the donation, Gartner was working on legislation directly affecting Archer Daniels Midland. "He pushed things awfully close to the edge, but it was absolutely legal," a former Andreas associate said. "The fact that he spent his whole life running yellow lights didn't bother us."

Driving along the Illinois plane, leaving Decatur on Route 40 East, you spot the giant stacks at ADM belching smoke and steam at the sheltering sky. But that's just the surface. There's a whole lot more going on underneath.

Indian Trails

Mick Andreas knew he had to work harder because he was the boss' boy. And he was no ambassador. Mick stood 5' 4", chubby, with a hunched posture that made him look sloppy even in a $600 suit. The best thing about ADM was it didn't matter who your daddy was or how well you combed your hair. (Mick's hair began thinning after he turned 30.)

"We don't have any organization chart or chain of command," Mick said about the company he grew up in. "If a guy from General

Motors ever came to work here, where you have to make decisions in a hurry—the wrong guess about the market can lose you millions of dollars in a day—he'd be shocked. If our corn man gets involved with beans, or our beans man with barges, that's fine with everybody. This is a company of Indian trails. Nobody not in the grain business can really have any idea how it works. I've been in it for more than 15 years, and I'm beginning to learn it. It's important to keep things secret, but I know of no case where anybody actually has spied on anybody. All our trading is done on the phone, and your word is your bond. When people come here for the first time and ask for instructions, I simply tell them to sit back, keep their eyes and ears open, and learn the Indian trails."

Mick blazed a lot of those trails himself. He went to work for ADM's purchasing department in 1971 and honed his deal-making skills at the Chicago Board of Trade. Dwayne Andreas believed that to run a business you had to know the business, so Mick also served time in the soybean processing division and the exporting group. He was later appointed as Assistant to the President, learning about life in the executive suite from ADM President James Randall. In 1985, Mick was named Vice Chairman of the company.

When he sat down with Mark Whitacre in 1990, Mick Andreas held the keys to the ADM kingdom in his plump little hands. Mark led the negotiating team for Degussa, a German chemical company thinking about going into partnership with ADM. No doubt about it, Mark and Mick agreed, the future of agriculture lay in biotechnology. From here on out America's amber waves of grain would be fertilized in a test tube.

Mark asked about the "seriousness" of ADM's commitment to biotech. Mick answered, "We're starting with a billion-and-a-half over the next five years. From there we'll do what it takes." Satisfied, Mark said the only thing holding Degussa back was the Japanese—Degussa didn't want to offend Ajinomoto, Japan's leading agrichemical producer. Mick said he had a good relationship with Ajinomoto and the competition wouldn't be a problem.

Degussa wasn't convinced, but Mark was. "Mick kept telling me how ADM lacked bureaucracy, how quickly things moved, how they were going to invest a lot of money in this new area—all things that very much turned out to be true."

Mick Andreas told his father he'd found the man to head their biotechnology division. At Cornell University, where Mark Whitacre earned his Ph.D. in nutritional biochemistry, he was still remembered for his warp-speed work habits. "He'd just swarm over a problem until it was solved. He was like a saw running on 220 volts instead of 110. We used to tease him about how wired he was," said Mark's dissertation director, Professor Gerald Combs. Mark wasn't brilliant, but he was committed. If he had to, he'd make a pallet on the lab floor, catching naps between experiments, eating cold pizza and washing it down with coffee until he got his answers. Professor Combs said, "Among all the students I have ever taught, Mark had the best ability to move from planning to action."

Mick heard the same things from Mark's old colleagues at Ralston Purina and Degussa. Mark was "a very driven...very intense person," said a Ralston Purina man. "It would be difficult to sit and relax with him." At Degussa, an office mate said, "Mark came to the office around 6:00 or 7:00 a.m. and finished his normal workload done by 9:30 or 10:00. Then he would come around bouncing ideas off everyone else. And he wouldn't leave until 6:30 or 7:00 in the evening." Buzzsaw Whitacre mastered Degussa's German-language program in two weeks. He built his reputation at Degussa with a two-year stint in the German offices, where he made deals with companies throughout Europe and established ties with producers in Korea and Japan.

Very soon, it was rumored, Mark would become the first non-German president of Degussa. Or, Mick Andreas suggested, he could be president of ADM. Dwayne Andreas was pushing 80, and President James Randall was 70. When the old guys retired, Mick would take over the chairmanship and name Mark president. In the immediate future, they'd build a world-class biotechnology operation. "I'll personally guide you into the company," Mick promised.

Dwayne Andreas doted on Mark as a "second son." They talked about growing up in a small town, the sense of community that comes from a life lived close to the soil. Mark hailed from Morrow, Ohio, a lively hamlet sitting at the crossroads of Highways 22 and 123. The Little Miami River forks at Morrow. Muntz Run borders the town on the north while Whitakers Run scribbles along the southern edge.

Mark told the Andreases he wasn't related to the Whitaker family, the Morrow pioneers whose name adorned Whitakers Run. Mark was adopted. His parents were killed in a car accident when he was two years old. Mark's stepfather, Marion Whitacre, owned the Morrow Chevrolet dealership. Marion spent his days shuffling between rows of trucks instead of corn, but still the townspeople called him "Farmer." Evelyn and Farmer Whitacre wore their Midwestern values on their sleeves, Mark said. They endorsed hard work and self-discipline, and they had no truck with nonsense. They adopted the orphaned baby Mark and raised him alongside their natural son because it was the right thing to do. The Whitacres nicknamed the boy "Corky" for the reddish-brown tint of his hair. He was a good student at Little Miami High, where he was elected senior class president.

The very picture of freckle-faced wholesomeness, Mark practiced his parents' folksy ways. He'd first asked a gawky girl named Ginger to marry him when they were both in seventh grade. Ten years later, after Mark was accepted to Cornell, Ginger said yes. If their lives had been a movie, Mark would've been played by Jimmy Stewart and Ginger would've been Ginger Rogers. By the time Dwayne Andreas brought them to Decatur, Illinois, Mark and Ginger had a boy and girl of their own, and they'd adopted two Japanese children, a boy and a girl.

The Whitacres needed a house, so Dwayne Andreas fixed them up with a colonial-style mansion in Moweaqua, Illinois. The estate's former owner? Dwayne himself. Dwayne had just bought a much larger property, literally next door to the place he was living. How about if he sold Mark and Ginger his old place? So did the Andreas and Whitacre families come to share a forested border, their homes a brisk walk apart.

The Whitacre family kept waiting for their carriage to turn into a pumpkin. Ginger and the kids helped the grounds staff tend to the stable of riding horses. But their favorites were the miniature ponies, who trotted alongside the squealing children like muscle-bound dogs. Mark built a fancy six-car garage to hold his collection of sports cars.

At ADM, the 32-year-old golden boy dressed in the obligatory double-breasted suit, though he jazzed up his ensemble with tasselled loafers and Escher-printed ties. A handlebar mustache, strawberry blonde like his wispy, usually tousled hair, lent Mark's face a certain dash. He kept several pairs of eyeglasses on hand, all variations of the horn-rimmed style favored by certain men in the 1980s, men who wanted to cultivate an intellectual appeal but still navigate the business track.

With their Andreas connections, the Whitacres immediately became known among the Moweaqua elite. Ginger and Mark helped out in toy drives and family relief projects. They gave $2,000 in scholarships for local seniors. When a paralyzed teenager needed a voice-activated computer, Mark discreetly arranged for its delivery and maintenance. Education superintendent Mark Gregory praised the Whitacres for their support of the sciences in Moweaqua schools.

Not that working for ADM was all dress-up and Santa Claus. Mark spent most of his time at company headquarters or in executive hotel suites from Mexico to Nagasaki. BioProducts was the very keenest edge of ADM's various businesses. BioProducts produced flavorings like monosodium glutamate and citric acid. The next frontier: synthesizing amino acids. Mark would be fighting Japanese competitors who had consistently prevented Dwayne Andreas from entering their markets. In the meantime, he'd be adapting to life inside the agricultural industry's premier corporation.

For now, Mick Andreas suggested, Mark ought to focus on building the amino-acid business and keep an eye on Terrance Wilson. Terry Wilson smoked one cigarette after the other and VP'd the Corn Processing division like a fiefdom. He breathed through his mouth between puffs, staring with haughty, impatient eyes at his interlocutors. The growl from Wilson's cadaverous face was so unnerving, his language so poison and profane, few underlings ever braved his bite. Besides his posted duties, Wilson quietly handled certain dirty business for the company— "like price-fixing," ADM vets told Mark. It was common knowledge Wilson had engineered informal "agreements" to prop up the price of citric acid.

Mark wasn't concerned. "I didn't give it much thought," he said later. "I was so busy getting my lysine business established." Lysine is an essential amino acid that grows thick, lean muscle in swine and poultry. A boosted animal yields 20 percent more meat at the butchery than one fed conventionally. Lysine belongs to the family of wonder drugs that gave the corporate farm movement its legs. It's also a product whose history is rooted in deception and the bloodiest of cutthroat competition.

Lysine became a hot agricultural product in 1969 when a Japanese company, Kyowa Hakko, developed a method for fermenting dextrose, which is derived from corn. The lysine was cooked in huge vats which one writer described as "the industrial equivalent of a cow's stomach," emerging at the end of the line as a thick powdery substance, like flour.

Kyowa Hakko's success was widely hailed, but its coming-out party didn't last long. Ajinomoto, the country's dominant agriculture company, did everything it could to filch the Kyowa Hakko formula. Ajinomoto needed to know what bacteria was driving Kyowa Hakko's fermentation process. Lysine is one of corn's quirkier byproducts. Without the right bacteria, you end up with gunk, "biochemical exudate," as techies call it.

Ajinomoto had to have the Kyowa Hakko bug. After several botched attempts, Ajinomoto spies hit paydirt in the Kyowa Hakko sewer system, where a sampling of the plant's waste products allowed Ajinomoto to identify the lysine-producing bacteria. Kyowa Hakko sued Ajinomoto for infringement in 1972 and won. By that time, however, Ajinomoto had developed its own lysine bug and politely offered to share the industry with its rival.

Two decades later, Dwayne Andreas wasn't waiting for an invitation to the lysine market. Even though he was nearing his 80s, the tanned, muscular millionaire still rose each morning at 5:30 to swim against the water jets in his swimming pool. "If you don't swim hard enough, you get slammed against the wall," he told visitors. Dwayne loved the odds of challenging the Japanese in a market like lysine, which they had pioneered and kept off-limits to Americans.

Dwayne told Mark Whitacre to put everything he had into lysine. ADM chemists had cooked up their own version of lysine, distinct from the formula used by the Japanese. You could literally see the difference: while the Japanese lysine looked like flour, ADM's recipe yielded tiny granules, like salt.

Mark bragged, "When we began our lysine business, we started in September 1989 and had the thing running by February 1991. That's pretty good. Our goal was to grow this into a massive business, and we really were on a roll—no doubt about it."

The only hurdle left? Actually producing an industrial-sized batch of lysine. Instead of salt pellets, ADM's high-dollar factory mostly issued a viscous ooze, the dreaded "biochemical exudate." More than 70 percent of the yield in any given batch turned to waste and the costs were running about double the market price. Mark combed the process for glitches, but found no explanation. He and his bosses speculated that industrial terrorists, probably Japanese, were sabotaging the operation.

The attack, if there was an attack, did not come unprovoked. Archer Daniels Midland had seriously impacted the world market for lysine, even with its vats oozing more waste than product.

ADM bought, stored, and shipped its own grain, mixed its own dextrose feedstock, and finally, processed its own lysine with other ingredients for a product sold directly to feed companies like Ralston Purina. Even with 20 years' headstart the Japanese could not match that degree of "vertical integration"—ADM's ability to move from raw materials to a finished product inside the company loop, cutting its time to market and saving millions of dollars in production expenses. To press its advantage, ADM sold lysine below its own substantially reduced cost, and the feed companies ate it up. Mark said, "We took market share so quickly. And as we started selling, prices started falling. Lysine fell from about $1.30 a pound to about 60 cents a pound."

What they lacked in volume they made up with punch, in a game called "gut the competitor." ADM was using its massive capital reserves to engage in what's called predatory pricing—a rich company sells its product at a loss in order to force its competitors out of business. If you've got deep enough pockets, you can defeat any challenger with predatory pricing; that's why it's illegal.

As Mark's lysine vats overflowed with gunk, it looked like the Japanese were striking back.

Fujiwara on the Phone

Mark boiled. He'd just been informed, halfway into 1992, that his BioProducts Division was being merged into the Corn Processing Division. Mark now reported to Terry Wilson, the chain-smoking *bete noir* who specialized in under-the-table deals. Nobody ever said the corporate world was built for fun, though. Mark dutifully reported to Wilson's office, cupping a stack of documents under his arm.

Terry Wilson was unimpressed. He cared not the least for Mark's figures and analyses. He never asked about the sales force or about Biotech's satellite offices in other countries. He showed no interest in the tons of gunk clogging the lysine pipes. Mark's new mentor wanted to know three things:

- *How big is the market?*
- *What's ADM's share of that market?*
- *Who are our competitors?*

Mark explained that besides its direct competitors—Japan's Ajinomoto mainly—ADM's lysine program had to deal with competition from other sectors of the market. Manufactured lysine can be replaced with natural lysine sources, such as soybeans, he told Wilson. If the price of soybeans falls low enough, feed companies will buy natural lysine because it's cheaper than synthetics. On the other hand, if the price of soybeans is high, synthetic lysine can scoop the market by charging a few pennies less per pound than soybeans. The price of soybeans is called the *shadow price.* Synthetic lysine prices need to hover just below the shadow price to produce maximum competition and maximum profit.

We have a healthy market share, Mark noted. Nearly a quarter of the world lysine market, totaling $650 million in yearly revenues, was sold by ADM. "Yes, well," said Wilson, expelling a gust of smoke from his lungs, "Now we need to take the business to a different tier." Forget everything you ever learned about running a business, Mark was told. Lesson Number 1, the gospel according to Terry Wilson:

> *The competitor is our friend, the customer is our enemy.*

Mark left the meeting amped out. "I didn't like this idea that I was going to be working with Terry," Mark said. "I took it as kind of a slap in the face." Mick Andreas and ADM president Jim Randall tried to soothe Mark's ire. "They assured me this wasn't a demotion. I wouldn't be working for Terry; I should look to Terry as someone to teach me some things about how ADM does business. It was phrased just that way: 'how ADM does business.'"

Meanwhile, Mark still had the gunk problem. Between under-achieving bacteria, ADM's scorched-earth sales strategies, and Terry Wilson muttering about the competition, Mark despaired. He updated his resume and let corporate headhunters know he was looking for work.

While he waited for the phone to ring, Mark got a call from a Mr. Fujiwara, an engineer at Ajinomoto in Tokyo. Mr. Fujiwara expressed interest in Mark's lysine problem. Mark said, "When I talked with him on the phone, he seemed to know a lot of stuff. He knew all about the contamination. He seemed to ask questions about things we were just learning ourselves."

In their first conversation, Fujiwara and Mark talked shop about the differences between granulated lysine versus powdered lysine—salt versus flour. Then Mark said he asked, kind of joking like, "Hey, you guys don't have somebody out here sabotaging our plant, do you?" Fujiwara didn't answer. "I decided that with the language difference maybe he hadn't quite understood what I was saying." Mark let it go.

But Fujiwara understood. He called back again and again, pressing Mark for the lowdown on the Americans' lysine while Mark asked about moles in the ADM lawn. Fujiwara didn't confirm Mark's suspicions, but he didn't deny them.

Mark went to Mick Andreas and said he thought he could lever Fujiwara into helping with the gunk problem. The Japanese engineer had opined that $10 million deposited in a Swiss bank might jog his thinking on the subject of industrial sabotage.

Mick Andreas ached to best the Japanese. To him this was a billion-dollar game with even taller stakes when you figured in intangibles like pride and honor. Mick drew inspiration from Michael Crichton's *Rising Sun,* a novel in which evil Japanese businessmen conspire against a California-based company. Mick passed copies of the book to several men on his staff. When Mark revealed his talks with Fujiwara, Mick said, "Forget about the mole."

"Get their technology," Mark remembered the junior Andreas saying. "Just think what the lysine technology would be worth to us. Sure, the mole too, if there's one out there. But we're in this business for a year; they're in it for 30 years, so they're bound to be further along than we are."

Mark said he made Fujiwara the offer, more than once, and that Fujiwara told him he'd mull it over. In the end, the man pleaded that he'd served 20 years at Ajinomoto. If he crossed over to ADM, he'd have to completely uproot his life, move from Tokyo to Decatur. So, no thanks, Fujiwara said.

Terry Wilson was finding a more receptive audience for his pitch. Mark got to see "the Terry method" eye-to-eye in sitdowns with Ajinomoto and Kyowa Hakko, first in Tokyo and later in Mexico City. "Terry made his opening pitch by proposing that we form an amino acids association. He said the association could be a joint effort at promoting and expanding the lysine business, the way a dairy association would promote milk." The Japanese looked curious but skeptical.

At the Nikko Hotel in Mexico City, Terry threw the next punch. "He got up. He had these flip charts on a tripod. He stood there and said: 'Okay, let's go through this business. Let's look at capacity. How much do you produce? Ajinomoto, how much is your capacity?' And they told him. And so did Kyowa. Then he asked me, 'Mark, what's ours?' He put the numbers up there and totaled them up, then turned the page over. Then he said: 'What's the market size we estimate in Europe, Latin America, Asia, and the U.S.?' And we all agreed on some numbers, and he totaled that up."

Wilson pointed out that the combined production capacity exceeded usage levels by 20 percent to 25 percent. He well knew that the gap had appeared when ADM doubled the world's output with its new plant, but no one forced the point. Wilson multiplied the usage levels by 60 cents a pound, the going price for lysine. Next he multiplied the same usage levels by $1.30 a pound, the going price before ADM came on the scene. The difference was $200 million. Wilson said, "Well, gentlemen, there's $200 million that we're giving to our customers. In other words, the customer is benefiting, not the people who spent hundreds of millions of dollars building these plants."

In case a drowsy executive with a language barrier might miss it, Wilson spoke slowly and firmly:

> The competitor is our friend; the customer is our enemy.

By October 1992, Mark was twisting in the wind. For three years he had thrown everything into his job at ADM, but he took little pleasure in the results. Besides the industrial terrorists raiding his lysine vats, he faced scoundrels inside his own company. Mark hated reporting to Terry Wilson, but he recognized that Wilson carried an awfully big stick. By Mark's account, he would've split for greener pastures by the end of the year except that he got an incredible offer.

We want you for the long haul, Mick Andreas assured his restless cohort. How does "Corporate Vice President" sound? Mark would oversee all Asian operations and retain his stewardship of biotechnology. Jim Randall reiterated his plans to retire before the new century turned over. He told Mark, "You are the top candidate to be the next president of this company."

Mark swallowed his ire, but his newfound calm barely lasted the week. On November 2, 1992 Mick Andreas pulled him into a small room just off the executive kitchen. According to Mark, Mick said: "Aw, man, Mark, you're not going to believe this. My dad has this friend at the FBI, and they're interested in this sabotage problem we have in the plant. I've just met with the FBI and they're asking about you and this Fujiwara, the sabotage problem."

Mick was nervous and thoroughly pissed at his father. The old man was calling in the cavalry while ADM troops were looting the fort. "The last thing we need is for the feds to start asking about our 'lysine association' with the Japanese," Mark exclaimed. Mick nodded, adding that by offering Fujiwara money to smuggle lysine technology, they had initiated a conspiracy. How hard would it be for the FBI to figure this out once they started snooping?

This wasn't the first time the Andreases had done business with the FBI. In 1988, the Bureau requested ADM's help with their investigation of the Chicago Board of Trade. Corruption was rampant in the commodities pits, agents claimed. Dwayne and Mick offered to have some of their agents make trades on the FBI's behalf and to outfit FBI agents as undercover traders. Apparently, when Dwayne heard about the Fujiwara character talking to Mark Whitacre, he called in his favor with the government and demanded an investigation.

Becoming the Mole

November 4, 1992. Mark was waiting at his home for Agent Brian Shepard to arrive. His stomach churned. He paced in his ground-floor office, finding it hard to breathe and harder to concentrate. Earlier in the day Mark had met Shepard at the FBI's shop in Decatur, a tiny office staffed only by Shepard and an administrative assistant. Brian seemed like "a super-nice guy" to Mark. ADM was going to put up $3 million to coax Fujiwara and the saboteurs out of their den. Mark would make the deal—not so different than any other business deal, really—and the FBI agents would do the rest. Brian Shepard had explained that Mark wouldn't carry exploding fountain pens or anything else from Sean Connery's props department. He'd carry on a few phone conversations and arrange a meeting.

Sometime between the afternoon meeting and 10 p.m. that night, Mark decided to tell Shepard about the price-fixing conspiracy. "I really believed I was doing a good deed. I thought I'd be able to fix the problem and stay with the company," he declared later. He told Ginger the story and asked her what he ought to do. This will affect all of us, Ginger agreed. Mark had some lower-altitude motivations also. He worried that the FBI tap would discover the price-fixing talks as well as the sabotage. Ginger said Mark had no choice. He had to tell or risk getting bit when the agents finally did discover the secret goings-on. Plus, he asked himself out loud, why should I lie and risk my liberty to save Mick Andrea neck, or Terry Wilson's?

In Mark's account, he turned on his company out of fear and because it was the right thing. He didn't want to be some nasty price-fixer. Mark said, "My philosophy was, let's get this plant going full ahead, become the low-cost producer, and kick butt. Don't make deals with competitors. Go out and earn the business and then take the prices up when you run everyone else out of the market." Price-fixing repulsed Mark. Predatory pricing, supported indirectly by billions in government subsidies, didn't bother him so much.

Mark claimed later he felt an instant bond with Agent Shepard. More likely he was gushing with relief. "I finally had a chance to talk to a third party about what had been going on," he said. When Shepard finally showed up at Mark's house on the night of November 4, Mark met him at the front door. Stepping outside and snapping the door shut, Mark said, "Let's talk out in the car." He explained as they walked to Shepard's car in the driveway that he thought ADM had bugged his house.

For the next four hours Mark wowed Shepard with stories of life inside the belly of the ADM whale. At 2 a.m. Mark was still huddled in Shepard's car, blurting one incredible accusation after the other. It was, Mark recounted sentimentally, the beginning of a beautiful friendship. Over the next few weeks, Shepard romanced his informant. They met two or three times a week, and Mark talked and talked and talked. Mark outlined what he knew about price-fixing in citric acid as well as lysine. He talked about ADM's penchant for buying their rivals' technology. He described the phone conversations with Fujiwara and recounted Terry Wilson's riveting lectures on how to gerrymander international markets. Mark grew more excited every time he talked with Agent Shepard. Three years of disappointment had drained some of the Buzzsaw's celebrated energy. Laying a trap for his archrival, Terry Wilson, suddenly recharged the old, frenzied Mark.

When Shepard asked for some evidence of the price-fixing conspiracy, Mark called "two guys" at Kyowa Hakko and got them talking. They mentioned the lysine association, and the $200-million deficit in the market caused by depressed prices. One of the guys even repeated Terry Wilson's mantra: *The competitor is our friend; the customer is our enemy.* Mark told Shepard this went on all the time. Citric acid already had price-fixing agreements, and business groups throughout ADM were forging "associations" with competitors.

Agent Shepard was impressed. He said if Mark was willing they could set up an investigation. He would need Mark to wear a wire. "Now it was getting close to Christmas. Brian pointed out to me that I basically only had two choices: 'If you stay with the company,' he said, 'You're going to be price fixing; you're going to be breaking the law.'

"'Or,' he said, 'you could leave the company and be fine. You haven't broken the law yet....' Then he said there was a third alternative. 'You could work with us and try to stop this stuff, which is actually a very serious crime....' He made it clear they couldn't force me because I hadn't yet broken the law."

Taping the Japanese was one thing, Mark said to himself, but my colleagues? Still, if he recorded the Japanese talking about Terry, it wasn't so different from recording Terry himself. Such are the rationalizations of the double agent: while ostensibly helping to sniff out an intruder, Mark would spy on his peers for the FBI.

"They gave me a small recorder with a wire on it, hooked to my inside coat pocket. There was a little mike at the end of the wire. I had nightmares that people would see the mike.... The thing that kept me going was that I was sure I was doing the right thing. I was not getting depressed at all yet."

"We Hope You Make a Lot of Money"

Mark tried to act nonchalant about the new wrinkles in his job description, but he couldn't stop himself from conjuring wild images. "I'm 0-14," he told one of the agents working with Brian Shepard, "twice as smart as 007." It wasn't the only delusion Mark was suffering. He wasn't that smart; and the nervous, twitching executive certainly lacked the fabled secret agent's suavity. His hands sweated, his neck veins throbbed, he spooked if someone approached him when he wasn't expecting it. Mark could be forgiven for a case of the jitters, though. He was under a lot of pressure. Around the world, in Mexico City, Paris, Tokyo, in Irvine, and Atlanta, he smuggled microphones and cameras into gatherings of the "Lysine Association."

Sometimes the proceedings took on a high intrigue—and low comedy—worthy of cinematic spies. While ADM reps huddled with executives from Ajinomoto, Kyowa Hakko and three other Asian companies in Atlanta, there came a knock at the door. The executives had flown into Atlanta for an agricultural trade show, but they had quickly ditched the exhibition hall for the meeting with ADM.

A sudden knock at the door shut down the conference table banter. Several seconds of silence.

Then Kanji Mimoto, leading the Ajinomoto delegation, rose from his seat: "Yes? FTC?" he asked, cupping his ear toward the door.

The table broke up laughing. It wasn't the Federal Trade Commission though. It was a bellhop—well, an FBI agent actually, disguised as a bellhop, delivering a bugged briefcase into the meeting. Prosecutors couldn't resist playing the segment in court. Mimoto's *"Yes? FTC?"* showed more in its guilty, nervous laughter than reams of expert testimony on the Sherman Antitrust Act.

Kanji Mimoto would eventually become the right-hand man of Mark Whitacre and Terry Wilson in the market conspiracy. Worldwide, the lysine market produced $650 million a year. Mimoto had been warned by his superiors, "Ajinomoto's lysine business is in crisis and may go under." He was also warned that he'd lose his job if the Americans won the lysine war. So Kanji Mimoto came to the Atlanta hotel ready to deal with Satan himself if necessary. Using the code name *Tani*, Mimoto prepared fake agendas for the Association meetings. In Paris he boldfaced "Animal Rights" as the main topic of discussion.

The ADM delegation knew better than to take Mimoto lightly. If we're going to do this thing, Mimoto asserted again and again, we're going to do it right. In one of the meetings tape recorded by Mark Whitacre, Mimoto complained about Sewon, a South Korea-based company that served about 14 percent of the lysine market. "They are not participating in the reporting and they won't discuss the quantity," Mimoto told his American counterparts.

"Write 'em a letter back and tell 'em to report," Mick Andreas retorted. Mick preferred the direct approach, threatening Kanji Mimoto, "You either take this deal, or I'm gonna crank up that plant and sell a heckuva lot of lysine."

Bringing along the other Asian producers outside Ajinomoto proved strenuous. Kanji Mimoto knew that the Korean-based Sewon couldn't handle the amount of waste-water required for the production figures Sewon had claimed. In a meeting in Atlanta, Mimoto challenged the Sewon reps. "Korea is belonging to the London dumping treaty," Mimoto pointed out, "and they cannot put the waste water into the sea. If you are making this product, where do you put the waste?"

The Sewon executive responded, "Illegally, or very cleverly, they can dump out the waste material to the ocean." This provoked a round of laughter, which subsided only as the participants agreed that using the Sea of Japan as an industrial toilet was "a smart idea."

Terry Wilson reminded the crowd, "If we can't trust each other in the end, this isn't going to work anyway.... We are not cowboys; we should be trusting and have competitive friendliness." He suggested the Association hire independent auditors to verify each producer's output and capacity. "We'll just rub out anybody who balks," Wilson said with a piece of a grin.

Wilson was also underscoring who controlled the Association. Kanji Mimoto and the other Asian producers were being dragged to the table by ADM's predatory pricing. Wilson pushed this button every time he got a chance. "Take our situation with citric acid," he ruminated at one gathering. "Prices had dropped as low as 58 cents a pound. After we formed a trade association and everyone worked together on the numbers, the price moved to 82 cents a pound."

Wilson told the Japanese the real culprits depressing the market were the large customers, like Ralston Purina, who played manufacturers off one another. "We are gonna get manipulated by the goddamn buyers," he warned. "They can be smarter than us if we let them be smarter.

"Come on," Wilson barked, revving up, "Let's put the prices on the board. Let's all agree that's what we're gonna do and then walk outta here and do it.... The customers are gonna tell you, 'I could buy it cheaper.' They'll, they'll outright lie to you. That's their job. You can believe 'em if you want to. If you trust us, and that is the big thing, if you trust us, you know we aren't doing it. They're gonna be giving their orders to somebody.... "

Wilson's prophecies were confirmed. Once the Association got underway, the price of lysine recovered. From its low of 60 cents a pound, the price rose to $1.20 by July of 1993. The market continued to fluctuate, but never again returned to the 60-cent days. And ADM did what it set out to do: by 1995, the Americans had locked in a better than 25-percent market share.

In a variation on Terry Wilson's mantra, Mick Andreas told one of the gatherings, "We have a saying at ADM. 'Keep your friends close, and your competitors closer.'" Mick ended one Association meeting with a valediction, something like a price fixer's prayer: "We hope you make a lot of money...and if you do, we will, too."

Mick contended it didn't matter what kind of bogus numbers the various producers were reporting. The point was to carve up the market by shares. "What we've got is a growth of about 14,000 tons a year. The question is, how are we going to share that growth? Isn't that the question?" Mick asked, glancing over his glasses at Kazutoshi Yamada, an Ajinomoto executive. When Mark Whitacre tried to comment on the production levels, Mick interrupted: "Their old figures, whether that's right or not, doesn't matter. The question is whether they'll agree to that much growth."

Mick coached Mark on the crass methods of international competition which are not exactly scientific. As Mark was about to meet with Ajinomoto on a follow-up, the markets had started falling again. Mick suggested, "You could just say to them, 'Look, these prices are so shitty...and you guys are so disorganized that I don't know what kind of shit you're managing.... Tell them how terrible it is that they never got the price up...how disappointed we are...that everything is fine except for those guys who fucked up the market," (Many of the tapes sound as if they were scripted by Chris Rock. At trial the defense argued that the profane talk would bias the jury against the defendants, and Judge Blanche Manning agreed. She ordered the tapes expurgated before the jury's audition.)

Mark Whitacre fidgeted and shuffled through many of the meetings, but he played his informant role to the hilt. He coaxed Mick Andreas into discussions of price and production quotas. When agent Brian Shepard told Mark they needed to get a piece of info on the record, Mark obliged. At a lysine meeting in Irvine, California, Mark reminded the attendants, "Terry talked about this the last time.... Remember, Terry said that in Paris." Mark awkwardly reconstructed Wilson's numbers, scribbling them onto a white-board for the hidden camera. "Remember?" he prodded Hirokazu Ikeda of Ajinomoto, "Terry said then we were at about 65 to 75 thousand tons."

Ikeda replied, "I don't know the truth of that."

No doubt, though, the ADM team knew precisely what they were doing. When Dwayne called in the FBI, Mick Andreas coached Mark to keep Brian Shepard away from all aspects of the Lysine Association talks. Terry Wilson also warned Mark that there'd be hell to pay if they were discovered. As he was handing Mark a report on the cartel's production quotas, Terry snarled, "I tell you, don't leave this in your fucking office, Mark. Really. Somebody out there could find it."

Mark thought he was acting like a good mole, and he thought he was bringing down Wilson. He was. He was also looping a rope around his own neck, painstakingly knotting the noose, and throwing the trap door open. Mark was working evidence into the record from the earliest, untaped meetings of the Association, those in the summer of 1992—from before the time he had sealed his immunity agreement with the government—evidence that could and would be used against him in a court of law.

Gutting the Whale

It didn't take Agent Brian Shepard long to realize that his inside man was treading on slippery feet. During November 1992, as he talked with Mark literally day and night, Shepard grew skeptical about the stories of Japanese saboteurs. Mark couldn't provide details about the plot, or produce the Fujiwara character, whose name did not appear on Ajinomoto's employee roster. While Mark's phone sat on his desk, not ringing, he flummoxed his story—"I called Fujiwara only once...I never call Fujiwara, he calls me...Fujiwara calls me, but only at my office...."

After several grillings and a botched polygraph test, Mark admitted in December that Mr. Fujiwara did not exist. Mark said, well, he wasn't making it up exactly. He had been speculating there *might* be a Japanese saboteur, and he'd sort of overdone it, and next thing he knew Dwayne Andreas had government agents swarming the ADM plant.

Perhaps Mark was trying to extort $10 million from Dwayne Andreas. The company later alleged that Mark concocted Fujiwara hoping to spook Dwayne Andreas into quietly paying a ransom for calling off the sabotage. Dwayne Andreas had a reputation as a man who let his money whisper in private things he'd adamantly deny in public. No reason Dwayne wouldn't cough up a few million to get a corporate spy off his back. Instead, cowboy Dwayne Andreas blew up everybody's plans—including his son's price-fixing conspiracy—when he called in the calvary.

An anonymous source at ADM told *Fortune*'s Ronald Henkoff that Mark had pulled other Fujiwara-like stunts. "The night of the first meeting with the FBI, Mark Cheviron, ADM's chief of security, gets a call from Mark Whitacre. Whitacre is panicked. He's wild. He says his daughter, who's at boarding school in Indiana, got a phone call from a Japanese person threatening her: 'If your father doesn't give us $2 million, you'll be in trouble.'"

Cheviron agreed to check it out, but the next day Mark asked him not to. He'd overreacted, Mark confessed. No one had actually called him about his daughter. Mark explained that he'd started to fret, and then *he called* his daughter to make sure she was okay, and she sounded worried. Mark said he'd merely expressed "concern" for his daughter's safety and the security division overreacted.

By November 1992, Mark was perpetually lying. He was lying to Dwayne and Mick. He was lying to lysine executives around the world. He was lying to Brian Shepard, and the Department of Justice. In late 1992, Mick tried to soothe Mark's hounded nerves by offering him a vice-presidency, which came with a boost in salary, responsibility, and prestige. The FBI may have ignored the alarm bells that should have gone off when they caught their informant in an outright lie. But dealing with informants is always nasty business. Brian Shepard figured he could contain Mark, using the wierdo's machinations to accomplish a greater good.

In late July 1995, the price-fixing investigation came to a head. Armed with warrants, flashing their badges and swaggering righteously, federal agents descended on ADM headquarters. By arrangement, Mark was to be questioned along with all the other execs, maintaining his cover. ADM had flown in a team of attorneys to get statements from management. Mark, with his own liar's logic, decided to tell his assigned attorney, a man named John Dowd, his little secret. "I'm the mole," Mark blurted. Dowd announced that since his firm had close personal ties with Dwayne Andreas, he wouldn't be able to represent Mark.

The very next morning, Mark claims, he got a call from "a friend at ADM." The person on the line said, "Hey, Dwayne told me your attorney just told him that you're the mole. You're the one who caused all this." The friend, according to rumor, was Howard Buffett, son of financier par excellence, Warren Buffett. The younger Buffett, agressively recruited onto the ADM board by Dwayne Andreas, resigned when it became apparent the company was going to take a hit on the price-fixing charges. At the time of the call Buffett apparently believed Mark was completely clean.

"Next morning," by Mark's account, "an ADM attorney met me in the office. He said, 'Mark, you're not supposed to be here today.' He told me I had two choices: I could leave the office. Or he could stay with me in the office. So I went home."

When the FBI and the Justice Department rolled into Decatur with their warrants, Mick Andreas and Terry Wilson pooh-poohed the charges against them. They claimed they were just playing along with cutthroat competitors. We're not talking about family farms here, they pointed out. There's a lot more to this undertaking than meets the eye. It's a huge animal with global dimensions. The high-tech agrimarkets in which ADM maneuvers are so filled with treacherous turns and insider manipulations only the initiated ought to pass judgment.

Whatever you think of us, Mick and Terry declared, we're simply businessmen charged with a nasty job. Mark Whitacre, on the other hand, took a government-funded camera and made selective recordings, editing innocent *negotiations* to make them look like a *conspiracy*. Feisty as ever, Mick Andreas declared, "No one is cowed or bowed" by Whitacre's accusations and tapes.

In July 1995, Mark got another call from his friend inside ADM. "He said, 'Jim Randall is telling people in accounting to pull invoices involving Mark Whitacre. They're going to go after you for embezzlement.'" Mark well knew which invoices President Randall was gathering. This was shaping up as a world-class character assassination—the Andreas fold wasn't just going to talk dirty about their rat, they were going to bury him.

Mark scurried to Brian Sheperd's office where he made an announcement. "ADM's going to accuse me of embezzlement.... For millions of dollars." How many? Several millions. Was it true? Yes and no, Mark said. He owned several offshore bank accounts in Switzerland, the Cayman Islands, and Hong Kong. He'd stashed money in these locales from ADM's biotech buildup. When your boss is spending $1.5 billion, scraping a million here and there for yourself is child's play. It's like sawdust on the floor. Mark had set up dummy companies, then slipped invoices from these companies into a large stack of capital expenditures.

But embezzlement isn't always embezzlement, Mark cautioned. "What ADM is calling embezzlement was actually a bonus scheme approved by top management." He claimed that ADM executives routinely inflated their group's invoices, with Dwayne and Mick Andreas' approval. The Andreas bonus progam compensated ADM executives without having to involve the IRS. The logic, Mark said, went something like this: *If we give it to you, we have to report it; but if you steal it from us, what do we know?* Dwayne Andreas was suggesting a *legal theft*, the kind of oxymoron that hits the cerebral cortex of a financial Frankenstein like a lightning bolt.

So Mick and Dwayne were in on the fraud? Yes and no, Mark cautioned. For example, in one instance, "I told Mick I was taking $500,000. But I really took $1.2 million. Mick wouldn't have liked that. He wouldn't have approved. He would've thought that that was... 'excessive.'" But Mark insisted that Mick had okayed the half-a-mill skim and suggested which projects to target. Mark couldn't be specific about Dwayne Andreas or Jim Randall, but he insisted the old guys knew what was going on.

In closed-door interviews with the FBI, Mark outlined a wide pattern of abuse. He said ADM's top echelon used company jets for personal use. None of these trips, worth millions *in toto*, were reported to the IRS or to ADM stockholders. Mark said the company housed visiting executives in apartments owned by Mick Andreas, who charged the company exorbitant rents. He accused Mark Cheviron, head of corporate security, of bugging the Decatur Club condominiums while a negotiations team from another company stayed there. And Mark stuck a few zingers into his account. He said Mick Andreas liked to snort cocaine, and provided the names of other people willing to swear they saw Dwayne's heir apparent nose-down in a molehill of coke. Mark said James Randall hired prostititutes to seduce men at Ajinomoto's Iowa subsiary, Heartland Incorporated, hoping to catch some industrially useful pillow talk from the Japanese executives.

ADM answered Mark's Bond-like tales of intrigue by filing embezzlement charges. Jim Randall publicly accused the former exec of taking $2.5 million just a day after Mark confessed to agent Brian Shepard. The invoices Randall was displaying showed Mark using a technology exchange as a smokescreen. In November 1992, just as Mark was embarking on his life as a corporate mole, ADM was working on a feed additive called threonine. Purchasing reps had secured a special strain of bacteria produced by a Swedish Company called ABP International. Around the same time, Mark drew up his own invoice for threonine technology, in the name of ABP *Consulting*, and slipped the paper into a long list of expenditures approved by the company's board of directors.

After Randall's initial charges, ADM twice revised their figures on Mark's skimming. He was accused of stealing $6.5 million, and later, $9 million.

Publisher David Levine, who runs an anti-corporate web site, named Mark the "Disgruntled Employee of the Year" for 1995. "Mr. Whitacre demonstrates that today, disgruntled employees can be found not only wedged into office cubicles, but in executive suites as well," Levine wrote. On the embezzlement, Levine smirked, "If he says he didn't steal the money, that's good enough for us until proven otherwise. But if he did, all I'd say is it beats nickel and diming the boss by rounding your mileage up on the monthly expense reports."

Brian Shepard and representatives from the Justice Department brought Mark further bad news on August 3. "They told me the deal to buy our house and pay my salary was off. ADM was dumping me onto the street. And now the FBI and Justice were dumping me onto the street too. The world was falling through." Justice prosecutors, furious over losing their star witness, decided to slap Mark with charges for fraud, money laundering, and tax evasion. Once a hero, Mark was being burned at the stake.

Mark wrote *The Wall Street Journal*, suggesting they investigate the Andreases' secret bonus program. "It's there!" he promised. "They give it; then use it against you when you are their enemy." He also gave extensive interviews to Ron Henkoff at *Fortune* magazine, repeating the same stories about Fujiwara he had told to the Andreases and to Brian Shepard, though he'd already admitted (to Brian Shepard, three years earlier) that he made Fujiwara up.

Mark decided to kill himself. He told his gardener, Rusty Williams, to come in late the next morning. Rusty showed up at 7 a.m. anyway, to find his boss unconscious in the garage, slumped in the back seat of his BMW, the building cloudy with carbon monoxide fumes. Rusty shook Mark and yelled for him to wake up. Gradually Mark started retching and coughing. Rusty helped Mark to the house, where Ginger Whitacre anxiously took over. The next day Mark was recuperating in a Chicago hospital.

In these dim circumstances, Mark might have hoped for some sympathy. He had ruined his life doing undercover work. The suicide attempt showed how far he'd gone. But not everyone saw things from Mark's point of view. According to some skeptics, Mark never intended to kill himself. He'd known the gardener would arrive as usual, because Rusty always shrugged off the Whitacres' suggestions that he take the day off. Furthermore, Mark had not shown any of the classic signs of suicide: He hadn't seemed withdrawn, pessimistic, especially irritable or morose, given the cirumstances. He and Ginger had just signed to buy a million-dollar house in Franklin, Tennessee, and Mark's job search looked promising.

These impressionistic musings aside, there were more substantial reasons to doubt Mark's commitment to making his final exit. None of the suicide notes Mark claims to have drafted were ever produced. He said his wife gave them to his doctor. Second, when Rusty the gardener happened upon the garage that Wednesday morning, he discovered Mark in his convertible BMW—with the top *down*. The car was parked inside a *six-car* garage. A smaller, two-car garage on the other side of the house would have offered much better chances of success.

In other evidence discounting the suicide attempt, a forensic pathologist suggested it was impossible to revive someone from carbon monoxide poisoning simply by shaking them, as Rusty said he'd done to awaken his boss. And when Ginger Whitacre "rushed" her husband to the hospital, she drove three hours to Chicago—"to a place that treats a lot of executives," in Mark's words—instead of choosing facilities within 20 or 25 minutes of the Moweaqua estate.

ADM stayed quiet about the latest bizarre rumblings from the Whitacre house until September, when F. Ross Johnson gave a speech to the business college at Emory University. Johnson had gained notoriety as a paragon of corporate greed when he attempted a leveraged buyout of RJR Nabisco, a doomed venture recorded in the bestselling *Barbarians at the Gate*. Just six years after from getting the boot from RJR, the freewheeling Johnson, who never spent $1 when he could spend $2, was named chairman of ADM's audit committee. During the question-and-answer session at Emory, Johnson told his audience, "It's a pretty exciting experience when you find that one of your top division presidents has been recording everything you've said for 2-1/2 years.... It's a mystery.... Start out with the idea that this guy was a Boy Scout and went to the FBI one day and said, you know, 'Hark, hark. These terrible people are thinking about fixing prices.'... It just never happens that way.... It turned out that the FBI, who have got some good scumbags in there, too—it's almost a criminal mentality—they came in and got the goods on this guy in one way or another, and for immunity, he signed this great long agreement, where he agrees not to commit any criminal acts without permission. And I said, 'My God, I can't believe that.'... But then, you know, he tried to commit suicide. But he did it in a six-car garage, which, I think, if you're going to do it, that's the place to do it."

The news from both camps sounded wackier all the time. In March 1996 came tales of intrigue among Mark's and Dwayne's gardeners. Remember that the Andreas and Whitacre estates abutted one another. Mark's gardener, Rusty Williams, met with Dwayne's gardener, Larry Morrell, in a grove of walnut trees that adjoined the two properties. Larry quizzed Rusty about the suicide and wondered what else Rusty might have observed around the Whitacre house. Larry said Rusty outght to come see Mr. Andreas: "We could make it worth your while." The next week Rusty did visit Dwayne Andreas, at Dwayne's home, and left with a signed copy of *Supermarketer to the World,* Dwayne's corporate sponsored biography.

To stage manage ADM's recovery, Dwayne turned to Brian Mulroney, Canada's former prime minister and a longtime Andreas compatriot. Mulroney's special committee met nearly once a week. In April 1996, the committee announced they had settled the class action suits brought by shareholders and feed companies with a $35-million payment. Ajinomoto and Kyowa Hakko kicked in $10 million a piece.

By November, Mulroney had Dwayne's mess swept up. ADM agreed to pay the largest criminal antitrust fine ever levied, $100 million, far surpassing the nearest comparable assessment of $15 million. The total included $30 million for fixing prices in the citric acid industry, an initiative similar to the lysine association talks, which had also been led by Terry Wilson, in consort with ADM VP Barrie Cox. Ajinomoto and Kyowa Hakko again offered

$10 million each, and Sewon agreed to pay $1.25 million. Kanji Mimoto, Masaru Yamamoto, and Jhom Su Kim, the negotiators for Ajinomoto, Kyowa Hakko and Sewon, respectively, paid personal penalties ranging from $50,000 to $75,000. All told, ADM and its Asian cohorts paid more than $200 million to settle the lysine scandal's dust. ADM's total costs, for violations in both the citric acid and lysine manufactories, would likely exceed $300 million, the company estimated.

Finally, Dwayne Andreas agreed to the unkindest cut of all. The entire management of ADM would be granted immunity from criminal charges, except for two men: Terry Wilson and Mick Andreas. After eight decades of swimming against the tide and spending trillions upon trillions of dollars to establish a dynasty, Dwayne Andreas had to give up his only son. There would be no succession. Sister Jeanne O'Laughlin of Barry University, whose endowment has enjoyed a bounty of Andreas support, mused, "To hurt the son is to wound the father. He's in some pain."

Indictments for price-fixing were handed down in December 1996 against Terry Wilson and Mick Andreas—and against Mark Whitacre. Prosecutor Scott Lazar, known as the top fighter inside the Chicago U.S. Attorney's office, charged Mark for the price-fixing meetings he'd attended between June and October 1992. Even if he had been acting under immunity later, Mark was playing the game before the FBI got there, Lazar argued. The price-fixing accusation was added to the charges against Mark filed by the Fraud Division in Washington, D.C., alleging 45 counts of criminal misconduct in various embezzlement schemes.

Meanwhile Mark was spending his days at a strip mall in Bannockburn, Illinois, where a biotech startup calling itself Future Health Technologies had converted a retail space into temporary headquarters. He, Ginger, and the kids lived in a modest home they rented by the month. The family had little to celebrate as the New Year's bells of 1997 wrangled with the snow.

Sucking it Up

Mark returned fire in January. In a suit filed with the District Court, he described a pattern of abuse committed against him by the FBI as a whole and by Brian Shepard in particular. Mark said Shepard hit him with a briefcase when he expressed his reluctance to continue with the investigation. Mark also called Ron Henkoff at *Fortune* and began stoking the publicity machine.

Mark said besides getting cuffed, he was enduring a psychological barrage. Shepard harried Mark to set up meetings, to elicit certain statements from the scheme's big players, to stop hemming and hawing and wringing his hands. By early 1993 the Bureau was getting plenty of incriminating soundbites on price-fixing in the lysine and citric-acid markets. But Brian Shepard demanded more. "High fructose corn syrup is your biggest line," he supposedly told Mark. "Cargill and ADM are definitely rigging that market. I need to hear Mick say it himself."

It wasn't Mark's division. But he says he asked Mick on tape, "Hey, HFCS is so hot right now. I guess we've got some agreements, like with our lysine associates, with Cargill?" But Mick bluntly rejected any such thing. "I could call Ernie Micek (Cargill's HFCS chief and future CEO) today, but he would hang up the phone if I tried to talk to him about what we could do to increase prices."

In his lawsuit Mark charged that when Agent Shepard heard Andreas' denial, he ordered Mark to ditch the recording. "He told me, 'I can't take this tape. If I take it I'm in a lot of trouble, because we have rules and regulations. But you're an informant. You work at ADM, not at the FBI. You don't have rules and regulations about what tapes you give me and what tapes you don't. You're a part of this case now too, and this isn't good, not for me, not for you. You take that thing home and destroy it.'"

Mark said he tried going around Shepard. "I also called Dean Paisley at the FBI's office in Springfield, Illinois. And his only comment was, 'Look, Brian's the agent that you're working with, and it's best if you take your issues up with him.'"

Five or six times Shepard refused to take the recordings, Mark said. But instead of destroying them, he and Ginger stashed them in a safe deposit box. They also began copying every single tape before handing it in. "Because I figured if there were certain tapes Brian was telling me to take back, what if there were also tapes I was giving him that he wasn't turning in himself? What happens if one day the whole case comes to a head and I remember something, but the government says, 'We never heard any of that stuff. It's bullshit.' Well, then I could pull out my copy."

After his August 1995 garage episode, Mark's personal physician began treating him for bipolar disorder. His lawsuit two years later charged that by denying him treatment, Shepard and the FBI had violated Mark's civil rights.

Mark's story was that Brian Shepard became obsessed with bringing down Mick Andreas. Nothing pierced Shepard's monomaniacal brain except getting to Mick. "Brian didn't give a crap about President James Randall. He didn't give a crap about Dwayne. All he cared about was Mick. He was jealous. Here was a guy of similar age. But Mick was very successful, whereas Brian's an agent in a one-man office in Decatur. Brian wanted to advance his own career, but at the same time he wanted to bring down Mick, who he thought was a spoiled rich kid driving Ferraris and Mercedes and living in a big house by the country club."

****

Mark thought he was playing hardball by filing his complaint against the FBI. But the strategy didn't work. Prosecutors not only didn't back down, they swung even harder. Early in the game Mark's FBI-recommended lawyer, James Epstein, had figured to have his client plead guilty on the embezzlement charge—Mark would serve a year or so on that, and draw time served on the conspiracy charge. But after enduring two years of Whitacre flim-flam, the government said all deals were off.

In 1997, Mark changed jobs and moved to North Carolina. He hired a new lawyer named Bill Walker to take care of things in the Illinois courts. Judging by the plea bargain Mark eventually signed, Walker won little sympathy from Mark's accusers. In October 1997, Mark entered a guilty plea to 37 counts of fraud. Don Mackay, chief of the Fraud Division, asked the judge for 6-1/2 to eight years jail time.

As his sentencing approached in early 1998, Mark dropped his suit against Brian Shepard and recanted his various public allegations. He said he had never possessed any secret tapes of Brian Shepard. "I did turn in every original tape to the FBI with no exceptions. The only reason I claimed agent Brian Shepard told me to destroy selected tapes was that I hoped it would convince ADM to drop the charges against me and my family."

Mark also repudiated a letter, one he had purportedly written and faxed to Epstein, informing the lawyer: "I still see more wrongdoing by the FBI than by ADM. I think that you should tell the Justice Department this stuff." In the letter, Mark claimed he had no choice but to enter a guilty plea because the feds had threatened to indict Ginger as a co-conspirator in the embezzlement, since her name was on the foreign accounts. Now Mark was saying that he'd never sent the letter to Epstein or asked him to alert the DOJ to its charges. However, Mark insisted that he'd been coerced into the plea to protect his wife.

These retractions only tightened the legal rope around Mark's neck. "You'll probably get what the prosecutors are asking for, and maybe more," Bill Walker warned his client. As Walker had told a reporter the day before, "The government doesn't appreciate how Mark has handled this situation."

Walker showed up in Urbana, Illinois, for sentencing on Wednesday, February 26, 1998, but Mark did not. A nervous Walker explained to the judge that his client had once again attempted suicide. Early Tuesday morning, at their North Carolina home, Mark's oldest daughter discovered her father in the garage, gulping fumes from the BMW's exhaust.

Mark had mailed a suicide note to a friend in Florida. "There was only one thing to do in order to give my family freedom," Mark wrote. "Selfish suicide is labeled a sin in the Bible. However, the Bible makes it clear that sometimes one has to sacrifice their own life to give life and freedom to others. This is what I am doing for my family."

Judge Harold Baker was unimpressed. Before the crowd in his small courtroom, Baker said he'd talked with law officers in North Carolina who thought Mr. Whitacre had again faked his suicide attempt, hoping to gain himself residence in a mental facility instead of prison. Baker demanded that Mark be arrested immediately and brought to Urbana for sentencing.

A week later, Baker lowered the boom. "To observe that Mr. Whitacre is not the usual felon who comes before this court is a gross understatement," Baker intoned. "The usual felon is a byproduct of Jim Crowism, segregation, and our society's chemical dependency. These felons, usually in their mid-20s, lack opportunities for education, employment, or success. But Mark Whitacre had every opportunity for success and capitalized on those opportunities. At times he displays what could easily be characterized as sociopathic behavior. It is difficult to know when Mr. Whitacre is lying and when he is being truthful," Baker despaired.

Mark, dressed in a dark blue suit, white shirt and red patterned tie, his jowls ballooned by 15 to 20 post-investigation pounds, gamely put on a remorseful face. For the first time he announced, "I take full responsibility for my actions.... I'd like to apologize to a lot of people in this room and a lot not in this room.... I apologize greatly," he said, the words jumbled by sobs. "Mostly, your honor, I'm here to accept my punishment."

Judge Baker, in a rare departure from prosecutor's recommendations, set that punishment at nine years. Since parole was abolished from the federal system in 1987, Mark had a long wait ahead. He would have to serve more than eight years before he could even be transferred to a halfway house.

A mental examination determined there was no reason for Mark to be committed, so he was returned to North Carolina for imprisonment. This at least allowed some proximity to his wife and children, who visited faithfully. As his trial for price-fixing began in Chicago during the summer of 1998, Mark opted not to attend the proceedings. He said he was worn out and claimed the Illinois prison system was a filthy pit run by a crew of sadists. Someone would undoubtedly let him know how the trial turned out.

****

His grousing aside, Mark decided to skip the trial for strategic reasons as much as anything. His absence spoke volumes, he and his attorney hoped, and left Mick and Terry Wilson twisting in the wind. Bill Walker never skipped an opportunity to point toward the defendants' table where Mick Andreas leaned heavily on his arms, and Terry Wilson sat with studied calm. Walker argued the government's charges against Mark constituted dirty dealing on their part. Mark's higher-ups had *come to him* with the "association" scheme, Walker said. Here was a young man, new to the company, just taking orders, who seized his first opportunity to alert the government to ADM's price-fixing conspiracy.

Speaking for the defense, Washington powerhouse attorneys John Bray and Reid Weingarten said the FBI had turned loose "a wild man" with a tape recorder. The lawyers supported Mark's contention that he had been suffering from manic depression and "extreme mental anguish." Who could trust such a creature? Brian Shepard had knowingly sent a sick, twisted personality (a Frankenstein's monster, if you will) into the world's corporate boardrooms. *Quel horreur!*

But while ADM's top-shelf attorneys wagged their fingers and shook their heads, there sat Kanji Mimoto on the witness stand for three days. Having paid a $75,000 fine and taken his lumps, the Ajinomoto executive confirmed, "We agreed on the sales price and also we agreed on the sales quantity." In a tape recording, Mimoto was heard telling Mark that the lysine producers should avoid meeting on U.S. soil whenever possible. "United States is, ah, very severe in control of antitrust activity," Mimoto warned, speaking in his halting but perfectly clear English. No doubt about it, Mimoto assured the jury, we knew what we were doing and we knew there would be hell to pay if we were caught. Prosecutors backed up Mimoto's testimony with 237 tapes and 250 boxes of documents.

The courtroom also heard from ADM VP Barrie Cox, who held immunity for helping to fix prices in the citric acid division. "Prices were low in Europe and around the world," Cox testified. "They were depressed, and they needed to be increased. We decided we should do something about it."

The three defense counsels all chose the minimalist route, given the hardcore documentation against them. Once the government closed its case, after a final round of damning testimony from Kyowa Hakko's Masaru Yamamoto, the trial was all but over. Bill Walker called no witnesses at all on Mark's behalf. He claimed the government had not proved its case. ADM's team called just one person to the stand, an employee of Weingarten's firm, Steptoe & Johnson. Akua Coppock, a senior legal assistant at the firm, described how she had reviewed a barnful of phone records showing that Mark Whitacre made "secret" calls to Mimoto, Yamamoto, and other Asian representatives, and to Terry Wilson. Not one of the dozens of calls were reported to Mark's handlers at the FBI, the ADM legal team asserted. Presumably this showed Mark pulling the strings in a wicked morality play.

The jury gave the defendants five days of their time, then returned unanimous verdicts, *guilty*, against all three defendants. Jury foreman Fritz DuJour said the audio and video tapes had clinched the verdict. The defendants had practically made the case against themselves by starring in the government's home movies. DuJour said the jury had a difficult time convicting Mark Whitacre, but they were satisfied the charges against him had been proved, even if they didn't seem completely fair. DuJour added the jury felt "dissatisfied" with the way Brian Shepard had handled his informant.

On a chilly December 17, 1998, Mick Andreas and Terry Wilson seemed unruffled as they heard themselves being convicted. Undoubtedly they had prepared for the worst. According to the *Chicago Tribune*'s Greg Burns, "Mick especially appeared at ease, chatting and smiling with his attorney, John Bray, while his wife, Sally, discussed holiday shopping with friends in the audience." Before the courtroom, Mick avowed, like a Ronald Reagan character facing court martial, "I love this country, Your Honor, and I thought I knew its rules. I didn't want to commit a crime and I didn't think I had committed one." Afterward, Mick stood outside the federal building on South Dearborn Street, allowing reporters a photo op while he hailed himself a cab.

At sentencing in July 1999, Judge Blanche Manning praised Mick and Terry as "wonderful men," but nevertheless confined them to prison for two years apiece. The sentence was remarkable, not just as the last blow against the Andreas dynasty, but as an indicator of the times. Traditionally less than half of antitrust convicts go to jail; when they do, they usually serve ten months or less.

Mark wasn't feeling so sanguine. Squawking over a speaker phone, Mark threw verbal darts at ADM and the FBI. "Life in prison has actually been better than life at ADM," he said. As for the feds: "They would have no case without me.... I risked my life and career for them, and I have yet to see anything."

Mark wasn't going to get any happier. Judge Manning designated him the legal "manager" of the conspiracy, the person steering its ultimate course. By this view, Mick and Terry were mere players, going along for the ride. The manager designation provided that Mark receive the toughest penalty of the three defendants. He was sentenced to 2-1/2 years, instead of the two years apiece served by his old superiors.

"She's taking a very, very bizarre view of the word *manager*," said Gerald Lefcourt, a former president of the National Association of Criminal Defense Lawyers, in response to Judge Manning's decision. "The vice chairman [Mick Andreas] is at the higher level of the conspiracy. Not to give him a managerial role and to give it to someone who carried out the price-fixing is pretty silly." Another legal observer commented, "I could not have imagined a whistle-blower, even this kind of self-destructive, unreliable whistle-blower, being turned on this harshly by the government. It doesn't bode well for future whistle-blowers."

Mark's actual sentence was extended by just 20 months, instead of the 30 months levied. With any luck he will see streetlights by mid-2010. He won't yet have turned 50. With advances in biotechnology, he could easily make 110, 115 years old. He'll just be hitting middle age.

****

In early 1999, Dwayne Andreas officially threw in the towel. He'd been gradually backing away from his regular duties for several years, while aggressively battling what he called the "fairy tales" of high crimes committed by him and his company. Dwayne had spent a lifetime swimming against the tide, but eventually he gave out. In his place, he appointed a nephew, G. Allen Andreas, who had earlier taken over ADM's presidency when James Randall retired—the job once promised to Mark Whitacre. Allen went from making a modest $600,000 salary as a VP in 1996, to almost

$2.25 million two years later when his uncle made him CEO. If it's not precisely the dynasty Dwayne had in mind, at least the head of Archer Daniels Midland still signs his name with a flourishing *A*.

It is certain that Dwayne Andreas will be remembered, if not always revered. *Tribune* writer David Greising opined, "Andreas is a complex man for a complex age, perhaps a perfect archetype for our era. His retirement marks the end of an age of corporate bossism as surely as the death of Mayor Richard J. Daley marked the end of the big-city boss."

No doubt ADM will not only survive this debacle, it will continue to prosper. Its lysine manufactory, with an original annual capacity of 100 million pounds, was expanded in 1998 to produce 350 million pounds a year. By the turn of the century, ADM alone will be producing 500 million pounds a year; Ajinomoto has expanded its Heartland operation in Eddyville, Iowa, by 50 percent; and Cargill has announced its intention to claim a piece of the lysine pie with a plant in Nebraska. As synthetics have almost totally replaced soybean-based lysine—eliminating the need to keep costs just below the so-called shadow price of natural sources—lysine's price per pound has jumped to $2.30 and higher, as high as $3. (Mark Whitacre and his co-defendants were sent to jail for insisting the market fall no lower than $1.20.)

At those prices, the "largest antitrust fine in history," a mere $100 million, feels like a comfortable cost of doing business. The world lysine market has grown to $700 million a year and is steadily approaching the $1 billion mark. Post-scandal ADM now controls fully half of that market. With a pre-tax profit margin of 20 percent, the house that Andreas built recouped the money it paid in fines and lawyers' fees in a few years' time.

Meanwhile it seems we've arrived at a new juncture of antitrust history. A new round of skirmishes between government forces and merger-mad corporations is shaping up as a war to rival the classic antitrust era, when Progessives battled US Steel and the railroad conglomerates. Twenty-five grand juries reviewed antitrust cases in 1998, and a slew of new convictions reduced the ADM fine to a mere footnote. The industrial equipment manufacturer UCAR International was fined $110 million; SGL Carbon Aktiengesellschaft, $135 million; BASF Aktiengesellschaft, $225 million. Currently, the record-holder for largest criminal antitrust fine ever is F. Hoffmann-La Roche Ltd., penalized $500 million.

We're learning, or we should be, that the laws of the Sherman Antitrust Act, designed to restrain Andrew Carnegie and John D.

Rockefeller, are not always sufficing when it comes to Dwayne Andreas and Bill Gates.

Whatever Happened to Mark Whitacre?

So what happened to Mark Whitacre? He taped stellar incriminations for the FBI and then was charged with the crime he exposed. Not only that, he was labeled the conspiracy's ringleader and drew the stiffest sentence. Judge Manning later ordered Mark to pay back the $1.17 million in salary and benefits he drew while working at ADM.

Mark created his own problem by talking himself into ground zero and then pushing the button. Once he made up Fujiwara and set him loose in the ADM rumor mill, Mark had to ride the waves. To appreciate the enormity of this little prevarication, you only have to consider who Mark worked for. Dwayne Andreas had enough high-level clout that it's not likely the feds would have come snooping without a big reason—like Dwayne's personal invitation. In short, none of Mark's maniacal tale would have happened if he hadn't babbled about a Japanese mad scientist.

Having queered things at ADM, and then queering them further by volunteering to narc on his colleagues, Mr. Whitacre proceeded to queer his deal with the FBI. It was no biggie, really, when Brian Shepard discovered Fujiwara was a phony. Most informants come with scummy baggage. *Realpolitik* says we'll deal with it at trial. But when Mark slunk in later, telling how he'd stashed millions in foreign bank accounts, somebody should've put a fork in his ass, 'cuz he was done. The FBI looked bad and the DOJ attorneys couldn't put Mark on the stand. Mark had just crowbarred three years' worth of federal investigation. If the government couldn't put him in the witness box, they'd put him in the chair of the accused.

Mark faced his crossroads when he joined the investigation. If he played it safe and confessed to Brian Shepard about the embezzlement, he'd lose the money. Almost $10 million. If he held on to the money he ran the risk ADM would ping him with it, sooner or later. That would mean ruin, and he would still lose the money. But, Mark figured, if he stayed hush, he at least had a chance—he could keep the money and enjoy a hero's welcome for exposing ADM's criminals. That's all a Frankenstein of Fraud needs, a chance.

People back in Morrow, Ohio, scratched their heads. They had been thrilled to hear their native son called "the Boy Wonder of modern agriculture," but consternated at the rumors and innuendo seeping from ADM headquarters. Morrow citizens must have been even more dizzied when they learned that Mark had been lying about things besides international intrigue. According to his corporate bio, Mark not only held a Ph.D. from Cornell, he had also earned an MBA from Northwestern University. In the wake of the scandal, investigators learned Mark had never attended that school. His business degree came from Kensington University, which awarded degrees by mail. It also came to light that what Mark was calling his doctorate in nutritional biochemistry was actually a doctorate in *nutrition.*

Imagine how Mark's hometown felt when they learned that Mark was an adopted child. That was big news in Morrow because it wasn't true. A reporter approached Marion "Farmer" Whitacre and asked him about adopting Mark. The 60-something truck dealer laughed. "He's not adopted," Farmer said, and walked away, lifting the Ralston Purina cap off his head and shaking it by the brim. Since college, Mark had been telling people he'd been orphaned at age two. He said a hideous car crash had killed his young parents and afterward the Whitacres took him in. Professor Combs at Cornell recalled, "Mark told me himself he was adopted." People at ADM thought Mark was adopted.

This particular lie of Mark's reveals what made him so dangerous. What could he have gained from repeating this absurdity? A little sympathy? Some fodder for the long plane ride to Tokyo? Why would he risk having someone at a dinner party casually mention "Mark's birth parents" to Ginger and expose his silly deception?

His personality may be inscrutable, but Mark is living in prison for one specific reason: *the money the money the money.* All the lies and double-crossings he could've gotten away with. He could have survived Fujiwara. He could have built a career after ADM. He could have continued raising a family, channeling his legendary work ethic into something grand. If he hadn't hoarded the money, he wouldn't have voided his immunity agreement and the government wouldn't have tried him for the conspiracy and he wouldn't have gone to jail. Mark might have done any number of things, all of them decent alternatives to 11 years in orange coveralls. But this fiend held on to the money.

Michael Milken

(1946 -)

CHAPTER 10

Man or Monster?
Michael Milken

"I had begun life with benevolent intentions and thirsted for the moment when I should put them in practice.... Now all was blasted. Instead of that serenity of conscience which allowed me to look back upon the past with self-satisfaction...I was seized by remorse and the sense of guilt, which hurried me away to a hell of intense tortures such as no language can describe."
—*The Creature*

Our imaginations are papered with his image—those creviced cheeks, the smirk, the hairpiece. Our library shelves sag with books about him. We are told: HE WAS A VERY BAD MAN. But Michael Milken sold pieces of paper, junk bonds. Was that alone so vile? Milken's minions counter the derision with a chorus of honorifics: HE WAS A GENIUS, A PROPHET, A REVOLUTIONARY.

These days, Milken portrays himself as a philanthropist. Even his for-profit work in education has a do-gooder aura about it. Can this be the same tyrant who reigned over the Predators' Ball? Whose admirers described him as "this eccentric monster brain?" During the summer of 1999, the once vainglorious Milken gazed from the cover of *BusinessWeek* magazine, fresh from a morning's meditation, proudly bald, talking family values and the social responsibility of corporations.

The Calling

He began as an angel of light. Mike Milken was a cheerleader for his high school football team in Encino, California, Class of 1963. His friends came from the same upper-crust, predominantly Jewish neighborhood where the Milken family lived. Mike spent his days and nights on the go, rushing from school to cheerleader practice to club meetings, arriving home after dark, still brimming with energy as he completed the next day's school assignments. Mike spent some evenings in the Milken home office where his father, Bernard, an accountant, was preparing his clients' tax returns. Mike was such a good boy: intelligent, positive-minded, high self-esteem. He not only refused to drink alcohol or smoke cigarettes, he went the teetotalers one better by boycotting caffeinated and carbonated beverages too. As a charter member of the Pepsi Generation, Mike wouldn't touch the stuff.

Following high school graduation, Mike and his seventh-grade sweetheart, Lori Hackel, both attended the University of California at Berkeley. You would never have known, visiting with this cookies-and-milk couple, that a social revolution was going on outside. Other students tumbled out of the classroom to dance half-naked in the street, flagging their arms like crosstown traffic, sticking flowers in their hair and into water pipes. Not Michael Milken. He was managing a portfolio of stocks and bonds which he owned with his father and his younger brother, Lowell, who was bound for law school.

Besides handling his family's investments, Mike also traded for several of Bernard Milken's clients. When he wasn't studying or pitching woo with Lori, he was reading annual reports, eager to prove his abilities in the so-called real world. He felt so sure of himself, Mike agreed to shoulder 50 percent of any losses his trading produced, though his clients kept 100 percent of any profits.

While his fellow students dropped acid and talked against the war in Vietnam, Mike was pondering a book he'd turned up in the Berkeley library, *Corporate Bond Quality and Investor Experience*. The author, W. Braddock Hickman, had compared the performance of high-risk bonds with the returns generated by investing in Wall Street's upper tier of businesses, known as blue-chip companies. In the usual scenario, a company that needs extra cash issues bonds, which are basically corporate IOUs: An investor purchases the bond for cash, say $80 for a bond with a $100 face value, and the company promises to make interest payments for, say, the next 15 to 30 years. At the end of the term, the company returns the principal. If everything has gone as planned, the interest payments have generated a profit for the investor. Companies whose history and assets suggest they can easily meet their interest payments and redeem the principal at the end of the term are deemed AAA by the ratings agencies. Less reliable companies receive lower ratings, but their bonds are still classified as "investment grade" bonds.

Then there are "those other bonds," the ones that stirred Mike Milken's brain. High-risk bonds are either shoved to the bottom of the investment heap—assigned a rating of BB, or C, for example— or they aren't rated at all. The financial establishment in Mike's day wouldn't spare a second glance at these low-rent companies who were starved for cash, which ironically enough was the same reason they were being snubbed for credit.

W. Braddock Hickman argued that high-risk bonds, if properly diversified, would pay better than blue-chip investments. To prove it, he evaluated the performance of corporate bonds from 1900 to 1943, sparking admiration in the fresh-faced Michael Milken. "Hickman had studied every bond for 43 years," Mike said, recalling his surge of inspiration. "He had done very thorough, original work, without machine support and the kind of databases that would be available today." Hickman showed that if a portfolio of high-risk/high-yield bonds produced large enough returns, investors could absorb a few losses and still do better than they would by sticking to safer, industry-certified investments. When blue-chip bonds were paying four to six percent, a diversified high-risk portfolio could earn nine or ten percent. Mike checked and rechecked the numbers. If Hickman was right, this obscure ten-year old study was the best kept secret in finance.

High-risk bonds were called by a handful of slang names and were drawn from several dusty corners of the corporate realm. *Fallen angels* were formerly A-rated companies whose debt had been downgraded. *Deep-discount bonds* were traded at a fraction of their face value (as low as ten percent or 20 percent), because the issuing companies had defaulted on their obligation to pay and might or might not redeem the bonds later. *Chinese paper,* a recent development, referred to debt being issued since the early 1960s in a wave of corporate mergers. Convinced that Hickman had nailed a blueprint for the future to his wall, Mike began sprinkling these rogue financial instruments throughout the portfolios he managed.

Mike and Lori were married just after his graduation in May 1968, and they immediately moved to Philadelphia, where Mike had been accepted at the prestigious Wharton School of Business. On the side, Mike took a position with a small firm called Drexel Ripley Harriman, where he began testing his faith in the corporate world's fallen angels. Mike quickly made a name for himself in Drexel's sales and trading department. After two years of full-time study and nurturing his obsession with the bond market, Mike left the Wharton School to join the staff at Drexel. He was short a paper required for graduation, but that wasn't important at the moment.

Of course people bought high-risk bonds in the days B.M. (Before Milken), but there was not a market *per se* for the products. Investors usually salted the bonds away and forgot about them until the date of maturity. Mike's vision was to put the bonds into play. Stalking through his usual 16- to 18-hour days, he sought out companies that had been underrated by the credit agencies. He'd find companies in bankruptcy court, possessing enough assets so that they could hold a desperation sale, pay off their delinquent bond debt, and get back into business. Mike bought the bonds of these companies for a cutthroat rate, then sold them to his customers.

Mike was taking a contrary position against the financial establishment. He argued that ratings agencies were mired in old ways of assessing risk. Banks and other lenders who followed those guidelines generally behaved too conservatively. The old guard was grossly underestimating the value and performance of many organizations. For example, when Penn Central Railroad looked as if it were sure to collapse, Mike scooped up Penn bonds from panicky investors for pennies on the dollar. Later, when Penn staged a strong turnaround and redeemed the bonds, Mike—and the investors he persuaded to join him—cried, "Gotcha!" Time and time again, Mike was proved right, as companies emerged from their nearly certain death. The financial world started to take note: a force was gathering in Philadelphia.

During this time, Mike laid the foundation for his soon to be legendary personality. In 1973 he was transferred to Drexel's office in New York City but chose to remain with Lori and their growing family in a Philadelphia suburb. That meant a two-hour commute each way, since Mike insisted on taking the bus instead of the train. He feared that he would be constantly greeted and chatted up by fellow Wall Streeters if he took the train, which made the journey in half the time, so Mike lugged a totebag full of annual reports and prospectuses onto the bus each morning. As reported by Connie Bruck in *The Predators' Ball*, Mike donned a most remarkable outfit for the ride:

> *On winter mornings the sky was still pitch black and the light on the bus was too dim for him to be able to read. He wore a leather aviation cap with the earflaps down; he had been bald for years, and although he wore a toupee his head always felt cold on these*

*frosty mornings. Now over his aviation cap he fitted a miner's
headlamp—strapped around the back of his head, with a huge
light projecting from his forehead.*

To look at him, he might've been a recently washed transient,
the totebag reposing all his worldly goods. But it was just Mike
Milken, who seemed to emerge from his dark tunnels of
contemplation only when he thought he'd found a new convert to
join him in the church of high-risk bonds. A co-worker told Bruck,
"Trading was perfect for Mike. You have to assess the many
complex forces at work on a particular transaction. And then the
question is, do you want to do it at this price—and do you have the
guts to act on it? For Mike, it's not even a guts question. It was
religion. If he didn't act on it, he was being unfaithful to his God."

Mike seemed to welcome the derision. It was he who first began
calling his pet products "junk bonds." "Mike was a bull in a china
shop," a Drexel executive said. "He was *terribly* arrogant. And he
didn't have the facility to shroud his ability, couldn't keep it from
being threatening and abrasive."

He might not have been the most popular guy in the office, but
Mike was just what Drexel's doctor ordered. The company had
been ailing for some time, limping along on the strength of its
heritage and a few blue-chip clients. Drexel traced its beginnings to
1838, when a Philadelphia portrait painter named Francis Drexel
entered the investment banking business. A resounding success,
the Drexel firm was merged with J.P. Morgan and Company in
1871. Later, when federal legislation forbade the same firm from
conducting both commercial and investment banking, Drexel and
Morgan went their separate ways. Despite this pedigree, Drexel
wasn't doing so well when Mike signed on. Clients were leaving for
better deals elsewhere; so were many key employees. The firm had
suffered losses in the stock market, and its bond department was
ailing too, because a slew of blue-chip companies were sliding—
against all conventional wisdom—into default. Drexel's merger with
Harriman Ripley in 1966 allayed some of the suffering; ditto the
merger with Firestone Tire and Rubber in 1970, which at least
brought $6 million into Drexel's capital-hungry coffers.

But Drexel wouldn't find its salvation until 1973, when I.W.
"Tubby" Burnham decided to whisk the old girl off her feet once
more. The 300-pound-plus Tubby had his own lineage to brag
about, being the grandson of I.W. Harper, who founded the Harper
Gin distillery. With a $100,000 loan from his grandfather, Tubby
started a brokerage house in 1935. While not a standout
performer, Burnham and Company had turned a profit every year

---

since its inception. Tubby saw the Drexel union as a way of moving into the tonier brackets of high finance and Drexel was growing desperate for a helpmate.

One of Tubby's first questions as he toured his new offices was, "Are there any Jews here?" Drexel was known as an old-line White Anglo-Saxon Protestant (WASP) business, which the decidedly Jewish Mr. Burnham resented a bit. Tubby learned from Drexel president Archibald Albright that there were a handful of the 250 employees who were of Jewish descent. "They're all bright, and one of them is brilliant," Albright said. Referring to that *one*, Albright speculated, "I think he's fed up with Drexel, and he may go back to Wharton to teach. If you want to keep him, talk to him."

Mike came characteristically to the point when Tubby Burnham approached him about signing on for good. "They won't give me any capital," Mike complained. He acknowledged that his so-called "junk bonds" weren't any more popular than he was, on the Street or inside Drexel.

Since joining Drexel three years before, Mike had set up a trading operation inside the firm that dealt in junk. The group of traders who supported the weirdo Milken were known in the hallways as "The Department." One insider recalled, "The high-grade bond guys considered him a leper. They said, 'Drexel can't be presenting itself as banker to these high-grade, Fortune 500 companies and have Mike out peddling this crap.'" But Mike smirked in the face of his enemies because he also knew that his sales were outpacing every other department. And, he argued to Tubby Burnham, those gains were produced with a pittance of speculative funds. Give me some real money and I'll spin your head around, Mike promised.

Tubby gave his *wunderkind* $2 million. Mike suddenly enjoyed virtually unlimited authority, with glancing oversight by upper management. He answered to Drexel president Fred Joseph and to Tubby Burham. Mike's compensation package was unrivaled in the financial world. According to James Stewart's *Den of Thieves*, Mike kept 35 percent of any profits generated by The Department. These profits Mike personally distributed among his people, according to his fiat. No one other than Mike was privy to the breakdown. He alone received finder's fees for any business that came to the firm through The Department, taking home 15 percent to 30 percent of the firm's profits on his deals.

Drexel's other departments showed mixed returns for 1973. Some eked out a profit, others admitted they'd lost money. The gains in any one area were offset by losses elsewhere, for a net zero. Mike on the other hand had taken Tubby Burnham's $2 million and doubled it. Effectively, then, the $2 million in profits that Drexel reported for 1973 came solely from The Department.

The revolution was at hand before many on Wall Street even suspected an uprising. Drexel's fallen angels were storming Heaven, and the powers-that-once-were were trembling in their suites. Mike celebrated in customary fashion, by getting up earlier, working harder, fighting more vociferously than ever, determined to become the unchallenged lord of finance.

The Coast

Mike Milken didn't invent junk bonds, but he did transform the junk market. Before Milken, companies whose credit rating fell outside the purview of the Street went begging to banks and insurance companies for their cash. Unfortunately the money came with strict covenants about what the borrower could and couldn't do with the funds. The banks and insurers wanted something to foreclose on if the company faltered. Alternatively, the company could issue new shares of stock. But the new issue diluted the value of each existing share, angering shareholders. Some companies were already in such trouble they knew it was useless to put any stock on the market, because no one would buy it.

Recognizing the implications of this dilemma and concocting a way out—therein lies the celebrated Milken genius. In the best capitalist fashion, he saw how his self-serving ambition to build a financial empire overlapped with the woes of underrated companies. Beginning in 1977, Mike's department didn't just buy and sell bonds, they began issuing new bonds.

Mike offered lower-rung companies the credit they had dreamed of, with little or no restrictions on how to spend the money. Again, Mike didn't pioneer the practice. He'd seen the Lehman Brothers firm easily sell some $250 million-plus in new junk bonds on behalf of four separate companies, all before the 1977 spring was out. Mike knew he could do even better; bond customers were calling him every day, thrilled with their returns, slavering for more. He later bragged, "Those investors who had confidence in '74 (when the market stumbled and many people bailed) achieved rates of return in excess of 40 percent. And it was their enthusiasm that fueled this market in 1977."

Mike took his plan to Tubby Burnham and to Drexel's president, Fred Joseph. Both men gave the green light. From the time he joined the firm in 1974, Fred was motivated by the same empire-building impulse that drove Mike's inhuman workdays. Fred was the son of a cab driver, from a family of Orthodox Jews who lived in one of the shabbier neighborhoods of Boston. He'd attended Harvard Business School on scholarship, making the contacts there that would land him an invite to E.F. Hutton, where he made partner in four years. Later Fred joined the Shearson firm, where he was named second in command. It took some courage to abandon his prestigious digs at Shearson for the less respectable environs of Drexel, but Fred had plans. Having climbed into the towers of power, he wanted his own castle. Fred promised Tubby Burnham they were going to build a world-class firm, turning the bluebloods at Shearson—and Salomon Brothers, and Goldman, Sachs—green with envy.

Mike merely nodded. He wasn't driving himself day and night to tread in the same old corporate ruts. Mike was crusading. At the same time, he was pragmatic enough to realize he'd never prevail without someone to run interference for him. Drexel Burnham's investment banking and brokerage arms didn't want to be associated with the bloody goings-on in The Department. But Fred Joseph showed a confident, recognizably patrician face to Wall Street traditionalists while Mike waged guerilla war with his junk bonds.

Mike led the firm into new junk-bond issues with $125 million in sales for 1977. Drexel bonds made up about 25 percent of the junk market. The next year, Drexel sold $440 million in junk, while its strongest rival posted just over $150 million. Mike attained these leaps because Fred Joseph and Tubby Burnham had committed the firm to acting as a "market maker." This meant that Drexel guaranteed the people who purchased its bonds that they would always be able to sell out if they chose to. Drexel would either find a buyer for the bonds, or do the buyback itself. Drexel wouldn't guarantee what *price* they'd pay, but they promised to move the bonds.

At first sight, the buyback agreement might look like a burden, committing the firm to rescuing its customers when their bonds started to fail; but in fact, acting as a market maker gave Mike greater powers than ever. He knew every player in the junk bond market, all the buyers, all the sellers. He could buy large stakes in a bond issue or make the issue himself, then easily unload the bonds to the growing list of investors ringing the Drexel phones. A deepening recession, skyrocketing interest rates, and corporate productivity lags were plaguing the business world. This weirdo Milken and his junk bonds looked pretty sweet.

Fred and Tubby knew they had backed the right man when Mike starting hauling chests of gold across the Drexel moat. For raising $30 million on behalf of Texas International—the first of Drexel's primary issues, in 1977—the firm charged a three percent underwriting fee, worth $900,000. Over the next two years, the market in new junk issues swelled to $2 billion, more and more of which came through Drexel, generating premium fees.

Another key strategy in Mike's campaign was to create junk-bond mutual funds, spreading investors' money into a variety of high-risk holdings, providing the scope and diversification necessary to fulfill the Hickman curve. Fred Joseph committed Drexel to this effort as well, spearheading the rise of the First Investors Fund for Income (FIFI). While FIFI was nominally run by one David Solomon, everyone knew that Solomon had studied at the feet of, and remained beholden to Mike Milken. Mike's rivals rushed out to create their own junk funds, worth $50 million or $100 million. By comparison, at the end of 1978, FIFI handled between $400 million and $500 million.

Finally, Mike whipped up a frenzied market in "secondary offerings." In these transactions, an institutional bondholder such as an insurance company sold its bonds to Drexel. Mike then fanned the paper out across his network, profiting on the "spread," the difference between what he paid the insurance company for the bonds and what he was able to unload them for. In some deals, Mike sold the bonds for three times his purchasing price, netting 30 percentage points in the spread, at a time when most dealers were content to take three or four points on a large sale. Mike could do this because the prices on secondary offerings bonds weren't posted anywhere. He was working in the financial equivalent of an open-air market, a setting in which Mike shifted prices and changed his positions as the tenor of each deal required.

Fred Joseph reflected on the headiness of those days. "All the other firms didn't have the confidence of having a Mike Milken who could sell this paper. So they had to look at spreadsheets, figure out what had been done, and do one just like it. But we could just sit there with our minds wide open, smoke pot, daydream, and say, 'What do you want?'"

In his intoxicated state, Fred readily assented to his star performer's most outrageous request ever. Mike wanted to move to California. His father had been diagnosed with cancer, and he wanted to be near him. Mike argued he could wage his campaigns just as well from the other coast; most of his days were spent talking on the phone, three and four conversations whirring at once, and tapping furiously on the keyboard of a trading terminal. If a deal required a face-to-face, he'd hop a plane.

Fred recognized that the best thing he and Tubby Burnham had ever done was stay out of this amazing man's way. The bosses happily stepped back this time too. In early 1978, word ricocheted through Drexel headquarters: A new group was forming, in California of all places. Yes, rumor mongers whispered, it's Milken. He was moving The Department, and he was recruiting others. A question harrowed many minds on the Drexel staff: *Will he take me with him?* Mike's group was the only one drawing bonuses worth cashing. The bond traders who had once been scorned by Drexel's investment bankers were swimming in money.

The handpicked retinue that followed Mike to Beverly Hills became known as "The Coast" in Drexel's New York offices, and produced bigger gains with each year that rolled around. In 1981, Mike's troops sold $1 billion in junk bonds for the first time; the total junk issues throughout the market that year totaled $1.5 billion, of which Drexel sold $1.08 billion. In 1983, Drexel issued junk worth $4.9 billion. Drexel bonds accounted for 70 percent of the junk market. Mike influenced, directly and indirectly, the other 30 percent.

Fred Joseph's dream of building a first-tier firm at Drexel was coming true. Thanks to The Coast, Drexel's profits rose from $2 million in 1973 to $6 million in 1979. In 1983, that number was $150 million, a sign, Milken's minions argued, that the dark economic days of the 1970s were done. President Ronald Reagan, running for his second term in 1984, declared, "It's morning in America."

However, The Coast looked better viewed from a distance—it wasn't even that nice a place to visit. There were plenty of perks, like Mike's offer to finance a new home for anyone moving west with him. Most importantly, there was money, money, money. Mike confided that while veterans in the investment banking department were drawing $100,000 a year, "No one who's been with me for the last five years is worth less than $20 million." He could say that with confidence because he personally distributed each employee's bonus on each deal.

As abundant and unprecedented as the money was, everyone knew that Mike kept more than his fair share. On one deal, dividing a profit spread of 30 points, Mike gave the trader who had pounded out the sale a measly 1/8 point ($1,250 on a $1-million sale). He stashed the other 29-7/8 ($298,750 on the same million) in his own account. Extending his control into every corner of his employees' lives, Mike required each person to put a portion of his or her earnings into several investment partnerships. The partnerships were administered by Mike's brother, Lowell, and only the Milken brothers knew precisely what was done with the monies. Mike even decreed, on a case-by-case basis, which partnership each employee would invest in and for how many shares. So, you might be worth $20 million but that didn't mean you had $20 million. *Mike* was holding a healthy chunk of that *for* you.

Your net worth didn't mean that much inside The Coast. Everyone was rich. And you didn't have time to spend 20 *thousand* dollars, much less millions. Mike liked to say, "I don't ask my employees to work any harder than I do myself." Coming from someone who gauged four hours' sleep an indulgence, that sounded like a strenuous demand. Office hours started at 4:30 a.m., which was 7:30 a.m. New York time, an hour and a half before the markets opened there. Non-stop scramble ensued until 8:00 p.m., by which time the markets in the East had been closed for three hours already. Mike's own day often stretched to midnight, though even then he seldom arrived back at the office later than 3:00 a.m., well in advance of his crew. Though he had discarded his miner's lamp, Mike still prowled the pre-dawn hours, determined to keep the edge over friend and foe alike.

It's no surprise that working with someone who obsessed about bonds and tranches of bonds from dewfall to dewfall wasn't all smiles. Mike conspicuously chose not to build himself a private office. Instead he occupied a black X-shaped desk that looked out across the trading floor. To Mike, it was a democratic gesture. Conveniently, though, the positioning allowed him to watch his traders constantly and to demonstrate to them his superior skills. Mike *occupied* his desk, spinning, pacing, and whirring. Certainly he was not sitting idle. When an office-party stripper showed up for Mike's birthday one year, he grinned and played along...until his phone rang. A member of his bond network was calling. While the woman shimmied her naked breasts above him, Mike crawled underneath his desk and took the call.

He drove his crew by piling demand on demand, by throwing temper tantrums, by yelling at employees who displeased him. The former cheerleader spared no kind word when an insult would do. In the environs of The Coast he was called "The King," partly in reverence, partly in jest. If a trader closed a deal at a lower price than Mike wanted, Mike would dog the person, asking again and again, "What was the spread on that? Why so thin? Why'd you let them ride you like that?"

And if you thought the King was a son of a bitch, then you'd judge his brother a full-fledged tyrant. Mike at least softened now and then, flashing his smirking grin. He once extended his condolences to an employee whose brother was dying by offering to pay the man's hospital bills. Not Lowell Milken. In 1979, soon after moving into Drexel's Wilshire Boulevard offices, Lowell distributed white envelopes to select members of The Coast. The document inside reviewed the mortgage loans which Mike had financed during the move from New York. Lowell, who had become a tax attorney while his brother stalked the bond market, demanded that all the loans be repaid immediately—without explanation or apology.

Lowell was the only person who could pull Mike away from his phone bank and trading station. Otherwise, Mike was hammering at three or four exchanges simultaneously. When he was questioned by the SEC about his work habits, Mike estimated that during 1982, he carried on about 500 phone conversations a day, many of them simultaneous. If you didn't make your point fast, you lost your chance to pick the Master's brain. A Drexel California associate told Connie Bruck he had maybe "two or three half-meaningful discussions" with his boss. "Those conversations lasted about 30 seconds, conversations where you're on the phone with him and you don't know if he's listening to you or talking to someone else, covering the mouthpiece. You're talking, you finish making your point, then he says (one of his most often-used expressions), 'I'm back.'"

"Mike's difficulty, gigantic, was that he simply didn't have the patience to listen to another point of view," another man said. "He would assume he had conquered the problem and go forward. He was useless in a committee, in any situation that called for a group decision."

Mike didn't have to listen. Everyone was listening to him, watching him, imitating him. He gained a cadre of new devotees and financial mercenaries in 1982, when the federal government deregulated the nation's savings and loans. Formerly, the New-Deal charters that created the S&Ls focused their activities around providing home loans. There were strict limits on how S&L owners could use depositors' funds, which were guaranteed by the federal government. Even if the institution failed, the government would reimburse each depositor up to $100,000. Specifically, S&Ls were barred from investing in anything but investment-grade bonds. But according to President Reagan's plan, stripping off the investment restrictions would allow S&Ls to compete with banks and other financial services companies. Inflation in the 1970s had crippled many S&Ls. They had been forced to pay higher interest rates on depositors' accounts, while their charters limited their investments to fixed-rate mortgages (returning five percent to seven percent) and top-rated bonds with similarly low rates of return. When you pay more on your deposits than you make on your loans, you're going to lose the farm. Either the feds would have to subsidize the S&Ls or turn them loose on the free range.

A host of rules and restrictions stayed in place after the deregulation, but these were routinely ignored by the "entrepreneurial minded" cowboys who accepted the Reagan challenge. From 1983 to 1988, savings and loans bought $14.4 billion in junk bonds, most of it through Drexel. These institutions became outposts of the Milken realm. He turned to them when he needed buyers for a bond issue; they looked to Mike when they got hungry for cash.

To demonstrate the incestuous ties binding Mike and the S&L bandits, consider the following example. One of Mike's early allies in the junk bond market was Carl Lindner, who decided in the early '70s to put his money where Mike's mouth was and got even richer for his trouble. One of Lindner's protégés, a man named Charles Keating, struck up his own relationship with Mike in the early '70s. Keating impressed Mike with his zeal for moneymaking and his personal commitment to what this country has since hailed as "family values." For some 20 years, Keating had spent his spare time agitating against pornography. He envisioned a Prohibition-like war on smutmakers and the twisted clientele who kept the porn rings spinning. Keating got himself appointed to the President's Commission on Pornography in 1969, but he was dismayed when the group's report suggested that local community standards ought to determine what images are bought and sold there, not the federal government. Keating published his own opinion, dissenting Supreme Court-like from the final report. For him, there was no tolerating porn.

In 1982, Mike raised $100 million for Keating, who used half of those funds to buy the Phoenix-based Lincoln Savings and Loan. On the Keating issues, Mike had demanded Drexel's usual three-percent underwriting fee, plus a ten-percent stake in Keating's largest holding company, American Continental Corporation (ACC). After the deal closed, Keating used $12 million of Lincoln deposits to buy out Mike's share of ACC. Federal regulators called this a "prohibited affiliated transaction." It might also be interpreted as a $12-million kickback in exchange for the $100 million in bonds.

Through his dealings at Drexel, Keating met Gene Phillips, a Dallas area businessman for whom Mike would eventually raise $1.2 billion. In a rash of transactions that later drove federal regulators batty, Keating and Phillips began dealing with each other's companies, using Mike's junk-bond operation as something like a hub.

With the proceeds of a Drexel junk-bond offering, Gene Phillips had his holding company, called Southmark, buy an insurance company called Pacific Standard Life. Then, in 1983, Pacific Standard purchased $18 million of Southmark's junk bonds. Pacific Standard bought its parent company's bonds with a loan from Charles Keating's Lincoln Savings and Loan.

Later, when regulators took over Lincoln, they found the money flowed both ways in the Keating-Phillips affair. While Pacific Standard had borrowed $18 million *from* Lincoln, the insurance company had also loaned money *to* Lincoln, totaling some $28 million. And Pacific Standard had purchased almost $1 million in junk bonds issued (through Drexel) by Keating's American Continental Corporation. This was the "you scratch my itch, I'll scratch yours" relationship that kept the S&Ls humming during their heyday.

To be sure, the junk bonds held by so many S&Ls did *not* cause the institutions to flop. This mistaken notion burnt its way into public opinion with the help of writers like Benjamin Stein. In Stein's portrayal:

> *The Drexel machine sucked the blood of its captive S&Ls like a vampire, draining the assets of their depositors dry. Plasma available through the federal deposit insurance blood blank could not even begin to replace their losses and huge transfusions would ultimately have to be drawn from taxpayers. For the Drexel Draculas, it was a feast.*

Unfortunately, there's more to the Milken/S&L connection than Mr. Stein could digest. The $14.4 billion in junk bonds held by S&Ls only accounted for a little more than one percent of the industry's $1.3 *trillion* in assets. Thing is, Mike Milken placed most of those bonds himself, and he placed them in a few S&Ls. His three favorites were *CenTrust Bank*, owned by a loyalist named David Paul, who invested $1 billion of CenTrust funds in junk bonds; *Lincoln Savings and Loan*, where Charles Keating authorized the purchase of $800 million in bonds between 1983 and 1988; and finally, the supreme Milken favorite, *Columbia Savings and Loan*, owned by Thomas Spiegel, with $3 billion in junk-bond holdings. But even these unholy triplets, bearing the most infamous names of the S&L scandal, were not toppled by Milken machinations.

Most S&Ls failed because they were too far gone when deregulation opened the gates on investments; they couldn't survive on the open market. It's true that a depressing number of the failures were caused by bloodsuckers—greedy come-lately owners who cared not a whit for making home loans at 9-1/2 percent per annum, and ceased to do so as soon as they got their hands on the S&L reins. Keating's shady dealings and his lavish lifestyle—brimming with homes, boats, jets, and million-dollar purchases of football tickets—were well documented during several trials in state and federal court.

Mike Milken didn't have the time or inclination to direct the misdeeds committed by Messrs. Paul, Keating, Spiegel, and others. But Mike staked them, funding their S&L purchases with Drexel bonds. Without a bankroll, Keating might still be sitting in the Arizona desert trying to define obscenity. These men returned the favor by acting as a $14-billion outpost for placing, and discreetly trading, Drexel junk bonds. In an act repeated time and again, a Milken-funded S&L warrior bought the bonds issued by his Milken-funded cohorts, who in turn dutifully bought some of the first warrior's bonds. Everyone supposedly slept more soundly, knowing they all had a little of each other's junk beneath their pillows. Often Mike overfunded a deal, that is, he issued $10 million more in bonds than the client originally asked for. Overfunding occurred with all Drexel clients, not just the S&Ls— and the overflow was earmarked for purchasing other Drexelites' junk bonds. Naturally there was no overt agreement requiring anyone to buy a single bond. That would've meant openly committing a crime.

Mike's role in the S&L scandal is far more subtle than that for which he's usually given credit. The artificial returns generated by his financial reach-around prolonged the amount of time men like Keating kept their S&L doors open. But to say that junk bonds and Drexel fees caused these businesses to fail overstates the case. According to federal regulators, criminal acts played a role in about 25 percent to 30 percent of the S&L failures. Among those acts were embezzlement, misuse of funds, improper investments with related parties, and other financial tricks like the so-called "land flips" in which the same piece of property was exchanged many times, among a single owner's subsidiaries and among the companies owned by several conspiring owners. On each flip, the seller recorded a profit and the buyer registered a significant increase in assets, a number which could reassure regulators and could be used as a loan collateral, producing cash money. When the American economy stumbled in the late '80s, hitting the overheated real estate market in particular, these S&Ls were doomed. A crash in the junk bond market from late 1989 through 1990 finished off the job, especially at Columbia Savings and its ilk, who had placed more depositor funds into high-yield bonds than the law allowed. These institutions were too dependent on their junk-bond holdings to maintain solvency.

Even so, the junk bonds, which were drawn against each owner's underlying businesses, not on the S&Ls, seemed to have held their value. According to the writers of *Inside Job* (Stephen Pizzo, Mary Fricker, and Paul Muolo), by August of 1990, "the federal government had inherited $3.7 billion in junk bonds seized from S&Ls." Government analysts predicted the bonds were worth half that price. In a depressed market, that was a fair estimate. But the junk bond market would recover after 1990, producing some losers and some winners. In the end, junk bonds fulfilled the Hickman curve as they had done throughout the century.

So Mike didn't drain his captive S&Ls. He snacked on an oversized bowl of fees and "affiliated transactions," perhaps. But the bonds all existed, unlike some of the phony land developments in which the S&L crooks claimed to have "invested" their deposits, and which turned out to be a few hand-painted signs staked in the middle of the desert.

Probably the worst thing Mike did in the S&L cases was *inflating,* not *draining,* the assets of these institutions. He was accused of using his unfettered access to the trading portfolios of Thomas Spiegel's Columbia Savings to stage phony trading losses in Columbia's portfolio near the end of the tax year—an act that significantly reduced the S&L's tax bill, leaving more money in the coffin, ...er, coffer, for Spiegel to loot.

Some would argue that the savings and loan crisis of the 1980s was a monster itself. And they might not be too far off, from where I viewed the situation. During that time, I was a practicing CPA fraud specialist. A decade previously, I was an FBI agent who concentrated on white-collar crime investigations. After I went into private practice, both the FDIC and the Resolution Trust company hired me on numerous occasions—first, to train anti-fraud specialists; and second, to evaluate several large S&Ls. The government wanted to know just how bad the fraud problems might be in those institutions. If I found indicia of fraud, I was to prepare a report of my findings for the regulators, who would in turn refer the matter to the FBI.

What I saw in the S&L files sickened me. Multi-million dollar loans were made to a variety of nefarious real-estate wheeler-dealers based on the thinnest documentation. In some cases, it was even difficult to determine who the borrower was. In one loan file I picked up at random, a check had been written to the borrower to loan him money on a real estate deal. But the appraisal on the $20-million disbursement came in three months after the check was cashed. I thought to myself: when I bought my $65,000 condo, the bank wouldn't disburse a dime until they had a written appraisal in their hands.

In short, I had no trouble finding fraud in the savings and loans I looked at. Just the opposite—every institution I examined was corrupt. The way these "problem" loans were handled on the books revealed why the S&L bandits got away with their crimes and avoided detection by the regulators. In a process that eventually became a "daisy chain," one savings and loan took care of the problems of another, and vice versa.

For example, say savings and loan "A" loaned friends and insiders $5 million. The loan would have stuck out like a sore thumb if it had been examined by the regulators, especially if it were in default. But "A" always had at least 30 days' advance notice of when the institution would be audited. So before that day arrived, "A" would "sell" the loan to savings and loan "B" and transfer all the paperwork to "B" in the process. In return, "A" would "buy" a loan of a similar amount from "B."

Now, both "A" and "B" have new loans. And new loans are much less likely to attract the scrutiny of regulators. Daisy chains weren't used by just two savings and loans—they were used by hundreds. In a process where bad paper was continually sold up and down in the line, the real problems were almost impossible to detect from the records.

Certainly the savings and loan crisis of the 1980s had an enormous impact on our economy. But I think one fact that went underreported is the sheer size of the criminal conspiracy. In the world of crime, a conspiracy between two people is the norm. Perhaps occasionally the number might reach ten conspirators. How about hundreds?

Accepting for a moment the estimate of the *Inside Job* authors, that the government lost between $1 billion and $2 billion on the junk bonds it inherited from failed S&Ls, it's still hard to see Mike Milken as a major player in this admittedly nasty bit of financial history. A couple billion dollars in junk-bond losses doesn't loom so large in the face of the $250 billion or $300 billion it cost to repair the industry. As a Frankenstein of Fraud, Mike didn't assault the S&Ls himself; instead, he created others who gave full rein to their greed. A therapist analyzing this family romance might call Mike an enabler.

****

In 1982, Mike led Drexel into the mergers and acquisitions business, or M&A as it was known on the Street. M&A was the perfect outlet for Mike. The most expensive restructuring in the history of business didn't arise from technological innovation or the creation of new industries; it was fueled by having one company take over another. Like the other creatures of Mike's celebrated financial "genius," the M&A business was built by recombining, relabeling, realigning existing materials, not by making anything original. In contrast to the wave of mega-mergers during the early '60s, the new wave involved relatively small organizations using wads of debt to buy companies ten or 20 times their size. Many Wall Street firms, such as Forstmann, Little and Kohlberg Kravis Roberts, had been building M&A divisions for some years. Kidder, Peabody and Salomon Brothers were just getting into the business. Mike saw in this new phase of merger mania the next opportunity for his junk-bond blitzers.

At first, Drexel allied with other firms who were performing leveraged buyouts, which came to be known as LBOs. The term refers to an acquisition funded mainly by debt. An LBO is a fancy name for a mortgage, the kind any homeowner makes for a first house: the buyer puts down a little cash, and makes a note for the rest. The note is guaranteed by the value of the property and the owner's expected cash flow. An LBO works the same way; but instead of the house and white picket fence, the borrower is buying a company. Drexel assisted other firms with LBOs by putting up the so-called "mezzanine" level of the financing package. The debt in a typical LBO consisted of top-level notes, which were secured by property and held first rank among creditors in case of a default. The mezzanine financing was constituted by junk bonds, which were unsecured and stood dead last in the creditors' line.

Drexel helped fund two LBOs for 1982 and two more during 1983, but Mike was itching to launch his own deals. In 1984, Drexel backed T. Boone Pickens in his attempted takeover of Gulf;

it funded Carl Icahn's bid for Phillips; and it made several other unsuccessful attempts to get some M&A action.

None of this helped Drexel's reputation among Wall Street traditionalists. Drexel had forced its way into the M&A game by dominating 70 percent and more of the junk bond market. Now, with Mike intimately guiding the deals, in some cases choosing the target company and the takeover client himself, Drexel was blasting its way into the "hostile" takeover. Also called a "raid," the hostile takeover is a leveraged buyout in which the buyer's offer is opposed by company management. The raider hopes to force the company's board and shareholders to accept an above-market price for their shares in exchange for voting out the existing managers and turning the company over to the raider's management.

After his botched attempts the year before, Mike backed a nobody named Nelson Pelz in the spring of 1985. Mike had scouted a company ripe for an LBO, the National Can Company. The market in cans was down, and the bottling business was about to bust, too. Mike, as he'd done since the early '70s, saw an opportunity where others saw scrap metal. He had tried to get another client, Victor Posner, to take over National Can, and when Posner bailed, no one else seemed to trust Mike's assessment of the can business. Mike had been holding Nelson Pelz in the wings for a while. Drexel had raised $100 million in junk bonds for Nelson's Triangle Industries the year before, specifically with a future LBO in mind.

By anyone else's logic, Nelson's Triangle Industries, a wire and cable manufactory worth about $51 million, would never be able to perform a $400-million buyout. You'd sooner run a Ford truck at a Panzer tank. But Nelson Pelz was all Mike had. "We were dying for a deal," Nelson said later. "We'd been sitting on the money for a year and a half." Mike wanted a deal, too. The final price tag for the National Can LBO was $465 million, of which $395 million came in the form of Drexel junk. Drexel fees on the job ran to $25 million.

Drexel's investment banking arm played an equal role with The Coast in the M&A deals, but it was Mike's bond traders who led Drexel to an unrivaled string of victories. Providing the financial equivalent of air cover, Mike pelted reluctant corporate boards and their shareholders with Drexel bonds. Mercenary dealmakers like Nelson Pelz and Ronald Perelman could suddenly bid like Rockefellers. These former corporate nobodies became known as "raiders," laying siege to companies that would never have considered them for a position in middle management.

As he had done with his once neglected high-yields, Mike whipped the mergers and acquisition business into a frenzy. Drexel did 73 deals for the year 1985, issuing some $6.7 billion in junk bonds. The nearest performer was Salomon Brothers, doing nine deals worth $1.4 billion. The 1985 profits at Drexel amounted to some $600 million. When raider T. Boone Pickens asked for $1 billion, Mike raised the money in a single weekend. The year 1986 was even wilder. Drexel as a firm conducted $4 *trillion* in transactions, producing $5 billion in revenues, which broke down to a pretax net income of $2 billion.

By virtue of his unrivaled revenue sharing plan, Mike's high-yield department received a bonus award of $700 million on its 1986 performance. Mike didn't exactly share the wealth, though. Since no one but he and Lowell knew how much the total bonus award was, no one could challenge how the Milken brothers divided up the money. Of the $700 million, Mike gave $150 million to his staff, keeping $550 million for himself. It was *his* market, after all.

Mike moved his troops and the corporate world at will. When MCI asked him to raise $500 million, Mike raised $1 billion. In tandem with Drexel's new M&A division, he developed a technique called "the Air Fund," later more euphemistically dubbed "the highly confident letter." By stating in a letter that Drexel was "highly confident" it could raise the funds, Mike sealed deals for $400 million or $500 million. In the raider wars, Mike's name was as good as cash—if he said the money would be there, it was there.

Along the way, of course, Mike was severely crunching the nation's securities laws. He didn't always commit outright violations, but he knew how to bend and pinch the code into strange shapes. When one of his creations, Victor Posner, mounted a hostile takeover of the Fischbach Corporation, Mike showed what he was capable of. Posner had settled a dispute with Fischbach's board in 1980 by signing a standstill agreement. Under the terms, Posner was barred from acquiring more than his 25-percent stake in Fischbach, unless someone else filed a 13(d) Form, announcing they had purchased at least ten percent of the company's stock. In effect, someone else had to put Fischbach "into play" before Posner could take another shot.

In late 1983, Posner discussed the Fischbach situation with Mike, insisting he had to merge the manufactory into his holding company, Pennsylvania Engineering. Mike agreed to help. Days later, an insurance company named Executive Life filed a 13(d), declaring its recent acquisition of ten percent of Fischbach stock.

Executive Life was owned by Fred Carr, a Milken mercenary who over several years put $7 billion of the insurance company's cash into Drexel junk bonds.

However, Posner, crouched to make his leap, was chagrined to discover that Fischbach had outmaneuvered him again. Fischbach's company lawyers delightedly pointed out that, yes, Executive Life had filed a 13(d), as the Posner agreement demanded. But since Executive Life was an insurance company, it should have filed a 13(g)—the difference between a *(g)* and a *(d)* meant the Executive Life offer was invalid. Pressing the technicality would buy Fischbach enough time for the company to rebuff Posner's attack.

While Posner buried his face in his hands, Mike spoke to another of his allies, Ivan Boesky. No one symbolized the rapacious image of the new players on Wall Street like Boesky. His attenuated jawbone, along with dark, close set eyes, gave him a lupine visage. Like others of his ilk, known as *arbitrageurs*, Ivan stalked companies that were besieged by corporate raiders. Once a deal was done, the arbitraguer sold "into the news" of the takeover or reorganization, which normally boosted the share price. Then, as now, a good arbitrageur makes money even when a company's stock drops in value, through a move called short-selling. To sell short, an arbitrageur "borrows" shares of stock from a current stockholder and sells the shares immediately (ten shares of the Doe Company, for example, at $100 a share). When the share price falls, the arbitrageur replaces the shares he borrowed and sold (for $100 each) with the cheaper ones (which have fallen to, let's say, $80 each). The difference between the initial sell price and the shares' replacement cost makes a profit for the arbitrageur (in this case, $20 a share).

As the Big Bad Wolf of arbitrage, Ivan Boesky built himself a command center worthy of a comic-book villain. As described by *The Wall Street Journal* editor James Stewart, "Each researcher and trader had a desktop television on which Boesky could project his image. At his own desk, Boesky had a large-screen television divided into two sections. On the upper screen he could project any image, including his own. The lower part of the screen was divided into 16 sections. TV cameras trained at each trader and researcher transmitted their images into those sections. Boesky could hear and see each of his employees at all times. Any unexplained absence, even a trip to the bathroom, would be immediately detected.... Electronic ticker tapes flashed across the walls of his office, and a digital clock displayed times in zones around the globe." Ivan's personal switchboard contained 160 direct lines, reaching Mike Milken and a host of others with one touch.

An arbitrageur could benefit enormously by cozying up to someone like Mike, who'd cornered the junk-bond market and was gradually dominating the M&A wars. Ivan Boesky agreed to trade according to Mike's directions at those times when Mike thought a target company needed a little under-the-table tweek so as to be properly positioned when the Drexel raiders came calling. By the terms of their unwritten agreement, Mike compensated Ivan for any losses. If Ivan's participation in a deal turned a profit, Mike shared half the gains.

To open up Fischbach for Posner's takeover, Mike told Ivan to buy enough stock to exceed the 13(d) limit. So Ivan loaded up the shares, filed the form, and *voila*, the doors of Fischbach opened. Posner finally got his company, which proceeded to lose money every year under his mismanagement. So hideous were his business practices, a federal judge later barred Victor Posner from ever again participating in a leveraged buyout. Drexel could've cared less what Posner did with the company. The Drexelites had carried off a hefty sack of fees, a third of which went directly to the "genius" Michael Milken, who made the whole thing possible.

Ivan Boesky, as it turns out, lost money on the stock. When Mike told him to buy, Fischbach shares were selling around $50. But the buyout came in at $42. Mike didn't abandon his buddy altogether. About six months after the deal closed, Ivan sold his shares on a London exchange for $45 a share (in New York, Fischbach was selling for $36 a share). No one noticed at the time, but the buyer who paid $9 a share more than necessary was Pennsylvania Engineering, the company owned by Victor Posner, whose way had just been cleared by Ivan's purchase. So Posner cashed Ivan out once the Fischbach deal was done.

Ivan often played the role of shield, or shock absorber, in the Milken machine. He posted losses in several of the large positions he bought at Mike's behest. For example, in 1984, the casino company Golden Nugget, one of Mike's oldest clients, acquired a large amount of stock in the entertainment conglomerate, MCA, in preparation for a takeover. When Golden Nugget decided not to go through with the takeover, the casino wanted to unload the stock it had acquired in MCA. If they tried selling on the open market, however, the market would bottom out—on the news that the takeover was a bust—and Golden Nugget would lose millions for their trouble. Mike persuaded Ivan to buy the MCA stock from Golden Nugget at a high market price. Ivan sustained about

$2 million in losses when he sold the shares later. But that was much less than what Golden Nugget would have suffered otherwise. Besides, Mike promised to square everything with Ivan in the end, and Mike always kept his promises.

According to Stewart's *Den of Thieves,* Mike compensated his wolfen partner with the coin of the Milken realm. "Because of his extraordinary control over the junk-bond market," Stewart writes, "Milken could buy back securities at artificially low prices from Drexel clients who had no way of knowing their actual value; sell them to Boesky at a small profit; have Boesky resell the securities to Drexel at a much higher price; and in turn resell them to Drexel clients at still higher prices." Of course, Drexel earned fees, and Mike took commissions, on each transaction. Mike also arranged losing bond trades on behalf of Ivan Boesky's Corporation, generating phony tax credits, which to a seasoned arbitrageur like Ivan look as juicy as cash.

For all his rapacity, Ivan Boesky despised the popular image of the corporate raider as some hambone-swinging Visigoth stumbling onto the grand estate. Ivan grew up in Detroit, where his father owned a few upper-register strip joints. As he became rich, Ivan used his money to surround himself with the trappings of culture, purchasing himself a membership in the Harvard Club, for example, though he'd only attended a few classes at Michigan State University. As one of the nation's richest men, Ivan couldn't be ignored, whatever his reputation. In 1986, he got himself invited to speak to the graduates of the University of California at Berkeley, the alma mater of his close friend, Mike Milken. At the ceremony, Ivan droned on about great American values, casting himself as an Everyman who had scrambled his way into power and money, while the graduates sat beneath their hoods, squinting into the sun and nodding at the old man's platitudes. Then, without warning, Ivan looked up from his prepared text, his voice shifting into a less artificial register.

"Greed is all right, by the way," he said. "I think greed is healthy. You can be greedy and still feel good about yourself."

Television news shows played the cut again and again. A big-time Hollywood director named Oliver Stone saw Ivan's speech and decided to use it in his next movie. In *Wall Street,* a Boesky-like son of a bitch named Gordon Gecko, played by Michael Douglas, wooed a crowd of hostile shareholders into his clutches with a simple, insidious refrain:

GREED IS GOOD.

Ultimate Monopoly

In May 1986, Michael Milken addressed a crowd of thousands, nearly every person there beholden to him for their wealth and well-being. The occasion was the annual high-yield bonds conference. Sponsored by and celebrating the ascent of Drexel, the conference was held at the Beverly Hills Hotel, an establishment partly owned by Ivan Boesky, who stood among those applauding so robustly that Mike could only smile and wave for several minutes. Also in attendance was Norman Pelz, last year's wannabe, now a corporate raider lugging $4 billion in booty, thanks to Mike helping him mount National Can. When Pelz took his turn on the dais, he paraphrased Winston Churchhill, gesturing to the throng of junk-bond millionaires, "Never have so few owed so much to so many." Joining Pelz and Boesky on the program were other dignitaries, like the industrialist tycoon Armand Hammer, who would deliver the conference's closing address; Senator Edward Kennedy, who said, "I'm here to listen and to learn;" and, via video, the actor Larry Hagman, who appeared as his J.R. Ewing character, touting the "Drexel Express titanium card." Packing a $10-billion line of credit, the Drexel Express card was indispensable for the acquisition-minded entrepreneur. "Don't go hunting without it," J.R. ordered, smirking for the self-satisfied congregants.

Originally a dry-as-dust gathering of Milken's minions in the 1970s, the junk-bond conferences had become a star-studded gala affair, with entertainers like Frank Sinatra and Diana Ross appearing live, joined by others doing pre-recorded bits in the J.R. Ewing vein. For the 1986 conference, Madonna licensed her "Material Girl" video to Drexel's marketing department, which overdubbed the song to include the line, "I'm a Double-B girl in a material world," referring to the "BB" rating of substandard bonds. Immediately following the Madonna video, that year's entertainer skipped onstage—Ms. Dolly Parton. If Madonna was a Double-B girl, then Dolly's chest made her the Queen of Junk.

Since 1984, the conference had been dubbed "The Predators' Ball," celebrating the vicious public image of the mergers-and-acquisition animal. There were still speeches at the conference, delivered by the latest Milken acolytes and invited guests, but mainly the event—as it grew into a genuine *event*—served as a chance for the attendees to brag about their conquests and to partner up for the next year's deals. The after-hours revelry in Bungalow 8 included vats of alcohol, an assortment of drugs, and call girls. "I understand CEOs," said Donald Engel, Drexel's man-in-charge of extracurricular pursuits. "CEOs don't care about money, power, or fame. They have all that. What they want is *pussy*. And I'm going to make sure they get it."

The Predators' Ball for 1986 spotlighted the latest minion, Ron Perelman. Ron made the perfect foot soldier in the Milken Revolution. For 15 years or so, he'd been quietly managing the money he came into with his first marriage, to Faith Golding of the Sterling Bank Goldings. In the meantime, using his own meager assets and his wife's good name as collateral, Ron had acquired several businesses, including the Technicolor company, which had expanded from its services to professional cinematographers into a not-so-profitable arm of one-hour photo processing. Like so many Hollywood paramours before him, Ron pushed his luck as far as it would go. When Faith sued him for divorce, she promised to reveal everything her detectives had discovered concerning Ron's extramarital affairs and questionable business dealings. Ron settled on Faith's terms.

Ron married his lover, gossip columnist Claudia Cohen, and went in search of a reputation. He'd always been "Mr. Faith Golding," now he was just plain Ronnie Perelman. But with financial backing from Mike Milken and The Coast, Ron acquired a bankrupt grocery chain called Pantry Pride, which had one chewy asset: a $300-million tax loss that carried forward into any new operations. If Ron merged the Pantry Pride shell with a genuinely functioning company like Revlon, the tax credit worked like a discount voucher, *$300 million off your next purchase of an extra-large corporation.*

Even in the Milken world, that was a meaningful amount of money—but not enough. Mike promised to supplement the tax discount with $350 million in cash, what Drexelites called a "war chest," which Ron would deploy in pursuit of some as yet undetermined venture. Since 1984, Mike had been raising funds for a few special clients, usually between $50 million and $100 million, then helping the client choose a target. For Ron Perelman, Mike broke his own war-chest record, raising $750 million. Ron's attorney said, "Milken kept calling me, saying he could sell $450 million, then $550 million, then $650 million. Finally, at $750 million, we decided to stop."

In the spring of 1985, Ron went calling on Michel Bergerac, the chairman of Revlon. Bergerac carried the mark of the Old Corporate Guard, in the same way that Ron embodied the New Barbarians crashing the gates. Bergerac knew something about Ron. They had a mutual acquaintance who had been safari hunting with Bergerac in Africa, a hobby Bergerac advertised by populating his Revlon executive suite with a menagerie of mounted trophies. Bergerac was described by Connie Bruck as "a courtly, somewhat imperious, urbane, witty Frenchman." He'd ridden the corporate merger wave of the 1960s as an agent for International Telephone and Telegraph, negotiating 100 acquisitions on behalf of the communications giant.

One of Ron's friends pictured the two men standing opposite one another, "Bergerac with his Chateau Lafitte, and Ronnie with his Diet Coke." Ron's poker-night attitude, complete with a large cigar that he liked to puff on every waking minute, inevitably puckered Bergerac's cultured visage. Ron seemed to welcome being cast as a raider, which in some corners of the corporate world was simply code, referring to an uprising of aggressive Jews who were bent on breaking down 40-some-odd years of industry building, as opposed to the cooperative Jewish men and women who made up Goldman, Sachs for example, working inside the system. Where financiers once thought of themselves as the constructors of conglomerates, a raider preferred to buy up a company using loads of debt, lay off all the management and employees he could spare; cut the salaries of everyone left; sell off divisions of the company as separate businesses; and, finally, sell off any assets not absolutely necessary for daily operation. These maneuvers produced enough cash to pay off all or most of the purchase debt. The raider was left with a few core businesses, which could be sold, or which could be leveraged...to launch another takeover.

Bergerac, in an interview for *The Predators' Ball*, summed up his first exchange with Ron Perelman. "He told me that the dream of his life was to buy Revlon. I said that was wonderful, but it was not for sale. He said he would bid in the low 40s. He said that he would do wonderful things for me. I said that I didn't have much taste for being bribed, and I said goodbye." Bergerac told others at Revlon they ought to have nothing to do with Ron Perelman or his non-entity of a company, "*Panty* Pride."

When Ron did make an offer in early September 1985, Bergerac and the Revlon board filed suit. The charges:

- Ron and Mike were already targeting Revlon when they raised the $750 million but failed to make that declaration to the company and the SEC, as required. Ron replied that he had been eyeing several companies when he talked to Michel Bergerac and only decided on Revlon in August.

- Ron and Mike tipped the arbitrage community to the upcoming offer for Revlon, causing the whole shareholder base of the company to shift. An average of 1.25 million shares of Revlon stock changed hands in the five days preceding Ron's offer.

- The debt portion of Ron's offer, $2.1 billion, violated federal rules restricting the amount of debt that can be used in a takeover. In Revlon's case, that number should not have exceeded $1.9 billion, the board argued. Ron answered that there were ways to calculate the debt that kept the number below the limit.

- Ron had ostensibly raised the entire $750 million for an acquisition. Instead he used $350 million to purchase Drexel-issued junk bonds. Revlon was now publicly alleging what people had whispered for years, that Drexel's clients were required, or heavily pressured anyway, to use some of the proceeds from their bond issue to purchase the bonds being issued by other Drexel clients.

It was a typically clumsy attempt to catch Mike Milken doing something wrong, one predicated on insinuation and technical violations, as opposed to hard-core evidence. A federal judge cleared Ron and Mike of all charges, and the deal was greenlighted.

The Revlon team wheedled and whined. Simon Rifkind, a Revlon board member since the 1950s, pointed to St. Bartholomew's Church on Park Avenue, asking, "If somebody could prove to you that the bricks of that cathedral could fetch a higher price in the market, would you dismantle it? I know, I know, today it is put'em together, break'em up— no cement anywhere." Michel Bergerac confessed that he cried at Revlon's final board meeting. "You must understand, people had a love for this company. It was like a woman being raped."

After decades of swearing allegiance to the profit motive, Bergerac and his pseudoaristocratic brethren were astounded to see men like Ron and Mike, who really meant it when they said they only cared about the money. There was no room in the Milken workshop for crying over spilt bricks or framing the corporate charter.

The proof of this doctrine came in its efficacy. Hosting the opening ceremonies of the Predators' Ball for 1986, Ron Perelman gleefully recounted his adventures as a Drexelite. The collective net worth of the room, he pointed out, was $3 *trillion* or $4 *trillion*. People said these parvenu tycoons acted as if they were spending Monopoly money. There were stories that raider Carl Icahn and his friends sometimes played the popular board game at Icahn's estate, hunched over a card table exchanging real 20s, 50s, and 100-dollar bills.

However, the game of Monopoly does *not* do justice to the raiders' financial daring. The board game does offer a primer on how financing used to work, in the good old days, B.M. Financial transactions on the Monopoly board are all tied to "real property," like the Marvin Gardens subdivision or the B&O Railroad. Players buy and sell this property, mortgage it for cash, charge each other rent to park on it, and so on. Banking is conducted on extremely conservative terms: mortgage values are assessed with no regard for inflation, and the tiny loan limits—$200 for one house in Marvin Gardens—are strictly enforced. There's plenty of finance happening around the board, but the exchange of money always signifies either a concomitant exchange of real property, or an act of consumption, like the "Luxury Tax" you have to pay because you wanted that tacky diamond ring. In the land of Monopoly, everything happens on and around the board. Just so, the Old Corporate Guard had always financed each other's ventures, confident that the money they passed back and forth symbolized the "real wealth" of tangible assets. If you really insisted, you could always drive out and view the widget warehouse or the knick-knack factory that represented your $10-million investment. Sure, there were speculators trading in paper, but they were a lousy bunch, a real Baltic Avenue kind of crowd.

Michael Milken changed the money game with his junk bonds. Some junk bonds, like those issued by Real Estate Investment Trusts, or REITS, which bundle many individual home mortgages into a lump-sum note, were supported by real property. Others were based on the future earnings of a company, which was a verifiable entity with production power and tangible assets. But the way Mike played the game, it eventually became irrelevant how much the assets were worth, or how reliable a company's future earnings were. If a company had trouble making its interest payments, Mike could "restructure" the debt, meaning he issued a new round of junk bonds to his network of obeisant buyers, giving the company more time to pay the debt and lowering—in some cases, *voiding*—the interest payments in the short term. Theoretically he could keep restructuring forever. Connie Bruck estimated that questionable refinancing arrangements kept about a billion and a half in junk bonds from going into default during the mid-'80s.

In building his so-called "war chests" Mike charged even further into these uncharted dimensions of pure finance. For these projects, the bonds were not backed by any existing assets or earnings, at least no specific ones. The money—in $50 million and $100 million increments—was earmarked for corporate raiders. Mike raised $750 million for Ronald Perelman before the two of them ever discussed a target. In Mike's world, the money was on the table before the deal was. The Milken loyalists who bought the bonds only asked two questions: "What's the spread?" and "When do you need the cash?"

Mike had generated a new game altogether, *Ultimate* Monopoly, in which the only backing necessary for financial success was the word of Michael Milken. Ultimate Monopoly worked like the video games that were starting to dot middle-class neighborhoods, digital universes with names like "Galaga" and "Pleiades," teeming with "smart bombs" and "hyperspace" buttons. Because Mike controlled his game so exquisitely he could forestall debt with more debt, the same way a smart bomb explodes all the enemy ships on a screen without harming the good guys. And he could raise billions of dollars at will through his loyalist network, the financial equivalent of hitting the hyperspace button and flashing into another dimension.

Michael Milken made money move faster, further, more ferociously than it had ever moved before. He reshaped the lodge-club financial markets of the late 1960s into the multimedia arcades of the new century.

****

With hindsight, it looks as if Milken's minions were asking for it. When you're known as a *predator*, as a *raider*, as a dealer in *junk*—and that's your friends talking—you've got a public relations problem. On May 12, 1986, the problem got bigger. That day, Dennis Levine, a member of Drexel's M&A team in New York, was arrested for insider trading. Levine had been feeding info to people at other firms about Drexel's deals and using the tips he got in exchange to make a string of lucrative stock trades. He told the SEC he could deliver much bigger players.

Mike was never accused of participating in Levine's scheme. But the two men had mutual friends...such as Ivan Boesky. Levine and Boesky had colluded on a slew of deals. *How far will Levine go when he starts naming names?* Wall Streeters wondered. The Levine affair was not mentioned on The Coast, not publicly anyway.

In July 1985, another Drexel M&A person, this time its star, Martin Siegel, was arrested for insider trading. Siegel was a blow-dried Adonis of the Manhattan money circuit, known for his good looks and winning ways. He had only recently come to Drexel, in late 1985, after building a successful M&A business for the firm of Kidder, Peabody. It was during his Kidder days that Siegel had been feeding a certain Big Bad Wolf named Boesky information about mergers in progress.

One of Drexel's investment bankers, to cheer himself and others, mounted and framed a quotation for display in his office that summer of 1986. The words had first been uttered by a competitor who despaired of ever challenging Drexel in the junk-bond market or the takeover business. In large, boldface letters, the sign declared:

> *Drexel is like a god...and a god can do anything it wants....*
> *They are awesome. You hate to do business against them.*

Cheerleading aside, Mike Milken had to be feeling his mortality. Nearly everyone knew where the government's trail was leading—to Boesky, for sure, and further. According to the testimony of several Drexel witnesses, including one of Mike's top traders named Jim Dahl, Mike held discreet conversations with key people in the office that summer, suggesting, without saying so overtly, that anything incriminating needed to be tossed in the dumpster. Mike supposedly pulled Dahl into a men's room, turned on the faucet, and quietly suggested that the government couldn't confiscate what one no longer possessed.

Boesky Day, as it would forever after be known, came on November 2, 1986. Like Levine who finked on *him*, Boesky also agreed to incriminate others in exchange for leniency. In fact, though he reaped an estimated $200 million in illegal profits, Ivan pled guilty to just two counts and received a year in prison. By way of comparison, Dennis Levine, who made about $10 million feeding the Boesky appetite, was sentenced to two years.

Mike knew his was coming; he just didn't know when. He guessed, correctly, that Ivan Boesky was trying to get him on tape when Ivan set up a meeting for the two of them not long after Boesky Day. Both men smiled nervously across the restaurant table, talking in circles and obscurantisms. Mike made no incriminating statements on the tape. He was almost happy a couple days later when he opened the notice that he'd been named a target of a federal investigation.

Mooradian's Error

For all its technicalities and arcana, the unraveling of this fraud case came about through the most ordinary, conventional means. David Levine was given up by the Bahamas bank where he had hidden his loot. In May of 1985, officials at Merrill Lynch received an anonymous letter from someone inside the bank. Though poorly typed, the message was clear enough.

> *Dear Sir: please be informed that two of your executives from the Caracas office are trading with inside information.A copie with description of ther trades so far has been submitet to the S.E.C. by separate mail.As is mention on that letter if us customers do not benefit from their knoledg, we wonder who surveils the trades done by account executives.Upon you investigation to the last consequecies we will provide with the names of the insider on their owne hand writing.*

To keep the Securities and Exchange Commission out of its highly discreet offshore banking practices, the bank offered up Dennis Levine. This brusque-mannered braggart liked to portray himself to accomplices as a financial gangster. Levine had masterminded the Caracas insider trading with the help of some well-placed aides at Merrill Lynch. Once the pressure was on, Levine immediately tossed the name of Ivan Boesky at the prosecutor's feet.

Discovering the evidence that linked Ivan to Mike Milken was an equally low-tech affair. During the spring of 1985, Ivan Boesky was formally shutting down his holding company, Hudson Funding. He was set at the same time to launch a new, publicly traded company called the Boesky Corporation, using $660 million in Drexel junk bonds as fuel. By Ivan's telling, Mike demanded that the two of them square their secret trading accounts before Ivan's legal team closed the books on Hudson Funding. It was safer, Mike suggested, to bury the transaction in the ledger of a defunct, privately held company, rather than bringing the debt into the Boesky Corporation, which was subject to public disclosure laws.

Mike's accountant at Drexel, Charles Thurnher, met with Ivan Boesky's accountant, a fidgety mustachioed Egyptian named Setrag Mooradian, or Set, as he was called. It was determined that Ivan owed Mike $5.3 million—the balance on the trades Ivan had made on Mike's behalf, minus the occasional losses Ivan had absorbed for the Drexel team, and minus the profits Mike had arranged for Ivan by staging bond trades. Set Mooradian, dreading the entire exchange and dying for a cigarette, wrote a single check to Mike's Drexel account for $5.3 million. The plan was that once the Hudson Funding attorneys approved the books for closing, Set would accrue the $5.3 million into a last-minute round of adjustments in the cash ledger.

But Set blew it. At ten minutes to four on the afternoon of March 21, 1986, Mooradian and a group of lawyers, led by one Peter Testaverde, gathered to look over the Hudson books. It should have been a snap. But Testaverde decided to make an issue of a $10,000 accounts payable. He wanted to know what the money was owed for. Set said he didn't know and didn't see why it mattered. As reported by James Stewart, Set Mooradian eventually blew a valve under the pressure.

"I'll need some documentation on this," Testaverde said.

"Oh come on, Pete," Mooradian replied, arguing that it wasn't enough money to worry with.

"I'll have to have some kind of backup, Set," Testaverde insisted.

Now Mooradian was agitated. "For God's sake, Pete," he said. "Why are you busting my balls on this? Why the fuck do you care about a little $10,000 when I've got $5.3 million sitting over here?"

Calmly, so as not to shatter the silence that had settled over the room, Pete Testaverde asked, "What $5.3 million?"

****

Between March 1989, when Mike was charged with 98 counts of insider trading, until mid-1991, when he pled guilty, the Milken name sprang from everyone's lips. Congress held hearings to discuss collapsing S&Ls, corporate raiders, and the scourge of junk bonds. Mike, and by association his brother Lowell, who was also named in the indictments, represented everything wrong with the Decade of Greed. The party was over, and somebody needed to pay up. Mike Milken was bad, just plain bad, bad for the corporate world, bad for the Street, bad for the country; he was even, some nervous Drexelites worried, "bad for the Jews," since Mike and the majority of his raider clients were Jewish.

In other corners, Mike's name was celebrated. A Drexel public relations campaign called him "a national treasure." Junk bonds were good for America, and "good for Americans," Drexel blah-blah-blahed in newspaper and television ads costing millions. A Drexel executive reflected later, "You have to understand what it was like, when Milken was the King. It was Camelot. Pure magic. We thought it would go on and on."

No such luck. Pleading guilty to six felony offenses, Mike said, "This long period has been extremely painful and difficult for my family and friends as well as myself. I realize that by my acts I have hurt those who are closest to me." He paused, swallowing his tears. "I am truly sorry," he concluded, thanking the court for its fairness in handling a complex case.

Gary Lynch, Director of Enforcement for the SEC, saw Michael Milken as the central figure in a Mafioso-like ring of dirty traders. Lynch offered to let Lowell Milken walk if Mike offered a guilty plea to the government's rap sheet. In negotiations, the original 98 charges were whittled down to six. However, in a bizarre judicial move, Judge Kimba Wood allowed Lynch to include the details of 70 "other crimes" in an attachment to the plea. Though Mike wasn't pleading to the "other crimes," the government would describe the acts for Judge Wood to consider during sentencing.

Author Daniel Fischel denounced the entire affair. In his book *Payback: The Conspiracy to Destroy Michael Milken and His Financial Revolution*, Fischel asked how could a defendant's sentence be based on crimes outside the legal charge? Fischel portrayed Mike as Jesus of Beverly Hills, nailed to the cross by a resentful, incompetent gang of federal agents. This Passion Play starred U.S. Attorney Rudy Giuliani as Pontius Pilate, the SEC's Gary Lynch as Herod, and Mike Milken as the junk-bond Savior, quietly defying the strongest government in the world.

In *Payback*, Fischel found the charges against Milken wanting. He did admit the prosecution's best case lay in the first four counts, covering Mike's relationship with Ivan Boesky. But Fischel dismissed the $5.3-million payment for "CONSULTING SERVICES" as the informal way two buddies chose to settle a series of perfectly legal transactions. That the buddies produced no convincing documentation for a one-time $5-million cash transaction, and the fact that one of the buddies admitted the payment was a sham mattered little to a true believer like Fischel. Even if the charges were true, Fischel argued, nobody got hurt. In the Fischbach deal, Boesky accumulated enough shares to break a technical roadblock; in the MCA situation, Boesky helped the Golden Nugget casino get rid of a block of shares it no longer wanted. Fischel pointed out that the underlying value of both companies remained intact.

Gary Lynch and his prosecution team argued that Mike's Ultimate Monopoly had endangered supply and demand—those evanescent, supposedly "natural" forces that keep a market economy humming. If a single man could break agreements between competitors by (secretly) commanding the actions of others, as Mike did when he directed Boesky's accumulation of Fischbach; if that man arranged kickbacks and bonuses for himself by (secretly) manipulating the stock of companies financed by his own firm; if that one man could (stealthily) move stocks and bonds across a range of portfolios, raising and lowering prices as it suited his needs; if one man could raise $1 billion in a weekend; if one man could do all that, then what happened to the free market?

The word *monopoly* applies literally to this discussion. Mike dominated the market in junk bonds, and using those bonds, he came to dominate the market fad in LBOs. No one else had ever forged a monopoly quite like that. Not J.P. Morgan, not several large Rockefellers (as Joyce Bennett called them), not anybody. So if Gary Lynch looked for novel ways to prosecute Mike Milken, it was because of the novel ways Mike had jiggled the financial markets.

Mike admitted to several crimes in his plea.

- He conspired with Ivan Boesky to manipulate stock prices and to profit from those manipulations.

- He shared in the profits of investment partnerships, run by his brother Lowell and others, when those partnerships traded in the stock of Drexel-backed companies.

- He created artificial tax losses for favored clients.

Most seriously, he so dominated the trading of junk bonds that he created a heretofore unprecedented monopoly, one for which the laws and regulations of the American system in 1989 were unprepared. This was an antitrust case unprosecuteable by existing jurisprudence.

****

Mike Milken chased an ambition on Viktor Frankenstein's scale, though he was obsessed with financial, not corporeal, matters. Mike reanimated the junk bond and created his very own market. By 1986 the Milken name had achieved a godlike status. He couldn't do *anything* he wanted, but he could do a lot, and he didn't ask permission. Mike Milken broke laws and collapsed moral fundamentals like he was stacking up folding chairs. Someday, it seemed, it would no longer be appropriate to say that Mike controlled the market. On that day, he would *be* the market.

Mike Milken remains a man of ambiguities, his blood flowing in cross currents. He stirred the sluggish markets of the late 1960s into an Information-Age frenzy, a state of constant motion in which the minimum speed is warp speed and no one knows, or worries much about, what lurks around the corner. The Internet market is the Milken market. Congress recently broke down the regulatory barriers separating banks, insurance companies, and trading firms, effectively ratifying the fundamental premise of the Milken "revolution"—that money ought to be transferred, transformed, and translated at will.

But the Michael Milken of the 21st century is not the one who plundered the markets of the 20th. Judge Kimba Wood sentenced him to ten years, which she later dropped to two years. When Mike was diagnosed with prostate cancer in 1991, 18 months into his sentence, he was released to receive medical treatment.

Since then the most hated man in America has somehow transformed himself into "that nice man," the one who teaches at Harvard and in high schools around the country, the one whose nice brother Lowell runs the Milken Foundation, the one who is currently aiming his laser-like brain at the nation's education system, exploring ways to make schools teach better and turn a profit at the same time. Yes, the selfsame King of the Predators' Ball has morphed into Mr. Chips.

As part of his cancer therapy, Mike has taken up yoga. He still gets up when it's dark outside, but instead of swiveling in front of a stock ticker or yammering on the phone, he's breathing and stretching, stretching and breathing, focusing his thoughts until they become no-thoughts, turning loose of himself until he has no self, courting the state of blissful nothingness called *nirvana*—the ultimate negative, the ultimate repose for the Monster of Debt.

Afterword:
Why They Were Monsters

It has been argued that capitalism itself is responsible for the monsters described in the preceding pages. Some would insist that, in our rush to turn the last century into the Age of Opportunity, we've overlooked a fundamental flaw in the logic of our commercial systems. The profit motive can turn into raw greed in the time it takes to wink.

Perhaps it would be better to describe these monsters as addicts. Just as the hopeless alcoholic knows the next drink will kill him, just as the smoker knows he's driving another nail into his coffin, just as the Frankenstein Creature seemed powerless to stop his bloody rampages, these financial addicts felt compelled toward their destructive behaviors by forces that bedeviled them.

Cassie Chadwick showed her loathsome tendencies early in life. Born Elizabeth Bigley, the near-deaf Lizzie endured a childhood of mockery because of her hearing and impaired speech. To compensate, Elizabeth simply stepped out of her own person and became someone else. By adolescence, she was already living in a dream world. She was regal; she was the daughter of aristocracy.

But living in a dream world turned out not to be cheap. After all, aren't fine breeding and fine possessions one and the same? They seemed to be so in Lizzie's demented mind. If she could surround herself with enough finery, she would be accepted as royalty. And if she were accepted as royalty, she would be surrounded with finery.

Never mind that she had to whore herself out in the early days to avoid starvation; it was all for a greater good. Because during this time, Elizabeth learned a very valuable life lesson: *sex* had a price limit—men were willing to pay only so much. But *greed* had no bounds; the more she offered her victims, the greater her rewards.

And reward herself, she did. As Elizabeth Bigley/Lydia Bagley/ Elizabeth Thomas/ Reuben Kip/ Alice Bertado/ Mrs. Bill Springsteen/ Mazie Bagley/ Madame La Rose/ Lydia Scott/Betsey Bagley/ Lylie Bagley/ Lylie Clingen/ Mrs. C. L. Hoover/ Lydia Devere/ Mrs. Richard Brown/ Florida Blythe/ Cassie Chadwick, she conned bankers and amateur financiers for several million dollars—a staggering amount of money at the turn of the 20th century. Except for the tricks she turned from time to time, Cassie's only known source of "revenue" was her borrowings. She could shift from fortune teller to brothel madam to millionaire heiress in the space of a single day if she had to.

Why was she successful? Two reasons, really. First, she had the sheer audacity such an intricate scam requires. Like Ponzi, no plan was too bold; no lie was too outrageous. By the age of 19, Cassie had already commissioned the printing of business cards announcing herself as "Lydia Bagley, Heiress to $15,000." Tacky, to say the least.

The second reason Cassie Chadwick was successful? She exercised unerring judgment in selecting her believers. She spoke the language of bankers and money managers, an act almost totally unknown to womanhood at that time. And she always tried to select greedy people to victimize. One of her first banking transactions was to borrow $25,000 and agree to pay back $30,000 in 90 days—an 80-percent annual interest rate.

Then she met a succession of bankers willing to believe her lies for the same or greater profits. The most glaring example was Cleveland banker Iri Reynolds, who decided it would have been an affront to Cassie to even look at the $11 million in "bonds" inside a sealed envelope she waved in his face. Had Reynolds taken the time to look, he would have easily uncovered her scam. But he too was hooked on Cassie's promises of big returns.

The same can be said of banker Charles Beckwith. She borrowed $35,000 by promising a donation of an equal amount to Oberlin College. Cassie eventually even promised she'd hire Beckwith and his ally at $10,000 annually to manage her affairs.

Over the next two years, Beckwith was duped out of a quarter of a million dollars.

In Cassie's case, all the money went to support the opulent lifestyle that was so necessary to convince her victims she really *was* worth the millions she was conning them out of. After all, the daughter of Andrew Carnegie *should* live like royalty. And how many people would have had the gall to claim to be the illegitimate daughter of one of the wealthiest men of the time?

****

It is hard to believe that the brilliant mind of Charles Ponzi didn't *really* understand pyramid mathematics, that no matter how long his scheme lasted, he was eventually doomed by the planet's finite population. But, like the addict he was, Ponzi continued anyhow. Certainly there were perks—the mansion on Fair Street, the Locomobile, the fine suits punctuated by a dazzling diamond stickpin, the clothing and gifts for Ponzi's precious Rose.

Ponzi was a freak before he ever landed on America's shores to seek fame and fortune. By the age of 21, he had worn out his welcome in his Italian homeland with his gambling, thieving, and forging. It is doubtful that Ponzi ever longed to make a legitimate income. One of Ponzi's colleagues, Dominico Defrancesco, succinctly said, "He never liked to work, and was always talking of millions and wearing a nice white collar and nice clothes."

Ponzi may well have been born a financial monster. After many failures, he was finally successful for a number of reasons. First and foremost, Ponzi's scheme had an air of legitimacy. Send a dollar to Italy. The dollar is exchanged for lira. The lira is used to purchase postal coupons in Italy. The postal coupons are sent to the United States, where they are exchanged for U.S. stamps. The U.S. stamps are then sold to discounters. The net result is a $2 profit for every $1 invested. Of course, Ponzi didn't use investors' money to buy coupons. Instead, he lived high and paid old debts with the money from new victims.

The second reason Ponzi was successful is because he lived at a time when individual investing was a fairly new concept. Certainly, in turn-of-the-century America, most working people had never invested before. That was especially true of immigrants, who generally had little formal education and even less ready cash. Ponzi preyed on the native pride and trust of his fellow Italians. It was easy to do in those days—no Securities and Exchange Commission, and no Federal Bureau of Investigation patrolling the financial frontier. Ponzi took in thousands a day while government officials wondered what they ought to, and could, do about it.

The third reason for Ponzi's success was because he was a practiced liar. He was so confident in his ability to lie his way out of trouble he didn't leave Boston when his scheme was unraveled. The problem with telling so many lies is that you start believing them. Even though his scheme was destined to fail from the outset, it is doubtful that Ponzi ever admitted that to himself. Had he done so, he would have taken the money and ran.

Like other Frankensteins of Fraud, Charles Ponzi's victims were his lifeblood. Some were greedy, others were just trying to make the best deal they could. Many of the people conned by Charles Ponzi remained loyal to him, even after he was tried and convicted. This is one characteristic that makes fraud difficult to pursue: it's almost impossible for some individuals to accept the fact that they have been duped.

All of Charles Ponzi's efforts to go straight were met with failure. He was a failure as the publisher of his investment newsletter; he was a failure as a landshark; he failed as the business manager of an airline; he failed as a landlord; he even failed as a hotdog salesman. If that weren't enough, despite his successes, he ultimately failed as a crook.

****

Ivar Kreuger's secret to business was "Silence, silence, and more silence." And for quite a while, silence covered the Swedish Match King's massive frauds. Indeed, who—in the 21st century—could single-handedly control the economic fate of major nations like Ivar Kreuger?

There were a number of factors at that particular moment in history that permitted Ivar Kreuger, and him alone, to decide how much he was worth. First, international ownership of companies started becoming more common at the beginning of the 20th century. Previously, most companies were privately owned in their native countries. But during Kreuger's rule, Swedish Match had financial ties with dozens of nations, each with its own exchange rate, currency, and accounting rules.

The international aspects of his business allowed Kreuger to play a financial version of the ancient shell game—where is the bean? In Kreuger's case, the bean was counted as many times as necessary. And that is obviously why silence was golden to Ivar Kreuger. Some parts of the huge Kreuger & Toll were real, some weren't. Some parts, it depended on the light; it was hard to say just what was real with Kreuger at the controls.

But the creation of phony assets was only one aspect of Kreuger's fraud. Recall that the Swedish Match King also said, "It doesn't matter what you make. Just so you make lots of them. And you control every one." The law tends to frown on monopolistic arrangements—for good reason. One critical aspect of commerce is a free market, where the selling price of goods and services is determined by a buyer and seller acting independently. But if the buyer and seller is the same person, he can charge whatever he wants. In his heyday, Kreuger controlled an astonishing 80 percent of the world's supply of matches.

Once people have the reputation of extreme wealth and power, it becomes more difficult to treat them like everyone else. Kreuger wasn't used to being questioned in great detail about his wealth, and he was quick to react if challenged. If an auditor, financier, government, or business acquaintance got too curious, Kreuger would just stop doing business with them.

On occasion when Kreuger was caught in a financial quandary, he would utter that line, "Just debit it to me personally." The tack worked for a long, long time. And it worked with the other Frankensteins in this book to one extent or another. By creating the *appearance* of wealth, one also creates the *appearance* of power, the power to control and even destroy the lives of those who would be too curious.

It is hard to say how much of Kreuger's fortune was obtained from his match industry versus how much money was "made" by pyramiding loans. I'm sure Kreuger didn't even know himself. And the accountants "auditing" his books certainly didn't know.

Kreuger used an accounting trick that has been employed by lesser fraudsters countless times: simply move the bad stuff from the main company to a "subsidiary." It is hard to find the dirt when it has been shipped somewhere else. The savings and loan crisis of the '80s was sustained largely the same way—bad loans were shipped from one S&L to another, depending on which institution was being examined at the time.

And the accountants, who don't want to bite the hand that feeds them, often take the word of the last person they should trust. Indeed, Price, Waterhouse would later observe that the Kreuger fraud was possible only because of "the loyalty or unquestioning obedience of officials."

Was the Kreuger bubble destined to burst? Of course. As long as the economy stayed on his side, Kreuger could have continued indefinitely. But when the banks in Austria and Germany failed and England abandoned the gold standard, Kreuger could no longer obtain the loans he needed to keep his schemes afloat.

In his place and time, Kreuger could have probably held on to the world's match market simply by competing. But for this monster, controlling the lion's share of the global market wasn't enough—he thought he had to have it *all*.

****

Philip Musica, a.k.a. Dr. F. Donald Coster, never bought his own line. Dr. F. Donald Coster was no fast-talking con artist. He was an authority. He took his masquerade as far as it would go, then pulled the trigger. With the speed of a muzzle blast, Musica was absolved of his earthly sins.

The explanation for Philip Musica's behavior lies with his family. After all, he was just doing what his mamma taught him, the same lessons Mamma Assunta taught her sons Robert, George, and Arthur. Like the Antars, a whole family of crooks. Were the Musicas and the Antars—and many others—biologically disposed to commit these fiendish crimes? The answer is yes and no.

Criminologists have noted that *some* criminal characteristics apparently have a genetic basis, but it is not strong, and it is heavily influenced by other factors. The eminent criminologist Edwin Sutherland (1883-1950) argued criminal activity was primarily a learned response. His *Theory of Differential Association* is the most widely accepted current theory of criminal behavior.

At its foundation, the theory suggests that criminal traits are learned in small groups and in intimate situations—such as family. And the learning process is divided into two major components: the techniques of committing the crime; and more importantly, the value system of the criminal. If a parent can convince his or her child that criminal activity is somehow justified, this becomes a critical factor in whether the offspring will adopt illegal behavior. So in the end, Mamma Assunta—like Viktor Frankenstein—created a monster.

****

Stanley Goldblum's lifelong dedication to building bulging muscles tells a lot about him. When his friend and partner Mike Riordan asked Goldblum he why spent so much time in his private gym, Goldblum's answer was simple: "To get big." The former sausage maker's approach to business was exactly the same—

bigger is better. In this case, Goldblum evidently figured out early that as long as Equity Funding kept growing the monster fraud beneath the surface could be buried indefinitely. From the time Goldblum entered the insurance business until his scheme was uncovered, it appears that Goldblum never made a legitimate profit. So like several other fiends in this book, Goldblum was no businessman; he just masqueraded as one.

Goldblum understood one fraud lesson well: to get investors and banks to give him their money, he had to produce the right *numbers.* The business—or lack of it—underlying the numbers was immaterial to Goldblum. He and his lieutenants created the precious numbers they needed out of thin air.

From that point, Riordan and Goldblum were pretty much hooked. Cooking the books has a cumulative and compounding effect. Unless the company makes enough profit to cover the crimes, they just get worse. Within three years of going public, Equity Funding had overstated its sales to Penn Life Insurance Company alone by $165 million. For Stanley and Mike, there was no looking back.

Mike Riordan extracted himself from the fraud only in death. Stanley Goldblum charged ahead, creating more *fake* deaths. From those he collected hefty insurance benefits, which further aided his scheme. It was Stanley's philosophy, as he told his aide-de-camp Fred Levin, "A public company doesn't lose money."

But Equity Funding was a public company in name only. In reality, it was Stanley Goldblum's dastardly creation. He ran it, he gave life to it, and he felt beholden to no one. Real public companies, on the other hand, are managed by a board of directors who represent the shareholders. At one of Goldblum's speeches, an analyst asked what he would do if his business decisions were opposed by a director. Goldblum's answer: "Get a new director."

Goldblum's board consisted of straw men, men whose ethics would go whichever way the winds of Goldblum were blowing. Still, Goldblum tried to be careful about what he said to whom; much of the dirty work was actually directed by his two closest aides, Fred Levin and Sam Lowell. They tried—as best they could—to keep employees below them isolated, so the underlings would not know they were aiding in the commission of a massive fraud.

In the end, Goldblum and a team of a hundred or so employees had created 64,000 phony policyholders and millions in fake revenue. He was brought down by one of his own—an employee with a grudge. Goldblum wasn't a nice boss, and in this instance, he eventually paid for it.

Those who expose massive frauds, though, often do so at their own risk. The fate of whistleblowers, in general, has not been a good one. Victims frequently want to slay the bearer of bad news. Ray Dirks, the Wall Street "hippie analyst" who exposed the Equity Funding fraud to the media was vilified in the press and in court. It took Dirks an entire decade to clear his name.

Like many other financial fiends, Stanley was probably too arrogant to believe he would ever be caught. Even after serving four years in prison, he hasn't learned. Twice since his release, Stanley has been accused of fraud. So the Creature lives on.

****

Robert Vesco, in addition to acting like a monster, looked something like one. With his heavily pomaded hair, deeply furrowed eyebrows, and a penchant for dark clothing, Vesco's countenance could be disturbing. When his demeanor was combined with his varied financial misdeeds, Robert Vesco could be downright scary.

From Vesco's humble beginnings in an auto body shop, he gradually worked his way toward self-employment. Selling became an all-consuming passion. Then after several years of business experience, it finally came to Vesco: he was put on earth to make deals. And make them he did.

Besides the legitimate aspects of Vesco's deals, there was one unspoken benefit. By taking advantage of the accounting complexities of merging companies, much financial chicanery could be hidden completely.

Financial power eventually turned Vesco into a Frankenstein. Indeed, some of Vesco's earliest supporters noticed a marked change in their protégé. According to one close friend, the situation with Vesco got "...worse and worse. His ambitions and designs eventually became overpowering." You could see it in other ways, too. In less than three short years, Vesco's five-acre estate had expanded to 80 acres.

Robert Vesco's political capital had expanded as well. He was an unabashed supporter of Richard Nixon, funneling several hundred thousand dollars to the now-disgraced president. Political contacts aside, the underlying problem with Vesco was that he wasn't making a legitimate profit. The companies he had acquired through mergers were—by and large—losers. Like several other Frankensteins in this book, many of Vesco's frauds were committed trying to prop up bad business decisions.

Vesco picked up some pretty freakish associates during his career: Bernie Cornfield, Don-Don Nixon, G. Gordon Liddy, Carlos Lehder-Rivas, Mohmmar Khaddaffi, Fidel Castro. Vesco's illegal take from IOS was about $500 million, which can provide a very nice lifestyle during 25 years on the lam. But finally, Bob Vesco met his match when he tried to defraud "The Beard." It looks like he'll spend the rest of his life in a Cuban prison, sans creature comforts.

Vesco's status as a financial monster is best illustrated by his conversation with Bernie Cornfield, who asked, "Bob, what about all those widows and orphans you're robbing?" Vesco replied, "They have their problems and I have mine."

****

It could be argued that "Crazy" Eddie Antar was also born to the business of lying and cheating. His father, Sam Antar, taught Eddie and the other family members well. By the time Eddie began his own business, cheating was not just a method to save on taxes. Dishonesty became a way of life. But Eddie didn't sell deception alone; it was truly a family affair. Many of Eddie's closest relatives actively participated in the multitude of frauds that found their way through the Crazy Eddie stores.

One of the most interesting aspects of the Crazy Eddie case was the fact that the family had a Plan—a plan to quit skimming money. It wasn't a plan to quit committing fraud; quite the opposite. The Plan consisted of going public, so the family could entirely change the dimension of its crime. Rather than cheat customers and taxing authorities, the Antar family decided to move on to investors, where the real money was. This move would accomplish two objectives: first, it would cover the past crimes; and second, it would greatly increase the family take. By gradually reducing the skimming each year, it appeared to potential investors that Crazy Eddie's was more profitable than it really was.

In terms of real dollars, the family skimmed at least $7 million. But their take from Crazy Eddie going public—which should have never happened—was $80 million. So the company assets were overstated, as were the profits. Eddie could have covered the skimming *if* the stores had been profitable. Eddie and his family could have worked their way out of the fraud *if* his idea of discount electronic superstores had given him a monopoly. Eddie did change the face of American commerce; before Crazy Eddie's, there were no Circuit City or Best Buy stores, and the other major chains that exist today. But unfortunately for Eddie, his competitors did not have to absorb the built-in cost of fraud—they started at ground zero instead of being millions in the hole.

So in the final analysis, this Frankenstein was uncovered like so many others are—through the competitive forces of capitalism. Those forces are every bit as strong as the laws of physics. Eddie Antar learned that lesson the hard way.

****

There was nothing new about Jack Bennett's "mission from God." Indeed, from the time of the Crusades to the era of Jim Bakker, religion has been used to justify countless unspeakable crimes. In Bennett's case, he was the product of an alcoholic father and a fervently religious mother. But he didn't become a drunken bum. Jack tried hard to please his mother by adopting the faith. He tried hard all his life to please other people, too. This is not an uncommon trait in the offspring of alcoholics. Jack Bennett was addicted to pleasing people, slurping their smiles and hugs by the case.

Jack Bennett tried to lead a model life. He married the right kind of girl—one that would please his mother. He pressed himself into the conformity required of a good boy, even enrolling in medical school to become the doctor his mother would be proud of. And although he didn't become a physician, Jack took the most valuable course of his life—how to develop an authoritative bedside manner.

Early in his fundraising career, when he was caught lying repeatedly to one of his benefactors, Don Wilkerson, Bennett explained, "Everything I've done here and said here was for the greater good. I just believe so fully myself that I am giving you the same assurances I feel in my deepest heart." In short, to achieve, you must believe. Recall though, that Wilkerson had a different feeling about Bennett: "I have never seen more deception and lying in all my years. And remember, I work with drug addicts and con artists."

Was Bennett self-delusional? Perhaps. More likely, he was simply a cunning and conniving thief and liar using faith as his cover. When the bounds of traditional faith restricted him too much, Bennett redefined himself as a "deinstitutional religionist." That way, Jack Bennett, not God, could make up his own Ten Commandments. Going to church provided Bennett with two important commodities: cash and contacts. The contacts Bennett made at church eventually led to the formation of New Era. But there he was again, attempting to fund projects using faith-checks which bounced. As his hot checks got bigger, Jack Bennett sought out bigger victims.

Bennett could drop some of the most famous names in the country like Ronald Reagan, Nelson Rockefeller, and Billy Graham, alongside Philadelphia luminaries like William Thatcher Longstreth. But it was the lesser-known names that brought Jack Bennett down. One Albert Meyer, accountant, first discovered Bennett was engaging in a Ponzi scheme. His news was not met with enthusiasm. And then there was Andy Cunningham, auditor. Bennett paid Cunningham—over a period of time—$76,000 to look the other way.

Once he was caught, Bennett figured out there were only two conclusions that could be drawn from his behavior—he was either crooked or crazy. He opted for the latter defense, even concocting delusional meetings with his anonymous "donors." But as a federal judge correctly noted, Jack Bennett's behavior was not irrational; it was exactly what you would expect from a calculating con man. Still, even after praying behind bars for several years, it is doubtful that this monster has come to accept the truth about what he did.

****

The names of history's turncoats are infamous: Judas Iscariot. Brutus. Benedict Arnold. And now Mark Whitacre, who spied on Archer Daniels Midland for the FBI. Of course, the FBI had its own troubles with Whitacre, which shouldn't have surprised anyone. Any seasoned law enforcement investigator will tell you the same thing: informants are not to be trusted. During the decade I spent as an FBI agent, we had a saying, "Anyone who will snitch *for* you will snitch *on* you."

In Whitacre's case, he was snitching to the FBI about his own co-workers, who were supposedly forming an illegal cartel with the Japanese. The motivation for the cartel allegedly came from Terry Wilson, Whitacre's immediate supervisor, who believed, "The competitor is our friend, the customer is our enemy."

People like Mark Whitacre become snitches for a variety of reasons. Revenge and greed top the list. But most informants pale in comparison to the damage wreaked by this fiend. By the time he finished, Mark Whitacre had nearly tanked the "Supermarket to the World."

Facts that came out later about Whitacre's early childhood might have predicted he would eventually become a financial monster. Claiming he was adopted at the age of two, Mark spent his early years in a midwestern farming community, where values such as hard work and honesty are highly valued. Mark had big plans to succeed. By the time he was barely grown, Whitacre had distinguished himself by earning a Ph.D. from Cornell.

Whitacre was already prone to lying when he volunteered to join the FBI's investigation. He was not adopted as he claimed. Mark said he had an MBA from Northwestern; not so. Whitacre said his Ph.D. was in biochemistry. That was a lie. Even Whitacre's Japanese contact, the mysterious Mr. Fugiwara, was made up. Those falsehoods did help Whitacre climb the corporate ladder. But when he got to the top, he fell.

Regardless of what Whitacre told the government, he really *was* trying to establish a global monopoly for his employer, ADM. And his strategy worked. ADM now owns fully half of the world market in lysine. A federal judge branded Whitacre not just a *participant,* but the *director* of the scam to inflate the prices of a $600 million-a-year industry.

After alienating nearly everyone around him, Whitacre was sentenced to a total of 12 years in prison, where he currently spends his days recanting his guilty plea to embezzlement, talking at his propeller pace about government conspiracies and cover-ups, wondering why the feds won't agree to call everything off and turn him loose. The monster turncoat Mark Whitacre has become a man-without-a-clue, perhaps a stranger even to himself.

****

There was nothing ordinary about Michael Milken. At a time when hippies across America were burning their draft cards and listening to Country Joe and the Fish, Milken was every parent's dream—the child who studied hard, did the right thing, and respected his elders. He didn't even drink carbonated beverages—much less alcohol.

And then there was his work ethic. While most people need a good night's sleep, Milken could get by on four hours or less. With that extra time, he was able to regularly put in 18 hours a day thinking, planning, plotting, reading. Even before Milken read Hickman's *Corporate Bond and Quality and Investor Experience*, he displayed every indication that he would be a very formidable businessman. W. Braddock Hickman's study—which indicated that "junk" bonds could be as safe and profitable as the blue-chip variety—had a profound effect on Michael Milken. He already displayed business savvy, and developing the market in "junk" bonds gave Milken the opportunity to prove his skills.

Milken began his career with Drexel in 1973, originally selling bonds. But by 1977, Drexel—under Michael's tutelage—was issuing the bonds themselves. Milken started with $2 million in Drexel capital. But by 1983, the market was at $4.9 billion in junk bonds, of which Drexel controlled 70 percent.

Milken's influence even extended to the merger-and-acquisition mania that spread throughout Wall Street in the 1980s. He backed a nefarious crowd of corporate raiders with his seemingly unending coffers, greatly influencing the market price of stocks. By 1986, Drexel had conducted *$4 trillion* in financial transactions in a single year. And for his efforts, Milken kept $550 million—not bad for 12 months of hard work.

Over the years Milken made some scary friends and associates: Ivan Boesky, Charles Keating, and David Paul, to name a few. Boesky came back to haunt Michael by turning state's evidence to save his own skin. But that's not what really convicted Milken. Like many criminal fraud cases, the charges Milken pled to were largely technical. He admitted to conspiring with Boesky to manipulate stock prices, secretly sharing in investment partnerships, and creating artificial tax losses for favored clients. But his crime, too, was building a monopoly. The extent of his financial control of markets in the United States was breathtaking, reaching into the trillions of dollars. Michael Milken undoubtedly wouldn't believe he struck out to be a monopolist. Nonetheless he continued to acquire financial power, figuratively slaying innocent people in the process. Still, Milken is different from other Frankensteins in this book. For one, there is no indication that he lived his life to satisfy his lust for possessions. Considering the money he made, Milken lived rather modestly. And he certainly didn't have the time to spend much of his fortune; he was too busy controlling the fortunes of the rest of us with his 120-hour work-weeks.

Unlike many of the monsters in this book, Milken did a lot of good, too. With junk bonds, he completely changed the way business is conducted in America. The positive impact on those businesses has provided employment and opportunity for untold thousands. So similar to Dr. Frankenstein's creature, Milken wasn't all bad. As a matter of fact, with his new life, many believe he is downright good.

Does Milken portend the 21st century white-collar criminal? If so, it's a scary thought: in the future, it may be almost impossible to tell who the real monsters are. But regardless of whatever physical form these creatures take tomorrow, we have only ourselves to blame. After all, human greed is the Viktor Frankenstein, the creator, of these financial fiends.

Select Bibliography

The Trial: Cassie Chadwick

"Chadwick." *Cleveland World*, March 12, 1905.

Chernow, Ron. "Philanthropy the Smart Way." *New York Times,* September 27, 1999.

Condon, George E. *Yesterday's Cleveland*. E. A. Seemann, 1976.

Crosbie, John. *The Incredible Mrs. Chadwick.* McGraw-Hill, 1975.

De Grave, Kathleen. *Swindler, Spy, Rebel: The Confidence Woman in Nineteenth-Century America.* University of Missouri Press, 1995.

Edelstein, Stewart I. "Cassie Chadwick Would Never Believe It." *Oberlin Alumni Magazine*, February 1971.

Ellington, George. *Women Of New York*. 1869. Arno Press, 1972.

Kennedy, Charles. *Fifty Years in Cleveland.* Weidenthall, 1925.

Kepler, Lou. "Cassie Chadwick." *Lorain Journal,* May 25, 1975.

Laning, Jay Ford. *The History and Story of the Doings of the Famous Mrs. Cassie L. Chadwick.* Laning, 1905.

Levins, Peter. "Coster-Musica Masquerade Recalls Cassie Chadwick's Amazing Career." *Chicago Sunday News,* January 1, 1939.

Mehling, Harold. "The Cassie Chadwick Story." *Cleveland News,* May 30, 1959.

Miller, Carol and Robert Wheeler. *Cleveland*. Indiana University Press, 1990.

Phillips, Wilbur. *Oberlin Colony: The Story of a Century.* Oberlin, 1933.

Prentice, Alison, et al. *Canadian Women.* Harcourt, Brace, Jovanovich, 1988.

Nash, Robert Jay. *Bloodletters and Bad Men.* Philadelphia: Lippincott, 1973.

Rigby, Cora. "Cassie Chadwick." *Pittsburgh Dispatch*, May 2, 1915.

Rafter, Nicole. *Partial Justice.* Northeastern University Press, 1985.

"Slop-over sympathy." *Oberlin News,* December 2, 1904.

U.S. v. Cassie L. Chadwick. Brief filed with the U.S. Court of Appeals, 6th Circuit, June 6, 1905.

Various articles from the *Cleveland Plain-Dealer*, 1905-1907.

Meet Mr. Ponzi: Charles Ponzi

Darby, Mary. "In Ponzi We Trust." *Smithsonian,* December 1998.

Dunn, Donald H. *Ponzi! The Boston Swindler.* McGraw-Hill, 1975.

Galbraith, Kenneth. *The Affluent Society.* Deutsch, 1977.

Herst, Herman Jr. "Ponzi was a Notorious Confidence Man." *Stamps*, December 9, 1995.

Knutson, Mark. "Charles K. Ponzi Website." www.usinternet.com/users/mcknutson.

Nash, Robert Jay. *Bloodletters and Bad Men.* Philadelphia: Lippincott, 1973.

Nash, Robert Jay. "They're Pros at Pulling Off Cons." *Wall Street Journal*, July 23, 1999.

Ponzi, Charles. *The Rise of Mr. Ponzi.* Ponzi, 194?.

Russell, Frances. "Bubble Bubble—No Toil, No Trouble." *American Heritage*, 1973.

Streissguth, Thomas. *Hoaxers & Hustlers.* Oliver Press, 1994.

"The Locomobile." www2.epix.net/~tdc/pages/autolink.html.

Various articles in the *Boston Post*, 1920.

Keeper of the Flame: Ivar Kreuger

Culture Jammer's Encyclopedia. www.syntac.net/hoax

Flesher, Dale L., Tonya K. "Ivar Kreuger's Contribution to U.S. Financial Reporting." *Accounting Review,* July 1986.

Flesher, Dale L. "Why America Has a Regulated Securities Market." *Phi Kappa Phi Journal*, Fall 1997.

Howard, Nat. "Royal Flushed." *D&B Reports*, November 1992.

"Kreuger. He Made the Match." *Time,* October 28, 1929.

Lindgren, Hakan. "The Kreuger Crash of 1932." *Scandinavian Economic History Review,* Spring 1989.

MacLeish, Archibald. "The Times were Right for Ivar Kreuger." *Fortune,* May-July 1933.

"Poor Kreuger." *Time*, March 21, 1932.

Rigby, Rhymer. "A Match Trade Made in Hell." *Management Today*, February 1997.

Shaplen, Robert. *Kreuger, Genius and Swindler.* New York: Knopf, 1960.

Citizen Coster: Philip Musica

Berger, Meyer. "The Story of F.D. Coster (Musica)." *New York Times,* December 25, 1938.

Bruce, Robert. "The Lessons of History Shed Light on the Present." *The Times of London*, July 15, 1999.

Claghorn, Kate Holladay. "The Foreign Immigrant in New York City" *Reports of the Industrial Commission, Volume XV.* United States Government Printing Office, 1901.

Helmstreet, Charles. *Nooks & Corners of Old New York.* Charles Scribner's Sons, 1899.

Keats, Charles. *Magnificent Masquerade.* Funk & Wagnalls, 1964.

Loomis, Carol J. "Lies, Damned Lies, and Managed Earnings: McKesson Again." *Fortune*, August 2, 1999.

MacDonald, Elizabeth. "Sensational '37 Fraud Produces Some Eerie Echoes at McKesson." *Wall Street Journal,* June 30, 1999.

"Philip Mariano Fausto Musica." *Dictionary of American Biography.*

Ris, Jacob, and Five Contemporary Photographers. "A Century Apart: Images of Spirit and Struggle." www.mcny.org/mcny/m30.htm

Shaplen, Robert. "The Metamorphosis of Philip Musica." *New Yorker,* October 22 & 29, 1955.

Stevenson, Robert Alston. "The Poor in Summer." *Scribner's Magazine,* September 1901.

Thompson, Larry D. "Early American Gangs." members.aol.com/tllillie/earlygangs/mz/index.html.

The Strong Man: Stanley Goldblum

Dirks, Raymond L. and Leonard Gross. *The Great Wall Street Scandal.* McGraw-Hill, 1974.

Dirks v. SEC. Supreme Court of the United States, 1983.

Friedman, Amy S. "Equity Funding—the Scandal of the Decade." *National Underwriter*, March 31, 1997.

Gaw, Jonathan, "Man Arrested in Alleged Scam of O.C. Lender." *Los Angeles Times,* February 17, 1999.

Hancox, David R. "Equity Funding: Could It Happen Again?" *Internal Auditor,* October 1997.

Macey, Jonathan R. "SEC's Insider Trading Proposal: Good Politics, Bad Policy." *Policy Analysis No. 101,* March 31, 1988.

Mannes, George. "Reliving Equity Funding, the Cal Ripken of Stock Frauds." www.thestreet.com, February 22, 1999.

"Once Burned, Twice Shy." *Wall Street Journal,* October 19, 1984.

Sansweet, Stephen J. "Man Who Presided Over Massive Fraud Picked to Head Firm." *Wall Street Journal,* September 7, 1984.

Seidler, Lee J., Frederick Andrews, and Marc J. Epstein. *The Equity Funding Papers: Anatomy of a Fraud.* Santa Barbara: Wiley, 1977.

Silverstein, Stuart. "L.A. Charges Doctor." *Los Angeles Times,* November 2, 1995.

_____. "New Charges Added in Workers' Comp Case." *Los Angeles Times,* June 1, 1996.

_____. "A Doctor, a Swindler and an Accused Stock Manipulator." *Los Angeles Times,* April 25, 1993.

Soble, Ronald and Robert Dallos. *The Impossible Dream.* Putnam, 1975.

The Outlaw: Robert Vesco

Arostegui, Martin. "Return of the Godfather." *National Review,* July 31, 1995.

Associated Press. "Trial Offers Peek at Cuban Justice System." *The Dallas Morning News*, August 21, 1996.

Barrett, William T. "I Work Hard." *Forbes,* March 18, 1991.

Bearak, Barry. "Mother Delivered Drug for Trip to Disneyland." *Los Angeles Times,* March 12, 1998.

Bardach, Ann Louise. "Vesco's Last Gamble." *Vanity Fair,* March 1996.

Collett, Mike. "Donald Nixon, After Weeks of Detention, Leaves Cuba." *Reuters,* July 3, 1995.

Chua-Eon, Howard. "The Predator's Fall." *Time*, June 19, 1995.

Farah, Douglas, "'Miracle Cure' Deal Trips Up Vesco." *Washington Post,* July 25, 1995.

Fletcher, Pascal. "Cuba Jails Fugitive U.S. Financier for 13 Years." *Reuters,* August 26, 1996.

Fuentes, Norberto. "Ghostly Blackmail." *Washington Post,* June 18, 1995.

Herzog, Arthur. *Vesco.* Doubleday, 1987.

Hutchison, Robert. *Vesco.* Praeger, 1974.

Knowlton, Christopher. "The Man Asking Iranscam's Tough Questions." *Fortune,* June 9, 1987.

Kutler, Stanley, ed. *Abuse of Power: The New Nixon Tapes.* Free Press, 1997.

Layaco, Richard. "The Judge Who Makes Everything His Business." *Time,* February 27, 1995.

Lippman, Thomas W. and Pierre Thomas. "Expected Handover of Vesco Poses Questions About Castro's Motives." *Washington Post,* June 10, 1995.

Marietta, Morgan. "The Historical Continuum of Financial Illusion." *American Economist,* March 22, 1996.

Massing, Michael. "There's Always A New Kingpin." *Washington Post,* June 25, 1995.

Mollins, Carl. "The Cuba Connection: Tough Talk in Washington may Hurt Canadian Companies." *Maclean's,* June 26, 1995.

Orr, Andrea. "Nixon Nephew says Cuba Detention 'Pretty Scary.'" *Reuters,* July 5, 1995.

Preston, Julia. "Cuba Sentences Officers To Death for Corruption." *Washington Post*, July 8, 1998.

Records of the United States Senate, 1969-1988.

Rinfret, Pierre A. *Untitled Memoirs.* www.rinfret.com/pr.html.

"The Fire Chief and the Fugitive." *New Yorker,* August 6, 1997.

Tricks, Henry. "Cuban Prosecution Demands 20 Years for Vesco." *Reuters,* August 4, 1996.

The Antar Complex: Eddie Antar

Antar, Sam E. Interviews, 1997-1999.

Antar, Sam M. Interviews, 1998.

Belsky, Gary and Phyllis Furman. "Calculated Madness." *Crain's New York Business Report,* June 5, 1989.

Crazy Eddie Annual Reports, 1984 – 1987.

"Crazy Eddie." Stock Analysis. Drexel, Burnham, Lambert. June 30, 1986.

"Crazy Eddie's Controlling Family a Small Conglomerate." *Discount Store News,* July 9, 1984.

"Crazy Eddie Takes Saner Approach to Biz." *Discount Store News*, August 22, 1988.

"Crazy Eddie Update." *The Motley Fool,* Tuesday, May 21, 1996.

Deborah Antar v. Solomon Antar.

Halverson, Richard C. "Crazy Eddie Pushes Southward." *Discount Store News*, March 16, 1987.

Hayes, Paul. Interviews, 1997.

Malanga, Steve. "Crazy Eddie: An Interview with Howard Sirota." *Crain's New York Business,* March, 27, 1995.

Ornstein, Gedajlov. "Crazy Eddie Insane Odyssey." www-rci.rutgers.edu/~gedajlov/ornstein/main.html.

SEC v. Sam M. Antar et al.

Sirota, Howard. Interview, 1998.

Simpson, Richard. Interview, 1998.

"Stable Jerry." *Forbes,* November 13, 1989.

Sutton, Joseph. *Magic Carpet: Aleppo-in-Flatbush.* Thayer-Jacoby, 1977.

USA v. Eddie Antar.

USA v. Mitchell Antar.

Ward, John. "Eddie Speaks." *Asbury Park Press*, March 13, 1997.

Weiss, Michael "Cult of Cheapness for Crazy Eddie." *Dallas Morning News,* February 28, 1988.

Weissman, Paul. Interview, 1997.

Loaves and Fishes: John Bennett

Faulkner, Gray. "Accountant Blows Lid Off New Era" *Practical Accountant*, July 1, 1995.

Fox, Charles D., IV and Benetta Y. Park. "How Fiduciaries can Avoid Another New Era Philanthropy Debacle. *Trusts & Estates,* May 1, 1997.

Frame, Randy. "New Era Bankruptcy." *Christianity Today,* September 16, 1996.

Goldberg, Richard. Interviews, 1999.

Hodges, Michael H. "Professor Exposed Foundation to Save Spring Arbor College." *The Detroit News*, May 19, 1995.

Mercer, Joyce. "Only 5 Colleges Posted Gains from New Era." *Chronicle of Higher Education,* June 30, 1995.

"New Era Founder Gets 10 Years." *The Christian Century,* October 22, 1997.

Nicklin, Julie. "At Lancaster Bible College, a 'New Era' Victim." *Chronicle of Higher Education,* June 2, 1995.

Peterson, Melody. "Maybe Pepsi has a Job for a Dogged Critic." *New York Times,* September 27, 1998.

Proceedings of and documents filed with the Grand Jury, U.S. District Court of Eastern Pennsylvania, 1995-1997.

Psychological analyses filed with the U.S. District Court of Eastern Pennsylvania, 1997.

Russell, Don. "Indianapolis Investment Whistleblower Loses Job over Coca-Cola Charges." *Philadelphia Daily News,* October 21, 1998.

Smith, Judy. Interviews, 1999.

Stecklow, Steven. Various articles reported for *Wall Street Journal*, 1995-1999.

U.S. v. John G. Bennett, Jr.

Various staff-written articles reported in the *Philadelphia Inquirer*, 1995-1999.

Wulf, Steve. "Scandal: Too Good to be True Big-Time Philanthropic Investors were Suckered when they put Faith, Hope in John Bennett's Charity." *Time*, May 29, 1995.

It's a Wonderful Life: Mark Whitacre

"ADM and the FBI Scumbags." *Time*, November 1995.

Burns, Greg. Various articles in the *Chicago Tribune*, 1995-1997.

Carney, Dan. "Dwayne's World." *Mother Jones*, July 17, 1995.

Eichenwald, Kurt. Various articles reported for the *New York Times*, 1995-1999.

Garland, Susan B. and Emily Thornton. "Justice's Cartel Crackdown." *BusinessWeek*, July 27, 1998.

Gunset, George. "Profile of Michael D. Andreas." *Chicago Tribune*, September 17, 1998.

Gunset, George. "Profile of Terrance S. Wilson." *Chicago Tribune*, September 17, 1998.

Henkoff, Ronald. Various articles reported for *Fortune*, 1995-1997.

Kahn, E. J., Jr. "The Absolute Beginning." *New Yorker*, February 16, 1987.

Kilman, Scott. "Archer Daniels Midland Saga." *Wall Street Journal*, July 9, 1998.

Lerner, Matthew. "ADM to Expand Biochemicals." *Chemical Market Reporter*, May 12, 1997.

Levine, Daniel. "Former ADM Executive Grabs First Annual Honor." www.disgruntled.com, January 1996.

Melcher, Richard A., Greg Burns and Douglas Harbrecht. "Executive Suite. It Isn't Dwayne's World Anymore." *Business sWeek*, November 18, 1996.

Mokhiber, Russell and Robert Weissman. "Antitrust in Me." *Focus on the Corporation*, December 15, 1998.

Quintanilla, Carl and Anna D. Wilde. "You Dirty Rat, Says Decatur, Ill., of Mole At Archer-Daniels." *Wall Street Journal*, July 13, 1995.

Sherrill, Robert. "A Year in Corporate Crime." *Nation*, January 1997.

Siklos, Richard. "Who Ya Gonna Call?" *The Financial Post Weekly*, October 19, 1996.

Spratling, Gary R. "International Cartels: The Intersection Between FCPA Violations and Antitrust Violations." American Conference Institute, December 9, 1999.

"This is Not Business Ethics 101." *Corporate Crime Reporter*, September 10, 1998.

"Unraveling the 'Best Documented Corporate Crime in American History.'" *The Agribusiness Reporter.* www.ea1.com/CARP/tiller/archives/april97.

U.S. v. Mark E. Whitacre.

U.S. v. Michael D. Andreas, Mark E. Whitacre, Terrance Wilson, and Kazutoshi Yamada.

Walsh, Sharon and Jackie Spinner. "ADM Informant's Personal Credibility Questioned." *Minneapolis Star Tribune,* August 14, 1995.

Whitacre, Mark. "My Life as a Corporate Mole." Interview with Ronald Henkoff. *Fortune,* September 4, 1995.

White, Ed. "Town Stands by ADM Mole." *Chicago Sun-Times,* July 14, 1995.

Wissman, Angela. "ADM Execs Nailed on Price-Fixing." *Illinois Legal Times*, October, 1998.

Man or Monster?: Michael Milken

Baker, Russ. "The Education of Mike Milken." *Nation,* May 3, 1999.

Bruck, Connie. *Predator's Ball.* Penguin Books, 1989.

Fischel, Daniel R. *Payback: The Conspiracy to Destroy Michael Milken and his Financial Revolution.* Harper Business, 1995.

Kinkead, Gwen. "Ivan Boesky." *Fortune,* August 6, 1984.

Michaels, James W., and Phyllis Berman. "My Story—Michael Milken." *Forbes,* March 16, 1992.

Morris, Kathleen. "The Reincarnation of Mike Milken." *Business Week,* May 10, 1999.

Pizzo, Stephen, Mary Fricker, and Paul Muolo. *Inside Job: The Looting of America's Savings and Loans.* McGraw-Hill, 1989.

Richter, Paul. "Ranking Milken Among the Rogues of Finance." *Los Angeles Times,* April 29, 1990.

Shapiro, Susan. *Wayward Capitalists.* Yale University Press, 1984.

Stein, Benjamin J. *License to Steal.* Simon & Schuster, 1992.

Stewart, James. *Den of Thieves.* Simon & Schuster, 1991.

"What to Make of Mike." *Fortune,* September 30, 1996.

Woody, Todd. "The Riddle of Knowledge Universe." *The Industry Standard,* July 13, 1998.

Zey, Mary. *Banking on Fraud.* De Gruyter, 1993.

About the Author

Joseph T. Wells, white-collar criminologist, is founder and Chairman of the Association of Certified Fraud Examiners, a 25,000-member professional organization.

Mr. Wells graduated with honors from the University of Oklahoma with a bachelor's degree in Business Administration, and spent two years on the audit staff of Coopers and Lybrand. In 1972, he was appointed a Special Agent of the FBI, specializing in the investigation of white-collar crime. Over the next ten years, he assisted in nearly 200 criminal convictions, including that of former U.S. Attorney General John Mitchell for his involvement in the Watergate case. In 1977, he was named Agent of the Year by the FBI.

In 1981, Mr. Wells left the FBI to form Wells & Associates, a consulting group of criminologists dealing with fraud detection and deterrence. In 1988, he became Chairman of the Association of Certified Fraud Examiners.

In addition to his administrative duties as Chairman, Mr. Wells writes, researches, and lectures to business and professional groups on white-collar crime issues. He was a Faculty Member of the Federal Financial Institution Examinations Council, a Visiting Scholar at the University of Nebraska, and is a Visiting Lecturer for the University of Texas.

Mr. Wells is the author of scores of articles and training programs on fraud. He has also written seven books: *Frankensteins of Fraud; The Fraud Examiners Manual (First, Second and Third Editions); Fraud Examination: Investigative and Audit Procedures; Occupational Fraud and Abuse*; and *The Accountant's Handbook of Fraud and Commercial Crime.*

Mr. Wells is the recipient of the Outstanding Contributor Award from the *Internal Auditor* magazine for his writing. He has been featured frequently in the national media, including *The Wall Street Journal, Forbes Magazine, The New York Times,* "ABC News 20/20," "Nightline," "NBC Nightly News," and "60 Minutes." In 1998 and 1999, he was named among the Top 100 Most Influential People in Accounting by *Accounting Today* magazine.

Mr. Wells is a member of the American Institute of Certified Public Accountants, the Institute of Internal Auditors, the National Criminal Justice Association, and the American Society of Industrial Security. He has served on the Practice Advisory Council of the American Accounting Association and the Ethics Committee of the Texas Society of CPAs. He has also served on the Board of Directors for CrimeStoppers.